MILLER'S
PICTURE PRICE GUIDE

1993

(Volume I)

Compiled and Edited by:
Judith and Martin Miller

General Editor:
Madeleine Marsh

MILLERS PUBLICATIONS

MILLER'S PICTURE PRICE GUIDE 1993

Created and designed by
Millers Publications
The Cellars, High Street
Tenterden, Kent TN30 6BN
Tel: (05806) 6411

Compiled and edited by
Judith and Martin Miller

General Editor: Madeleine Marsh
Editorial and Production Co-ordinator: Sue Boyd
Editorial Assistants: Gail Jessel, Marion Rickman, Jo Wood
Production Assistant: Gillian Charles
Advertising Executive: Elizabeth Smith
Advertising Assistants: Sally Marshall, Liz Warwick
Index compiled by: DD Editorial Services, Beccles
Design: Stephen Parry, Jody Taylor, Darren Manser, Tim Arundel

A CIP catalogue record for this book is
available from the British Library

ISBN 1-85732-981-3

Typesetting by Mainline Typesetters Ltd, St. Leonards-on-Sea
Illustrations by G.H. Graphics, St. Leonards-on-Sea
Colour origination by Scantrans, Singapore
Printed and bound in England by Bath Press, Avon

CONTENTS

Edgar Meyer (1853-1925)
Austrian
A Procession Entering a Church on the Italian Coast
Signed and dated 'Rom 84', watercolour and gouache
52¾ x 41¼in (134 x 105cm)
£3,400-3,700 *S*

Arthur Joseph Meadows (1843-1907)
British
The Old Bridge, Verona
Signed; signed and inscribed with title on a label on the reverse, oil on panel, unframed
12 x 8in (30.5 x 20cm)
£3,300-3,600 *S*

Acknowledgements

The publishers would like to acknowledge the great assistance given by our consultant editors:

Martin Beisly, Christie's, 8 King Street, St. James's, London SW1
Gary Blissett, Gavels, 3 Commercial Courtyard, Settle, North Yorks.
Simon Carter, Polak Gallery, 21 King Street, St. James's, London SW1
Edwin Collins, Coltsfoot Gallery, Hatfield, Leominster, Herefordshire
John Denham, John Denham Gallery, 50 Mill Lane, London NW8
David Gilbert, Driffold Gallery, The Smithy, 78 Birmingham Road, Sutton Coldfield
Haynes Fine Art, The Bindery Gallery, 69 High Street, Broadway, Worcs.
Charles Hind, Sotheby's, 34-35 New Bond Street, London W1
John Martin, Thompson Gallery, 38 Albemarle Street, London W1
Roy Miles Gallery, 29 Bruton Street, London W1
David Moore-Gwyn, Sotheby's, 34-35 New Bond Street, London W1
Commander J. Morton Lee, Cedar House, Bacon Lane, Hayling Island, Hampshire
John Noott, John Noott Fine Paintings, 31 High Street, Broadway, Worcs.
Caroline Oliphant, Bonhams, Montpelier Street, Knightsbridge, London SW7
Mark Senior, 240 Brompton Road, London SW3
John Somerville, Sotheby's, 34-35 New Bond Street, London W1
John Steeds, Graham Gallery, Highwoods, Burghfield, Nr Reading, Berks.
Susan Sterling, Christie's, 8 King Street, St. James's, London SW1
William Thuiller, 180 New Bond Street, London W1

John Linnell (1792-1882)
British
David
Signed and dated 1871, oil on canvas
28 x 39in (71 x 99cm)
£3,600-4,000 *C*

About this book

Miller's Picture Price Guide presents a unique and comprehensive survey for professionals and enthusiasts alike of how pictures of every style, medium, period and price have performed in the market-place throughout the past year.

The Guide has been designed to make it as "user-friendly" as possible: you don't have to know the date or artist of a work in order to find it in the book. Instead, turn to the subject area you are interested in, for example, landscapes, and then to the specific area you want, such as Paris. Within the Paris section you will then find works depicting Paris, arranged chronologically so that you can compare paintings of a similar theme and period and see at a glance how a particular subject has been portrayed throughout the centuries, how styles have changed and how prices compare. Alternatively, if you are interested in specific painters, by consulting the index you can obtain a list of all the pages on which their works appear.

For each picture shown *Miller's Picture Price Guide* provides the name of the artist, with dates and nationality where known, the title of the picture (or, if it has none, a brief description), the medium, dimensions, price and source code, which can be cross-referenced to the Key to Illustrations on page 10.

The pictures and captions are supplemented by introductions to each section and extra information on specific artists or works. Comments from leading picture dealers, auctioneers and art experts provide both an historical context and an overview of market trends. A glossary of terms, a bibliography and Directories of Galleries and Specialists are also included.

It is worth bearing in mind that *Miller's Picture Price Guide* is a GUIDE to prices rather than a definitive price list. The price ranges have been carefully worked out by Miller's experts to reflect the current state of the market-place, but remember that no two pictures are ever exactly the same. The price of a painting depends on the artist, subject, rarity, quality and condition, but is also affected by who is selling the painting, how many people want to buy it and where and when it is sold.

No guide to pictures can ever be complete, but we have tried to be comprehensive and wide-ranging. However, if there is a painter or a particular subject that you would like us to include, please let us know: we rely on feedback from the people who use the guide to tell us how to make it as interesting and informative as possible.

Paul Signac (1863-1935) French Montélimar – La Petite Place
Signed and titled, watercolour and pencil
4¾ x 7⅞in (11.8 x 20cm) **£5,000-5,400** *S*

INDEX TO ADVERTISERS

Paul Maze (1887-1979)
French
Tea by the Pond
Signed, pastel
16 x 25in (40 x 62.5cm)
£7,600-8,000 *S(S)*

Key to Illustrations

Each illustration and descriptive caption is accompanied by a letter-code. By reference to the following list of Auctioneers (denoted by *) and Dealers (•), the source of any item may be immediately determined. In no way does this constitute or imply a contract or binding offer on the part of any of our contributors to supply or sell the goods illustrated, or similar articles, at the prices stated. Advertisers in this year's directory are denoted by †.

A †• Alma Gallery Ltd., 29 Alma Vale Road, Bristol BS8 2HL. Tel: (0272) 237157
AC • The Art Collection Ltd., 3-5 Elystan Street, London SW3 3NT. Tel: 071-584 4664
AdG • Adam Gallery, 13 John Street, Bath BA1 2JL. Tel: (0225) 480406
ALL * Allen and Harris, Bristol Auction Rooms, St. John Place, Apsley Road, Bristol. Tel: (0272) 737201
AMC • Anna-Mei Chadwick, 64 New King's Road, London SW6 4LT. Tel: 071-736 1928
B/Bd * Boardman, Station Road Corner, Haverhill, Suffolk. Tel: (0440) 703784
BAR †• Barnes Gallery, 8 Church Street, Uckfield, East Sussex TN22 1BJ. Tel: (0825) 762066
BB • Beaton-Brown Fine Paintings, 20 Motcomb St., London SW1X 8LB. Tel: 071-823 2240
BCG †• Betley Court Gallery, Betley, Nr. Crewe, Cheshire CW3 9BH. Tel: (0270) 820652
Bea * Bearnes, Rainbow, Avenue Road, Torquay, Devon. Tel: (0803) 296277
BG • Beardsmore Gallery, 22-24 Prince of Wales Road, Kentish Town, London NW5. Tel: 071-485 0923
BJP • Beverley J. Pyke, The Gothic House, Bank Lane, Totnes, Devon. Tel: (0803) 864219
Bne †• Bourne Gallery Ltd., 31/33 Lesbourne Road, Reigate, Surrey RH2 7JS. Tel: (0737) 241614
Bon * Bonhams, Montpelier St., Knightsbridge, London SW7. Tel: 071-584 9161
BOU • Boundary Gallery, 98 Boundary Road, London NW8. Tel: 071-624 1126
BuP • Burlington Fine Paintings Ltd., 12 Burlington Gardens, London W1X 1LG. Tel: 071-734 9984
BWe * Biddle and Webb, Ladywood Middleway, Birmingham. Tel: 021-455 8042
C * Christie's, 8 King Street, London SW1. Tel: 071-839 9060
Cae • Caelt Gallery, 182 Westbourne Grove, London W11 2RH. Tel: 071-229 9309
CAm * Christie's Amsterdam, Cornelis Schuystraat 57, 107150 Amsterdam. Tel: 020 642011
Ce/CE †• Century Gallery, 100/102 Fulham Road, London SW3 6HS. Tel: 071-581 1589
CG †• Coltsfoot Gallery, Hatfield, Leominster, Herefordshire HR6 0SF. Tel: (056 882) 277
CH †• Christopher Hull Gallery, 17 Motcomb St., London SW1X 8LB. Tel: 071-235 0500
Ch • Churzee Studio Gallery, 17 Bellevue Road, London SW17 7EG. Tel: 081-767 8113
ChG • Charterhouse Gallery Ltd., 14 Birds Hill, Heathand Reach, Leighton Buzzard, Beds. LU7 0AQ. Tel: (052 523) 379
CNY * Christie's New York, 502 Park Avenue, New York, NY10022. Tel: 212 546 1000
CoH * Cooper Hirst Auctions, The Granary Saleroom, Victoria Road, Chelmsford. Tel: (0245) 260535
C(R) * Christie's Rome, c/o Christie's (International) S.A., 3 Via Manin, 20121, Milan. Tel: (392) 2 900 1374
C(S) * Christie's Scotland Ltd., 164-166 Bath Street, Glasgow. Tel: 041-332 8134
CSK * Christie's South Kensington Ltd., 85 Brompton Road, London SW7. Tel: 071-581 7611
DC • David Cooke, Old Post House, Playden, Rye, East Sussex TN31 7UL. Tel: (0797) 280303
DG • Dean Gallery, 42 Dean Street, Newcastle-upon-Tyne NE1 1PG. Tel: 091-232 1208
DK †• David Ker Fine Art, 85 Bourne Street, London SW1. Tel: 071-730 8365
DM †• David Messum Fine Paintings Ltd., The Studio, Lordswood, Marlow, Bucks. SL7 2QS. Tel: (0628) 486565
DN * Dreweatt Neate, Donnington Priory, Donnington, Newbury, Berks. Tel: (0635) 31234
Dr †• Driffold Gallery, 78 Birmingham Road, Sutton Coldfield, West Midlands. Tel: 021-355 5433
EH * Edgar Horn's, Fine Art Auctioneers, 46-50 South Street, Eastbourne. Tel: (0323) 410419
EJ • E. Joseph (Booksellers), 1 Vere Street, London W1M 9HQ. Tel: 071-493 8353
EW • East West, 8 Blenheim Crescent, London W11. Tel: 071-229 7981
FCG • Flying Colours Gallery, 35 William Street, West End, Edinburgh EH3 7LW. Tel: 031-225 6776
FdeL †• Fleur de Lys Gallery, 227A Westbourne Grove, London W11 2SE. Tel: 071-727 8595
FL • Fine Lines Fine Art Ltd., The Old Rectory, 31 Sheep Street, Shipston on Stour, Warwicks. Tel: (0608) 62323
G • Gavels, 3 Commercial Courtyard, Settle, North Yorks. Tel: (0729) 824015
GeC • Gerard Campbell, Maple House, Market Place, Lechlade-on-Thames, Glos. Tel: (0367) 52267
GG †• Graham Gallery, 1 Castle Street, Tunbridge Wells, Kent TN1 1XJ. Tel: (0892) 526695
Go †• Goldmark Gallery, Orange Street, Uppingham, Rutland, Leics. Tel: (0572) 821424
Gra • Graham Gallery, Highwoods, Burghfield, Nr. Reading, Berks. Tel: (0734) 832320
GrG †• Graves Gallery, 3 The Spencers, Augusta Street, Hockley, Birmingham. Tel: 021-212 1635
G6 • Gallery 6, 6 Church Street, Broseley, Shrops. Tel: (0952) 882860
HF • Harper Fine Paintings, Overdale, Woodford Rd, Poynton, Cheshire. Tel: (0625) 879105
HFA • Haynes Fine Art, The Bindery Gallery, 69 High Street, Broadway, Worcester WR12 7DP. Tel: (0386) 852649
HG • Holland Gallery, 129 Portland Road, London W11 4LW. Tel: 071-727 7198
HHG • Hampton Hill Gallery, 203-205 High Street, Hampton Hill, Middlesex TW12 1NP. Tel: 081-977 1379/5273
HLG †• Hayloft Gallery, Berry Wormington, Broadway, Worcs. Tel: (0242) 621202
HSS * Henry Spencer and Sons, 20 The Square, Retford, Notts. Tel: (0777) 708633

HOU • Houldsworth Fine Art, 4-6 Bassett Road, London W10 6JL. Tel: 081-969 8197

HOP • Stephanie Hoppen Ltd., 17 Walton Street, London SW3 2HX. Tel: 071-589 3678

I †• Malcolm Innes Gallery, 172 Walton Street, London SW3 2JL. Tel: 071-584 0575 and 67 George Street, Edinburgh EH2 2JG. Tel: 031-226 4151

JB • John Bonham & Murray Feely Fine Art, 46 Porchester Road, London W2. Tel: 071-221 7208

JD †• John Denham Gallery, 50 Mill Lane, London NW6. Tel: 071-794 2635

JGG • Jill George Gallery, 38 Lexington Street, London W1R 3HR. Tel: 071-439 7343

JML †• J. Morton Lee, Cedar House, Bacon Lane, Hayling Island, Hants. PO11 0DN. Tel: (0705) 464444 (by appointment)

JN †• John Noott Fine Paintings, 14 Cotswold Court, Broadway, Worcester. Tel: (0386) 852787

JSD • J. Steven Dews Fine Art, 66-70 Princes Avenue, Kingston-upon-Hull, North Humberside. Tel: (0482) 42424

JS • James Starkey Fine Art International, Highgate, Beverley, North Yorks. Tel: (0482) 881179

KG †• Kilvert Gallery, Ashbrook House, Clyro, Hay-on-Wye, Hereford HR3 5RZ. Tel: (0497) 820831

KHG • Kentmore House Gallery, 53 Scarcroft Hill, York YO2 1DF. Tel: (0904) 656507

KT • Kidson Trigg, Estate Office, Friars Farm, Sevenhampton, Swindon, Wilts. Tel: (0793) 861072

L * Lawrence Fine Art Auctioneers, South Street, Crewkerne, Somerset. Tel: (0460) 73041

Lan • Lantern Gallery, Hazeland House, Kington St. Michael, Chippenham, Wilts. Tel: (0249) 75306

LB †• Laurence Black Ltd., 45 Cumberland Street, Edinburgh EH3 6RA. Tel: 031-557 4545

L&E * Locke & England, Black Horse Agencies, 18 Guy Street, Leamington Spa, Warwicks. Tel: (0926) 889100

LG • Lamont Gallery, 65 Roman Road, London E2 0QN. Tel: 081-981 6332

LH • Laurence Hallet. Tel: 071-828 8606

LW * Lawrences Auctioneers, Norfolk House, 80 High Street, Bletchingley, Surrey. Tel: (0883) 743323

MAY • The Mayor Gallery, 22a Cork Street, London W1. Tel: 071-734 3558

MG • Mark Gallery, 9 Porchester Place, Marble Arch, London W2 2BS. Tel: 071-262 4906

MP • Michael Parkin Gallery, 11 Motcomb Street, London SW1. Tel: 071-235 8144/1845

MS • Mark Senior, 240 Brompton Road, London SW3. Tel: 071-589 5811

NGG • New Grafton Gallery, 49 Church Road, London SW13 9HH. Tel: 081-748 8850

O • Fine Art of Oakham, 4/5 Crown Walk, Oakham, Leics. Tel: (0572) 755221

OEG • The Open Eye Gallery, 75/79 Cumberland Street, Edinburgh EH3 6RD. Tel: 031-557 1020

OL * Outhwaite & Litherland, Kingsway Galleries, Fontenoy Street, Liverpool. Tel: 051-236 6561

OLG †• On Line Gallery, 76 Bedford Place, Southampton, Hants. SO1 2DF. Tel: (0703) 330660

Om • Omell Galleries, Goswell Hill, 134 Peascod Street, Windsor, Berks. SL4 1DR. Tel: (0753) 852271

ONS • Onslows, Metrostore, Townmead Road, London SW6. Tel: 071-793 0240

P * Phillips, 101 New Bond Street, London W1. Tel: 071-629 6602

PaHG • Paul Hayes Gallery, 71 High Street, Auchterarder, Perthshire. Tel: (0764) 62320

PBG †• Penn Barn Gallery, By The Pond, Elm Road, Penn, Bucks. HP10 8LU. Tel: (0494) 815691

P(F) * Phillips Folkestone, 11 Bayle Parade, Folkestone, Kent. Tel: (0303) 455555

PHG †• Peter Hedley Gallery, 10 South Street, Wareham, Dorset. Tel: (0929) 551777

Pol • Polak Gallery, 21 King Street, St. James's, London SW1Y 6QY. Tel: 071-839 2871

P(S) * Phillips Son and Neale, 49 London Road, Sevenoaks, Kent. Tel: (0732) 740310

QAG †• Queen Adelaide Gallery, 76 High Street, Kempston, Bedford MK12 7BS. Tel: (0234) 854083

RdeR †• Rogers de Rin, 76 Royal Hospital Road, London SW3. Tel: 071-352 9007

RM/RMG • Roy Miles Gallery, 29 Bruton Street, London W1. Tel: 071-495 4747

S * Sotheby's, 34-35 New Bond Street, London W1. Tel: 071-493 8080

S(Am) * Sotheby's Amsterdam, Rokin 102, 1012 KZ Amsterdam. Tel: 020 627 5656

SC • Simon Carter Gallery, 23 Market Hill, Woodbridge, Suffolk. Tel: (0394) 382242

SCG • Sport and Country Gallery, Northwood House, 121 Weston Lane, Bulkington CV12 9RX. Tel: (0203) 314335

SH • Sheila Hinde Fine Art, Idolsford House, Nr. Billingshurst, W. Sussex. Tel: (0403) 77576

SJG • St. James's Gallery, 9b Margaret Buildings, Brock Street, Bath BA1 2LP. Tel: (0225) 319197

S(NY) * Sotheby's, 1334 York Avenue, New York NY 10021, USA. Tel: 212 606 7000

S(R) * Sotheby's Rome, Piazza d'Espana 90, 00186, Rome, Italy. Tel: 396 6841791/6781798

SRB †• Susan and Robert Botting, Rosedene, 38 Firs Avenue, Felpham, Sussex. Tel: (0243) 584515

S(S) * Sotheby's Sussex, Summers Place, Billingshurst, West Sussex. Tel: (0403) 783933

S(SC) * Sotheby's, 112 George Street, Edinburgh EH2 2LH. Tel: 031-226 7201

TG • The Titus Gallery, 1 Daisy Place, Saltaire, Shipley, West Yorks. Tel: (0274) 581894

Tho • Thompson Gallery, 38 Albemarle Street, London W1X 3FB. Tel: 071-499 1314

ULG †• Upton Lodge Galleries, 6 Long Street, Tetbury, Glos. GL8 8AQ. Tel: (0666) 53416 Also at Avening House, Avening, Tetbury

VCG • Vicarage Cottage Gallery, Preston Road, North Shields NE29 9PJ. Tel: 091-257 0935

Wa • Waterman Fine Art Ltd., 74a Jermyn Street, London SW1Y 6NP. Tel: 071-839 5203

WG • Walker Galleries, 6 Montpelier Gardens, Harrogate, Yorks. Tel: (0423) 567933

WO • Wiseman Originals Ltd., 34 West Square, London SE11 4SP. Tel: 071-587 0747

WrG • Wren Gallery, 4 Bear Court, High Street, Burford, Oxon. Tel: (0993) 823495

WT • William Thuiller, 180 New Bond Street, London W1. Tel: 071-499 0106

WWG • Wilkins and Wilkins Gallery, 1 Barrett Street, London W1A 6DN. Tel: 071-935 9613

WyG • Wyllie Gallery, 12 Needham Road, London W1. Tel: 071-727 0606

Wyk • Wykeham Gallery, 51 Church Road, London SW13 9HH. Tel: 081-741 1277

General Cataloguing Terms

With every picture, Millers has followed the basic description provided by the auction house or dealer. As all the auction houses stress in their catalogues, whilst full care is taken to ensure that any statement as to attribution, origin, date, age, provenance and condition is reliable and accurate, all such statements are statements of opinion only and not to be taken as fact.

Where possible Millers have added the dates and nationality of the artist. In each instance these details refer only to the given name of the artist and not necessarily to the work itself.

The conventional cataloguing system used by the auction houses has been maintained:

A work catalogued with the name(s) of an artist, without any qualification, is in their opinion, a work by the artist (where the artist's forename(s) is not known, this is replaced by a series of asterisks, sometimes preceded by an initial.

"Attributed to . . ."
In their opinion probably a work by the artist, but less certainly than in the preceding category.

"Studio of . . ." "Workshop of . . ."
In their opinion a work by an unknown hand in the studio of the artist which may or may not have been executed under the artist's direction.

"Circle of . . ."
In their opinion a work by an as yet unidentified but distinct hand, closely associated with the named artist, but not necessarily his pupil.

"Follower of . . ." "Style of . . ."
In their opinion a work by a painter working in the artist's style, contemporary or nearly contemporary, but not necessarily his pupil.

"Manner of . . ."
In their opinion, a work in the artist's style, but of a later date.

"After . . ."
In their opinion, a copy of a known work by the artist.

"Signed . . ." / "Dated . . ." / "Inscribed . . ."
In their opinion signature/date/inscription are from the hand of the artist.

"Bears Signature . . ." / "Bears date . . ." / "Bears inscription . . ."
In their opinion, signature/date/description have been added by another hand.

Measurements: Dimensions are given height before width.

Select Glossary

Acrylic: A synthetic emulsion paint.

Airbrush: A small mechanical paintsprayer permitting fine control and a smooth finish.

Allegory: A work of art conveying an abstract theme or subject, under the guise of another subject.

Aquatint: Etching technique in which a metal plate is sprinkled with resin and then bathed in acid which bites into any uncovered areas. According to the amount of acid used and the density of the particles, darker or lighter shading is obtained.

Bistre: A brown pigment made from charred wood, often used as a wash on pen and ink drawings.

Cartoon: A full size early design for a painting (Henry VIII in male portrait section – p274).

Collage: A work of art in which pieces of paper, photographs and other materials are pasted to the surface of the picture.

Conversation piece: A group portrait with the sitters placed informally as in conversation.

Drawing: Representation with line.

Dry-point: The process of making a print by engraving directly on copper with a sharp needle.

Edition: The run of a print published at any one time.

Engraving: The process of cutting a design into a hard surface (metal or wood) so that the lines will retain the ink.

Etching: A technique of printmaking in which a metal plate is covered with an acid-resistant substance and the design scratched on it with a needle revealing the metal beneath. The plate is then immersed in acid, which bites into the lines, which will then hold the ink.

Fête Champètre: A rustic festival or peasant celebration – also known as a Kermesse in Dutch and Flemish works.

Fête Galante: Ladies and gentlemen at play often in a parkland setting.

Genre: Art showing scenes from daily life.

Gouache: Opaque watercolour paint.

Grisaille: Painting in grey or greyish monochrome.

Icon: A religious painting on panel usually by a Greek or Russian Orthodox artist, its subject and representation conforming to established traditions.

Impression: An individual copy of a print or engraving.

Lithograph: A print made by drawing with a wax crayon on a porous prepared stone which is then soaked in water. A grease-based ink is applied to the stone which adheres only to the design. Dampened paper is applied to the stone and is rubbed over with a special press to produce the print.

Medium: The materials used in a painting, i.e. oil, tempera, watercolour, etc.

Mezzotint: The reverse of the usual printing process – the artist begins with a black ground, a metal plate that is completely roughened, and the design is polished or burnished into it, thus the image remains white whilst the background takes all the ink.

Mixed Media: Art combining different types of material.

Oils: Pigment bound with oil.

Panel Painting: Painting on wood.

Pastel: A dry pigment bound with gum into stick-form and used for drawing.

Pendant: One of a pair of pictures.

Plein-air: A landscape painted outdoors and on the spot.

Plate: The piece of metal etched or engraved with the design used to produce prints.

Print: An image which exists in multiple copies, taken from an engraved plate, woodblock, etc.

Provenance: The record of previous owners and locations of a work of art.

Recto: The front of a picture.

Sanguine: Red chalk containing ferric oxide used in drawing.

Silk screen: A print-making process using a finely meshed screen, often of silk, and stencils to apply the image to paper.

State: A term applied to prints – to the different stages at which the artist has corrected or changed a plate – and the prints produced from these various 'states', which are numbered first state, second state, third state, etc.

Still Life: A composition of inaminate objects.

Tempera: A medium for pigment mostly made up of egg yolk and water, commonly used before the invention of oil painting.

Tondo: A circular painting.

Topographical painting: A landscape in which the predominant concern is geographical accuracy rather than imaginative content.

Triptych: A set of three pictures, usually in oils, with hinges allowing the outer panels to be folded over the central one – often used as an altarpiece.

Vanitas: An elaborate still life including various elements such as a skull, symbolising the transcience of earthly life.

Verso: The back of a picture.

Wash: A thin transparent tint applied over the surface of a work.

Watercolour: Transparent, water soluble paint, usually applied on paper.

Woodcut: Print made from a design cut into a block of wood.

Alan Franklin Transport

LANDSCAPES

There are more landscapes sold at auction and by dealers than any other category of painting. Though 17th, 18th and in particular 20thC pictures are all strongly represented in the salerooms and as such in the present guide, by far the greatest number of works fall into the 19thC. Much of this section is devoted to painters of the Victorian and Edwardian eras – to their vision of the natural world which in many instances remains as commercially popular today as it was in their own times.

Looking through the landscape section as a whole gives one a review of the range, type and price of pictures sold over the past year. Any number of factors can help make the landscape on your wall a desirable object in the salerooms.

Obviously with landscapes, as with all other types of painting, artist, quality and condition are major considerations in today's market where, as almost every dealer we have talked to has stressed, it tends to be the better quality pictures that are still holding their own.

Subject is all important. Certain views seem to have a perennial appeal. 'Mountains are the beginning and end of all natural scenery,' noted John Ruskin in Modern Painters, and pictures of Scottish mountains, Alpine scenery, and mountains miscellaneous all make their appearance. Seas, lakes and lochs (often with watering cattle) are continuously popular subjects whilst at the less dramatic end of the scale, cottage gardens and rural harvest scenes predominate. Famous beauty spots such as Venice and the Bay of Naples have been endlessly painted and are always in demand whilst early topographical views of Asia, the Americas and other more exotic locations can command high prices because of their rarity. Content is vital in a landscape: the more interesting the view, whether through its own natural merits, or by the addition of figures, a snowstorm or a sunset, the higher the price.

Guiseppe de Angelis (17thC)
Italian
A View on Ischia
Signed, oil
12 x 17¾in (30.5 x 45cm)
£1,550-1,750 *C(S)*

17th Century

Circle of Paul Bril (1554-1626)
Flemish
Coastal Scenes with Christ Calling St Peter to Walk on the Waves; and the Calling of St Peter (a pair)
Oil on copper
4¼ x 8½in (10.7 x 21.6cm)
£6,100-7,000 *S*

Circle of Jan Both (1618-52)
Dutch
Mountainous Italianate Landscapes (a pair)
Oil on canvas
19⅜ x 20¾in (49.2 x 67.9cm)
£13,300-14,200 *C*

According to one of his contemporaries, J. van Sandrart, Jan Both made such sensitive representations of noon, evening and sunset, that by looking at his paintings one could assess, almost to the hour, the time of day. Both was amongst the most popular of all the Italianate landscape painters and the warm golden light of his paintings was reflected in the work of many followers.

Remigio Cantagallina (1582-1630) Italian
A View of Val Urbano
Black chalk, pen and brown ink, blue and brown wash
7 x 10in (18.4 x 25.5cm)
£3,400-3,700 *C*

Jan Joost Cossiau (1660-1732/4)
Dutch
A Wooded Landscape with a Shepherdess and a Hunting Party
43 x 33¼in (109.3 x 84.5cm)
Oil on canvas
£7,200-7,900 *C*

Dutch School (17thC)
A Wooded Landscape with a House
Black lead, grey wash
7⅛ x 11in (18.2 x 27.9cm)
£1,300-1,700 *S(NY)*

Did you know?
MILLER'S Picture Price Guide will build up year by year to form the most comprehensive photo-reference library available

Follower of Anton Goubau (1616-98) Dutch
Peasants on a Wooded Track by a Ruin
11⅝ x 13¾in (30 x 35cm)
Oil on canvas
£2,500-2,800 *C*

Jan Van Goyen (1596-1656) Dutch
A Winter Landscape with Skaters on a Frozen River
Signed, oil on panel
5¼ x 10¼in (13.5 x 26.3cm)
£102,000-115,000 *S*

In the 1620s, to which period this picture can almost certainly be dated, Goyen developed the tonal qualities that so distinguish his work: a use of monochromatic and muted colours that suggest an atmosphere as much as a subject. A fine and highly respected painter who began his craft at the age of ten, Goyen also dabbled in many other professions, working as dealer and auctioneer and speculating in both property and tulip bulbs. In spite or perhaps because of these various activities, he died penniless.

Follower of Jan Van Goyen (1596-1656) Dutch
Landscape with Peasants
Oil on panel
14¾ x 19½in (37.5 x 49.5cm)
£10,500-11,000 *S*

Gillis Claesz d'Hondecoeter (1570-1638) Dutch Landscape with Christ on the Road to Emmaus
Oil on panel 13½ x 24in (33.5 x 61cm)
£22,500-25,500 *S*

Follower of Filippo Lauri (1623-94)
Rumanian
Putti with Flora in the Grounds of an Italian
Villa
Oil on canvas
25½ x 38¾in (64.7 x 98.4cm)
£4,500-5,000 *C*

Jacobus Sibrandi Mancadan (1602-80)
Dutch
Landscape with a Goat Herd Resting by his Flock
Signed with monogram, oil on panel
13¼ x 24½in (33.5 x 62.4cm)
£25,500-30,000 *S*

Klaes Molenaer (1630-76)
Dutch
River Landscape with Figures
Oil on panel
18½ x 24½in (47 x 62.3cm)
£10,500-11,500 *Bon*

Joos de Momper the Younger
(1564-1635) Dutch
Mountainous, Coastal Landscape with
Travellers at Rest
Oil on panel
18¼ x 29in (46.5 x 73.7in)
£102,000-115,000 *S*

The present work has been dated to c1600-10, and the figures attributed to Jan Brueghel the Elder.
At auction it trippled its original estimate, showing the strong market for old masters of good quality and provenance

Frederic de Moucheron (1633-86)
Dutch
Italianate Landscape with Travellers on a Path
Oil on canvas
25¾ x 31¼in (65.5 x 79.5cm)
£7,900-8,500 *Bon*

Circle of Joachim Patenier (1485-1524)
Flemish
St Anthony Abbot in a Rocky Landscape
Oil on panel
8½in (21.6cm) diam
£12,200-13,000 *S*

Pieter de Neyn (1597-1639)
Dutch
Landscape with Figures by a Cottage
Oil on panel
15½ x 22in (39.5 x 56cm)
£10,000-10,500 *S*

Circle of Mathys Schoevaerdts (c1655-after 1694)
Flemish
Wooded Landscape with Figures
Oil on panel
7¾ x 9⅝in (19.7 x 24.5cm)
£2,700-3,200 *C*

Follower of Jacob van Ruisdael (17thC)
Dutch
A Wooded River Landscape with Cottage
Oil on canvas
29 x 25⅞in (73.7 x 63.5cm)
£5,300-5,900 *C*

Jacob Salomonz van Ruisdael (1630-81)
Dutch
A Bosky Landscape with Cattle
Indistinctly signed and dated,
oil on panel
22 x 33in (56 x 84cm)
£28,000-33,000 *S*

Herman Saftleven (1609-85)
Dutch
Rhenish River Landscape
Signed and dated 1664,
oil on panel
6 x 14in (15.2 x 35.6cm)
£15,500-16,500 *S*

Attributed to Philips Wouvermans (1619-68)
Dutch
Dune Landscape
Bears monogram,
oil on canvas
20¼ x 26in
(51.5 x 66cm)
£18,200-19,500 *S*

Thomas Wyck (1616-77) Dutch
Peasants in an Italianate Courtyard
Oil on panel
13¾ x 18¼in (35 x 46.5cm)
£6,100-6,700 *S*

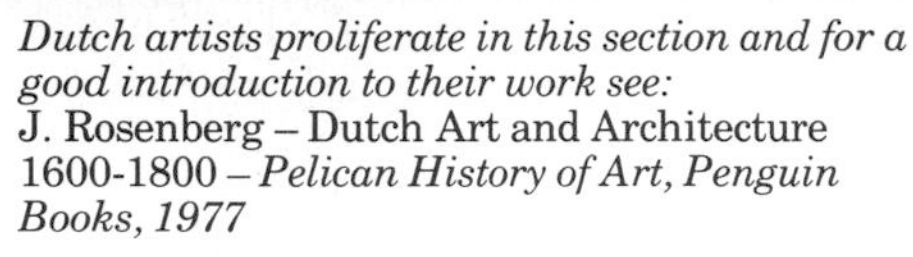

Dutch artists proliferate in this section and for a good introduction to their work see:
J. Rosenberg – Dutch Art and Architecture 1600-1800 – *Pelican History of Art, Penguin Books, 1977*

18th Century

Circle of George Barret (1728-84) British River Landscapes with Fishermen (a pair)
Oil on canvas 23¾ x 30¾in (60.4 x 78cm)
£650-750 *C(S)*

Robert Adam (1728-92)
British
A Romantic Landscape with a Ruined Castle
Inscribed on verso: Drawn by Mr Adams the Architect
Pen and brown ink and grey washes over pencil
12¼ x 15¼in (31 x 39cm)
£2,800-3,100 *S*

George Barret (1728-84)
British
Italianate Landscape with Travellers Resting by a River
Inscribed, oil on canvas
12 x 14½in (30.5 x 36.5cm)
£5,600-6,100 *S*

Follower of Adriaen Bloemaert (1609-66)
Dutch
A Wooded River Landscape with Travellers on a Bridge
Oil on panel
31⅞ x 21¾in (81.1 x 55.2cm)
£3,400-3,700 *C*

Circle of Karel Beschey (b 1706)
Flemish
A River Landscape with Peasants at a Ferry Crossing; and a companion piece (a pair)
Oil on canvas
13⅜ x 16¾in (34 x 42.4cm)
£9,000-9,600 *C*

Attributed to Jean Simon Barthelemy (1743-1811)
French
Italianate Landscape with Buildings
Brown red chalk
13½ x 18⅞in (34.1 x 48cm)
£1,400-1,700 *S(NY)*

François-Joseph Casanova (1727-1802) Italian
A Runaway Wagon in a Storm
Black chalk, brown wash 14½ x 19¾in (36.8 x 50.2cm)
£3,500-3,800 *S(NY)*

Giovanni Battista Busiri (1698-1757) Italian
The Ponte Sant'Angelo, Rome; and three other landscape studies Black chalk, pen and brown ink 6½ x 9in (17.1 x 22.8cm)
£2,500-2,800 *C*

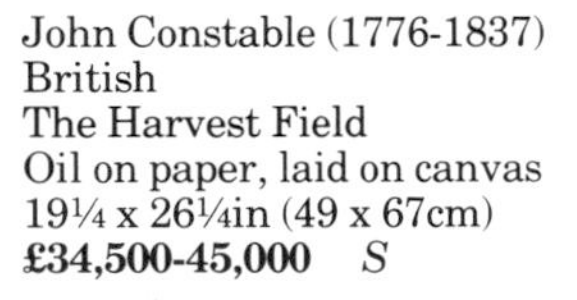

John Constable (1776-1837)
British
The Harvest Field
Oil on paper, laid on canvas
19¼ x 26¼in (49 x 67cm)
£34,500-45,000 *S*

Recently discovered, this painting is one of two versions from which Constable made an etching in 1797. Probably painted within a year of 'Moonlight Landscape with Hadleigh Church' (private collection) which, bearing the date 1796, is the earliest known oil by the artist, this must be one of his first paintings. (Also see Constable in Landscapes 19thC.)

After Susannah Drury (18thC)
Irish
The East Prospect of the Giants Causeway, County of Antrim, Ireland; the West Prospect . . .
by F. Vivares (a pair)
Engravings, published by Drury, Dublin 1743-4,
margins obscured by the mount, some defects at the edges, minor staining and foxing,
16 x 27in (41 x 69cm)
£650-750 *C(S)*

'Cozens is all poetry . . .,' wrote Constable in a letter in 1821, 'the greatest genius that ever touched landscape.' After Paul Sandby, Cozens was the most influential watercolour artist of the 18thC, and a major inspiration to both Turner and Girtin. His continued importance is emphasised by the fact that this present picture of Lake Albano (a popular subject with the artist), more than tripled its auction estimate. The work is not only a classic example of the artist's atmospheric style, but came with a matchless provenance: from the possession of artist Thomas Girtin (see below), to G. W. Girtin and then by descent to the present owner. It had been widely exhibited and illustrated over the years in relevant literature. Hugely admired in his own time and today, Cozens suffered the 'traditional' fate of genius and died incurably insane.

John Robert Cozens (1752-97) British
Lake Albano and Castel Gandolfo, Sunset
Watercolour over pencil
17 x 24½in (43 x 62cm)
£200,000-220,000 *S*

Thomas Gainsborough (1727-88) British
Study of a Wooded Landscape with a Country Lane Black and white chalk on buff paper
6¼ x 8in (15.5 x 20.5cm)
£4,000-4,500 *S*

Thomas Gainsborough (1727-88) British
Upland Landscape with Cows and Sheep
Grey washes and white over and offset outline on buff paper
Inscribed to the reverse in William Esdaile's hand at the bottom left '1833 WE Dr Monro's sale N040X', and at the bottom centre 'Gainsborough' 10½ x 12½in (26.6 x 31.7cm)
£13,000-14,000 *L*

Genoese School (18thC) An Extensive River Landscape with Pilgrims by a Gatehouse Oil on canvas 14⅛ x 23⅛ (35.9 x 58.7cm)
£1,400-2,000 *C*

German School (late 18thC)
Wooded River Landscape with Figures
Oil on canvas
36½ x 45¾in (92.7 x 116.2cm)
£4,500-5,000 *S(NY)*

Follower of Henrick Frans van Lint, lo Studio (1684-1763) Flemish
An Extensive Winter Landscape; and an Italianate Landscape (a pair) Oil on copper
6⅛ x 8⅝in (15.5 x 22cm) **£5,000-5,500** *C*

Thomas Girtin (1775-1802)
British
Kirstall Abbey, Yorkshire
Signed and dated 1802, watercolour over pencil heightened with bodycolour
12½ x 20½in (31.5 x 52cm)
£83,000-90,000 *S*

Thomas Girtin (1775-1802)
British
A Bridge, Possibly in Wales
Watercolour over pencil
3 x 4¾in (7.5 x 12cm)
£3,600-4,000 *S*

William Hodges (1744-97)
British
Figure Approaching an Indian Temple
Oil on canvas
40¾ x 49¼in (103.5 x 125cm)
£21,000-25,000 *S*

In the 1770s, Hodges enrolled as draughtsman on Captain Cook's second expedition to the South Pacific where he was greatly inspired by the exotic scenery. In 1779 he went to India and painted many of his most distinguished landscapes. He returned six years later with a considerable fortune and in 1795, gave up painting for banking. It turned out to be an unwise decision. His bank rapidly collapsed and he died barely two years later.

Thomas Hearne (1744-1817)
British
Romsey Abbey, Hampshire
Watercolour over pencil
5½ x 8in (14 x 20cm)
£1,700-2,000 *S*

A. Hammond (late 18thC)
British
Spithead from the Isle of White
Signed and dated 1782,
watercolour over pencil
19 x 32½in (48 x 70cm)
£2,000-2,500 *S*

Bernard Gottfried Manskirch (1736-1817)
German
A River Landscape with Children Fishing by a Cottage; A Landscape with a Ruined Castle (a pair)
Oil on canvas
53¼ x 63¼in (135.5 x 160.6cm)
£15,000-17,000 *C*

William Marlow (1740-1813)
British
An Italian Landscape with Ruins and Cattle
17 x 21in (43 x 53.3cm)
£4,500-5,000 *Bon*

Theobald Michau (1676-1765) Flemish
A River Landscape with Boats near a Village
Oil on panel
14¾ x 24½ (37.5 x 62cm)
£40,000-45,000 *S*

A. Nasmyth (1758-1840)
British
The Falls of the Clyde
Oil on canvas
32¾ x 44in (183 x 112cm)
£33,000-36,000 *DK*

George Morland
(1763-1804) British
Landscape with
Boy Fishing
Signed, oil on panel
17 x 14in
(43 x 35.5cm)
£2,300-2,600
S

In a letter of condolence to Nasmyth's widow, Sir David Wilkie recalled his friend's achievements: 'He was the founder of the landscape painting of Scotland and by his taste and talents took the lead for many years in the patriotic aim of enriching his native land with the representations of her romantic scenery.' Nasmyth worked as a painter of portraits and conversation pieces until the 1790s when, according to his son, his friendship 'with men of known reforming views' (including the poet Robert Burns) caused his aristocratic patrons to abruptly withdraw their patronage. Curiously, however, his political views did not stop them from commissioning his other works. By the 1800s Nasmyth was working not only as a landscape painter, but also as a landscape consultant and architect.
'Typically Nasmyth's pictures incorporate one of the peculiar charms of the Scottish landscape, the presence in a single view of cultivation and the habitation of man, together with an expanse of water and wild hills, the domain of untamed nature. In the serene light in which he presents them, these two things are in harmony.' Duncan MacMillan (see Biblio)

George Morland (1763-1804) British
Fishermen Unloading their Catch Signed, oil on canvas
7¾ x 11¾in (19.5 x 30cm)
£4,700-5,000 *S*

George Morland (1763-1804)
British
The Bell Inn in Winter with Sportsmen
Signed, oil on canvas
6½ x 8½in (16 x 21.5cm)
£2,600-3,000 *S*

Jean-Baptiste Pillement (1728-1808)
French
Coastal Landscape with Figures Looking at a Sunset
Signed, pastel, possibly dating c1770-80
15¼ x 23in (38.9 x 58.4cm)
£9,500-10,200 *S(NY)*

According to Bryan's Dictionary of Painters (see Biblio), Pillement specialised in 'landscapes and fancy subjects . . . composed and coloured in a theatrical, gaudy style.' These dramatic tendencies clearly appealed to Royal patrons, and he was appointed painter to Marie Antoinette and to the last King of Poland.

John Rathbone
(1750-1807)
British
Landscapes with
Cattle (a pair)
Oil on canvas
13½ x 17in
(34 x 43cm)
£4,500-5,000 *S*

Paul Sandby (1730-1809)
British
Figures on a Lane before Rochester Castle
Pen, ink and watercolour
19⅜ x 24⅞in (49.5 x 63.2cm)
£5,300-6,000 *C*

Ramsay Richard Reinagle (1775-1862)
British
Classical Landscape
Signed, oil on canvas
22½ x 27¾in (57.1 x 70.5cm)
£5,500-7,000 *I*

Philip Reinagle (1749-1833)
British
A Couple Reading Poetry
Beneath a Tree
Pencil and watercolour
14¼ x 20½in (36.4 x 52cm)
£800-900 *C*

Hubert Robert (1733-1808)
French
Figures by a Cottage
Signed, red chalk counter proof
14¼ x 11¼in (36.3 x 28.7cm)
With two other counterproofs
£3,500-4,000 *S(NY)*

Robert, like many other artists of the 18thC, made extensive use of counterproofs. A counterproof was made by wetting the verso *of a chalk drawing and pressing a damp sheet of paper onto the* recto*, producing a duplicate in reverse of the original. The method was regarded as a means of fixing the chalk on the original. Counterproofs were valued for their smoothness and evenness. The museum of Besançon has a collection of Robert's counterproofs. Many of them, like the present drawing, are signed.*

Roman School (18thC)
Landscape with Figures Near
a Waterfall
Oil on canvas
35½ x 45¾in (90.5 x 116.2cm)
£9,000-9,600 *S*

Circle of Johann Christian Vollerdt (1708-69)
German
Shepherds in extensive Italianate Landscapes with Waterfowl on a River (a pair)
Oil on canvas
22⅝ x 29½in (57.5 x 75cm)
£22,500-25,000 *C*

Follower of Antonio Zocchi (18thC?)
Italian
An Italianate Landscape with Pilgrims Resting by a Cascade
Oil on canvas
31 x 35¼in (78.7 x 89.5cm)
£3,100-3,600 *C*

Joseph Mallord William Turner (1775-1851)
British
Knaresborough Castle, Yorkshire
Watercolour over pencil
3 x 4¾in (7.5 x 12cm)
£5,600-6,200 *S*

Paul Sandby (1730-1809)
British
Figure with Horse,
Donkey and Dog in a Landscape
Signed with initials and dated 1796,
watercolour over pencil
15¼ x 21½in (39 x 54.5cm)
£1,800-2,400 *S*

Joseph Mallord William Turner (1775-1851) and
Thomas Girtin (1775-1802)
Radicofani in Tuscany
Inscribed, pencil and watercolour
6 x 9½in (15.3 x 24.2cm)
£3,400-3,800 *C*

The diarist and artist Joseph Farrington (1747-1821) recorded that 'Girtin drew in outlines and Turner washed in the effects.' Dr Monro employed both artists to make copies after other artist's works, in particular John Robert Cozens.

19th and early 20th Century

John Clayton Adams (1840-1906)
British
At Winterfold near Ewhurst, Surrey
Signed and dated 1889, oil on canvas
42½ x 60¼in (108 x 153cm)
£15,500-16,000 *BuP*

John White Abbot (1763-1851)
British
A Cottage near Holne
Initialled, inscribed, numbered and dated July 16 1800
Pen and brown ink and watercolour
6 x 8⅜in (15.3 x 21.2cm)
£7,200-7,600 *C*

John Clayton Adams (1840-1906) British
Harvest Time
Signed, oil on canvas
20 x 30in (50.8 x 76.2cm)
£9,500-9,800 *HFA*

Edward Arden (Tucker) (c1847-1910)
British
Borrowdale, Cumbria
Watercolour
12 x 16in (30.4 x 40.6cm)
£325-350 *G*

'In the local art market, in spite of the recession, there is still a strong demand for pictures by specific artists who worked in specific areas of the North of England,' notes dealer Gary K. Blisset from Gavels, who submitted the present work. 'This has been maintained due to the dedication of a certain number of keen collectors. Such areas of collecting are the Lake District artists (including the Tucker family), Yorkshire artists and the Liverpool school.'

John White Abbot (1763-1851)
British
Near Holne, on the Dart, with Benshetor in the distance, Devon
Initialled, inscribed, numbered and dated July 16 1800
Pen and grey ink and watercolour
8½ x 6in (21.5 x 15.2cm)
£8,300-8,800 *C*

Francis Abel William Taylor Armstrong (1849-1920)
British Mountainous Lake Landscape
Initialled and dated '94 Oil on canvas
13 x 20½in (34 x 52cm)
£200-230 *ALL*

Hendrick van de Sande Bakhuysen (1795-1860)
Dutch
Figures in a Winter Landscape
Signed, oil on panel
19 x 25¼in (48 x 64cm)
£3,900-4,500 *S*

Thomas Baker of Leamington (1809-69) British On the Holyhead Road, near Corwen, North Wales
Signed and inscribed, pencil and watercolour with touches of white heightening
7¼ x 10¼in (18.5 x 26cm)
£1,600-2,000 *C*

David Bates (1840-1921)
British
Near Tenbury
Signed and dated 1904, pencil and watercolour with scratching out
14 x 20¾in (35.6 x 52.7cm)
£1,900-2,400 *C*

Richard Beavis (1824-96)
British
La Moisson, Près Boulogne-sur-Mer
Oil on board
9 x 13in (23 x 38cm)
£2,800-3,000 *JN*

William Bennet (1811-71) British Cattle Watering by a River
Signed and dated 1865, pencil and watercolour with scratching out 6¾ x 9½in (17.2 x 24.2cm)
£1,600-2,000 *C*

Adolf Blankenburg (19thC) German Panoramic Views of Loretto, Hungary; A View of Silenstadt with the Leitha Mountains in Hungary (a pair) Both inscribed, signed and dated 1858, oil on canvas 13½ x 44in (34.5 x 112cm)
£6,700-7,200 *S*

Charles Bentley (1806-54) British
The Hood Gate
Inscribed and numbered on the reverse of the mount, watercolour with scratching out
12½ x 9¼in (32.3 x 23.5cm)
£1,600-2,000 *C*

Samuel John Lamorna Birch (1869-1955)
British
Crossing the Footbridge
Signed and dated 1899, watercolour and gouache
9¾ x 13½in (24.5 x 34.5cm)
£1,050-1,250 *S(S)*

Henry John Boddington (1811-65) British Sheep Dipping
Signed, oil on canvas
12 x 16in (30.5 x 40.6cm)
£3,900-4,050 *HFA*

Boddington was a member of the famous Williams family of painters, a number of whom appear later in this section. Artist and specialist in moonlight scenes, Edward Williams (1782-1855) fathered six sons all of whom followed the family profession. 'They all paint landscapes extremely well,' commented the supplement to Bryan's Dictionary in 1866, 'but commercially the pictures of A. Gilbert, H. Boddington and Sidney Percy take the lead.' Boddington, like two of his brothers, decided to change his surname in order to avoid otherwise inevitable confusion, and took on his wife's maiden name. He concentrated on views of the Thames and Wales, exhibiting at Suffolk Street, The Royal Academy and the British Institute. Ruskin praised his works for their honesty and love of the countryside and his pictures were admired for what one critic described as their 'daringly fresh' portrayal of nature

William Kay Blacklock (1872-c1940)
British
A Woman Feeding Ducks by a Windmill
Signed and dated '99, pencil and watercolour with touches of white heightening
10 x 7in (25.3 x 17.7cm)
£700-750 *C*

Hercules Brabazon Brabazon (1821-1906)
French
Palermo, Sicily
Signed, coloured chalks on paper
7 x 10½in (18 x 27cm)
£1,200-1,500 *S*

Willem Bodeman (1806-90)
Dutch
A Dutch Canal Landscape with Figures in a Barge
Signed
21 x 26in (53.3 x 66.1cm)
£8,000-8,500 *CSK*

Locate the source

The source of each illustration in Miller's can be found by checking the code letters below each caption with the list

W. J. J. C. Bond (1833-1928) British
Peggoty's Home, vide David Copperfield
Signed and inscribed, oil on canvas
22¾ x 34in (57.5 x 86cm)
£1,500-1,700 *S*

Eugène Boudin (1824-98)
French
La Rade de Villefranche, Vue du Quai de la Marine
Signed and dated '92, oil on canvas
16 x 22in (40.6 x 55.8cm)
£45,200-50,000 *C*

William Bradley (active 1872-89)
British
Where Peaceful Waters Flow
Signed and dated 1883,
pencil and watercolour
22 x 35in (56 x 89cm)
£2,700-3,000 *S(S)*

Alfred de Breanski (1852-1928)
British
Where the Water Lillies Grow
Signed, oil on canvas
24 x 36in (61 x 91.4cm)
£16,000-16,600 *HFA*

Alfred de Breanski (1852-1928)
British
Scottish Landscape
Signed, oil on canvas
20 x 30in (50.8 x 76.2cm)
£8,500-8,750 *HLG*

Alfred de Breanski (1852-1928)
British
The Hills of Scotland – Sunset
Signed and inscribed, oil on canvas
30 x 50in (76.2 x 127cm)
£24,000-24,950 *HFA*

'Sunsets are quite old fashioned,' declared Oscar Wilde in 1891. 'They belong to the time when Turner was the last note in art.' Wilde might have disapproved of the sunset, but the average Victorian patron liked nothing better than a landscape bathed in a rich and rosy glow. Breanski was the master of this art, he specialised in highland scenery (another immensely popular theme), in lush and luminous portrayals of Scottish lochs at sundown, often with cattle wading in the water. His paintings appear regularly on the market, and the prices they command demonstrate their continuing appeal

Gustave de Breanski (1856-1898)
British
Whitby
Signed, oil on canvas
24 x 36in (61 x 91.4cm)
With a companion 'Bambugh' a pair
£1,650-1,850 *Bon*

Brother of the above, Gustave specialised in coastal scenes in a more impressionistic style than Alfred

Robert Bridgehouse (19thC)
British(?)
Landscape with Cattle and Figures; Fisherfolk on the Shore (a pair)
Signed and dated 1869, oil on canvas
11½ x 17¾in (29 x 44cm)
£600-650 *S(S)*

Henry Barlow Carter (1803-67)
British
A Perilous Sea
Signed and dated 1856, watercolour with scratching out
12¼ x 18¼in (31 x 46cm)
£1,200-1,400 *S*

Attributed to Vincenzo Cabianca (1827-1902)
Italian
A View of a Town on the Roman Coast
Oil on canvas
12 x 15¼in (31 x 39cm)
£9,000-9,500 *S*

Walter Waller Caffyn (d 1898)
British
Old Lane, Minster, Near Ramsgate
Signed and dated 1894, oil on canvas
24 x 16in (61 x 40.5cm)
£1,600-2,000 *S*

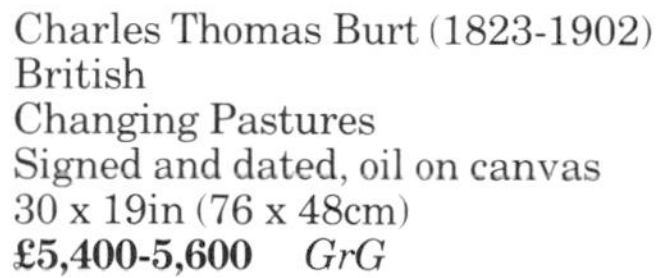

Charles Thomas Burt (1823-1902)
British
Changing Pastures
Signed and dated, oil on canvas
30 x 19in (76 x 48cm)
£5,400-5,600 *GrG*

Guiseppe Carelli (1858-1921) Italian Costa Sorrentina
Signed and inscribed, oil on panel 13¼ x 20in (33.5 x 51cm)
£4,500-5,000 *C*

George Chinnery (1774-1852)
British
A Chinese Family at the Water's Edge
Watercolour over traces of pencil and brown ink
4 x 6in (10.5 x 15.5cm)
£5,000-5,500 *S*

Chinnery spent much of his life working abroad, first in India, then in China. According to Martin Hardie (see Biblio), his travelling was possibly stimulated by the desire to escape from his Irish wife, to whom he was not happily married. 'Mrs Chinnery's appearance cannot be exaggerated,' Chinnery declared some years after he had abandoned her. 'She was an ugly woman thirty years ago. What in the name of the Graces can she be now?' Whilst he made his living predominantly as a portrait-painter in oils and miniatures, he drew for pleasure and his fluent and atmospheric watercolours capture the scenery and native life of Asia 'with great descriptive skill, sometimes brilliantly.' The British Museum holds examples of his Indian work and the Victoria and Albert Museum large numbers of his Chinese drawings

Richard Harry Carter (1839-1911)
British
A Winter's Day near The Lizard
Signed and dated 1870, watercolour with scratching out
15½ x 27¾in (39.5 x 70.5cm)
£680-750 *S(S)*

T. E. Churnside (active turn of the century)
British
River Landscape
Watercolour
10 x 15in (25.4 x 38cm)
£200-225 *AC*

Vittore Antionio Cargnel (1872-1931) Italian
Figures by a Church in Winter
Signed, oil on canvas
19¼ x 28¾in (49 x 73cm)
£9,000-9500 *S*

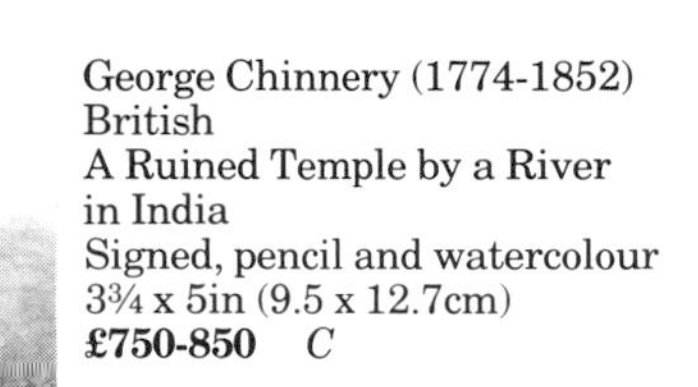

George Chinnery (1774-1852)
British
A Ruined Temple by a River
in India
Signed, pencil and watercolour
3¾ x 5in (9.5 x 12.7cm)
£750-850 *C*

James Hughes Clayton (active 1891-1929)
British
Wayside Cottages
Signed and dated 1898, watercolour
16 x 25in (40.6 x 63.5cm)
£1,000-1,200 *L*

William Stephen Coleman (1829-1904)
British
Playing on a Grassy Bank
Signed, watercolour heightened with bodycolour
over traces of pencil
8½ x 6½in (21.5 x 16.5cm)
£2,000-2,300 *S*

Condition is a major factor in a picture's price

George Cockram (1861-1950)
British
The Approach to Idwal Nant, Ffrancon
Watercolour over pencil
13½ x 20½in (34.3 x 52cm)
£200-250 *OL*

George Vicat Cole (1833-93)
British
A Straw Cart Crossing a Stone Bridge
Signed and dated 1868, oil on canvas
30 x 48in (76 x 122cm)
£4,700-5,200 *S*

Thomas Collier (1840-91) British A View in Arundel Park, Sussex
Signed and dated 1879, watercolour over pencil heightened with bodycolour
23½ x 35¾in (59.5 x 81cm)
£2,300-2,500 *S*

John Constable (1776-1837)
British
Water Meadows near Salisbury
Pen and brown ink, squared in pencil and incised watermark (Flincher and Sons 1823)
9 x 12½in (22.9 x 30.2cm)
Together with another study of trees
£2,800-3,100 *C*

The reverse of the present drawing is prepared with grey chalk for transfer, and is a pen and ink outline drawing of the subject that Constable exhibited at the Royal Academy in 1830. The picture is now in the Victoria and Albert Museum.

'The sound of water escaping from mill-dams, etc, willows, old rotten planks, slimy posts and brickwork. I love such things. Shakespeare could make everything poetical; he tells us of poor Tom's haunts among "sheep cotes and mills." As long as I do paint, I shall never cease to paint such places. . . Those scenes made me a painter and I am grateful.'
John Constable, letter to the Rev John Fisher, 1821

David Cox (1783-1859)
British
A Herdsman at the Door of a Priory
Signed and inscribed, pencil and watercolour
6¼ x 8⅝in (15.9 x 21.8cm)
£1,600-2,000 *C*

David Cox (1783-1859)
British
Changing Pasture
Signed and dated 1850-51, oil on canvas
23 x 33in (59 x 84cm)
£11,500-12,500 *S*

The provenance of Cox's work presents an interesting sidelight on the fluctuating values of a work of art. In 1858 it was purchased by a friend of the artist, along with another work for £28. In 1882, the painting was brought by Agnews for 1,400 gns and in 1934, sold at auction by Sotheby's for £540.

David Cox (1783-1859)
British
Barden Tower on the River Wharfe near Bolton Abbey
Pencil and watercolour
3¼ x 5⅛in (9.5 x 13cm)
£1,000-1,250 *C*

Henri-Edmond Cross (1856-1910)
French
Pins au Bord de la Mer
Stamped with the initials (Lugt 1305a)
Watercolour and pencil
6¼ x 9⅞in (16 x 25cm)
£3,600-4,000 *S*

Thomas Creswick (1811-69)
British
Woodland Scene with Lady Approaching a Cottage
Signed, oil on canvas
16in (40.6cm) diam
£400-600 *BWe*

George Cuitt (1789-1854)
British
View near Llangollen, North Wales
Bears inscription and dated 1826, oil on panel
11 x 13¾in (28 x 35cm)
£950-1,200 *S(S)*

J. Valentine Davis (1854-1930)
British
'Branches bare and rushes sere, now sadley mark the waning year'
A Scene in the Norfolk Broads of Fens; Swans on a River (a pair)
Both signed and one inscribed, oil on board
12½ x 19in (32 x 48cm)
£2,800-3,300 *S*

Charles François Daubigny (1817-78)
French
Spring on the Oise
Signed and dated 1877, oil on panel
16 x 26¼in (41 x 67cm)
£1,700-1,900 *S*

Hans Dahl (1849-1937)
Norwegian
Sailing in a Fjord
Signed, oil on canvas
21¾ x 16½in (55 x 42cm)
£2,500-2,900 *S*

François Diday (1802-77)
Swiss
A View of Lake Geneva, La Tour-de-Peilz and Vevey
Signed, oil on canvas
39¾ x 47in (93.5 x 119cm)
£18,500-20,000 *S*

Edward Duncan (1803-82)
British
Tantallon Castle with the Bass Rock in the Distance
Signed and dated 1869, pencil and watercolour with scratching out
32 x 26in (81.3 x 66.1cm)
£5,000-5,500 *C*

The Rev William Dickie (19thC?)
British
Loch Achray and Ben Venue
Signed, oil on canvas
18 x 30in (46 x 76cm)
£750-850 *S(SC)*

Alexander Brownlie Docharty (1862-1940) British
Loch Morar, Winter
Signed, oil on canvas
17½ x 24½in (44.5 x 62.5cm)
£1,400-1,800 *S(SC)*

W. R. Dommerson (b 1850)
Dutch
Zonneburgh on the River, Spaarn, Holland
Oil on canvas
11 x 15in (28 x 38cm)
£3,200-3,450 *FdeL*

Sir Alfred East (1849-1913) British
Shepherd with his Sheep in a River Landscape
Oil on canvas
36 x 52in (91.5 x 132cm)
£750-800 *C*

Johannes Bartholomaus Duntze (1823-95)
Dutch
A Village in Winter with Skating Figures
Signed and dated 1881, oil on canvas
14 x 19¼in (36 x 48.9cm)
£11,700-12,000 *Pol*

'With certain exceptions, good Victorian paintings have remained comparatively steady throughout the recession,' notes Simon Carter of the Polak Gallery. 'They seem to have been less affected than other more speculative areas of the market. Over the past year it has tended to be the better pictures that have sold, and it is often the case that the Victorian artists popular today, were those who were successful in their own times.'

Henry Earp Snr (1831-1913)
British
Rookford Bridge, Surrey
Signed and dated 1894,
watercolour heightened
with white
14 x 21in (36 x 54cm)
£900-1,000 *S*

Jules Dupré (1811-89)
French
A River Scene
Signed, oil on canvas
7 x 9½in (18 x 24cm)
£4,500-5,000 *S*

Georg Engelhardt (1823-83)
German
A Pastoral Scene in the Mountains
Signed, oil on canvas laid down on board
26½ x 37½in (67 x 95cm)
£2,800-3,200 *S(S)*

Sir Alfred East (1849-1913)
British
The Vines, Amberley, Sussex
'The Winter is past, the rain is over and gone, the flowers appear on the earth, the time of the singing of birds is come.'
Signed and dated 1897, oil on canvas
36 x 51in (91.5 x 134.5cm)
£10,500-11,000 *Pol*

English School (19thC)
A Barge in a Wooded River Landscape
Oil on canvas
16¾ x 27½in (42.5 x 70cm)
£1,200-1,500 *CSK*

English School (mid-19thC)
A Wooded Landscape, possibly in New Brunswick, Canada
Oil on canvas
27 x 33in (68.7 x 83.3cm)
£1,900-2,300 *CSK*

Although the artist is unidentified, this work exceeded its auction estimate, pictures of Canada being rare and as such desirable.

John Fairlie (active mid-19thC)
British
River Landscape
Signed with initials and date 1845
28 x 36in (70 x 90cm)
£2,000-2,300 *HSS*

The present work was removed from the Peacock Hotel, Rowsley, Derbyshire, originally the property of the Dukes of Rutland.

William Evans of Eton (1798-1877)
British
Cliveden from the Thames, Bucks
Watercolour over pencil
heightened with bodycolour
10 x 14in (25 x 35.5cm)
£1,700-2,000 *S*

R. Favelle (19thC)
Winter Landscape with Figures
on a Frozen River
Signed and dated 1864,
oil on canvas
24 x 36in (60.9 x 91.4cm)
£1,800-2,000 *CSK*

Anthony Vandyke Copley Fielding (1787-1855)
British
Kilburne Castle, Loch Awe, Argyllshire
Watercolour with scratching out
11½ x 15¾in (29.2 x 40cm)
£2,700-3,000 *C*

William Banks Fortescue (d 1924)
British
Newlyn
Signed, oil on canvas
12 x 19in (30.5 x 48.2cm)
£700-900 *L*

Anthony Vandyke Copley Fielding
(1787-1855)
British
A Ruined Abbey
Signed and dated 1850
12¼ x 18½in (31.5 x 47cm)
£8,500-9,500 *AG*

Blandford Fletcher (19th/20thC)
British
Fladbury Lock, Evesham – the Avon, Worcestershire
Signed, oil on canvas
20 x 27in (51 x 68.5cm)
£1,300-1,500 *S*

Anthony Vandyke Copley Fielding (1787-1855)
British
Dunderaw Castle, Loch Fynne, Inveraray
Signed, pencil and watercolour with scratching out
10½ x 14⅜ (26.7 x 36.5cm)
£2,300-2,500 *C*

Fielding was an extremely popular painter in the 19thC. He specialised in views of the Sussex Downs, mountainous landscapes and portrayals of the sea. 'No man has ever given, with the same flashing freedom, the grace of a running tide under a stiff breeze, nor caught with the same grace and precision, the curvature of the breaking wave, arrested or accelerated by the wind,' wrote Ruskin, a great admirer of his work. Though Fielding had many of the qualities of a 'considerable artist', he also had the defects of a successful one. According to Hardie (see Biblio) in later years his art became 'facile, dextrous, but not always sincere', the artist churning out smooth and standardised works, guaranteed to please but never to perturb his many Victorian patrons who could commission a Copley Fielding and know exactly what they were getting for their money.

Myles Birket Foster (1825-99)
British
Witley Common, Surrey
Signed with monogram, pencil, watercolour and bodycolour
8¾ x 12¾in (22.2 x 31cm)
£3,100-3,400 *C*

Myles Birket Foster (1825-99) British
A Cottage, Hambledown, Surrey
Signed with monogram, pencil, watercolour and bodycolour
8¾ x 12¾in (22.2 x 31cm)
£3,100-3,400 *C*

Birket Foster trained as a wood engraver, producing illustrations for Punch and the Illustrated London News. Circa 1859, he began to concentrate on watercolours and enjoyed a successful career. He travelled the continent painting many views and landscapes (in particular of Venice), but became best known for his watercolours of Surrey, where he built a house (at Whitley) in 1863. A supremely 'pretty' painter, hence his perennial popularity, Foster was an observant, meticulous and technically gifted artist. 'Under all the sugary surface of sentiment and prettiness lies a hard core of sound and honest craftmanship,' notes Hardie (see Biblio). 'We may deplore the sentiment, but we shall be narrow-minded if we fail to respect the artistry.'

Henry Charles Fox (1860-1913)
British
A Goose Girl Watering her Flock
Signed, watercolour heightened with white
14½ x 21½in (36.2 x 54.6cm)
and a companion piece
£980-1,150 *Bon*

Myles Birket Foster (1825-99)
British
On the Thames
Signed with monogram, watercolour over pencil, heightened with white
7¼ x 10½in (18.5 x 26.5cm)
£4,300-4,700 *S*

Condition is a major factor in a picture's price

Henry Charles Fox (1860-1913)
British
Dell Quay, Sussex; Boxham Mill, Sussex (a pair)
Signed and dated 1904, watercolour
13¾ x 20½in (35 x 52cm)
£950-1,150 *S(S)*

Theodore Fourmois (1814-71)
Belgian
Wooded Landscape
Signed and dated 1841
27¼ x 35¼in (69 x 89.5cm)
£4,200-4,600 *S(S)*

Robert Gallon (1845-1925)
British
Cookham Church on Thames
Signed, oil on canvas
17 x 13in (43 x 33cm)
£2,500-2,800 *S*

William Fraser Garden (1856-1921)
British
Hemingfold Mill, Huntingdonshire
Signed and dated '91, pencil and watercolour
7½ x 11in (19.1 x 28cm)
£1,900-2,200 *C*

Guglielmo Giusti (1824-1916)
Italian
Marina Piccola, Capri and the Faraglioni
Signed, gouache
10 x 15¾in (25.3 x 40cm)
£1,300-1,500 *Bon*

Robert Gallon (1845-1925)
British
A Highland Loch
Signed, oil on canvas
36 x 38in (91.4 x 71.2cm)
£2,700-3,000 *C*

Eugenio Gignous (1850-1906)
Italian
A Wooded Marsh Landscape at Sunset
Signed, oil on board
14½ x 24½in (36.8 x 61.6cm)
£9,400-10,000 *C*

Attributed to Winkworth Allen Gay (1821-1910)
American(?)
Wooded Landscape with Rabbits in the Foreground
Bears signature, oil on canvas
48 x 34½in (12.2 x 87cm)
£800-1,000 *Bon*

Vincent van Gogh (1853-90)
Dutch
Les Canots Amarrés
Oil on canvas
20½ x 25⅝ (52 x 65cm)
£1,450,000-1,650,000 *S*

The present work was painted at Asnieres on the outskirts of Paris in the spring or early summer of 1887. Van Gogh spent much of that summer working on the banks of the Seine often accompanied by Paul Signac, and paying frequent visits to his friend, the artist Emil Bernard, who had a studio in his parent's garden at Asnieres.
In the introduction to Lettres de Vincent van Gogh à Emile Bernard, *published in 1911, Bernard gives the following account of van Gogh's painting expeditions. 'He started off with a large canvas fastened to his back. This he divided into as many sections as the number of motifs; in the evening he brought it back completely filled, and it was like a little walking museum in which all the emotions of the day had been recorded. There were little sketches of the Seine filled with boats, islands with blue swings, fashionable restaurants with multicoloured sunshades, with pink sweetbrier... I revelled in their charm, all the more because I then lived in those surroundings, because they were the object of my own solitary wanderings, and because they reflected the spirit of what I sensed in them.*
For van Gogh, the two years (1886-88) he spent in Paris, were an important transitional period from the dark realism of his native Holland works to a freer, lighter more impressionist palette.

Alfred Augustus Glendening (active 1861-1903)
British
A Fisherman by a Flint Bridge, Mountains Beyond; and Cattle Watering in a Mountain Lake Landscape (a pair)
Signed with initials and dated '67, oil on canvas
8 x 7in (20.2 x 17.8cm)
£2,500-2,800 *C*

Carleton Grant (active 1885-89)
British
Lakeside Scene
Signed and dated, watercolour
20 x 13in (52 x 34cm)
£1,700-1,850 *GrG*

William W. Gosling (1824-83) British A Hot Day in the Harvest Field
Signed and dated 1877, oil on canvas
33 x 63in (83.8 x 160cm)
£20,000-22,000 *C*

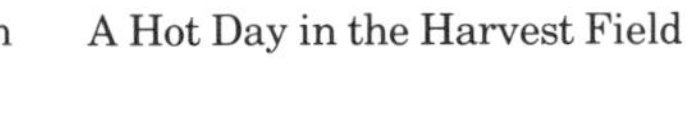

Charles Gregory (1849-1920)
British
In the Gendryth Valley, Cornwall
Signed and dated '87, pencil and watercolour heightened with white
13¾ x 20⅜in (35 x 51.8cm)
£830-950 *C*

James Stephen Gresley (1829-1908)
British
Driving Cattle by a Cottage; Cattle on a Bridge (a pair)
Signed, watercolour
8 x 11in (20 x 28cm)
£1,250-1,300 *S*

Frank Gresley (1855-1936) British
In a Bluebell Wood Signed
23½ x 17¼in (59 x 43.5cm)
£800-1,000 *S(S)*

James Stephen Gresley (1829-1908)
British
A Highland Landscape
Signed and dated 1879
17 x 25in (43 x 63cm)
£500-650 *HSS*

John Atkinson Grimshaw (1836-1893)
British
Mountain Solitude
Signed and dated 1885, oil on canvas
24 x 42in (61 x 107cm)
£9,000-10,000 *C*

Armand Guéry (1850-1912) French
A Shepherd with his Flock on a Path by Haystacks
Signed, oil on canvas
18 x 23⅞in (45.7 x 60.6cm)
£2,900-3,300 *C*

Théodore Gudin (1802-1880)
French
The Return of the Fishermen
Signed and dated 1826, oil on canvas
22 x 32in (56 x 81cm)
£3,000-3,400 *C*

Sir James Guthrie (1859-1930) British
The Shore, Helensburgh
Signed and dated '90, pastel
12¼ x 19¾in (31 x 50cm)
£5,600-6,000 *S(SC)*

In the 1880s Guthrie's landscapes were strongly influenced by the 'plein air' painting of Bastien Lepage. By the time the present work was produced however, he had already embarked upon his career as a portrait painter, so successful that he was to end up President of the Royal Scottish Academy. Though his commitment to naturalism rapidly disappeared from his oils, it still surfaced in his pastels. In 1890 he produced a whole series of landscapes and seascapes based round the town of Helensburgh. 'He attained a delicacy and bloom of tones and values, surprising in a dry medium and obtained in a way difficult to analyse,' Sir James Caw, writing about this series in 1932.

Armand Guillaumin (1841-1929)
French
Chemin à Damiette
Signed, painted c1886, oil on canvas
21¼ x 25½in (54 x 64.8cm)
£36,000-40,000 *C*

John Atkinson Grimshaw (1836-1893)
British
Scarborough by Moonlight from the steps of the Grand Hotel
Oil on board
10 x 14¾in (25.4 x 36.2cm)
£7,200-8,000 *C*

Charles Harmony Harrison
(1842-1902)
British
A Silent Pool
Signed and dated 1884, watercolour heightened with bodycolour
15 x 32¾in (38 x 83cm)
£1,200-1,500 *S(S)*

Henri-Joseph Harpignies (1819-1916)
French
A View of a Village
Signed and dated 1882, oil on panel
20½ x 32¾in (52 x 82cm)
£10,000-10,500 *S*

Louis Adolphe Hervier (1818-79) French A French Rural Landscape with a Woman by a Cottage
Signed 14 x 20in (35.5 x 48cm)
£650-850 *C(S)*

Richard Hilder (1813-48)
British
A Gypsy Encampment
Signed, oil on canvas
21 x 17in (53.2 x 43.2cm)
£1,500-1,700 *CSK*

Herman Herzog (1832-1932)
German
An Alpine River in Spate
Signed and dated 1897, oil on canvas
37 x 51in (94 x 129.7cm)
£3,500-4,000 *CSK*

Johannes Hilverdink (1813-1902)
Dutch
The Watchers
Signed and dated 1878, watercolour
25 x 13in (63.5 x 33cm)
£1,450-1,600 *QAG*

J. Holland Snr (active 1831-79)
British
Windmills Near Swankeston Bridge, Derbyshire
Signed, oil on canvas
£450-490 *BWe*

Joseph Holor (active 1834-66)
North Wales Lake Landscape
Signed, oil on canvas
9½ x 15½in (34 x 44.5cm)
£300-350 *ALL*

William Hull (1820-80)
British
Sheep Washing – Enton Mill, Surrey
Signed, watercolour with scratching out
16 x 22⅞in (40.8 x 58.1cm)
£2,300-2,600 *C*

Christiaan Immerzeel (1808-86)
Dutch
A Winter Landscape with Peasants Conversing by a Windmill
Signed, oil on panels
12 x 15½in (30.5 x 40cm)
£3,300-3,700 *CAm*

Circle of Arthur Joy (19thC)
Dutch
Figures in a Wooded Landscape
Bears signature Arthur Joy, oil on panel
22½ x 31¼in (58 x 79cm)
£2,000-2,300 *S*

Thomas Swift Hutton (c1875-1935)
British
A Stormy Day on the Northumberland (coast) – Seaton Sluice
Signed and inscribed
11 x 20in (28 x 51cm)
£800-900 *A*

Henry John Kinnaird
(active 1880-1920)
British
A Sussex Lane
Signed and inscribed,
watercolour heightened
with bodycolour
9½in x 13¼in (24 x 34cm)
£1,100-1,400 *S(S)*

Henry John Yeend King
(1855-1924)
British
A Lane in Surrey
Signed, oil on canvas
18 x 24in (45.5 x 61cm)
£1,600-1,900 *S*

Benjamin Williams Leader (1831-1923) British
On the Teme at Bransford Bridge,
Worcestershire
Signed and dated 1865, oil on board
16 x 24in (40.6 x 61cm)
£12,500-12,900 *HFA*

Leader abandoned a career in engineering for art and became a hugely successful painter. His picture February Fill-Dyke (Birmingham Art Gallery), painted in 1881, is one of the most famous paintings of the Victorian period, 'the popular equivalent in landscape of Millais's Bubbles', notes Victorian expert Jeremy Mass (see Biblio). Leader was greatly admired for his 'truth to nature', and the faithful exactitude of his landscape views.

Walter Langley (1852-1922) British
Figures on a Quayside, Polperro Harbour,
Cornwall
Signed, watercolour
14 x 10in (35.5 x 25.4cm)
£2,100-2,500 *L*

Edward Lear (1812-88) British
Umbrella Pines Near Cannes
Signed with monogram, watercolour over pencil heightened with bodycolour over gum arabic
4 x 7in (10 x 17.5cm)
£10,200-10,500 *DK*

Edward Lear (1812-88)
British
Constantinople from Ayoub
Signed: Edward Lear del/ Constantinople from Ayoub/ Sept. 1848/1856, pen and brown ink heightened with bodycolour on grey paper
11½ x 17½in (29 x 45cm)
£12,200-13,000 *S*

Charles Henri Joseph Leickert (1818-1907)
Belgian
A Dutch Winter Landscape
Signed, oil on canvas
17¼ x 23¼in (44 x 59cm)
£6,700-7,500 *S(S)*

Lear first visited Corfu in 1848 and the island made a deep impression on him. The present watercolour was painted on his second trip when he returned to Corfu in December 1855. The artist was delighted to be back on his favourite island and wrote to his friend Chichester Fortescue, 'Anything like the splendour of olive grove & orange garden, the blue of sky & ivory of church & chapel, the violet of mountain, rising from peacockwing-hued sea, & tipped with lines of silver snow, can hardly be imagined.'

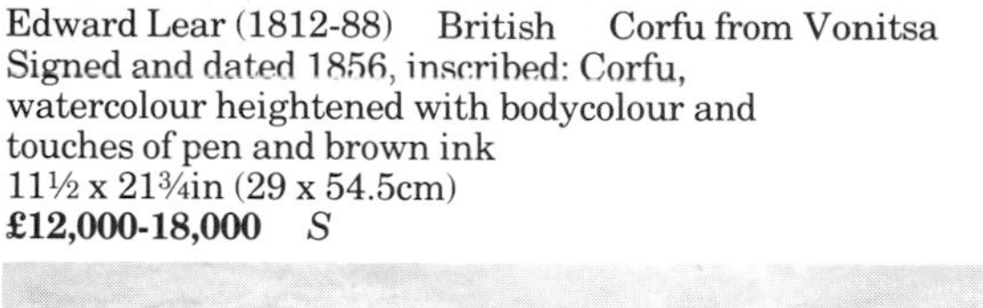

Edward Lear (1812-88) British Corfu from Vonitsa
Signed and dated 1856, inscribed: Corfu, watercolour heightened with bodycolour and touches of pen and brown ink
11½ x 21¾in (29 x 54.5cm)
£12,000-18,000 *S*

William Leighton Leitch (1804-83) British
Glen Finlas, Perth Watercolour
10¼ x 14½in (26.1 x 36.8cm)
£220-270 *Bon*

Leitch taught watercolour painting to Queen Victoria and many other members of the royal family.

William Linton (1791-1876) British
On the Lune, Sedburgh, Yorkshire
Oil on board
11 x 16½in (30 x 42cm)
£1,200-1,500 *S*

Charles James Lewis (1830-92) British
At the Back of the Mill
Signed and dated 1889, oil on canvas
24 x 49½in (61 x 118cm)
£4,500-5,000 *S*

George Lucas (active 1890-99) British
Harvest Time Signed and dated, watercolour
28 x 21in (70 x 54cm)
£2,500-2,650 *GrG*

William McTaggart (1835-1910)
British
The Farm
Signed and dated 1865, watercolour
9½ x 14¼in (24 x 36cm)
£1,800-2,000 *S(SC)*

Pompeo Mariani (1857-1927) Italian Shooting Duck
Signed, oil on canvas
28½ x 36¾in (72.4 x 93.4cm)
£10,500-11,000 *C*

Pompeo Mariani (1857-1927)
Italian
A Wooded Lake Landscape
Signed, oil on panel
29½ x 19in (75 x 48.2cm)
£7,200-7,600 *C*

James Edwin Meadows (1828-88)
British
A Country Footpath
Signed and dated 1855, oil on canvas
13¾ x 12in (35 x 30.5cm)
£750-900 *S*

Arthur Joseph Meadows (1843-1907)
British
Palanza Lago Maggiore
Signed and dated 1896, oil on canvas
12 x 20in (30.5 x 50.8cm)
£11,000-11,500 *BuP*

William Mellor (1851-1931)
British
On the Wharfe, Bolton Woods, Yorkshire
Signed and inscribed, oil on canvas
15 x 26in (38.1 x 66cm)
£750-800 *EH*

Henry Milburn (19thC?)
French?
Figures and Cattle in a Wooded River Landscape
Signed, oil on panel
10⅛ x 12¼in (25.3 x 31.5cm)
£1,300-1,600 *CSK*

Claude Monet (1840-1926)
French
Le Bassin D'Argenteuil
Signed and dated '75, oil on canvas
21¼ x 29in (54 x 74cm)
£490,000-550,000 *S*

Joel Isaacson describes this painting in his book on Monet as follows: 'The small boats and the hulking boat-hiring house in the foreground are set darkly against the view down-river at the end of the day. The boathouse was moored at the foot of the bridge on the Petit-Gennevilliers shore. This is seen, with its readily identifiable red houses and poplars, on the left. Monet did two longer-range views of the site from a high vantage-point, presumably on the bridge, in 1874 (Wildenstein, nos 334 and 335).'
This work fetched well below its lowest estimate of £600,000 when auctioned at Sotheby's last year, reflecting the downturn in the impressionist market.
Joel Isaacson, Claude Monet, Observation et Réflexion, *Neu '78.*

Sir David Murray (1849-1933) British
A Shady Pool
Signed and dated '89, watercolour
13¼ x 19¾in (33.5 x 50cm)
£2,300-2,700 *S(SC)*

Charles Morgan (active 1892-1911)
British
Harbour Scene
Oil on canvas
12 x 17in (30 x 44cm)
£600-650 *GrG*

Isobel Naftel (active 1857-91)
British
Sutton Scotney, Hants
Signed and dated 1886, pencil and watercolour heightened with white
10¼ x 14in (26 x 35.5cm)
£3,100-3,500 *CSK*

William Oliver (1804-1853) British
View on the River Inn near Swartz, Tyrol
Signed and dated 1849, oil on canvas
18¼ x 29½in (46.3 x 74.9cm)
£4,100-4,400 *C*

Sir Charles D'Oyly (1781-1845)
British
The Great Fig Tree at Bodh Gaya, India
Oil on canvas laid down on board
27½ x 34in (70 x 86.5cm)
£17,000-20,000 *S*

Bodh Gaya is situated in Northern India in the province of Bihar, seven miles south of the town of Gaya which lies south east of Benares. It is an important site for Buddhists since it was in the temple at Bodh Gaya that Buddha attained enlightenment. This painting dates from shortly after D'Oyly's trip to Gaya from 18th December 1824 to 2nd January 1825.

David Teniers the Younger (1610-1690)
Flemish
An Open Landscape with Travellers on a sandy Track
Signed with monogram, oil on panel
8 x 13in (20.3 x 33cm), and a companion, a pair
£28,000-30,000 *Bon*

Attributed to Jacob Koninck I (c.1610/15-after 1690)
Dutch
Extensive Landscape with a River and Mountains in the Distance
Oil on canvas
33 x 46¾in (83.8 x 118.7cm)
£19,000-20,000 *S(NY)*

Attributed to Adriaen van de Velde (1636-1672)
Dutch
Wooded Landscape with a Watermill and two Figures on the Banks of the River.
Oil on panel
21 x 16¼in (53.3 x 41.3cm)
£15,500-17,000 *S(NY)*

Attributed to William Ashford (1746-1824)
British
A Wooded River Landscape
Oil on canvas, in a carved wood frame
37 x 47in (94 x 119.5cm)
£9,500-10,000 *S*

George Barret Sen (1728-1784)
British
Hauling Timber through a Wood
Bodycolour
23 x 17¾in (58.4 x 45.1cm)
£4,000-4,200 *S(NY)*

Circle of George Barret (1728-1784)
British
Italianate Landscape with Travellers resting by a River
Oil on canvas
43 x 59in (108.5 x 149.5cm)
£6,200-6,700 *S*

Abraham Louis Rodolphe Ducros (1748-1810)
Swiss
The Falls of Tivoli
Pen, grey ink, watercolour and gouache on laid paper
26¾ x 41½in (68 x 105.4cm)
£17,000-18,000 *Bon*

George Lambert (1700-1765)
British
Italianate River Landscape with Figures in the Foreground
Signed and dated 1763, oil on canvas
26 x 39in (66 x 99cm)
£10,000-10,500 *S*

Bernard Gottfried Manskirch (1736-1817)
German
An extensive Landscape with Children playing by a River
53 x $68^{3}/_{4}$in (134.6 x 174.5cm)
£9,000-9,300 *C*

George Morland (1762-1804) and John Rathbone (1750-1807)
British
Rustics on a Path with a Distant View of London from Blackheath
Oil on panel
$8^{1}/_{2}$ x 12in (21.5 x 30.5cm)
£2,700-3,000 *S*

Alexander Nasmyth (1758-1840)
British
Near Inver, Sutherlandshire
Signed, oil on canvas
$26^{1}/_{4}$ x $34^{1}/_{2}$in (67 x 87cm)
£10,000-10,500 *S*

Paul Sandby (1730-1809)
British
A Bridge over a River, Wales
Gouache
$15^{3}/_{4}$ x $19^{3}/_{4}$in (40 x 50cm)
£4,200-4,500 *S*

Joseph Vernet (1714-1789)
French
Morning Landscape with Fishermen, and a Calm Sea in Moonlight:
A pair of paintings both signed and dated 1778, oil on canvas
Each: 119½ x 98in (303.5 x 260cm)
£880,000-1,000,000 *S(NY)*

John Varley (1778-1842)
British
Richmond Hill, Surrey
Watercolour over pencil heightened with bodycolour
10 x 14¾in (25.5 x 37cm)
£6,700-7,000 *S*

Francis Towne (1740-1816)
British
Lake Coniston, Lancashire
Pen and grey ink over pencil and watercolour on wove paper
6 x 18½in (15.5 x 47cm)
£25,000-30,000 *S*
Towne made many studies of the Lake District and was greatly inspired by its scenery. The present work (his only recorded view of Lake Conniston) shows the lake's northern end, looking west towards the Old Man of Coniston.

John 'Warwick' Smith (1749-1831)
British
Pont Rhianellt near Llangollen
Watercolour over pencil with touches of gum arabic
5 x 8¼in (13 x 21cm)
£2,300-2,500 *S*

Johann Christian Vollerdt (1708-1769)
German
Landscapes with a Manor House by a River, and with Figures and a Farmhouse on a Hill beside a River: a pair of paintings
Both indistinctly signed and one dated 1760, oil on canvas
Each: 23¼ x 29½in (59.1 x 74.9cm)
£22,000-25,000 *S(NY)*

David Bates (1840-1921)
British
A Glade in the New Forest
Signed and dated 1909, oil on canvas
16 x 24in (40.5 x 61cm)
£4,550-4,750 *Dr*

Alfred de Breanski, Snr.
(1852-1928)
British
The Valley of the Tay
Signed, oil on canvas
24 x 36in (60.5 x 91.5cm)
£5,800-6,200 *S*

Johann Ludwig Bleuler
(1792-1850)
Swiss
A View of the Château de Loufen
Stachelberg, Switzerland
Gouache
13¾ x 20in (35 x 51cm)
£5,600-6,000 *S*

Consalvo Carelli (1818-1900)
Italian
Peasants and a Herd of Goats
in a Landscape
Signed and inscribed *NAPOLI,*
watercolour
13½ x 20½in (34.5 x 52cm)
£5,300-5,500 *S*

Eugène Boudin (1824-1898)
French
La Somme près D'Abbeville- Clair de Lune
Signed and dated '94, oil on canvas
$21^{1}/_{4}$ x $17^{3}/_{4}$ (54 x 45cm)
£18,000-20,000 *S*

Gustave Courbet (1819-1877)
French
Sentier dans les Rochers
Signed, oil on canvas
15 x $18^{1}/_{8}$in (38.1 x 46cm)
£17,000-19,000 *C*
Painted c.1876

Jean Baptiste Camille Corot (1796-1875)
French
Le Pêcheur près de la Rive Tirant
son Epervier
Signed, oil on canvas
$13^{1}/_{4}$ x 16in (33.5 x 40.5cm)
£36,000-40,000 *S*
Executed c.1871

Eugène Delacroix (1798-1862)
French
Au Bord du Sebou
Signed and dated 1858, oil on canvas
$19^{1}/_{2}$ x $23^{1}/_{2}$in (50 x 60.7cm)
£400,000-410,000 *S*

Onorato Carlandi (1848-1939)
Italian
Olive Trees in a Landscape
Signed and inscribed Tivoli, watercolour
19¾ x 14in (50.5 x 35.5cm)
£1,800-2,000 *S*

Sir Alfred East (1849-1913)
British
In Provence
Signed and dated '96, oil on canvas
10 x 14in (25.4 x 35.5cm)
£1,250-1,350 *Dr*

Alfred Augustus Glendenning Snr (active 1861-1903)
British
Sunset over the Farm
Signed, oil on canvas
16 x 24in (40.5 x 61cm)
£4,300-4,500 *Dr*

Charles Cousin (19thC)
French
Haymaking in Normandy
Signed, oil on canvas
8 x 13½in (20 x 34cm)
£1,700-1,850 *SCG*

Alfred Augustus Glendenning Snr (active 1861-1903)
British
Capel Curig, North Wales
Signed, oil on canvas
13 x 23in (33 x 58.4cm)
£11,000-11,500 *HLG*

Henry Charles Fox (b.1860)
British
End of the Day
Signed and dated 1913
15 x 21½in (36 x 51cm)
£1,650-1,850 *CG*

Remigius van Haanen (1812-1894)
Dutch
Figures by a Channel
Oil on canvas
$19^{3}/_{4}$ x $24^{3}/_{4}$in (50 x 63cm)
£6,700-7,000 *S*

Heinrich Höfer (1825-1878)
German
Travellers on a Mountainous Path by the Staubbachfall near Lauterbrunnen
Signed and dated München 1876, oil on canvas
24 x $32^{3}/_{4}$ (61 x 83cm)
£19,000-21,000 *S*

Barend Cornelis Koekkoek (1803-1862)
Dutch
Figures in a Winter Landscape
Signed and dated 1842, oil on panel
$29^{1}/_{4}$ x $37^{1}/_{2}$in (74 x 95cm)
£190,000-200,000 *S*

Georg Emil Libert (1820-1908)
Danish
Fishing on a Fjord
Signed and dated Kobn 1846, oil on canvas
$35^{1}/_{2}$ x $52^{1}/_{4}$in (90 x 133cm)
£1,900-2,100 *S*

Karl Heffner (1849-1925)
German
A Wooded River Landscape
Signed, oil on canvas
$27\frac{3}{4}$ x $37\frac{1}{2}$in (70.5 x 95.3cm)
£5,000-5,300 *C*

Henry John Kinnard (Active 1880-1908)
British
Goring, Sussex
Signed and inscribed, watercolour
$13\frac{3}{4}$ x $20\frac{1}{2}$in (34 x 51cm)
£3,750-3,950 *SCG*

Robert Angelo Kittermaster Marshall (1849-1923)
British
Near Wableton, Hants
Signed
$13\frac{1}{4}$ x 23in (33.5 x 58.5cm)
£1,800-2,000 *S(S)*

Benjamin Williams Leader (1831-1923)
British
The Old Church, Whittington, Worcester
Signed and dated 1887, oil on canvas
20 x 30in (51 x 76cm)
£6,700-7,000 *S*

Edward Lear (1812-1888)
British
View from Saint Hospice, France
Signed, watercolour over pencil
$5\frac{1}{4}$ x 14in (13 x 35.5cm)
£6,000-6,300 *S*

James Edwin Meadows (1828-1888)
English
Haymaking in Hampshire
Signed, oil on canvas
29¾ x 48in (75.6 x 122cm)
£6,100-6,500 *Bon*

William Manners (active 1889-1910)
British
Rural Landscape
Signed, watercolour
9½ x 13½in (24 x 34cm)
£1,700-1,850 *SCG*

William Henry Mander (active 1880-1922)
British
A Landscape
Signed and dated 1913, oil on canvas
12 x 19in (30.5 x 48 cm)
£2,300-2,450 *HLG*

Charles Rolt (1845-1867)
British
Boy by a Stream
Signed and dated 1852, watercolour
12 x 8in (30.4 x 45.7cm)
£420-445 *Gra*

Henry H. Parker (1858-1930)
British
Evening-Backwater on the Thames, Henley
Signed, oil on canvas
24 x 36in (61 x 91cm)
£8,400-8,600 *S*

Thomas Mackay (19thC)
British
The Village Street
Signed, watercolour and bodycolour
with scratching out
7½ x 11½in (19 x 29cm)
£2,100-2,300 *S(S)*

Thomas Miles Richardson Jr. (1813-1890)
British
Sunset on Derwentwater from above Lodore
Signed and dated *1845*, watercolour over traces of pencil heightened with touches of bodycolour
24¼ x 39½in (64 x 100cm)
£8,500-8,800 *S*

Joseph Thors (active 1863-1900)
British
Summer Landscape
Signed, oil
20 x 30in (50.8 x 76cm)
£3,600-3,750 *Dr*

Frederick Waters Watts
British
(1800-1870)
River Landscape with Fishermen and a distant Village
Oil on canvas
21½ x 28¼in (54.5 x 72cm)
£6,100-6,500 *S*

George Clarkson Stanfield (1828-1873)
British
Fishing Boats on the Mosel with a Castle beyond; and Fishing Boats on the Mosel with a Town and Castle beyond A pair, signed and dated 'G.Clarkson Stanfield, 51' and 'G.Clarkson Stanfield, 52' respectively; oil on canvas
14½ x 21in (35.5 x 53.3cm)
£5,600-6,000 *CSK*

David Bomberg (1890-1957)
British
Ronda Valley
Oil on board
28 x 36in (71 x 91.5cm)
£40,000-45,000 *S*

Jean Dufy (1899-1964)
French
Paysage à Preuilly sur Claisse
Signed, oil on canvas
21¼ x 25½in (53.9 x 64.7cm)
Painted c1930
£7,100-7,500 *C*

Erich Kahn (1904-1980)
British
Landscape with Figures and a Building
Signed with monogram E.K 1952, oil
22 x 30in (56 x 76cm)
£2,900-3,000 *JD*

Robert Henri (1865-1929)
American
Cottages, Achill Island, Co. Mayo
Signed and dated 1913, oil on panel
12½ x 16in (32 x 41cm)
£4,500-4,800 *S*

Robert Bevan (1865-1925)
British
Weeping Ash
Signed, oil on canvas
28 x 23in (71 x 58.5cm)
£24,000-25,000 *C*
Painted in 1923

Odette Dumaret (1913-1989)
French
Les Grands Arbres
39½ x 32in (100 x 81cm)
£5,800-6,000 *CE*

Dame Laura Knight (1877-1970)
British
The May Tree
Signed, oil on canvas
30 x 40in (76 x 102cm)
£41,000-45,000 *C*
Painted c.1914-1915

André Lhote (1885-1962)
French
Personnages dans un Paysage
Signed, oil on canvas
19¼ x 25¼in (49 x 64cm)
£11,200-11,700 *S*

Albert Lebourg (1849-1928)
French
Bord d'étang de Chalou-Moulineux
Environs d'Etampes
Signed, oil on canvas
21¼ x 31⅞ (54 x 81cm)
£11,200-11,700 *S*

Maximilien Luce (1858-1941)
French
Au Bord de la Route
Signed and dated 1905, oil on canvas
15 x 17⅞in (38 x 45.5cm)
£21,000-25,000 *S*

Henri Martin (1860-1943)
French
Paysage du Lot
Signed, oil on canvas
27½ x 38⅝in (70 x 98cm)
£45,000-50,000 *S*

James McIntosh Patrick (b.1907)
British
Oak Trees in May, Carse of Gowric
Signed, oil on canvas
21½ x 25in (54.5 x 63.5cm)
£11,400-12,000 *Bon*

Francis Picabia (1879-1953)
French
Bords du Loing
Signed, oil on canvas
19⅝ x 24in (50 x 61cm)
£21,000-25,000 *S*
Painted C.1904-1905

Henri Le Sidaner (1862-1939)
French
Le Vieux Pont sur L'Elle
Signed, oil on canvas
26 x 32in (66 x 81.5cm)
£42,800-50,000 *S*
Painted in Quimperlé in 1923

Theo van Rysselberghe (1862-1926)
Belgian
Landscape in Yellow and Purple
Signed with monogram, oil on canvas
18 x 22in (46 x 56cm)
£24,000-28,000 *Bon*

Maurice Utrillo (1883-1955)
French
Paysage à La Lessive
Signed, gouache on card
15¼ x 19¾in (38.5 x 50cm)
£16,000-18,000 *S*
Executed c.1920

Maurice de Vlaminck (1876-1958)
French
Maison au Bord de Riviere
Signed, oil on canvas
13 x 17in (33 x 43.2cm)
£35,000-40,000 *S(NY)*

Edouard Vuillard (1868-1940)
French
Petite Maison à Saint-Jacut
Stamped with the signature (Lugt no.2497a), distemper on paper mounted on canvas
19¾ x 25½in (50.2 x 64.8cm)
£26,000-29,000 *S(NY)*

Alfons Walde (b.1891)
Austrian
Haüser in Winterlandschaft
Oil on board
17 x 13in (43 x 33cm)
£10,500-11,000 *S*

Harry Sutton Palmer (1854-1933)
British
Stratford-on Avon
Signed, watercolour
14¼ x 20½in (36 x 52cm)
£2,400-2,700 *S*

Samuel Palmer (1803-1881)
British
Cypresses at the Villa D'Este, Tivoli
Watercolour over pencil heightened with bodycolour, gum arabic and scratching out 20¼ x 28in (51 x 71cm)
£22,500-27,500 *S*

This watercolour shows the famous cypresses of the Villa d'Este, with the water organ to the right and a distant view of Rome beyond. Palmer was entranced by the Villa d'Este which he visited with his wife in the late 1830s. 'The Villa d'Este is enchantment itself,' he wrote in 1838, 'the grounds are small but have work for months. Michael Angelo built the house and his inspiring angels seem to have laid out the gardens and designed the fountains.'.

Henry H. Parker (1858-1930)
British
Pangbourne on Thames
Signed and inscribed, oil on canvas
20 x 30in (51 x 76cm)
£19,500-20,000 *BB*

Henry H. Parker (1858-1930)
British
A Surrey Cornfield
Oil on canvas
20 x 30in (51 x 79cm)
£12,000-12,500 *JN*

Henry H. Parker (1858-1930)
British
Near Marlow on Thames
Signed and inscribed, oil on canvas
16 x 27in (40.6 x 68.6cm)
£4,650-4,850 *WG*

Sidney Richard Percy (1821-86)
British
Lake Landscape with Cattle
Signed, oil on canvas
24 x 40in (61 x 101.6cm)
£2,700-3,000 *C*

Waller Hugh Paton (1828-95)
British
Invermoriston
Signed, inscribed and dated 1887, watercolour heightened with bodycolour
9½ x 14in (24 x 35.5cm)
£1,200-1,500 *S(SC)*

James Baker Pyne (1800-70)
British
Borrowdale
Signed and dated 1849, oil on canvas
26 x 36in (66 x 91.5cm)
£2,800-3,100 *S*

According to the supplement to Bryan's Dictionary of Painters and Engravers (1866), Pyne was articled to an attorney, but on coming of age, threw up the profession of the law, for the more poetic but more precarious pursuit of landscape painting. He specialised in marine and lake subjects 'remarkable for their delicate treatment . . . atmospheric effects, and aerial perspective.'

James Price (active 1842-76)
British
Shepherd with Sheep and Dog in Lane
14½ x 25½in (36.8 x 63.5cm)
£1,000-1,150 *CG*

James Poole (1804-86)
British
A Highland Wooded River Landscape
Signed, oil on canvas
23¾ x 36¾in
(60.3 x 93.3cm)
£1,350-1,500 *Bon*

Alfred Powell (late 19thC)
British
Rye
Watercolour
10 x 14in (25.4 x 35.5cm)
£2,000-2,200 *MS*

Georg Anton Rasmussen
(1842-1914)
Norwegian
Figures on a Beach in a Fjord
Signed and dated 1883, oil on canvas
26½ x 19¼in (67 x 49cm)
£3,400-3,800 *S*

Samuel Reid (1854-1919)
British
Boating on Kelsey Manor Lake
Signed, oil on canvas
18 x 24in (45.5 x 61cm)
£2,800-3,100 *S(SC)*

George Melvin Rennie (1802-60)
British
Dinnet Moor
Signed and inscribed, oil on canvas
16 x 24in (41 x 61cm)
£900-1,000 *S(SC)*

Alfred William Rich
(1856-1921)
British
On the South Downs
Signed, watercolour
4 x 6in (10.1 x 15.2cm)
£400-450 *MS*

Thomas Miles Richardson Jr (1813-90) British Goatfell, Glen Rossie, Isle of Arran
Signed and dated 1847, watercolour over pencil heightened with white, inscribed on label attached to backboard: No 3./'Goatfell. Glen Rossie'/Isle of Arran/T. M. Richardson Jnr./ London./1847 28 x 39½in (71 x 100cm)
£4,500-5,000 *S*

Percy Robertson (1868-1934)
British
The South Coast
Signed, watercolour
14 x 22in (35.5 x 55.8cm)
£1,550-1,650 *MS*

C. Edward Roe (19thC)
British
An Extensive Country View
Signed and dated 1884, oil on canvas
33⅜ x 35⅜in (59.4 x 89.8cm)
£425-500 *Bon*

Oscar Ricciardi (1864-1935) Italian Marina Grande, Capri
Signed, oil on canvas 10¼ x 15¼ (26 x 38.7cm)
£2,100-2,500 *C*

Frederico Rossano (1835-1912) Italian
A Country Farmstead
Signed, oil on canvas
23½ x 19½ (59.7 x 49.6cm)
£15,500-17,000 *CSK*

Nicolaas Johannes Roosenboom (1805-80)
Dutch
Figures in a Winter Landscape
Signed with initials, oil on panel
8 x 12in (20 x 30.5cm)
£2,800-3,100 *S*

Tom Rowden (1842-1926)
British
Perranporth near Newquay, Cornwall
Signed, watercolour
12 x 18in (30 x 46cm)
£500-525 *BCG*

William Shayer (1788-1879)
British
Unloading the Catch
Oil on canvas
18 x 24in (46 x 61cm)
£12,000-12,500 *JN*

Daniel Sherrin (active late 19thC)
British
Children in a Landscape
Signed, oil on canvas
19½ x 29½in (49.5 x 75cm)
£1,050-1,200 *S(S)*

Henry Shirley (1843-70)
British
Sorting Fish
Signed, oil on canvas
14 x 23in (36 x 59cm)
£1,000-1,200 *S*

William Simpson (1823-99)
British
Temple of Martund, Kashmir
Signed, inscribed and dated 1862, pencil and watercolour heightened with white
13¾ x 19¾in (35 x 50.3cm)
£3,100-3,500 *C*

Henry J. Sands (active 1883-99)
British
Hazy Summer
Signed, oil
16 x 20in (40.6 x 50.8cm)
£600-650 *Dr*

John Falconer Slater (1857-1937)
British
Farmyard with Horse, Cart, Man, Chickens, etc
Signed, oil on panel
22 x 18in (55.9 x 45.7cm)
£2,000-2,200 *DG*

Edward Smith (19thC)
British
A Coastal Scene at Llanstephan, Carmarthenshire
Signed and dated 1837, oil on canvas
24 x 33in (61 x 84cm)
£3,600-4,000 *S*

Jan Jacob Coenraad Spohler (1837-1923)
Dutch
The Ferry
Signed, oil on canvas
24½ x 32½in (62 x 82.5cm)
£13,400-15,500 *S*

John Brandon Smith (1848-1884)
British
Waterfall on the Dulas, South Wales
Signed, oil on canvas
17¼ x 13½ (44 x 34cm)
£2,100-2,400 *S(S)*

Thomas Spinks (active 1872-80)
British
An Angler in a River Valley below a Ruined Abbey
Signed, oil on canvas
13½ x 19½in (34 x 49.5cm)
£800-900 *S(S)*

Henry John Sylvester Stannard (1870-1951)
British
The Return of the Market Cart
Signed, watercolour
20 x 35in (61 x 88.9cm)
£12,500-12,950 *HFA*

Follower of George Clarkson Stanfield (1793-1867)
British
Peasants on the Shores of a North Italian Lake
Bears indistinct initials, oil on canvas
23¼ x 42¼in (59 x 107.5cm)
£1,500-1,800 *S(S)*

James Stark (1794-1859) British Hampstead Heath
Oil on canvas 17½ x 23¾in (44.5 x 60.5cm)
£7,500-8,500 *S*

Ada Stone (active 1879-1904)
British
A Country River Landscape
Signed, oil on canvas, a pair
23¼ x 19in (59 x 48.3cm)
£600-700 *Bon*

Arthur Claude Strachan (active 1885-1929)
British
Streatley Mill
Signed, inscribed and numbered 120 on reverse; watercolour heightened with white and gum arabic 11¾ x 18⅜in (29.9 x 46.7cm)
£2,100-2,500 *C*

Jakob Suter (1805-1874)
Swiss
The Mer de Glace from Mount Anvers, Switzerland
Signed and dated 1829, watercolour
6¾ x 9¾in (17 x 24.5cm)
£1,400-1,700 *S*

William Thomas Such (active 1847-57)
British
The Woodcock's Haunt
Signed and dated 1856, oil on canvas
36 x 48in (91.5 x 122cm)
£4,200-5,000 *S*

John Gutteridge Sykes (b1866)
British
Cornish Landscape
Watercolour
26 x 19in (66 x 48cm)
£800-900 *GrG*

Joseph Thors (active 1863-1900)
British
The Path by the Pond
Oil on canvas
20 x 16in (51 x 40.5cm)
£4,800-4,950 *JN*

Paul Desiré Trouillebert (1829-1900)
French
A View of Romarantin in the Loire Valley
Signed, oil on canvas
14½ x 21¾in (37 x 55cm)
£20,000-25,000 *S*

Franz Richard Unterberger (1832-1902)
Austrian
Rocca d'Amalfi
Signed and inscribed 'Bruxelles' and titled 'Rocca d'Amalfi, Italia', oil on canvas
32 x 27¼in (81 x 69.5cm)
£21,000-25,000 *S*

The present work doubled its auction estimate when sold at Sotheby's sale of 19thC continental pictures in March 1992. Like many of the works on offer it went to a private buyer. The sale was notable for the presence and expenditure of Italian bidders, creating high prices for several works of Italian interest and bringing a welcome boost to the continental sale and the British art market.

J. A. Henderson Tarbet (19thC)
British Loch Achray, Ben Venue
Signed, bears title on a label on the frame, oil on canvas
20 x 27in (51 x 68.5cm)
£800-850 *S(SC)*

Adrianus Vrolijk (1834-62) Dutch
A Landscape with Cows by a River
Signed and indistinctly dated, oil on panel 18½ x 26in (47 x 66.5cm)
£3,800-4,200 *S*

Charles Vacher
(1818-83)
British
Thebes
Signed, inscribed
and dated 1863,
pencil and watercolour
13¾ x 35⅞in
(34.9 x 91.1cm)
£1,250-1,450 *C*

Robert Holland
Walker (active
1892-1920)
British
On the Lea,
Warwickshire
Signed, oil on
canvas
7 x 10in
(17 x 25cm)
£420-470 *BCG*

Edward Wilkins Waite (1854-1924) British The Old Water-Mill Signed, oil on canvas
20 x 30in (50.8 x 76.2cm) **£10,000-10,500** *C*

Edmund George Warren (1834-1909)
British
The Way to the Village
Signed and dated 1866, watercolour heightened with bodycolour
9¾ x 14in (25 x 35.5cm)
£4,500-4,800 *S*

Edgar E. West (active 1857-81)
British
Looking Across the Severn Valley
Signed, watercolour heightened with bodycolour
27½ x 48in (70 x 122cm)
£1,600-2,000 *S*

Linnie Watt (active 1875-1906)
British
The Harbour at Concarneau
Signed and inscribed, oil on canvas
12½ x 18½in (31.75 x 46.3cm)
£5,750-6,250 *BuP*

Arthur White (1865-1963)
British
A Rural Landscape with Two Women Holding Baskets of Washing in the Foreground, Thatched Cottages Beyond
Signed
10 x 14in (25 x 35.5cm)
£230-250 *HSS*

George Augustus Williams
(1814-1901)
British
The Cowherd's Rest
Signed with monogram,
oil on canvas
14 x 20in (35.5 x 51cm)
£1,300-1,500 *S*

Edward Charles Williams (1807-81)
British Gypsies by the Way
Bears title on a label on the stretcher,
oil on canvas
20 x 28in (51 x 71cm)
£6,000-6,500 *S*

Walter Williams (1835-1906)
British
Estuary Landscape at Sunset with Figures, Cattle, Moored Ship and Cottage in the Foreground
Signed and inscribed 'Plymouth 1850', oil on canvas
19½ x 31½in (48.75 x 78.75cm)
£2,000-2,400 *P(S)*

Samuel Williamson (1792-1840)
British
Pastoral Landscape
Signed, oil on canvas
24 x 33in (61 x 84cm)
£3,750-3,950 *FdeL*

G. Wright (19thC)
British
A Woodland View with Sheep in the Foreground
Signed, oil on canvas
20 x 30in (50.8 x 76.2cm)
£230-280 *Bon*

20th Century

Maxwell Ashby Armfield (1882-1972)
British
Relics of Palma, Mallorca
Tempera on gesso-prepared board
15½ x 20in (39.5 x 51cm)
£2,300-2,600 *C*

Lucien Adrion (1889-1953) French
Village Street
Signed, oil on canvas
19¾ x 34¾in (50.2 x 60.3cm)
£1,300-1,500 *S(NY)*

G. Warner Allen (1916-88)
British
The Spires of Oxford
Signed with monogram and dated 1948, oil
23½ x 19½in (60 x 50cm)
£1,100-1,300 *LH*

Mary Armour (b1902)
British
Steeple Brae
Signed and dated 'Mary Armour 57'
Oil on canvas
23 x 32¼in (58.5 x 82cm)
£750-850 *C*

Alexandre Altmann (b1885)
Russian
A Village
Signed, oil on canvas
23¼ x 28in (59 x 71.5cm)
£3,400-3,700 *S*

John Ambrose (20thC) British Mousehole
Signed, oil 12 x 15in (30.5 x 38.1cm)
£700-800 *GeC*

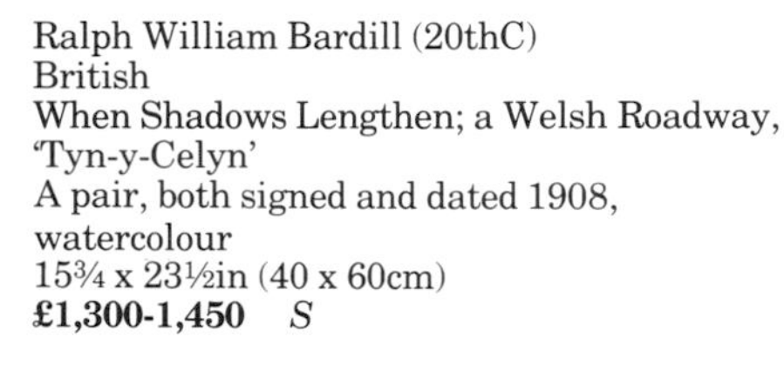

Ralph William Bardill (20thC)
British
When Shadows Lengthen; a Welsh Roadway, 'Tyn-y-Celyn'
A pair, both signed and dated 1908, watercolour
15¾ x 23½in (40 x 60cm)
£1,300-1,450 *S*

S. J. Lamorna Birch (1869-1955)
British
June – The Fallen Woods of Fetternear
Signed, oil on canvas
24 x 30in (62 x 77cm)
£6,550-6,750 *AdG*

John Bratby (b1928) British
Blackheath
Signed, oil on canvas
36 x 48in (92 x 112cm)
£1,800-2,000 *C*

Painted in 1953-54. This is a view from the top of Blackheath Hill, painted from the artist's former home at 42 Dartmouth Row.

Owen Bowen (1873-1967)
British
A Yorkshire Farm
Signed, oil on canvas
16 x 24in (40.6 x 61cm)
£3,300-3,500 *WG*

Edwin Byatt (b1888)
British
A Farmstead
Signed
27¼ x 35½in (69.5 x 90cm)
£1,500-1,600 *S(S)*

Christo (b1935) Rumanian
Packed Coast (project for the West Coast 15 Miles Long)
Signed, titled and dated 1968, plastic sheeting, string, gouache and pencil on a photograph on paper laid down on board
28 x 22in (71 x 56cm)
£13,500-14,500 *S*

Sue Campian (b1944)
British
Down the Valley, Frigiliana
Signed and dated '91
32 x 36in (61 x 91.5cm)
£700-800 *Bon*

Sir Winston Churchill (1874-1965)
British
A Lake, Norfolk
Signed with initials, oil on canvas
24 x 20in (61 x 51cm)
£35,500-40,500 *S*

Winston Churchill was a traditionalist when it came to painting, both in his own work and his appreciation of others. In a speech to the Royal Academy in 1959, Sir Alfred Munnings recalled the following interchange: 'Alfred,' asked Churchill, 'if you met Picasso coming down the street, would you join with me in kicking his something, something, something?' 'Yes sir, I would,' replied the artist fervently. When Graham Sutherland painted his portrait, Churchill and his circle were famously outraged. 'The portrait is a complete disgrace,' fumed Lord Hailsham. 'It is bad-mannered; it is a filthy colour . . . Churchill has not got all that ink on his face – not since he left Harrow, at any rate.' Churchill refused to let the portrait be hung in Parliament and eventually his wife destroyed it.

Fred Cumming (b1930)
British
Etretat, Normandy
Signed, oil on board
16 x 16in (40.6 x 40.6cm)
£1,600-1,700 *NGG*

'There is a difference in attitude between purchasing contemporary and 19thC or earlier pictures', explains dealer John Noott who covers both areas. 'People buying a contemporary work, be it for £200 or £1,200 tend not to think so much about investment. They see something, they love it, and if they can afford it, they buy it. There is always a chance that the artist might subsequently become famous and the work itself more valuable, but that is not the prime motivation. Nevertheless, he adds, 'contemporary works are good value in today's recessionary market. The bulk of my artists haven't put their prices up for three years and you can get quality work for less money than in many other fields.'

Edward Dawson (20thC)
British
The Picnic – Springtime
Signed, oil
7½ x 9½in (19 x 24cm)
£450-470 *JN*

Marcel Dyf (1899-1985)
French
La Ferme aux Peupliers
Signed, oil on canvas
18 x 21¾in (45.8 x 55.3cm)
£3,400-3,800 *C*

David Donaldson (20thC)
British
Church at Buisson
Signed, oil on canvas
30 x 30in (77 x 77cm)
£14,500-15,000 *OEG*

John Donaldson (b1945)
British
Tournesols
Signed, oil on canvas
18 x 24in (46 x 62cm)
£1,750-1,850 *Om*

Manuel Garcia y Rodriguez (1863-1925)
Spanish
By the Water Mill
Signed and dated 1920, oil on canvas
26 x 16in (66 x 40.6cm)
£3,600-4,000 *C*

Gregory Davis (20thC) British
Vines, Autumn Morning, South West France
Oil 16 x 22in (40.5 x 56cm)
£1,050-1,200 *JN*

Richard Eschke (1859-1944)
German
The Young Piper
Signed and dated 1901, oil on canvas
24 x 30½in (61 x 77.5cm)
£2,300-2,600 *S*

A. Moulton Foweraker (1874-1955)
British
A Spanish Landscape
Signed, watercolour
13 x 20in (33 x 51cm)
£2,300-2,500 *JN*

Emile Othon Friesz (1879-1949)
French
La Montagne Sainte Victoire
Signed, watercolour on paper
18⅛ x 24in (46 x 61cm)
£8,000-8,500 *C*

Henry Charles Fox (b1860)
British
In the Springtime
Signed and dated 1910, watercolour
25½ x 39½ (64.7 x 100.3cm)
£2,800-3,000 *CG*

This watercolour was exhibited in the R.A. in 1910 and was sold for £105.

Wilfrid-Gabriel de Glehn (1870-1951)
British
Bathing in the Avon, Wiltshire
Signed
22¼ x 28in (56.5 x 71.1cm)
£5,500-6,000 *CSK*

William Mervyn Glass (20thC?)
British
Iona
Signed with initials, oil on canvas laid down on board
12½ x 15½in (32 x 39.5cm)
£2,500-3,000 *S(SC)*

William Fraser Garden (1856-1921)
British
The Ferry Boat Inn, Holywell
Signed and dated 1909, watercolour
7¾ x 11in (19.7 x 28cm)
£550-650 *Bon*

Mervyn Goode
British
February Shadows on the Bridge
Signed, oil
20 x 20in (51 x 51cm)
£825-875 *Bne*

John Gleich (b1879)
German
On the Ganges
Signed 'J. Gleich', oil on canvas
28½ x 40in (72.5 x 102cm)
£9,500-10,000 *C*

Spencer Frederick Gore (1878-1914) British
Garth House, Hertingfordbury Painted c1908,
oil on canvas 12 x 16¼in (30.5 x 41cm)
£6,500-6,800 *C*

Gore was a founder member of the Camden Town Group and a key participant in many of the events and movements that shaped British art between 1900 and 1914. Gore died just before the outbreak of the First World War, at the age of only 35, when in pursuit of his art, having got wet while out painting and contracted pneumonia. In an essay 'A Perfect Modern', his friend and early mentor, Walter Sickert, praised his abilities to create beautiful pictures not only from lovely scenes, but from the most unpromising and ugly material. 'Gore had the digestion of an ostrich. A scene, the dreariness and hopelessness of which would strike terror into most of us, was for him a matter for lyrical and exhilerated improvisation. . . The artist is he who can take a flint and wring out a star of roses.'

Philipp Graf (b1874)
German
A River Valley in Spring
Signed and inscribed, oil on panel
9¼ x 12in (23.5 x 30.5cm)
£2,800-3,000 *C*

Frederick Gore (b1913)
British
Olive Grove, Majorca
Signed, oil on canvas
32 x 40in (81 x 101.5cm)
£5,300-5,600 *C*

Rigby Graham (b1931) British
The Sadness of Passing Time Oil
24 x 24in (61 x 61cm)
£3,300-3,500 *Go*

Rigby Graham could be seen as a figure of hope to all neglected and despairing artists. 'For thirty five years his work was almost completely ignored and found very few buyers.' explains dealer Mike Goldmark. 'Suddenly over the past two years he has been "discovered". The art magazine Modern Painters *wrote a piece about him, as did Frances Spalding. Suddenly there were a whole load of articles and this year there will be a television documentary. Graham's reputation is now assured and his prices are rising correspondingly.'*

George Leslie Hunter (1879-1931)
British
A Tower
Signed, oil on board
27 x 19in (68.5 x 48cm)
£7,200-8,000 *S(SC)*

Josef Herman (b1911) British Carrying the Sack
Oil on board 10½ x 12½in (27 x 32cm)
£850-950 *Bon*

Forrest Hewit (1870-1956)
British
Mont Orgeuil, Jersey
Signed, oil on canvas
19 x 23in (48.2 x 58.4cm)
£450-500 *G*

Rowland Hilder (b1905) British Oak Farm, East Anglia
Signed, pencil, watercolour, bodycolour and coloured crayons
13½ x 21in (34 x 53.5cm) **£850-950** *C*

Though born in the United States, Hilder's work is essentially British. He came to England on the Lusitania at the age of 10 and later studied etching and drawing at Goldsmith's School of Art. Painter and illustrator, he was known for his pictures and drawings of Kent and the English landscape. He worked on the Shell Guide to Flowers *and in 1958 produced the pictures for the* Shell Guide to Kent, *the first of the series. 'His paintings of Kent look back to a pre-industrial age,' wrote Francis Spalding, 'and have done much to sustain the myth of rural England.'*

Eric Hesketh Hubbard (1892-1957)
British
The Bridge at Richmond, Yorkshire
Signed, oil on canvas
17½ x 23½in (44.4 x 59.6cm)
£1,175-1,275 *G*

David Jones (1895-1974)
British
The Park
Signed, watercolour
24 x 19in (61 x 48cm)
£5,600-6,000 *S*

Augustus John (1878-1961)
British
Mas de Galeron
Signed, oil on canvas
19¾ x 23¾in (50 x 60cm)
£10,000-11,000 *S*

Painted c1938. Dorelia John rented the Mas de Galeron, near St Remy-de-Provence in 1936, as a studio for Augustus and he first went there in September 1937. The family returned to the Mas – the local word for a small farmhouse – every summer until September 1939 when they had to leave precipitately, having dismissed too lightly the threat of war, catching the last boat from Le Havre and reaching England the day before war was declared.

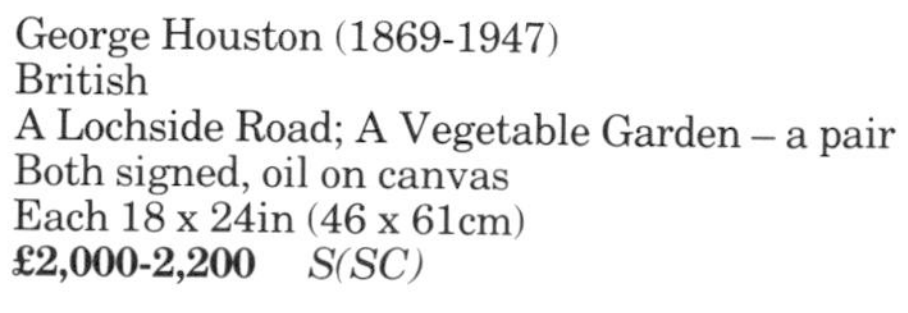

George Houston (1869-1947)
British
A Lochside Road; A Vegetable Garden – a pair
Both signed, oil on canvas
Each 18 x 24in (46 x 61cm)
£2,000-2,200 *S(SC)*

Pyton Stepanovich Keller (b1909)
Russian
On the Green Island
Signed and dated 1966, oil on card
19 x 25¼in 48 x 64cm)
£450-480 *S(SC)*

James Kay (1858-1942)
British
Afterglow on the Clyde
Signed, watercolour and bodycolour over black chalk
11¼ x 15in (28.5 x 38cm)
£500-550 *S(SC)*

Alan Carr Linford (20thC) British
St. Margaret's Bay, Kent
Signed, oil on canvas
18 x 25¼in (45.7 x 63.6cm)
£1,600-1,800 *RdeR*

Alois Kalvoda (1875-1934)
Czech
An Autumn Landscape with a Lake
Signed, oil on canvas
58¾ x 59in (149 x 150cm)
£4,500-4,800 *S*

Vladimir Mikhailovich Klynov (b1932)
Russian
Winter
Signed and dated 1961, oil on card
19¾ x 27½in (50 x 70cm)
£450-650 *S(SC)*

Vladimir Mikhailovich Klynov, born 1932, Rostov-on-Don. Graduated from V. I. Surikov Art Institute, Moscow, 1959, studied under D. K. Mochalsky. Member of the Union of Artists of the USSR since 1963. Lives in Rostov.

André Lhote (1885-1962) French Village en Automne
Signed, oil on canvas 14 x 19¾in (35.6 x 50.2cm)
£5,900-6,500 *S(NY)*

William Lee-Hankey (1869-1952)
British
The River Conway, North Wales
Signed and inscribed, oil on canvas
24 x 30in (61 x 76cm)
£4,500-4,800 *C*

Enrique Marin (19th/20thC)
Spanish
A Laden Donkey
Signed and inscribed 'Granada', watercolour
17¼ x 12½in (44 x 32cm)
£1,200-1,500 *S*

Emilie LeJeune (1885-1964) French
Le Hameau Provençal Signed and dated '40, oil on canvas
10⅝ x 13¾in (27 x 35cm) **£1,200-1,400** *C*

Norah McGuiness
(b1903) British
The Black Gate
Signed with initials
and dated, oil on
canvas
11½ x 15in
(29 x 38cm)
£1,400-1,600 *C*

Vitaly Alexandrovich Markin (b1924)
Russian A Stretch of the Don River
Signed and dated 1991, oil on card
19¾ x 27½in (50 x 70cm)
£300-325 *S(SC)*

Vitaly Alexandrovich Markin, born 1924, village of Sredny near Rostov. Graduated from M. B. Grekov Art School, Rostov, 1949 and Polygraphic Institute, Moscow, 1962. Member of the Union of Artists of the USSR since 1957. Lives in Rostov.

Albert Marquet (1875-1947) French Le Port d'Alger
Signed, oil on canvas 10¾ x 16⅛in (27 x 41cm)
£51,000-55,000 *C*

Painted c1940.

Henry Morley (1869-1937) British
A Shepherdess Driving her Flock out of a Farmyard
Signed, with a sketch of a ewe and lambs applied to the reverse, oil on panel
11 x 15in (28 x 38cm)
£370-420 *AG*

Paul Maze (1887-1979)
French
Canal, France
Signed and dated 1955, pastel
21¾ x 29½in (53.1 x 72.5cm)
£8,500-8,800 *S(S)*

John Maclauchlan Milne (1885-1957)
British
White Cottages, Aran
Signed, oil on canvas
17 x 23in (43 x 58.5cm)
£6,400-6,700 *C*

Tom McPherson (b1967)
British
To the Bridge
Signed on reverse, oil on canvas
23 x 40in (59 x 102cm)
£240-280 *Bon*

Campbell A. Mellon (1876-1955)
British
Haddiseoe Cut, St Olaves, Nr Oulton Broad, Norfolk
Signed and inscribed, oil on panel
9 x 12in (23 x 30.5cm)
£450-500 *C*

Sir Cedric Morris (1889-1982)
British
Olive Trees
Signed and dated '26, oil on canvas
21 x 25in (53 x 63.5cm)
£3,500-3,700 *C*

Christopher Richard Wynne Nevinson (1889- 1946)
British The Bypass
Signed, oil on canvas
18 x 22in (46 x 56cm)
£3,400-3,700 *C*

Sir Alfred Munnings (1878-1959) British
Brightworthy Fords, Withypool, Exmoor
Signed, dated and inscribed on the reverse 'To Willoughby Hancock from A. J. Munnings 1942, Brightworthy Fords, Withypool'
Oil on panel 19½ x 23¾in (49.5 x 60cm)
£11,600-12,000 *C*

Munnings moved to Exford on Exmoor following the requisitioning by the army of Castle House, Dedham in 1941.

John Scorror O'Connor (b1913) British
Moon Over Middleton Dyke
Signed, oil on canvas
24 x 30in (61 x 76cm)
£350-400 *Bon*

Michel Marie Poulain (20thC)
French
Small Hill Village
Signed and dated 1945, oil on panel
33½ x 34in (85 x 87cm)
£720-800 *Bon*

Jose Palmeiro (b1903)
Spanish
Le Port de Nice
Signed, and dated '64, signed, inscribed and dated 1965 on reverse, oil on canvas
24 x 32in
(61 x 81.5cm)
£1,000-1,200 *Bon*

John Anthony Park (1880-1962)
British
Cornish Fishing Village
Signed, oil on panel
17½ x 21½in
(44.5 x 54.5cm)
£900-1,000 *Bon*

J. McIntosh Patrick (b1907) British Strathmore from Tullybaccart Signed, watercolour 19 x 28in (48.2 x 71.1cm)
£5,300-5,500 *LBL*

Tony Peart (20thC) British The Churchyard
Oil and wax on canvas
16 x 18in (41 x 46cm)
£850-900 *VCG*

James Priddey (1916-1980)
British
Snow's Hill, Broadway
Signed, watercolour
21 x 13in (54 x 34cm)
£500-550 *GrG*

Paul Rebeyrolle (b1926)
French
Landscape
Signed and dated 1953, oil on panel
37½ x 38½in (95 x 98cm)
£2,200-2,400 *Bon*

Ian Renshaw (b1967) British October
Signed with initials and dated '90
37½ x 44½in (95.5 x 113cm)
£600-800 *Bon*

James Riddel (1857-1928)
British
The Mill Stream
Signed and dated '08
15½ x 19¾ (39.5 x 50cm)
£2,000-2,200 *S(S)*

Peter Roberson (20thC)
British
A Group of Whitewashed Cottages with a Valley Spreading Beyond
Signed and dated 44/65, watercolour
10½ x 14in (26.5 x 35.5cm)
Together with 12 other watercolours of English views
£100-120 *Bon*

Herbert Royle (1870-1958)
British
Hay Making
Signed, oil
20 x 24in (50.8 x 61cm)
£4,300-4,500 *WG*

At the turn of the century Sargent was perhaps Britain's most popular and prolific portrait painter, his works proving a comprehensive and masterly record of late Victorian and Edwardian Society ('To die before being painted by Sargent is to go to heaven prematurely,' commented Saki ironically). However, by 1907, the year before the present work was painted, Sargent had had enough of portraiture. 'Ask me to paint your gates, your fences, your barns . . . but not the human face,' he begged Lady Radnor and with the declaration 'No more mugs!', he gave up all but charcoal portraits and turned to landscapes, decorative works and increasingly to watercolour. He spent much time painting on the continent, often in the company of Wilfrid and Jane de Glenhn and a favourite location was Purtud in the Swiss Alps, where he spent three successive summers. The Alpine streams and ponds feature prominently in works from this period.

John Singer Sargent (1856-1925)
British
Reflections: Rocks and Water executed in 1908
Watercolour and bodycolour
9½ x 11¾in (25 x 30cm)
£32,000-35,000 *C*

Tony Brummell Smith (20thC)
British
Menorcan Landscape
Signed, oil on canvas
24 x 30in (61 x 76.2cm)
£800-850 *WG*

Ruskin Spear (1911-1990)
British
Village with Hills Beyond
Signed, oil on canvas
12 x 14in (30.5 x 36cm)
£300-350 *Bon*

Norman Smith (20thC)
British
The Lane at Letcombe Regis
Signed, pastels
20 x 26in (50 x 66cm)
£800-880 *JN*

Leonard Russell Squirrell (1893-1979)
British
A Sunlit Valley
Signed and dated 1932, watercolour over pencil
11¾ x 8¼in (30 x 21cm)
£570-650 *S(S)*

Born in Ipswich and a founder member of the Ipswich Art Club, Leonard Squirrell specialised in topographical local views and in aquatints and etchings of East Anglia, the Lake District and Scotland. 'Though he suffered from deafness, a speech impediment and nervousness, his hand rarely faltered,' noted critic Frances Spalding, and Squirrell's work is distinguished by its precise and confident clarity.

Ben Tobias (1901-1985)
British
St Ives Harbour
Signed and dated 1957 and inscribed, oil on canvas, laid on board
15½ x 19½in (39.3 x 49.5cm)
£700-800 *L*

Graham Sutherland (1903-1980)
British
Michaelmas
Signed in pencil, etchings, with margins
3⅜ x 2⅞in (8.6 x 7.3cm)
£400-450 *Bon*

Louis van Staaten (20thC)
Dutch
Wind and Water
Signed, watercolour
12 x 16in (30 x 40cm)
One of a pair on the same theme
£500-550 each *BCG*

William R. S. Stott (20thC) British
The Ferry
Signed and indistinctly dated 1935 (?), oil on board
19½ x 15½ (49.5 x 39.5cm)
£850-950 *S(S)*

Julian Trevelyan (1910-1988)
British
The Watermill
Signed, inscribed and dated 'Norwich 1928', oil on canvas
14 x 18in (35.5 x 45.8cm)
£1,000-1,200 *C*

Walter J. Watson (b1879) British
On the Llugwy, North Wales; On the Glaslyn, North Wales
A pair, both signed and dated 1921; both signed and inscribed with title on the reverse, oil on canvas
Each 16 x 26in (41 x 66cm)
£5,000-5,600 *S*

José Antonio Velasquez (20thC)
Mexican(?)
Iglesia
Signed and dated 'Honduras/CA 1958', oil on canvas
21¼ x 27¼in (54 x 69.2cm)
£1,950-2,500 *S(NY)*

Ethelbert White (1891-1972)
British
Bridge over the Burn, Co Down
Signed, black chalk and watercolour
10¼ x 13½in (26 x 34cm)
£500-550 *S(S)*

William Page Atkinson Wells (1872-1923)
British
Carting Kale
Signed, oil on canvas
19½ x 23½in (49½ x 59½cm)
£1,000-2,000 *S(SC)*

Carel Weight (b1908) British The Way to the Sea
Signed, oil on board 20 x 24in (50.8 x 61cm)
£4,900-5,000 *NGG*

Maurice Canning Wilks (active 1930s-40s) British
Curragh, Atlantic Drive, Co Donegal
Signed 15¾ x 17¾in (40 x 45cm)
£950-1,050 *S(S)*

Norman Wilkinson (1878-1971)
British
Near Hythe
Signed, Fine Art Society label verso dated April 1955, oil on canvas
17½ x 23¾in (44.4 x 60.3cm)
£3,000-3,300 *P(S)*

Rex Whistler (1905-1944) British
Bosco Sacro (G.B. sketchings)
Inscribed with title and dated 'June 29th', pen and black ink and watercolour
6¼ x 9¾in (16 x 25cm)
£1,600-2,000 *S*

Mary Yates (b1891)
British
Wind over
Northumbrian
Landscape Pastel
9½ x 13½in
(24 x 34cm)
£120-140 *AC*

CITIES, TOWNS AND STREETSCENES

17th and 18th Century

There is a wide range of different cities, towns and sites included among the following works. Certain locations such as London, Venice, Paris and Rome are such popular subjects with artists throughout the centuries that they have been alloted specific sections within Miller's Picture Price Guide. In addition to the capital cities, other towns came into and dropped out of fashion at certain periods. For example, as the sequence of illustrations shows, in the first half of the 19thC artists gravitated towards the towns of Northern France – Calais, Honfleur, Beauvais, Amiens, with their fortifications, cathedrals and medieval buildings. A hundred years later, the painters were heading down south to Nice, Antibes and the French Riviera, in search of the colours and scenery of the Mediterranean.
High prices can be obtained for pictures of more unusual or exotic locations in Asia or the Americas, their supply being limited by the fact that until the late 19thC, there were only a very few professional artists working outside Europe. But in this area, as in all others, market prices have been affected by the recession and a number (although by no means all) of the pictures included from auction houses, sold at or below their lower estimates.

Bernardo Bellotto (1724-80)
Italian
Perspective de la Facade de la Gallerie Roïale de Dresden
Etching, 1749
21⅝ x 33¼in (55 x 84.6cm)
£3,750-4,000 *S(NY)*

Gasparo Galliari (1760-1818) Italian
A View of a Quay from an Arcade, a Harbour beyond
Black chalk, pen and brown ink, grey wash, restorations
8¼ x 11¾in (21 x 30.2cm)
£2,100-2,500 *S(NY)*

Pieter Bout (1658-1702) Flemish
A Townscape with many Figures in a Market Place beside a Canal, a River beyond
Oil on canvas 11½ x 16½in (29.2 x 42cm)
£4,500-5,000 *Bon*

Attributed to John Flaxman (1755-1826) and Georgiana Hare Naylor (1755-1806)
British
A Panoramic View of Bologna
Pencil, pen and brown ink and watercolour, three joined sheets
56⅛ x 11¾in (142.5 x 29.9cm)
£5,600-6,000 *C*

The attribution to Georgiana Hare Naylor and John Flaxman is made by analogy to the view of Lake Nemi, with an idea for a Roman Villa, sold at Christie's on 10th July 1990, where a similar attribution was based on an inscription on a label on the back by Georgiana Maurice, Georgiana Hare Naylor's step-daughter. Georgiana, first wife of Francis Hare Naylor, was a partner of Flaxman while he was in Italy from 1787 to 1794, in particular commissioning the outline drawings illustrating the Iliad and Odyssey. She was the daughter of the Bishop of St Asaph.

Simone Pomardi (1760-1830) Italian
A View of the Piazza dei Miracoli, Pisa
Signed and inscribed 'Vue de la Place de Pise', pen and black ink and watercolour heightened with touches of gum arabic
18 x 28¾in (46 x 73cm)
£3,800-4,200 *S*

Attributed to John Russell (1745-1806) British
A View of Guildford High Street, Surrey
A sign on the left inscribed '1765/HALL', watercolour over pen and grey ink on laid paper with original wash line mount
11½ x 16¼in (29 x 41cm)
£1,400-1,600 *S*

Dominic Serres (1722-93) British
The Intendant's Palace, Quebec; and the Bishops House with the Ruined Town of Quebec, the St Lawrence beyond
A pair, one signed 'D. Serres 1760', the other 'D. Serres P. 1760', oil on canvas
Each 13¼ x 20½in (33.6 x 52cm)
£42,000-50,000 *S*

19th Century

Gustave Bauernfeind (1848-1904) German
Praying at the Western Wall, Jerusalem
Signed and inscribed 'G. Bauernfeind, Jerusalem', oil on canvas laid down on board
51 x 39½in (129.5 x 100.3cm)
£225,000-250,000 *C*

Bauernfeind travelled 3 times to the Middle East, prior to his permanent settlement in Jerusalem in 1896. Three other pictures by Bauernfeind of 'Jews at the Wailing Wall' are known, including his last work painted in 1904.
Views of Jerusalem are a popular subject in the saleroom and the price of the present work was the highest seen for a work by Bauernfeind in recent years, though below the upper estimate of £300,000.

Guilliume Bechmann, publisher (19thC)
Views of Moscow
A series of hand-coloured tinted lithographs in modern composition frames
9½ x 12in (24.2 x 30.4cm)
£1,600-1,800 *C(S)*

Thomas Shotter Boys (1803-74) British
The Gateway at Calais, France
Signed and dated 1830, watercolour heightened with bodycolour and scratching out 8½ x 6½in (21.5 x 16.5cm)
£5,300-5,600 *S*

Ernest Briggs (1866-1913)
British
A Stormy Day in Whitby Harbour
Signed, watercolour
16 x 24in (40.6 x 61cm)
£2,700-2,800 *WG*

William Callow (1812-1908) British
A Watergate at Honfleur, France
Signed and inscribed on the boat 'Honfleur', pencil and watercolour heightened with bodycolour on oatmeal paper
10⅝ x 8⅛in (27 x 20.7cm)
£3,600-4,000 *C*

Paul Braddon aka James Leslie Crees (active 1880-93)
British
Islington Row, Bham
Signed and dated, watercolour
21 x 15in (54 x 38cm)
£400-425 *GrG*

James Cadenhead (1858-1927)
British
Princes Street
Signed and dated 1881, watercolour heightened with bodycolour
38½ x 24½in (97.8 x 62.2cm)
£3,600-4,000 *C(S)*

William Callow (1812-1908)
British
Ross-on-Wye, Herefordshire
Watercolour heightened with bodycolour and scratching out
10½ x 19½in (27 x 49.5cm)
£3,600-4,000 *S*

Miles Edmund Cotman (1810-1858)
British
The South Gate, Great Yarmouth, Norfolk
Watercolour over pencil
7¼ x 9in (18.5 x 23cm)
£5,600-6,000 *S*

Thomas Colman Dibdin (1810-93) British
Amiens Cathedral; and Rouen Cathedral
(a pair) Both signed and dated 1873, pencil, watercolour, bodycolour and gum arabic
31½ x 21⅝in (80 x 54.8cm)
£7,200-7,600 *C*

David Cox (1783-1859)
British
Old Calais Fortifications, France
Watercolour over pencil heightened with bodycolour
8½ x 6¼in (21.5 x 15.5cm)
£5,300-5,700 *S*

Day and Haghe, publisher (c1864)
British
The Clifton Suspension Bridge
Lithograph with original hand colouring, by Hawkins after Jackson
£325-350 *Lan*

John Dobbin (1815-84) British Townscape of Prague, Bohemia
Signed and dated 1873, watercolour 12 x 22in (30 x 55cm)
£480-520 *EH*

Patrick Downie (1854-1945) British
A Paisley Street Scene Oil on board
6¾ x 9½in (17 x 24cm)
£1,400-1,600 *S(SC)*

Stanhope Alexander Forbes (1857-1947)
British
Old Newlyn
Signed and dated 1884, oil on canvas
15 x 12in (38 x 30.5cm)
£51,000-55,000 *C*

In an undated letter to his mother, probably in February 1884, Forbes states that 'I have a little street scene in progress, houses, steps, etc, a whole host of sketches of boats, boys, sea and other fishy things. I am more pleased with the place artistically each day, and have no idea of going elsewhere this year.'
Forbes first visited Newlyn in Cornwall in 1884, and was a founder member of the Newlyn School, an important force in British art in the 1880s and 1890s. Influenced by the developments in French art, Forbes wanted to bring 'a breath of fresh air in the tired atmosphere of the studios'. The artists of Newlyn painted daily life in the Cornish fishing villages, showing everyday people, outdoors and in their own environment, which the painters themselves shared.
The present work more than double its upper estimate at auction.

John Fulleylove (1847-1908)
British
The Piazza del Campo, Siena
Signed, inscribed and dated 1880-81, pencil, watercolour and scratching out
31 x 23in (79 x 58.3cm)
£3,800-4,000 *C*

Circle of Anthony Vandyke Copley Fielding
(1787-1855)
British
Pulteney Bridge, Bath
Pencil and watercolour with scratching out
8½ x 11⅝in (21.6 x 29.5cm)
£2,700-3,000 *C*

Pulteney Bridge was built in 1770 by Sir William Pulteney to Robert Adam's design.

Thomas Grant (active 1868-79)
British
A View of Edinburgh from Calton Hill looking West across the City Prison towards the Old Town and the Castle
Signed and dated 1875, oil on canvas
45 x 74½in (114.2 x 189.2cm)
£7,200-7,800 *C(S)*

William Biscombe Gardner (c1847-1919)
British
The Pantiles, Tunbridge Wells
Signed and inscribed, watercolour
6¾ x 10in (17.2 x 25.4cm)
£2,900-3,200 *Bon*

Gerolamo Gianni (b1837)
Italian
Valetta Harbour, Malta
Signed and dated 1886, oil on board
8½ x 21in (21.5 x 53.3cm)
£4,200-4,500 *C*

James Whitelaw Hamilton (1860-1932) British
A Continental River Signed, oil on canvas
17 x 21in (43 x 53cm) **£1,500-1,700** *S(SC)*

Rudolf Kargl (19thC)
Austrian
Street Scene, Hohensalzburg
Signed, watercolour
11 x 8in (28 x 20cm)
£800-900 *GrG*

Ludwig Hermann (1812-81)
German
A View of Town on a River
Signed, oil on canvas
24¾ x 37in (65.5 x 94cm)
£5,600-6,000 *S*

Italian School (19thC)
A View of Florence
Indistinctly signed on the stretcher, oil on canvas
11 x 15¾ (28 x 40cm)
£2,600-2,900 *S*

Charles Euphrasie Kuwasseg (1838-1904) French Joinville-le-Pont
Signed and dated 1872, inscribed on stretcher, oil on canvas
22¼ x 39⅜in (56.5 x 100cm) **£36,000-38,000** *BuP*

Edward Lear (1812-88) British Catania
Inscribed three times and dated 18 June 1847, and numbered 153, pen, brown ink and gouache
12½ x 18¾in (31.8 x 47.6cm)
£6,200-6,600 *Bon*

Henry Martin (active 1880-94)
British
Coastal Village Scene
Signed and dated, oil on canvas
12 x 9in (30 x 22cm)
£1,000-1,250 *GrG*

Francis Nicholson (1753-1844)
British
A View of Scarborough from the Beach, looking across the Town towards the Castle
Pen and grey ink and watercolour
11½ x 16¼in (29.3 x 41.3cm)
£2,000-2,300 *C(S)*

Attributed to Johann Jakob Meyer (1787-1858)
Swiss
Views of Swiss Landscapes and Towns
Nine, all titled on the border, all pen and ink and watercolour heightened with gum arabic
Each 2½ x 4in (6.5 x 10cm)
£4,700-5,200 *S*

This group includes views of the temple La Fusterie in Geneva, of Morges near Lausanne, a view of Lucerne looking towards the Glaris mountains, of Meilen and the Lake of Zurich, a street scene in Berne and a village near Locarne by Lake Maggiore.

Louise Rayner (1832-1924)
British
Old Houses, Shrewsbury
Signed, pencil, watercolour and bodycolour
8¾ x 13⅝in (22.2 x 34.7cm)
£4,700-5,000 *C*

William Prinsep (19thC)
British
Canton, Street behind the Factories, a Kolao or Cook's Shop
Signed and dated 1839, watercolour
9¼ x 11¼in (23.5 x 29.3cm)
£3,200-3,500 *DN*

Carl Onken (1846-1934)
German
A View of Tivoli near Rome
Signed, oil on canvas
19¼ x 24¾in (49 x 63cm)
£4,000-4,400 *S*

Samuel Prout (1783-1852)
British
Loading the Coach at the Trois Piliers, Beauvais
Pencil and watercolour
9 x 13in (22.8 x 33cm)
£1,000-1,300 *C*

After the ending of the Napoleonic wars and the final signing of peace in 1816, the continent was again opened up to English artists. One of the many to cross the channel was Samuel Prout. He visited Europe in 1819, and from that date onwards specialised in the portrayal of continental towns, architecture and street life. His work was extremely popular with a public eager for pictures of foreign views and Ruskin considered him unbeatable in his depiction of 'the crumbling character of stone'. More recent critics however, have been less enthusiastic. '[Prout],' notes Martin Hardie (see Biblio), 'became one of those capable practitioners who, having found that his sweetened recipe of crumbling buildings and lively figures was efficacious and soothing, prescribed it with persistent monotony'.

Louise Rayner (1832-1924)
British
Hastings
Signed, watercolour heightened with white
20¼ x 13½in (51.5 x 34cm)
£4,200-4,500 *S*

Louise Rayner (1832-1924)
British
Old Hastings
Signed, watercolour heightened with bodycolour
14¾ x 21¼in (37.5 x 54cm)
£6,700-7,200 *S*

Thomas Miles Richardson Jnr (1813-90)
British
The City of Durham
Signed and dated 1860, watercolour over pencil heightened with bodycolour, gum arabic and scratching out
30 x 51¼in (76 x 130cm)
£15,500-17,500 *S*

David Roberts (1796-1864) British Dieppe
Inscribed and dated 'Aug 1828'
Pencil, pen and brown ink and watercolour heightened with white, on grey paper
9 x 12⅛in (22.9 x 30.7cm)
£3,400-3,800 *C*

Spanish School (late 19thC)
Andalucian Houses
Indistinctly signed, oil on panel
12 x 6⅝in (30.5 x 16.8cm)
£2,700-3,000 *C*

Thomas Sewell Robins (1814-80) British
On the Rhine, Cologne
Signed with initials, inscribed 'Bayen Thurn' and dated 'Cologne 1860'?, watercolour heightened with white
14½ x 21½in (36.8 x 54.6cm)
£900-1,000 *CSK*

George Thomson (1860-1939) British
The Monument
Signed and dated 1897, indistinctly inscribed on a label on the frame 'The Monument', oil on canvas
30 x 22in (76 x 56cm)
£3,900-4,200 *C*

G*H* Thompson (active 2nd half 19thC)
British
Sunrise – The Arundel Tower, Southampton
Signed and dated '83, oil on canvas
14 x 18in (35.5 x 46cm)
£900-1,000 *S*

Max Uth (1863-1814) German
A Girl in a Village Street
Signed 'Max Uth', oil on canvas
29 x 33in (73.8 x 83.8cm)
£1,000-1,200 *CSK*

José Villegas y Cordero (1848-1922)
Spanish
Feeding Poultry in a Backstreet
Signed, oil on canvas
27½ x 15½in (70 x 39cm)
£3,400-3,700 *S*

John Varley Jnr (d1899) British
Azabu, Tokio; and Akabane and part of Shiba Park, Tokio: a pair
Signed, oil on panel
Each 11 x 13½in (28 x 34.2cm)
£11,500-12,500 *BuP*

Linnie Watt (active 1875-1906)
A Truffle Hunter in a Brittany Street
Signed, oil on canvas
21½ x 15in (54.6 x 38.1cm)
£5,750-5,950 *BuP*

George Weatherill (1810-90)
British
The Upper Harbour, Whitby
Signed, watercolour
9½ x 13½in (24.1 x 34.3cm)
£4,300-4,500 *WG*

Pictures of Whitby, Scarborough, Hastings and other English coastal towns were a popular theme of period watercolours.

Lewis John Wood (1813-1901)
British
Abbeville Cathedral
Signed, oil on canvas
21¼ x 18in (61.6 x 45.7cm)
£2,200-2,500 *Bon*

George Weatherill (1810-90) British
Whitby
Signed, watercolour
10¼ x 16¾in (26 x 42.5cm)
£6,700-7,000 *S*

20th Century

Ian Armour-Chelu (20thC) British
The Cathedral at Albi against an Evening Sky
Signed, watercolour 10 x 15in (26 x 39cm)
£650-675 *PHG*

Locate the source

The source of each illustration in Miller's can be found by checking the code letters below each caption

Henri Alphonse Barnon (20thC)
French
Marseilles – le Port
Signed, oil on canvas
24 x 29in (61 x 74cm)
£9,300-9,500 *JN*

Walter Bayes (1869-1956)
British
Corner of the Street, Dieppe
Oil on board
21 x 16½in (53 x 42cm)
£2,700-3,000 *C*

David Bomberg (1890-1957)
British
A View of the Mount of Olives
Signed and dated 25, oil on board
20 x 26in (51 x 66cm)
£47,000-50,000 *S*

Bomberg left London for Palestine in April 1923, supported by the Palestine Foundation Fund which had commissioned him to record the work of the Pioneer Development camps in the Holy Land. Arriving in Jerusalem he found 'a Russian toy city, punctuated by its red roofs, jewelled with the gildings of the Mosque spires – set against hills – patterned with walls encircling the Christian holy places – the horizontal lines accentuated by the perpendicular forms of the minarets'. After an abortive trip to Petra in 1924, he started to paint this aspect of the city, setting up his easel on the roofs of the Austrian Post Office (now the Christian Information Centre) or of his friends' homes nearby, looking over the roof-tops of the Old City and the Temple Mount Bomberg was to find some of his most loyal and enduring patrons in Jerusalem.

Sir Frank Brangwyn (1867-1956)
British
A Street in Worcester, South Africa
Signed with initials and dated 91, oil on panel
17 x 12¾in (43 x 32.5cm)
£5,800-6,200 *S*

The artist visited South Africa in 1891 with his friend William Hunt, after being commissioned by the Japanese Gallery in Bond Street. The pictures from the trip were exhibited at the Japanese Gallery in March 1892.

Joan Kathleen Harding Eardley (1921-1963)
British
Glasgow Tenement
Signed, gouache
6⅞ x 8⅞in (17.3 x 22.5cm)
£5,600-6,000 *C(S)*

Did you know?
MILLER'S Picture Price Guide will build up year by year to form the most comprehensive photo-reference library available

Mary Fedden (b1915)
British
Isle of Gozo
Signed and dated 1950, oil on canvas
19 x 23in (48 x 58.5cm)
£1,100-1,300 *C*

Orlando Greenwood (1892-1989)
British
The Antique Shop
Signed with monogram and dated 1919, oil on canvas
50 x 38in (127 x 96.5cm)
£6,600-7,000 *S*

Frederick Gore (b1913)
British
Isle-sur-Sorgue
Signed and dated 1984, oil on canvas
30 x 36¼in (76 x 92cm)
£3,900-4,200 *C*

Ashley Hold (b1964)
British
Winter Afternoon, Falmouth
Signed and dated on reverse, oil on board
20 x 20in (51 x 51cm)
£500-600 *Bon*

Frederick Gore (b1913)
British
Place du Clos, Cavaillon
Signed, oil on canvas
28 x 36½in (71 x 93cm)
£4,200-4,500 *C*

Noel Harry Lever (1889-1951)
British
A Continental Landscape
Signed, watercolour
14 x 10in (35.5 x 25.4cm)
£700-800 *G*

Noel Harry Lever (1889-1951)
British
Figures by a Gateway to a Spanish Town
Signed, watercolour heightened with bodycolour
10½ x 14⅜in (26.6 x 36.5cm)
£700-800 *C(S)*

Martin Lewis (20thC)
American
Shadow Dance (McC. 97)
Signed in pencil, annotated in pencil with the title, 1930, from the edition of drypoint, with sandpaper ground, on laid paper, with margins
9⅜ x 10⅞in (23.8 x 27.7cm)
£8,000-10,000 *S(NY)*

John Miller (?)
British
Rhu from the Artist's Studio
Signed
24 x 20in (61 x 50.8cm)
£320-400 *C(S)*

Frank Henry Mason (1876-1965)
British
Scarborough
Signed and dated 1909, watercolour
19 x 29in (49 x 74cm)
£5,000-5,400 *S*

Glenn O. Coleman (20thC)
American?
Minetta Lane
Signed in pencil, stamped 'SEP 27 1929' in lower right corner, lithograph
11¼ x 11⅛in (28.5 x 28.1cm)
£1,100-1,300 *S(NY)*

Condition is a major factor in a picture's price

Laurence Stephen Lowry (1887-1976)
British
The Football Match
Signed and date 1949, oil on canvas
28 x 36in (71 x 91.5cm)
£125,000-140,000 *S*

C. W. Nevinson (1889-1946)
British
New York by Night
Signed and dated 1920, oil on canvas
38 x 19in (96.5 x 48cm)
£38,000-40,000 *DK*

Walter Nessler (20thC)
German
View of Salzberg
Signed and dated 1957, watercolour
15 x 19½in (38 x 49.5cm)
£600-650 *JD*

Dennis Page (20thC)
British
Umbrian Market
Signed, watercolour
8½ x 11¼in (21 x 29cm)
£275-295 *Wyk*

Charles Sheeler (b1881)
American
Delmonico Building (Gordon checklist 4)
Signed and dated in pencil 1926, lithograph
9¾ x 6¾in (24.8 x 17.2cm)
£7,600,8,000 *S(NY)*

John Sloan (b1871)
American
Easter Eve, Washington Square (M. 222)
Signed in pencils and inscribed '100 proofs' (60 were printed), 1926, etching and aquatint
9⅞ x 8in (25 x 20.3cm)
£2,300-2,500 *S(NY)*

Sloan rarely used zinc plates because of their tendency to wear down. He used a zinc plate for Easter Eve and added aquatint when he felt the lines had been 'bitten too deeply and coarsely'. The result is a skilful combination of etching and aquatint that captures the early evening light of rainy New York day.

John Piper (b1903)
British
Weymouth
Signed and dated 1934, gouache
14½ x 18in (37 x 46cm)
£2,300-2,600 *Bon*

John Sloan (b1871)
American
Night Windows (M. 152)
Signed and titled in pencil, 1910, inscribed '100 proofs' (110 were printed), etching
5⅛ x 6¾in (13.1 x 17.3cm)
£2,600-2,800 *S(NY)*

Oskar Rabin (b1928)
Russian
Kuartal A. B-Zh.
Oil on canvas
19 x 28in (48.2 x 71.1cm)
£450-500 *G*

Locate the source

The source of each illustration in Miller's can be found by checking the code letters below each caption

Georges Stein (20thC)
French
A Street, Bern
Signed and inscribed, oil on canvas
18½ x 26in (47 x 66cm)
£6,100-6,400 *CSK*

Maurice Utrillo (1883-1955) French
La Maison de Mimi Pinson, rue du Mont-Cenis
Signed, oil on canvas
20½ x 29½in (52.1 x 74.9cm)
£98,000-110,000 *S(NY)*

LONDON

The huge variety in subject matter of the pictures of London sold over the past year, emphasises why the city has always been such a popular theme with artists. Pictures include: famous sights, urban back streets, parks, lively shipping scenes and quiet Thameside views; something for every type of painter and purchaser.

William James (active 1754-1771) British
A View of Westminster from Adelphi Terrace, with the Royal Barge and Other Shipping
Oil on canvas 28½ x 48½in (72.5 x 123cm)
£23,000-26,000 *S*

18th Century

Giovanni Antonio Canal, il Canaletto (1697-1768)
Italian
The Old Horse Guards, London, from St James's Park, with numerous ladies and gentlemen and guards on parade
46 x 93in (117 x 236cm)
£9,300,000-10,000,000 *C*

In July 1749 Canaletto took out an advertisement in the Daily Advertiser 'Signor Canaletto hereby invites any Gentleman that will be pleased to come to his house to see a picture done by him being a view of St James's Park, which he hopes may in some manner deserve their approbation any morning or afternoon at his lodgings.' The advertisement appears to have worked and the work was purchased by John Robartes, 4th Earl of Radnor, who pronounced it 'the most capital picture I ever saw of that master'.
The painting received considerable publicity in spring 1992 when it was purchased by composer Andrew Lloyd Webber, thus keeping in Britain this most celebrated view of London.

Thomas Priest (18thC)
British
Capriccio View of Chelsea Hospital on the Thames
Oil on canvas, laid on panel
19½ x 28¾in (49.5 x 73cm)
£2,500-2,800 *S*

Attributed to Joseph Nicholls (active 1726-1755)
British
A View of the River Thames from the Terrace of Somerset House Looking Towards St Paul's Cathedral and Old London Bridge; and a View of Westminster Abbey and the House of Commons beyond
Oil on canvas
30 x 50in (76.2 x 127cm)
£34,000-38,000 *C(S)*

19th Century

Daniel Turner (active 1872-1901)
British
View of London from the Thames with the Palace of Westminster and Westminster Abbey
Oil on panel
8¾ x 12½in (22 x 32cm)
£1,600-2,000 *S*

Alfred Bennet (1861-1916)
British
The Houses of Parliament from the Embankment
Signed, dated August 17. 96', pencil and watercolour with touches of white heightening
9¼ x 14in (23.5 x 35.6cm)
£650-750 *C*

Edwin Thomas Dolby (active second half 19thC)
British
Victoria Tower, Westminster
Signed, dated 1884, watercolour
9¼ x 6¼in (23.5 x 15.8cm)
£200-250 *Bon*

Arthur Gilbert (1819-95)
British
Greenwich from the Park
Signed
13½ x 20in (34 x 51cm)
£1,850-2,000 *S(S)*

John Atkinson Grimshaw (1836-93)
British
Gillbeck Bridge, London
Signed and dated 1881, oil on board
12 x 20in (30.5 x 50.8cm)
£13,450-13,850 *HFA*

Frederick E. J. Goff (1855-1931)
British
Westminster Abbey
Signed and inscribed with title, watercolour
4½ x 6in (11.4 x 15.2cm)
£450-480 *EH*

Thomas Bush Hardy (1842-97)
British
On the Thames
Signed and dated 1890, watercolour over traces of pencil heightened with bodycolour
8½ x 27¼in (22 x 69.5cm)
£2,600-2,900 *S(S)*

After Thomas Hosmer Shepherd (1792-1864)
British
Regent's (or London) Canal
Six coloured aquatints with etching
9½ x 14½in (24.5 x 36.5cm) each
£1,800-2,000 *S(S)*

20th Century

Suzanne Cooper (active 1936-1938)
British
Bloomfield Terrace, Pimlico
Signed, oil on canvas
20 x 24in (50.8 x 61cm)
£1,000-1,250 *SCG*

James Boswell (1906-71) British
The Siege of Sidney Street
Signed lower right Boswell, signed again and inscribed on the reverse The Siege of Sidney Street James Boswell 28 Parliament Hill, London NW3, oil on canvas
30 x 40in (76 x 102cm)
£500-700 *C*

The Siege of Sidney Street
A band of Russian anarchists living in London planned a jewel robbery in December 1910 as a result of which three policemen were shot dead and four wounded. The gang escaped, but several members were later apprehended and on 2nd January 1911 police were told that two of the anarchists were hiding at 100 Sidney Street, off the Mile End Road in the East End. The siege of the house by the police became a famous event in the annals of East End crime. The Scots Guards were called from the Tower, Winston Churchill (the Home Secretary) turned up to watch. Eventually the house burst into flames, the fire killing both gang-members and injuring several firemen. All the anarchists were eventually acquitted.

Robert Bevan (1865-1925) British
King Henry's Road, London
Signed and inscribed on a label attached to the frame Robert Bevan, 14 Adamson Road, NW3
Title King Henry's Road, NW, oil on canvas
18 x 22in (46 x 56cm)
£18,000-20,000 *C*

John Donaldson (b1945)
British
Dusk on the South Bank
Oil on canvas
28¾ x 36in (73 x 92cm)
£3,000-3,250 *OM*

Charles Ginner (1878-1952)
British
The Dome of the Brompton Oratory
Signed, pen and black ink and watercolour
15 x 12in (38 x 30.5cm)
£6,200-6,800 *S*

Cecil Arthur Hunt (1873-1965)
British
Three landscapes: Passing Shower in Calabria; The Thames Below Wapping; The Bridge Sospel
Signed, pencil and watercolour heightened with white
10¾ x 14¾in (27.5 x 37.5cm)
£1,400-1,600 *S(S)*

Henry and Walter Greaves (1846-1930)
British
Church Street, Chelsea
Signed and dated H & W Greaves 1903, pencil, watercolour and bodycolour
19¾ x 25½in (50 x 65cm)
£4,700-5,000 *C*

This work was originally commissioned from the artist for the sum of 23 shillings.

Alan Carr Linford (20thC)
British
House Boats at Chelsea Reach
Oil on canvas
23½ x 35½in (59.6 x 90.1cm)
£2,250-2,500 *RdeR*

Westminster Palace, from the South Bank – Winter Afternoon

George Leslie Hunter (1877-1931)
Rottenrow, Hyde Park,
London
Signed, brush and black
ink and crayon
16¾ x 22½in (42.5 x 57.3cm)
£7,200-7,800 *S(SC)*

Dorothea Sharp (1874-1955)
British
Children at the Peter Pan Monument,
Kensington Gardens
Oil on panel
14 x 10in (36 x 25.5cm)
£3,100-3,400 *C*

Frank Scarborough (active 1896-1939) British
The Pool of London Watercolour
20 x 30in (50.8 x 76.2cm)
£3,300-3,500 *MS*

Carel Weight (b1908)
British
Walham Green: Evening
Signed, oil on canvas
24 x 36in (61 x 91cm)
£9,500-10,500 *S*

Jolan Polatschek Williams (b?-d1984)
Austrian
Hampstead Street Scene
Oil
16 x 20in (40.5 x 51cm)
£700-750 *JD*

Cornelis Christian Dommersen (1842-1928)
Dutch
Dutch Canal Scenes
A pair, both signed and dated 1876, oil on canvas
Each 14½ x 11½in (37 x 29.5cm)
£11,100-11,600 *S*

Hubertus van Hove (1814-1865)
Dutch
A view of Amsterdam Market
Signed, and indistinctly dated 1860, oil on panel
16 x 24½in (41 x 62cm)
£13,300-13,700 *S*

Willem Koekkoek (1839-1895)
Dutch
Washerwomen by a Canal
Signed l.r., oil on canvas
18 x 24in (46 x 61cm)
£17,100-17,600 *S*

Jan Hendrik Verheyen (1778-1846)
Dutch
Figures near a Church
Signed and dated 1810, oil on panel
18 x 23¼in (46 x 59cm)
£5,000-5,300 *S*

David Cox (1783-1859)
British
Fishermen on the Thames looking towards Westminster and Lambeth
Signed on an oar, *1823/D Cox*, watercolour
10 x 14½in (25.5 x 37cm)
£11,700-12,200 *S*

Raoul Dufy (1877-1953)
French
Londres
Signed, titled and dated 1929, watercolour
19⅝ x 25½in (50 x 65cm)
£11,200-11,600 *S*

Louis H.Grimshaw (1870-1943)
British
Westminster Bridge
Signed, oil on board
11¾ x 18in (30 x 45.5cm)
£10,500-11,000 *S*

Sir Claude Francis Barry (20thC)
British
The Houses of Parliament-A Wartime Nocturne 1941
Signed
29 x 37½in (74 x 95cm)
£4,100-4,400 *S(S)*

Edouard Cortès (1882-1969)
French
On the Champs-Elysées, Paris
Signed, oil on canvas
10½ x 13½in (26.5 x 34.5cm)
£5,000-5,300 *S*

Eugène Galien-Laloue (1854-1941)
French
On a Grand Boulevard at Dusk,
Porte St Martin, Paris
Signed, Gouache
7½ x 12¼in (19 x 31cm)
£9,500-10,000 *S*

Eugène Galien-Laloue (1854-1941)
A View of the Assemblée Nationale and the
Pont de la Concorde, Paris
Signed, gouache
10¼ x 18in (26 x 45.5cm)
£7,200-7,500 *S*

Maurice Utrillo (1883-1955)
French
La Place du Tertre et le Sacré-Coeur
Signed and dated 1922, oil on canvas
23⅝ x 28¾in (60 x 73cm)
£144,000-150,000 *S*

Karl von Bergen (1794-1835)
German
Piazza Barberini, Rome
Indistinctly signed and dated 'Carl. . .
Roma 183', oil on canvas
$39^{3}/_{4}$ x $54^{3}/_{4}$in (101 x 139cm)
£29,000-32,000 *C*

Cavaliere Ippolito Caffi (1809-1866)
Italian
Fishermen by the Tiber with the Castel
Sant Angelo and St. Peter's beyond,
Rome
Signed, oil on board
9 x 12in (23 x 30.5cm)
£30,000-33,000 *C*

Friedrich Mayer (1792-1870)
Swiss
A View from Rome
Signed and dated *Roma 1841,* oil on canvas
22 x $31^{1}/_{4}$in (56 x 79.5cm)
£14,500-16,000 *S*

Roman School, First Half 19th Century
View of St Peter's Cathedral, Rome
Oil on canvas
$20^{1}/_{2}$ x 33in (52 x 83.8cm)
£27,500-30,000 *S(NY)*

Jacob Alt (1789-1872)
German
A View of the Forum; a View of the Arch of Vespasianus, Rome
A pair, both signed ad inscribed *Rom,* oil on panel
Each 14½ x 21¼in (37 x 54cm)
£17,000-19,000 *S*

Hubert Robert (1733-1808)
French
Italian Peasants resting among Roman Ruins: A pair of paintings
Both oil on canvas
Each: 39 x 58in (99.1 x 147.3cm)
£227,000-240,000 *S(NY)*

Carlo Grubacs (1829-1919)
German
A view of the Doges Palace and the Piazzetta;
Figures on the Piazza San Marco, Venice
A pair, both signed, oil on canvas
Each 8¾ x 12½in (22 x 32cm)
£15,500-18,000 *S*

William James (active 1754-1771)
British
Venice, the entrance of the Grand Canal;
and A View of the Grand Canal
A pair, both oil on canvas
Each 19¼ x 29in (49 x 74cm)
£22,500-25,000 *S*

Samuel Prout (1783-1852)
British
Canonica, Venice
Signed and dated 1807, pencil and watercolour with scratching out
17 x 12½in (43.2 x 31.8cm)
£1,600-1,800 *C*

Federico del Campo (late 19thC)
Peruvian
San Samuele, Venice
Pencil and watercolour on paper, laid down on canvas
9⅞ x 7in (25.1 x 17.9cm)
£2,800-3,000 *C*

Edward Pritchett (active 1828-1864)
British
By the Doge's Palace, Venice
Signed, oil on canvas
24 x 20in (60.9 x 50.8cm)
£13,500-14,000 *Pol*

Antoine Bouvard (d.1956)
French
The Grand Canal with the Rialto Bridge, Venice
Signed, oil on canvas
20 x 25½in (50.8 x 64.8cm)
£8,900-9,200 *C*

Wilfred Knox (born c.1885, active 1920's-30's)
A Suburb of Venice
Signed, watercolours, heightened with white
12 x 18in (30.4 x 45.7cm) **£1,000-1,100** *FL*

Maurice Bompard (1857-1936)
French
An Antiquarian Shop in Venice
Signed and inscribed *Venise 1894,* oil on canvas
31½ x 25¼in (80 x 64cm)
£4,000-4,300 *S*

Manuel Barron y Carrillo (1814-1884)
Spanish
Panoramic views of Seville
Four, signed and dated *Seville 1849,* oil on canvas
Each 26½ x 41in (67 x 104cm)
£180,000-200,000 *S*

Gabriele Carelli (1820-1900)
Italian
From the Garden of A'O'Clla, outside Tangier
Signed and inscribed *Tanger,* watercolour
7 x 14½in (17.5 x 37cm)
£1,450-1,600 *S*

Eugène Napoléon Flandin (1803-1876)
French
A view of the Suleymaniyeh and the Golden Horn, Instanbul
Signed and dated 1852, oil on canvas
52½ x 103in (132 x 262cm)
£46,500-50,000 *S*

William Holman Hunt (1827-1910)
English
The Walls of Jerusalem
Signed with initials and dated 1869, watercolour
10 x 19½in (25.5 x 49.5cm)
£21,000-24,000 *S*

Franz Theodor Aerni (1853-1918)
German
Rue du Marché
Signed and dated *Rom '86*, oil on canvas
43½ x 29in (110.5 x 74cm)
£22,500-27,000 *S*

Fred Yates (b.1922)
British
Corner Tea Shop- Penzance
Signed, oil
12 x 16in (30 x 41cm)
£300-325 *Dr*

Paul Emile Lecomte (b.1877)
French
Marché aux Fleurs
Signed, oil on canvas
25 x 36½in (63.5 x 92.8cm)
£3,100-3,300 *CSK*

Stanhope Alexander Forbes (1857-1947)
British
The Fountain Tavern
Signed and dated 1939, oil on canvas
20 x 25in (51 x 63.5cm)
£10,000-10,500 *C*

Paul Signac (1863-1935)
French
Marché à Antibes
Signed, inscribed and dated 1919, watercolour and pencil on paper laid down on card
11⅝ x 16½in (29.5 x 41.8cm)
£24,000-26,000 *C*

Myles Birket Foster (1825-1899)
British
Richmond Hill, Surrey
Signed with monogram, watercolour heightened with bodycolour and scratching out
4 x 5½in (10 x 14cm)
£6,200-6,600 *S*

Frank Will (1900-1951)
French
Après-midi à Dennemont
Signed and dated 1929, charcoal and watercolour
19½ x 25½in (49.5 x 64.5cm)
£2,300-2,500 *S*

Edward Seago (1910-1974)
British
Chestnut Trees, Champs Elysées, Paris
Signed, oil on canvas
26 x 36in (66 x 91.5cm)
£22,500-25,000 *C*

Carl Moll (1861-1945)
Austrian
A View of the Gardens at Schonbrunn, Vienna
Signed, oil on panel
13½ x 13½in (34.5 x 34.5cm)
£26,500-28,500 *S*

Attributed to Abraham Louis Rodolphe Ducros (1748-1810)
Swiss
The Gardens of the Palazzo Doria Pamphili, Rome
Pen, brown ink and watercolour heightened with white, inscribed 'Villa Pamphili à Rome'
20½ x 27¾in (52 x 70.5cm)
£4,100-4,500 *Bon*

Victor Charreton (1864-1937)
French
Jardin de Ville en Printemps
Signed, oil on canvas
$18^{1}/_{8}$ x $21^{1}/_{2}$in (46 x 54.6cm)
£15,500-17,500 *S(NY)*

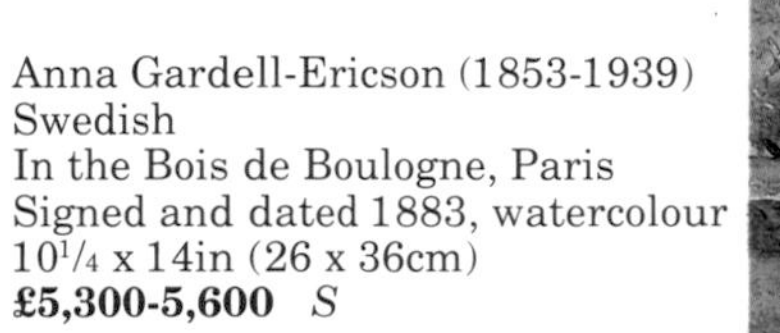

Anna Gardell-Ericson (1853-1939)
Swedish
In the Bois de Boulogne, Paris
Signed and dated 1883, watercolour
$10^{1}/_{4}$ x 14in (26 x 36cm)
£5,300-5,600 *S*

Lillian Stannard (1877-1944)
British
Glorious Summer
Signed, watercolour and bodycolour
$9^{1}/_{2}$ x $13^{1}/_{4}$in (24.5 x 34cm)
£1,600-1,800 *S(S)*

Ralph Todd (1856-1932)
British
An Old Breton Courtyard
Watercolour
20 x $13^{1}/_{2}$in (51 x 33cm)
£3,200-3,500 *WrG*

Louis Belanger (1736-1816)
French
A Mansion in a Park
Signed and dated 1792, black chalk, bodycolour
13¼ x 18⅞in (33.7 x 48cm)
£5,700-6,100 *S(NY)*

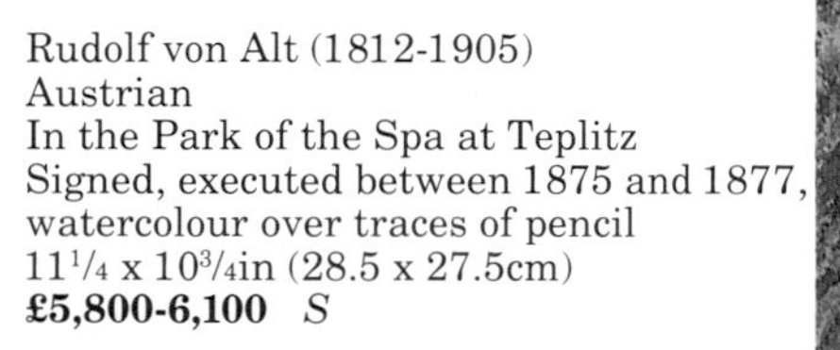

Rudolf von Alt (1812-1905)
Austrian
In the Park of the Spa at Teplitz
Signed, executed between 1875 and 1877, watercolour over traces of pencil
11¼ x 10¾in (28.5 x 27.5cm)
£5,800-6,100 *S*

John Atkinson Grimshaw (1836-1893)
British
In Autumn's Evening Glow
Signed bottom left, oil on canvas
11½ x 17¾in (29 x 45cm)
£13,500-14,000 *TG*

Henry Brian Ziegler (1798-1874)
British
Views of Bedgebury Park, Kent, the seat of the Law family
A pair, both inscribed on labels attached to the reverse, oil on board
Each 9½ x 13in (24 x 33cm)
£8,300-8,700 *S*

John Brett (1830-1902)
British
Saint's Bay, Guernsey
Signed and dated 1885, oil on canvas
24 x 48in (61 x 122cm)
£10,000-10,500 *S*

Ralph Todd (1856-1932)
British
A Sandy Cove near the Lizard
Watercolour
9¾ x 13½in (22.5 x 34cm)
£850-950 *WRG*

Edmund Kanoldt (1845-1904)
German
Sappho at the Leukate Mountains (Lesbos)
Signed and dated 1879, oil on canvas
55¾ x 39¾in (136.5 x 101cm)
£8,900-9,300 *C*

Consalvo Carelli (1818-1900)
Italian
Fisherfolk in Capri
Signed and inscribed *Capri,*
oil on panel
10¼ x 15¾in (26 x 40cm)
£7,800-8,200 *S*

Konstantin Lomikin (b.1924)
Russian
The Seaside, Crimea, 1976
Oil on canvas
19 x 27in (48.2 x 68.5cm)
£4,000-4,500 *RMG*

Henri Manguin (1874-1949)
French
Le Golfe de St.Tropez
Signed, oil on canvas laid down on board, painted in 1924
12¾ x 17⅞in (32.5 x 45.5cm)
£16,700-17,500 *C*

Paul Desiré Trouillebert (1829-1900)
French
A Windy Day by the Sea
Signed, oil on canvas
8½ x 10½in (21.5 x 26.5cm)
£5,300-5,600 *S*

Lucien Neuquelman (1909-1988)
French
Beaulieu sur Mer
Signed, inscribed on the stretcher *La propriété de David Niven à Beaulieu,* oil on canvas
21¼ x 25½in (54 x 65.7cm)
£4,800-5,200 *C*

Pierre Bonnard (1867-1947)
French
Marine à Arcachon
Signed, oil on board
$18^{1}/_{4}$ x $15^{1}/_{8}$in (46.5 x 38.5cm)
£57,000-65,000 *S*

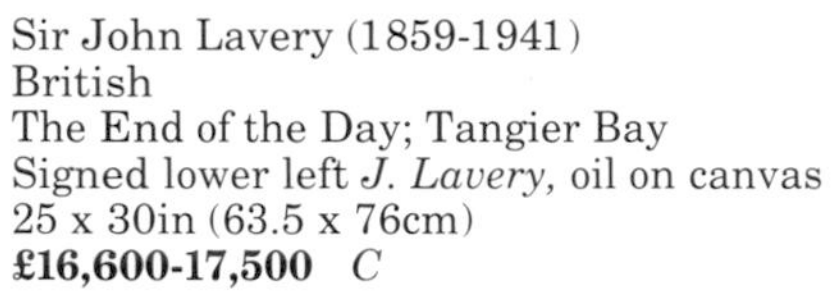

Sir John Lavery (1859-1941)
British
The End of the Day; Tangier Bay
Signed lower left *J. Lavery,* oil on canvas
25 x 30in (63.5 x 76cm)
£16,600-17,500 *C*

Maxime Maufra (1861-1918)
French
Marine
Signed, oil on canvas
$18^{1}/_{8}$ x $21^{5}/_{8}$in (46 x 55cm)
£4,700-5,000 *C*

Jack Butler Yeats (1871-1957)
British
Sligo Bay
Signed, oil on panel, painted c.1922
9 x $13^{1}/_{4}$in (23 x 33.5cm)
£23,200-25,000 *C*

DUTCH AND FLEMISH TOWNS AND STREETSCENES

A selection of some of the views that have appeared during the past season (also see Towns General).

18th and 19th Century

Jan Anthonie Langendyk (1780-1818)
Dutch
The Fish Market in Rotterdam: Winter
Signed and dated 1805, black chalk, pen and black ink, grey wash heightened with white, brown ink framing lines
12 x 17¾in (30.5 x 45.1cm)
£2,700-3,000 *S(NY)*

Jan Anthonie Langendyk (1780-1818)
Dutch
The Flower Market in Rotterdam: Summer
Signed and dated 1804, black chalk, pen and black ink, grey wash, black ink framing lines
12 x 17¾in (30.5 x 45.1cm)
£2,400-2,700 *S(NY)*

19th and 20th Century

Johannes Franciscus Spohler (1853-94)
Dutch
A Dutch Canal Scene
Signed, oil on canvas
17¼ x 13¾in (44 x 35cm)
£7,500-7,800 *S*

Cornelis Christian Dommersen (1842-1928)
Dutch
The Flower Market, Brussels
Signed and dated 1886, oil on canvas
25½ x 22in (65 x 55½cm)
£8,000-8,400 *S*

William Raymond Dommersen (1875-98)
Dutch
At the Fish Market
Signed and dated 1884, oil on panel
14½ x 12¼in (37 x 31cm)
£3,100-3,400 *S*

Willem Koekkoek (1839-95)
Dutch
A Dutch Street Scene
Signed, oil on panel
11¼ x 16in (31 x 41cm)
£9,100-9,500 *S*

Cornelis Springer (1817-91)
Dutch
The House of Admiral Martin van Rossum in Zaltbommel
Signed and dated 1860, oil on canvas
29⅝ x 38¼in (75.2 x 97.2cm)
£97,000-105,000 *C*

David Schulman (1881-1966)
Dutch
An Extensive View of Amsterdam with the Central Station and the St Nicholaas Church beyond
Signed, oil on canvas
19¾ x 27½in (50 x 70cm)
£4,300-4,600 *CAm*

Albert Hemelman (1883-1951) Dutch
An Extensive View of Amsterdam with the St Nicholaas Church and Trains Entering the Central Station
Signed and dated 1926, oil on canvas
43⅞ x 64¼in (111 x 163cm)
£5,100-5,500 *CAm*

PARIS

This section devoted to protrayals of Paris is dominated by works from the 20thC. The two 'Paris painters' who have appeared most frequently in the saleroom over the past year are Eugene Galien-Laloue and Edouard Cortes. Prolific and popular, they both specialised in decorative street scenes capturing Paris of the 1900s, creating a vision of elegant shoppers, glowing lights, trams and hansom-cabs, their pictures almost invariably set in winter, as though that were the only possible season for the fashionable metropolitan.

17th Century

Circle of Didier Barra, called Monsù Desiderio
(1590-1650)
French
A Capriccio View of Paris with the Tour de Nesle and the Louvre from the Top of the Ile de la Cité
38¾ x 68⅞in (98.5 x 175cm)
£10,500-11,500 *C*

19th Century

Richard Redgrave (1804-88) British Pont de la Concorde, Paris
Signed l.r: Ricd Redgrave, watercolour over pencil
4¼ x 11¾in (10.5 x 30cm)
£4,500-4,800 *S*

Paul Vogler (1852-1904) French
La Place Clichy à Paris
Signed, inscribed and dated Xbre 1870,
oil on panel 12¼ x 11¾in (31 x 29.5cm)
£2,000-2,200 *S(S)*

Edouard Cortès (1882-1969)
French
L'Arc de Triomphe
Signed, oil on canvas
13 x 18in (33 x 45.7cm)
£6,300-6,700 *S(NY)*

20th Century

Eugene Galien-Laloue (1854-1941)
French
A Busy Boulevard Under Snow
at the Porte St Martin, Paris
Signed, gouache
7¼ x 12¼in (18.5 x 31cm)
£8,600-9,000 *S*

Eugène Galien-Laloue (1854-1941)
French
Quai Montebello,
with Notre Dame beyond,
Paris
Signed,
charcoal and bodycolour on card
10¾ x 13¾in (27.3 x 35cm)
£6,100-6,400 *C*

Armand Guérin (b1913)
Swiss
Montmartre and Place de la Concorde
Each signed, oil on masonite
10½ x 13½in (26.7 x 34.3cm) each
£400-450 *S(NY)*

Armand Guérin (b1913)
Swiss
Paris Street in Winter
Signed, oil on masonite
18 x 21½in (45.7 x 54.6cm)
£350-400 *S(NY)*

Willy James (b1920)
Montmartre, le Moulin de la Galette
Signed, oil on canvas
21⅝ x 15⅛in (55 x 38.3cm)
£2,300-2,500 *C*

John Linfield (20thC)
British
The Carousel, Montmartre
Oil
10 x 12in (25.5 x 31.5cm)
£375-395 *JN*

Christopher Richard Wynne Nevinson (1889-1946)
British
Latin Quarters
Signed in pencil, etching
13¾ x 9⅞in (34.9 x 25.1cm)
£150-175 *Bon*

Constantine Kluge (20thC)
Le Quai du Louvre
Signed, oil on canvas
32 x 39½in (81.3 x 100.3cm)
£2,600-2,900 *S(NY)*

Georges Stein (early 20thC)
French
Elegant Figures before the Arc de Triomphe, Paris
Signed, watercolour, coloured chalks and bodycolour on card
15¾ x 19¾in (40 x 50.7cm)
£2,700-3,000 *C*

Théo Tobiasse (20thC)
French
View of Notre Dame
Signed, inscribed 'Paris que j'aime' and dated 74, oil on canvas
13 x 16in (33 x 40.6cm)
£5,700-6,000 *S(NY)*

Chaim Soutine (1894-1944)
Russian
Vue de Montmartre
Signed, oil on canvas
26 x 32in (66 x 81.3cm)
£145,000-155,000 *S(NY)*

Painted c1918-1919 sometime between the artist's first trip outside Paris to Cagnes in 1918 and just prior to his move to Céret in 1919.

Claude Venard (b1913)
French
Rooftops of Paris
Signed, oil in canvas
38 x 51in (96.5 x 129.5cm)
£1,900-2,200 *S(NY)*

VENICE

In compiling this year's Picture Price Guide, Millers has received more pictures of Venice than any other single location. Venice has always acted as a magnet to artists from every nation, some simply passing through, others making a whole career from portraying its palazzi and canals. Venice must surely be the most painted city in the world. Pictures in this section run from the 1700s to the present day, celebrating the unique beauty of the place and demonstrating, unlike other cities, how little it has changed throughout the centuries.

Francesco Albotto (1722-57)
Italian
Venice, the Entrance to the Grand Canal
Oil on canvas
22½ x 31¾in (57 x 80.5cm)
£19,000-20,000 *S*

18th and 19th Century

William James (active 1746-71) British
The Entrance to the Grand Canal, Venice
Oil on canvas
29 x 48¾in (74 x 124cm)
£34,000-40,000 *S*

Giacomo Guardi (1764-1835)
Italian
Figures Conversing in a Campo by a Church, the Lagoon beyond
Black chalk, pen and brown ink, grey wash
18 x 12in (46.5 x 31cm)
£7,200-7,800 *C*

Attributed to Giacomo Guardi (1764-1835)
Italian
The Arsenale, Venice
Pen and black ink and watercolour
4¼ x 6½in (11 x 16.5cm)
£900-1,000 *CSK*

Follower of Michele Marieschi (1696-1743)
Italian
San Giorgio Maggiore, Venice with the Doge's Palace Beyond
Oil on canvas
24¼ x 38¼ (61.6 x 97.2cm)
£7,200-7,600 *C*

Michele Marieschi (1710-44) Italian
The Doge's Palace, the Piazzetta and the Prisons, Venice, from the Bacino di San Marco, S. Maria Della Salute beyond
21⅞ x 33½in (55.5 x 85cm)
£51,000-60,000 *C*

19th and 20th Century

William Callow (1812-1908)
British
Palaces near the Entrance of the Grand Canal, Venice
Signed and dated 1847, pencil and watercolour heightened with bodycolour and scratching out
29¾ x 23in (75.7 x 58.3cm)
£10,500-11,500 *C*

Callow first visited Venice in the summer of 1840 and began to exhibit Venetian views at the Old Watercolour Society in the next year. His second visit was in 1846, on his honeymoon, having married Harriet Anne Smart on 2nd July of that year.

Antonietta Brandeis (b1849)
Austrian
A View of the Piazzetta and S. Maria Della Salute; A View of the Doge's Palace and the Piazzetta, Venice
A pair, both signed, oil on panel
Each 6¾ x 9½in (17 x 24cm)
£11,500-12,000 *S*

Eugenio Buono (19th/20thC)
Italian
Gondolas laden with Flowers and Vegetables on the Grand Canal, Venice
Signed, oil on panel
5 x 10½in (13 x 27cm)
£1,400-1,600 *S*

Attributed to Francesco Tironi (d1800)
Italian
The Zattere from the Giudecca, Venice
20¾ x 32in (52.7 x 81.2cm)
£15,500-16,000 *C*

Federico del Campo (19thC)
Italian
The Santa Barbara Canal, Venice
Signed, oil on panel
7 x 11in (17.5 x 28cm)
£9,500-10,000 *S*

Myles Birket Foster (1825-99) British
Venice Signed with monogram, watercolour heightened with white
5½ x 3¾in (14 x 9.5cm) **£5,000-5,500** *S*

Thomas Bush Hardy (1842-97)
British
After a Shower, Venice
Watercolour
14 x 10in
(35.5 x 25.4cm)
£2,300-2,500 *MS*

Writing in 1850, novelist and critic William Thackeray expressed his boredom with the seemingly endless portrayals of Venice and Italy churned out by the artists of the period. 'How long are we to go on with Venice, Verona, Lago di So-and-So, and Ponte di What d'ye-call-em?' he complained. 'I am weary of gondolas, striped awnings, sailors with red night (or rather day), caps, cobalt distances and posts in water. I have seen too many white palaces standing before dark purple skies, black towers with gamboge atmosphere behind them.'

Italian School, 19thC, in the manner of Canaletto
A View of San Marco, Venice
Oil on canvas
24¾ x 19¼ (62.8 x 48.8cm)
£3,000-3,400 *Bon*

Vincent Stoltenberg Lerche (1837-92)
Norwegian
Carnival Masqueraders Boarding a Gondola
Signed and dated ddf 70,
pencil and watercolour
14½ x 10½in (36.8 x 26.6cm)
£2,100-2,400 *CSK*

James Holland (1800-70)
Gondoliers Beneath the Rialto Bridge, Venice
Signed on a box on the quayside with monogram and dated 63, watercolour over pencil heightened with bodycolour
12½ x 21¼in (32 x 54cm)
£2,800-3,400 *S*

'I stood in Venice on the Bridge of Sighs;
a palace and a prison on each hand,
I saw from out of the wave her structures rise
As from the stroke of the enchanter's wand.'
Childe Harold's Pilgrimage – Canto IV

Byron's description of the 'dying Glory' of Venice, published in 1818, sets the tone for many of the highly coloured and richly romantic visions of the city produced throughout the 19thC.

***Miala (19thC)
Italian
On the Blue Lagoon, Venice
Signed, oil on canvas
24½ x 51in (62 x 130cm)
£2,700-3,000 *S*

Alfred Pollentine
(active 2nd half 19thC)
British
St Mark's Square, Venice
Signed and dated '79,
oil on canvas
30 x 50in (76 x 127cm)
£4,900-5,400 *S*

Franz Richard Unterberger (1838-1902) Belgian
Fondamenta Zorzi, Campiello S. Barbara, Venice
Signed, oil on canvas
51½ x 43¾in (130.8 x 111.1cm)
£53,000-60,000 *C*

The 19thC audience was interested not only in the building of Venice but in portrayals of its people. The sections of the Picture Price Guide devoted to men, women and children include examples of Venetian beauties and children, genre pictures rather than topographical views.

George Owen Wynne Apperley (b1884) British
Vegetable Market, Venice
Signed and dated 1905, watercolour
14 x 10in (36 x 25cm)
£900-950 *BAR*

Edward Pritchett (active 1828-1864)
British
The Grand Canal, Venice
Signed and dated 1838, oil on canvas
18 x 26in (45.5 x 66cm)
£12,200-13,000 *S*

Samuel Prout (1783-1852)
British
The Doge's Palace, Venice
Inscribed 'Ducal Palace, Venice', pencil, pen and grey ink, grey wash heightened with white
10½ x 14⅝in (26.7 x 37.2cm)
£550-600 *C*

Henry Pember Smith (1854-1907)
American
Guidecca Canal
Signed, oil on canvas
14 x 20in (35.6 x 50.8cm)
£1,400-1,600 *S(NY)*

Francesco Zanin (19thC) Italian
Napoleon III Visiting Venice in 1869
Signed and dated 1869, oil on canvas
29 x 43in (73.6 x 109.2cm)
£36,000-38,000 *HFA*

'The connoisseur who was not a mere tourist could only tolerate a view of Venice which was more than just a view,' notes Haynes Fine Art, who submitted the present work. Italian artist Zanin solved this problem by producing an historical painting, celebrating the visit of Napoleon III to Venice in 1869. In welcome addition to the usual gondolas, the paddle steamer in the foreground is believed to be the same one which was used for the opening of the Suez Canal by the Empress Eugénie.

Alfred Bendiner (20thC)
Venice
Signed and titled, watercolour on paper
15½ x 22½in (39.4 x 57.2cm)
£320-360 *S(NY)*

Antoine Bouvard (d1956)
French
The Doge's Palace, Venice
Signed, oil on canvas
19 x 25in (48.2 x 71.1cm)
£16,500 16,000 *HFA*

Bob Brown (20thC)
British
The Flower Market, Venice
Oil on canvas
29 x 36in (74 x 92cm)
£1,800-2,000 *Ch*

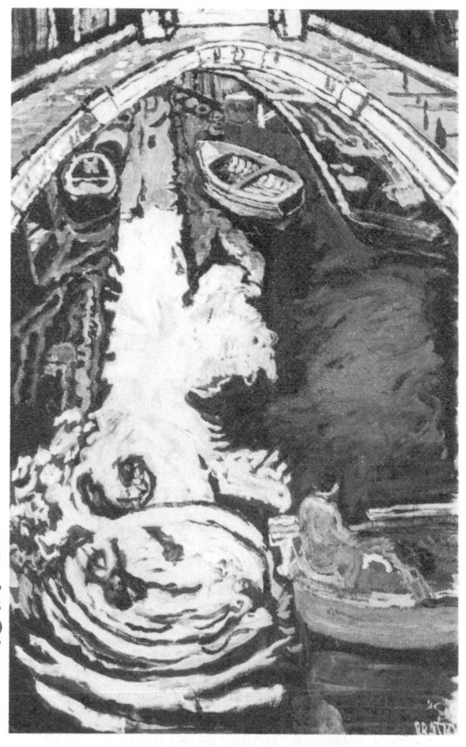

John Bratby (1928-1992)
British
Disturbed Water, Venice
Signed and dated 88, oil on canvas
48 x 30in (122 x 76cm)
£1,000-1,200 *C*

Emma Ciardi (1879-1933)
Italian
Mattino in Canal Grande
Signed and dated 1923, oil on panel
14½ x 19½in (36.8 x 49.5cm)
£18,800-19,800 *C*

Wilfrid de Glehn (1871-1951)
British
On the Canals, Venice
Signed, oil on canvas
30 x 25in (76 x 64cm)
£80,000-85,000 *DM*

Frank Henry Mason (1876-1965)
British
A Scene on the Venetian Lagoon, and another, a pair, The Dogana and S. M. della Salute
13 x 17½in (33.5 x 45cm)
£4,300-4,500 (the pair) *JML*

Robert King (b1936) British
Grand Canal, Venice
Signed, gouache
17⅞ x 25¾in (45 x 65.4cm)
£2,300-2,500 *BuP*

Did you know?
MILLER'S Picture Price Guide will build up year by year to form the most comprehensive photo-reference library available

Antonio Maria de Reynar Manescau (1859-1937) Spanish
The Monument to Bartolomeo Colleoni in Campo SS Giovanni e Paolo, with the Scuola Grande di S. Marco Beyond, Venice
Signed, oil on board
6 x 8in (15.2 x 20.3cm)
£4,200-4,500 *C*

Rubens Santoro (1859-1942) Italian
Gondolas on the Grand Canal with S. Maria della Salute and Punta della Dogana, Venice
Signed, oil on canvas 10¼ x 17¾in (26 x 45.1cm)
£25,000-28,000 *C*

ROME

Roman and classical ruins, antique and architectural fantasies.

'Antiquity has not ceased to be the great school of modern painters, the source from which they draw the beauties of their art,' claimed the great French painter Jacques Louis David in 1799.
This section is not only devoted to pictures of Rome, the central stop on every grand tour of Italy, but to pictures of classical ruins, some actual Roman sites, some architectural fantasies, others a mixture of the two. Many of the pictures are entitled 'Capriccio', a term describing a landscape or architectural scene combining real and imaginary features, and a genre of painting that was popular in the 18thC. A number of the capriccio illustrated on the following pages went over their estimate at auction.

Hendrik Frans van Lint, called Monsù Studio (1684-1763)
Flemish
The Vatican from Monte Mario
13 x 17⅛in (33 x 43.5cm)
£45,000-55,000 *C*

Ippolito Caffi (1809-66)
Italian
A View of the Forum, Rome
Signed and dated 1830, oil on canvas
13¼ x 22¾in (34 x 58cm)
£47,000-52,000 *S*

Circle of Domenico Quaglio (c1786-1837)
German
Rome from the Tiber with Castel San Angelo
Indistinctly signed, oil on board
8½ x 11½in (21.5 x 29cm)
£3,600-4,000 *S*

Salvatore Guarina (b1882)
American
The Tiber, Rome
Signed, oil on canvas
25 x 30in (63.5 x 76.2cm)
£1,500-1,800 *S(NY)*

Karl August Lindemann-Frommel (1819-91)
German
A View of Rome
Signed and dated Rom 1872, oil on canvas
36¼ x 70½in (92 x 179cm)
£26,000-28,000 *S*

Linnie Watt (active 1875-1906)
British
On the Pincio, Rome
Signed and inscribed, oil on board
9 x 13in (22.8 x 33cm)
£4,000-4,250 *BuP*

17th Century

Studio of Viviano Codozzi (1603-72) and
Domenico Gargiulo (1612-79)
Italian
Architectural Capriccio with Figures
A set of 4, oil on canvas
28¼in (73cm) diam
£14,500-16,000 *S*

Follower of Giovanni Ghisolfi
(1632-83)
Capriccio Landscapes with
Classical Ruins
A pair, both oil on canvas
laid on board,
octagonal
48 x 43¼in (122 x 110cm)
£17,000-19,000 *S*

Paul Vredeman de Vries
(c1567-after 1630)
Dutch
A Palace Courtyard with David and Bathsheba
Oil on canvas
38½ x 52¼in (98 x 133cm)
£16,000-18,000 *S*

18th Century

Circle of Abraham-Louis-Rodolphe Ducros (1748-1810) and Giovanni Volpato (1733-1803)
Swiss and Italian
Views of Rome: The Temple of Concord and the Arch of Septimius Severus; and The Arch of Janus
Watercolour over etched outline
14¼ x 18in (36.3 x 45.7cm)
£1,200-1,800 *S(NY)*

Follower of Gian Paolo Panini (1691-1765)
Italian
Capriccio of Roman Ruins
Oil on canvas
35½ x 37¾in (90.5 x 95.7cm)
£24,000-28,000 *S*

Follower of Antonio Joli
(1700-70)
Italian
The Temple of Neptune, Paestum
30 x 40in (76.2 x 101.7cm)
£9,000-9,400 *C*

Bolognese School (18thC) Capriccio of Classical Buildings with the Triumph of David and the Return of Jepthah
A pair, oil on canvas 48¾ x 78in (124 x 198cm)
£27,000-32,000 *S*

Although unattributed, this highly decorative pair of paintings went considerably over their upper estimate when auctioned by Sotheby's in January 1992.

Antonio del Drago (active end 18thC)
Italian
The Temple of the Sybil, Tivoli
Signed and dated 1790, watercolour heightened with white, over etched outline, on paper mounted on canvas
23¾ x 33¼in (60.3 x 84.5cm)
£2,000-2,300 *S(NY)*

19th Century

Wilhelm Beurlin (19thC) German
A Mediterranean Landscape with Ruins
Signed and dated 1855, oil on canvas
36½ x 44in (93 x 112cm)
£3,000-3,400 *S*

Arthur John Strutt (1819-88) British
The Roman Compagna
Signed and dated, Rome 1886, oil on canvas
11¼ x 18¼in (28.6 x 46.3cm)
£1,500-1,800 *CSK*

Thomas Peploe Wood (1817-45)
British
Roman Fantasia
Signed and dated 1839, oil on board
12 x 17in (30 x 44cm)
£850-950 *BCG*

One of the few oils painted by this Staffordshire artist.

NAPLES

Naples was another essential stop on the Italian Grand Tour and views of this fashionable beauty spot abound in the salerooms and the galleries. Many pictures of the Italian coastline are also included in the main landscape sections and the following is just a selection of certain Neapolitan views sold over the past year.

Gioacchino La Pira (19thC) Italian
A View of Naples;
A View of Amalfi
A pair, signed, gouache
12 x 18in (30.5 x 46cm)
each **£3,000-3,200** *S*

Giuseppe Giardiello (late 19thC) Italian
Napoli dal Granatello
Signed, oil on canvas laid down on board
19 x 26in (48.2 x 66cm)
£3,100-3,500 *C*

After Pietro Fabris (1754-92) Italian
Sir William Hamilton, Campi Phlegraei, Observations on the Volcanoes of the Two Sicilies. A series of 19 different views including: View of the Eruption of Snow Covered Vesuvius coloured etchings, black ink borders within grey wash outer borders
8¼ x 15½in (21 x 39.5cm)
£3,800-4,200 *CSK*

Joseph Wright of Derby (1734-97) British
Vesuvius from Posillipo Oil on canvas
17 x 22½in (43 x 57cm) **£16,000-18,000** *S*

Wright's fascination with Vesuvius stems from a visit made in October 1774. He wrote of the volcano, 'Tis the most wonderful sight in nature . . .'. This work relates closely to a larger painting of the late 1780s.

Edward Lear (1812-88) British
A View of the Bay of Naples
Signed, indistinctly inscribed and numbered 37.W, black chalk heightened with white
8⅝ x 15in (22 x 38cm) **£2,000-2,400** *Bon*

Neapolitan School (19thC)
A View of Naples and Vesuvius
Oil on canvas 14½ x 24in (37 x 61cm)
£6,800-7,500 *S*

Italian School (19thC/20thC)
An Album of Views of Naples and Pompeii
Various media including 4 gouache, 4 oil on paper and 13 pencil heightened with white gouache on tinted paper, various sizes
£5,300-6,000 *S*

Also included in the album is a group of 17 albumen prints of statuary including a good image of Pompeii with a standing figure, each approx 6.8 x 9.4in (17.5 x 24cm).

Friedrich Mayer (1792-1870) Swiss
A View of the Bay of Naples and Vesuvius
Oil on canvas 22 x 31¼in (56 x 79.5cm)
£24,000-28,000 *S*

The present work more than doubled its auction estimate in November 1991.

James Baker Pyne (1800-1870)
British
A Temple Near Naples
Signed, inscribed Napoli, dated 1853 and indistinctly numbered 35-, oil on canvas laid down on board
24¾ x 34¾in (63 x 88.5cm)
£1,800-2,200 *S*

This is either Temple of Venus (no 352) or Temple of Diana (no 353) in Pyne's notebooks. Both were painted for Agnews.

Robert Paton Reid (1859-1945) British
Amalfi
Signed c1910, oil on canvas board
12 x 16in (30.5 x 40.5cm)
£2,000-2,200 *PaHG*

Achille Solari (b1865)
Italian
Capri from the Amalfitan Coast; and the Bay of Naples from Posillipo
A pair, 1 signed, oil on canvas
10¼ x 15¾in (26 x 40cm)
£3,000-3,400 *C*

Oscar Ricciardi (b1864)
Italian
A View Across the Bay of Naples; Neapolitan Fishermen; Sunset Over the Duomo, Venice
A set of 3, each signed
15½ x 8½in (39.4 x 21.6cm)
£2,800-3,200 *Bea*

Charles Rowbotham (1823-75)
British
The Bay of Sorrento; Pozzuoli, Bay of Naples
A pair, both signed and dated 1892, watercolour
5½ x 10in (14 x 25.5cm)
£3,600-4,000 *S*

Camillo de Vito (19thC)
Italian
Vesuvius Erupting at Night
A pair, both signed and titled, gouache
11¾ x 16½in (30 x 42cm)
£4,200-4,600 *S*

PARKS AND GARDENS

The current interest in gardening that is reflected in the increased number of garden-related magazines and television programmes is also seen in the picture market. This section is predominantly composed of 20thC works, many contributed by dealers specialising in what one gallery described to Miller's as 'contemporary but traditional' artists – a field that many seem to consider far safer in these recessionary times than 'contemporary and modern'.

Robert Adam (1728-92)
British
Design for a Classical Bridge
Grey washes over pen and black ink on original wash line mounts
14¼ x 18¼in (36 x 46.5cm)
£5,800-6,400 *S*

Peter de Wint (1784-1849)
British
An ornamental Garden Fountain surrounded by Trees
Pencil and watercolour with scratching out
11¼ x 9⅜in (28.6 x 23.8cm)
£3,000-3,400 *C*

Ronald Bone
(20thC)
British
Pegging Out
Acrylics
11 x 10in
(28 x 25.5cm)
£725-775
JN

William Lionel Clause (1887-1946)
British
Well in Sunlit Courtyard
Signed
16½ x 12in (42 x 30.5cm)
£460-480 *SCG*

Jean-Honoré Fragonard (1732-1806)
French
The Cascade at the Villa Aldobrandi, Frascati
Red chalk
14⅛ x 18½in (35.4 x 47cm)
£63,000-70,000 *S(NY)*

Paul Dawson (20thC) British
Wicker chair, ball and teddy
Signed, watercolour
12½ x 17½in (32 x 44.5cm)
£550-595 *JN*

Jean Dufy (1888-1964)
French
Séville, la Fontaine et le Patio
Signed, oil on canvas
21½ x 13in (54.6 x 33cm)
£7,800-8,300 *C*

Prof Fred Duberry (b1926) British
Dark Pink Profusion
Signed, oil on board
10¾ x 8¾in (27.3 x 22.2cm)
£550-600 *NGG*

Condition is a major factor in a picture's price

Ella du Cane (19th-20thC) British
A Garden on the Italian Coast with Capri in the Distance
10½ x 17in (26.8 x 43.2cm) **£500-550** *Bon*

George Samuel Elgood (1851-1943)
British
The Garden Walk
Signed, watercolour heightened with bodycolour
9¼ x 14in (23 x 36cm)
£1,600-2,000 *S*

Jane de Glehn (1873-1961)
British
The Escutcheon of the Emperor Charles V, the Generalife Palace, Granada
Signed and dated 1912, oil on board
19¼ x 15¼in (49 x 39cm)
£28,000-29,000 *DM*

Wilfrid de Glehn (1871-1951)
British
A Garden in Spain
Signed and dated 1912, oil on canvas
25 x 30¼in (64 x 77cm)
£60,000-70,000 *DM*

Ettore Roesler Franz (1845-1907)
Italian
Villa d'Este, Autumn
Signed, pencil and watercolour on card
12½ x 30in (31.7 x 76.2cm)
£3,500-3,800 *C*

Thomas H** Hunn (1861-1941)
British
Rose Garden, Clandon
Signed, inscribed and dated 1910, watercolour
11 x 15in (28 x 38.1cm)
£600-700 *DN*

Caroline Leeds (b1931) British
The Garden at Lectoure Signed, oil on canvas
10 x 12in (25.4 x 31cm) **£500-550** *BuP*

René Legrand (b1847) French
A Summer's Day Signed, oil on canvas
20 x 28in (51 x 71cm)
£1,000-1,200 *S(S)*

Emile Lejeune (1885-1964)
French
Le Jardin Exotique
Signed and dated 1940,
oil on canvas
28¾ x 23⅝in (73 x 60cm)
£3,400-3,700 *C*

James Matthews
(late 19th/early 20thC)
British
Summer Garden
Signed, watercolour
13½ x 20½in (34 x 52cm)
£1,150-1,250 *SH*

Richard Pikesley (20thC) British La Place Napoleon (detail)
Oil on canvas 12 x 14in (31 x 36cm)
£420-460 *Ch*

Colin Newman (20thC) British
The Arbour
Signed, watercolour
14 x 20in (35.5 x 51cm)
£950-1,000 *JN*

Tom Mostyn (1864-1930) British The Garden
Signed, oil on canvas 24½ x 29½in (62 x 75cm)
£450-550 *C*

Beatrice Parsons (1870-1955)
British
Crocuses, Rose Hill, Falmouth in the Background
Signed, watercolour
11¾ x 15½in (29.8 x 39.4cm)
£1,550-1,750 *Bon*

Tony Brummell Smith (20thC)
British
Child in a Garden
Signed, pastel
13 x 15in (33 x 38cm)
£350-400 *WG*

Enrique Serra y Auque (1859-1918)
Spanish A Woodland Lake at Malmaison Signed and inscribed 'Malmaison Paris', oil on canvas
36¼ x 26½in (92 x 67cm)
£2,500-2,700 *S*

Eva Walbourne (20thC) British
Summer Garden
Signed, oil on canvas
11½ x 15¾in (29 x 40cm)
£900-1,000 *SH*

Lilian Stannard (1877-1944)
British
The Old Garden Gateway
Signed, watercolour
13½ x 9½in (34.2 x 24.2cm)
£2,100-2,400 *Bon*

Olga Wisinger-Florian (1844-1926)
Austrian
The Apple Orchard
Signed, oil on canvas
51½ x 71¼in (131 x 181cm)
£50,000-55,000 *S*

After studying under Melchior Fritsch and August Schaeffer in Vienna, Wisinger-Florian became closely associated with the Austrian 'Impressionist' movement led by the influential landscapist Emil Jakob Shindler. Within this group, Wisinger-Florian, along with Maria Egner and Carl Moll, became one of the most significant Austrian artists of the late 19thC. She worked and travelled extensively in Europe and North America, exhibiting in London, Paris, Chicago and her native Vienna.

Josephine Trotter (b1940)
British(?)
Looking up to the Balcony
Signed, oil on canvas
18 x 14in (45 x 35cm)
£625-675 *NGG*

THE ENGLISH COUNTRY COTTAGE

Though perhaps not receiving such an enthusiastic response in the auction rooms as in the recent past, there is always a market for these late 19th/early 20thC pictures of English country cottages and their flower-filled gardens bathed in perpetual sunshine. Decorative, colourful and seductively sentimental, they epitomise the idealised view of rural life.

John Abernethy Lynas Gray (early 20thC) British
Feeding Chickens on a Country Lane Signed and dated 1912 11¼ x 18in (28.5 x 46cm) **£900-1,000** *S(S)*

Henry Hadfield Cubley (active 1882-1904)
British
Signed, watercolour
15 x 11in (38 x 28cm)
£250-300 *BCG*

Alfred de Breanski Jnr (1877-c1945)
British The Open Door
Signed and dated 'III-XI' on the reverse, oil on canvas
22 x 16in (56 x 41cm)
£2,400-2,700 *S*

Helen Allingham (1848-1926)
British
Thatched Cottage beyond
Signed, watercolour
6¼ x 9⅛in (15.8 x 23.2cm)
£250-280 *Bon*

Helen Allingham was queen of the cottage garden school. Writing in 1931, W. Graham Robertson encapsulated the appeal of her work; 'Her lovely little transcripts of the Surrey lanes and woodlands . . . are delights to the eye and lasting memorials of the fast-vanishing beauty of our countryside. In a few more years they will seem visions of a lost Fairyland, a dream world fabulous and remote as Lyonesse or Atlantis, but they are no false mirages but beautiful truth; few painters have penetrated so close to the soul of the English Country.'

Theresa Sylvester Stannard (1898-1947)
British The Cottage Garden, a pair
Both signed
Each 6¾ x 9¾in (17 x 25cm)
£1,500-1,700 *S(S)*

Tom Lloyd (1849-1910)
British
The Cottage on the Marsh
Signed and dated 1906, watercolour
8½ x 18½in (21.5 x 47cm)
£900-1,000 *Bea*

Theresa Sylvester Stannard (1898-1947)
British
A Thatched Cottage in Summer
Signed, watercolour and bodycolour
10 x 13½in (25 x 33.7cm)
£1,400-1,600 *L*

The Stannards were a whole family of cottage garden painters whose members included Henry John Sylvester, his brother Alexander Molyneux, his sisters Emily and Lilian, and his daughter Theresa.

Arthur Claude Strachan (b1865 – active 1885-1929)
British
A Worcestershire Cottage
Signed and numbered 121 on reverse, watercolour heightened with bodycolour and scratching out
11¾ x 18½in (29.9 x 47cm)
£2,700-3,000 *C*

Trevor Haddon (1864-1941)
British
A Rural Landscape with a Girl sweeping a Cottage Step, Geese in the foreground, and Trees beyond
Signed
20 x 13in (50 x 33cm)
£600-700 *HSS*

Sir Ernest Arthur Waterlow (1850-1919)
British
A Berkshire Cottage
Signed, watercolour heightened with bodycolour
7 x 10in (17.5 x 25.5cm)
£1,000-1,100 *S*

Thomas Nicholson Tyndale (?)
British
A Surrey Cottage
Signed, oil on canvas
12¾ x 9in (32.5 x 23cm)
£1,500-1,700 *S(S)*

Arthur Stanley Wilkinson (c1860-1930)
British
Sewing by a Cottage Door; Preparing to Go Out, a pair
Both signed, watercolour heightened with white
Each 10¾ x 15¼in (27.5 x 39cm)
£1,200-1,400 *S*

Arthur Stanley Wilkinson (c1860-1930) British
A Cottage Garden with a Mother and Child standing by the Door
Signed, pencil, watercolour and bodycolour
13¾ x 20¾in (34.9 x 52.7cm)
£1,200-1,400 *C*

HOUSES AND BUILDINGS: PICTURES, DRAWINGS AND ARCHITECTURAL DESIGNS

The market for architectural drawings which peaked in the 1980s, largely thanks to the demand from interior decorators, is still depressed. According to Miller's sources, many specialist dealers have either gone out of business, retired or changed direction. Sotheby's abandoned their sales of architectural drawings in 1990 when prices plummeted. 'There is very little on the market compared to 3 or 4 years ago, and I'm lucky if I see 1 architectural drawing a week,' says their expert Charles Hind. 'We find that if something of great quality comes in we can still sell it, but there is little demand for works that aren't really choice.' For collectors, however, this could be an advantage. 'The heat has gone out of the market,' notes Hind. 'If you are keen-eyed, it is a good time to buy and run of the mill things are far cheaper than they were 5 years ago'.

Thomas Daniell (1749-1840)
British
View of the Amrooah Gate, Sumbul
Numbered and inscribed 'Amrooah Gate Sumbul May 19, 1789', black lead, pen and brown ink, brown wash, watermark fleur-de-lys inside a crowned ornamental cartouche
14¾ x 21⅛in (37.5 x 53.4cm)
£800-1,000 *S(NY)*

Circle of Michele Sanmicheli (1484-1559) Italian A Design for a Palace
Red chalk, pen and brown ink, brown wash; and 2 drawings by a French hand
11⅛ x 16⅞in (27.8 x 42.2cm)
£5,500-6,000 *C*

English School, c1730
A Prospect of Hartland Abbey
Inscribed in the margin 'An East Prospect of Abbey in Devonshire ye Seat of Paul Orchard Esqr., Colonel of ye Northern Bataln. of Devon. . .', pencil and grey wash
6½ x 9½in (16.5 x 24.2cm)
£600-700 *C*

Paul Orchard (1682-1740) was the son of Charles Orchard (1651-1706) of Aldercombe, Cornwall, a collector of customs, and his wife Katherine, née Prust. He was married 3 times, the first marriage being to Mary, the daughter of Nicholas Luttrell of Hartland Abbey, in 1702.

Giacomo Guardi (1764-1835)
Italian
The Courtyard of the Loco Pio at San Canziano Black chalk, pen and brown ink, grey wash, watermark 3 crescents in a cartouche
18 x 12in (46.4 x 31.4cm)
£7,000-8,000 *C*

J. Hindley (c1760-c1820)
British
The Pantheon at Ince Blundell Hall, Lancashire
Signed and dated 1790 in the margin, pencil and grey wash on paper laid down on linen
10⅛ x 15⅛in (25.7 x 38.3cm)
£1,200-1,500 *C*

Ince Blundell Hall was the home of Henry Blundell (1724-1810) who built the pantheon to house his splendid collection of antiquities, said to be unequalled by any similar collection in the country.

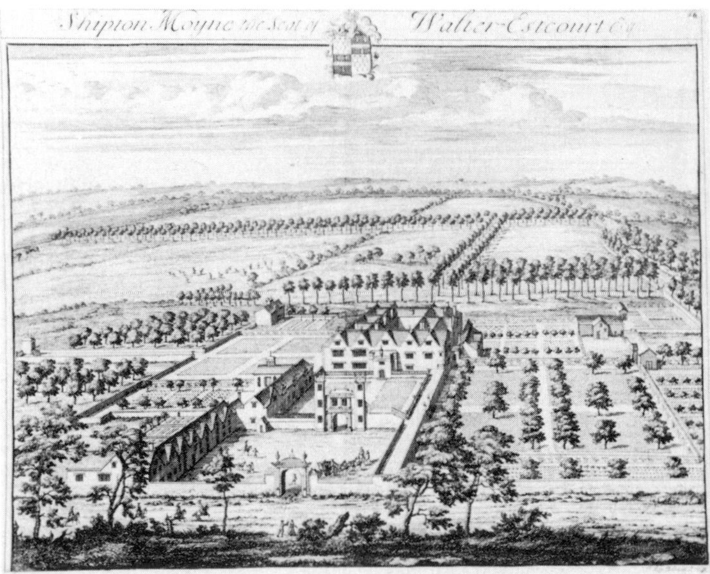

J. Kip (18thC)
Dutch
Shipton Moyne, the seat of Walter Estcourt Esq
Copperplate engraving drawn and engraved by J. Kip, from Robert Atkins Ancient and Present State of Gloucestershire, 1768
14¼ x 17½in (36.3 x 44.7cm)
£125-150 *Lan*

After J. C. Nettles (?)
British
The Assembly Rooms, Bath
Aquatint with original hand colouring, published 1806
£200-225 *Lan*

Peter Frederick Robinson (1776-1858)
British
Two Projects for the Earl of Ailsbury's House, Tottenham Park, Wiltshire, dated 1819 and 1920; along with a group of other designs (35), all signed and extensively inscribed 'P F Robinson Archt./29 Brook Street.', the majority pencil, pen and grey ink and watercolour, unframed
£4,500-5,500 *C*

Thomas Malton (1748-1804)
British
Oriel College, Oxford, with St Mary's Church in the Distance
Pen and ink and watercolour, watermark J. Whatman
12½ x 18in (32 x 46cm)
£4,000-4,400 *C*

Rev Thomas Streatfield (1777-1840)
British
The South Front of Wilton House and the Palladian Bridge
Inscribed on the reverse 'Wilton', pen and grey ink and watercolour
8 x 12in (20 x 30.4cm)
£700-750 *C*

The seat of the Earls of Pembroke. An Elizabethan house re-designed under the influence of Inigo Jones and John Webb and erected 1647-49 after the fire had partially destroyed Isaac de Caus's earlier façade. The Palladian bridge erected in 1737 was designed by the Earl of Pembroke and Roger Morris.

Rudolf von Alt (1812-1905)
Austrian
The Cemetery at Gastein
Signed and dated '889, watercolour
11 x 10½in (28 x 27cm)
£5,500-6,000 *S*

This is one of several versions of the same subject executed by the artist in 1889.

Anthony Vandyke Copley Fielding (1787-1855)
British
Prestbury Priory
Signed and dated 1840, pencil and watercolour
7¾ x 11½in (19.7 x 29.2cm)
£750-850 *Bon*

Lewis William Wyatt (1777-1853)
British
Perspective View of a Design for the South Front, Tatton Park, Cheshire
Watercolour over pencil
18 x 26¾in (45.5 x 68cm)
£3,800-4,200 *S*

John Atkinson Grimshaw (1836-93) British
Yew Court, Scalby, near Scarborough
Signed and indistinctly dated 187-, oil on board
18½ x 29in (47 x 74cm)
£13,300-14,000 *S*

John Adey Repton (1775-1860)
British
East Barsham Manor, Norfolk, from the High Road and from the Abbey Barn; a pair
Grey wash over pencil
Each 10¼ x 17in (26 x 43.5cm)
£4,500-5,000 *S*

East Barsham Manor was built about 1520 for Sir Henry Fermor and is elaborately decorated with carved brick. Neglected from 1760, restoration only began in 1919. The ruinous part was made habitable again in 1938.
John Repton was the eldest son of Humphry Repton, the landscape designer, and was apprenticed to the architect William Wilkins of Norwich.

David Cox (1783-1859)
British
Haddon Hall, Derbyshire
Signed and dated 1845,
watercolour over pencil
heightened with bodycolour
8 x 17¾in (20.5 x 45cm)
£4,200-5,000 *S*

Jeremy Barlow (20thC)
British
Chez Nico
Signed, oil
11¾ x 15¾in (30 x 40cm)
£600-650 *A*

Richard Jack (20thC)
British
Palais des Papes
Signed, oil on board
20 x 24in (51 x 61cm)
£2,200-2,400 *AdG*

Jessie Alexandra Dick (?)
British
The Glasgow School of Art
Signed, watercolour
15¼ x 12in (39 x 30.5cm)
£2,300-2,600 *S(SC)*

Laurence Stephen Lowry (1887-1976)
British
Old House
Signed and dated 1953, oil on canvas
10 x 18in (25.4 x 45.7cm)
£14,500-16,000 *C*

Isolated or derelict houses feature strongly in Lowry's work and are a symbol of his own sense of loneliness and personal isolation. Lowry once remarked 'I'm a very lonely man. But I like to be lonely', adding 'Had I not been lonely, I should not have seen what I did.'

T. L. Vesper (c1870-1920)
British
Project for the National Museum of Wales
Inscribed 'Design for the National Museum of Wales', pencil and watercolour
10¼ x 21in (26 x 53.3cm)
£350-450 *C*

A competition to design the National Museum of Wales was held in March 1910. The winning designs were by Alfred Dunbar Smith and Cecil Brewer, T. L. Vesper's project being awarded second premium.

Attributed to John Bakker (active 1696-1712)
Dutch – active in Britain
The Interior of Canterbury Cathedral: a view of the choir and chancel looking east, with members of the chapter and congregation seated in the foreground
Oil on canvas
48½ x 39½in (123 x 100.5cm)
£15,500-16,500 *S*

This rare view of the choir of Canterbury Cathedral dates from c1705. It shows the cathedral having recovered from the ravages of the Cromwellian period when it was used as a stable and armoury and when tombs and stained glass were desecrated. On Sunday 26th May 1660, Charles II attended a service at the cathedral and, as Clarendon commented, the cathedral was found to be 'much dilapidated and out of repair, yet the people seemed glad to hear the Common Prayer again'. Dr Thomas Turner, the new Dean, set about repairing the cathedral and almost £8,000 was spent in the next decade.

Jules Victor Genisson (1805-60)
Belgian
Figures in the Choir of a Cathedral
Signed and dated 1849, oil on canvas
46¾ x 38½in (119 x 98cm)
£2,000-2,300 *S*

Heinrich Hübner (b1869)
German
An Interior with Flowers
Signed, oil on canvas
27½ x 31½in (70 x 80cm)
£3,500-3,800 *S*

Hubert Robert (1733-1808)
French
Washerwoman in an Egyptian Temple
Black chalk, pen and grey ink, grey and brown wash, watermark device
22 x 13½in (55.8 x 33.6cm)
£6,100-6,500 *C*

The woman carrying water is inspired by a figure in Raphael's 'Fire in the Borgo'.

Charles Spencelayh (1865-1958)
British
2nd June 1953
Signed and dated 2-6-53, oil on canvas
30 x 22in (76 x 56cm)
£2,000-2,300 *C*

Peeter Neeffs the Elder (c1578-c1659)
Flemish
A Gothic Church Interior
Signed on the base of the pillar, oil on canvas
16¾ x 23¾in (42.7 x 58.7cm)
£20,000-25,000 *S*

The figures are by another hand. An attribution for them to Gillis Peeters has been suggested.

Gerry Ball (20thC)
British
In the Outhouse
Signed, watercolour
13 x 10in (33 x 25cm)
£700-750 *Bne*

Charles Spencelayh (1865-1958)
British
Grandfather's and Grandmother's Treasures
Signed and dated 1945, oil on canvas
16¼ x 20¼in (41 x 51.5cm)
£18,000-20,000 *S*

Locate the source

The source of each illustration in Miller's can be found by checking the code letters below each caption

Henry Spernon Tozer (active late 19thC)
A Surrey Kitchen near Farnham; and
Kitchen at the Woolpack Inn, Surrey: a pair
One signed and dated 1885, oil on canvas
8 x 10in (20 x 25.5cm)
£1,300-1,500 *S*

MARINE PAINTINGS

'In spite of the recession, the market in marine pictures is still encouraging,' claims John Morton Lee, specialist in marine watercolours. 'In my area, I would estimate that for the finest works, prices have risen by 10% over the past year and good quality pictures, even if they are not going up, are still holding their own. I would advise the new collector to go for quality ALL the time and to beware of buying pictures just because they are so-called fashionable names. If anything is undervalued at the moment, it is the earlier marine watercolours of the 1780-1830 period. Over the last decade, prices have remained static compared to those of later works, and they can offer great opportunities to the careful buyer.'

Ludolf Bakhuysen (1631-1708)
German
Warships off the Dutch Coast
Oil on canvas
26 x 37in (66 x 94cm)
£37,500-39,500 *JN*

17th Century

Attributed to Lorenzo Castro
(active late 17th and early 18thC)
Spanish
An Engagement between Levantine Galleys and a Turkish Man of War
Oil on canvas, in a carved wood frame
26¼ x 44in (67 x 111.5cm)
£7,500-8,000 *S*

Hendrik Martensz Sorgh (1610/11-70) Dutch Shipping on the Zuider Zee
Signed in the centre on the flag: HM Sorgh.
Bears a seal, possibly that of van Loe of Gelderland, on the reverse of the stretcher, oil on canvas
28½ x 42¼in (72.3 x 107.5cm)
£23,000-25,000 *S*

Abraham Storck (c1635-after 1705)
Dutch
Capriccio Mediterranean
Harbour Scene
Signed and dated 1679, oil on canvas
51 x 79in (132 x 200.5cm)
£70,000-80,000 *S*

Samuel Atkins (active 1787-1808) British
A Frigate at Anchor, smaller craft nearby
Signed, watercolour
11¼ x 15¾in (28.5 x 39.5cm)
£2,500-3,000 *JML*

Anthonie van Borssom (1630-77)
Dutch
A Moonlit Coastal Landscape with a Fisherman drying Nets in the foreground, and various Pinks setting sail
Signed, oil on panel
11¼ x 12¾in (28.5 x 29.8cm)
£20,000-25,000 *Bon*

Richard Beauvoir (18thC?)
British
A Part of the Walls of Southampton
Signed, inscribed and dated 1768 on original mount: and another similar view, watercolour
6 x 8¾in (15.2 x 22.2cm)
£500-600 *Bon*

Like many marine artists, Pocock spent much of his career at sea before becoming a professional painter. As a merchant sea captain, he made several voyages to America and, when writing up his ship's log, would always include a little wash drawing, recording the day's weather and events. From the early 1780s, he devoted himself to painting, his practical experience at sea recommending him to many naval clients. During the Napoleonic wars he concentrated on sea-battles. The present work shows the capture of the French frigate Piedmontaise which was taken by the frigate San Fiorenzo, commanded by Captain Hardinge, in March 1808. Hardinge was killed in the action.

Nicholas Pocock (1740-1821) British
The Capture of the French Frigate Piedmontaise
Signed and dated 1809, oil on canvas
32½ x 46½in (83 x 118cm) **£8,300-8,800** *S*

Thomas Allen (d1772-73)
British
The Storm during Queen Charlotte's Voyage to England: together with an engraving by P. C. Canot after the present painting, published by Inigo Bowles, trimmed to margins,
oil on canvas
15¼ x 23in (38.7 x 58.5cm)
£2,700-3,000 *Bon*

Thomas Allen's best known works are his depictions of the voyage and arrival in England in 1761 of George III's bride, Charlotte of Mecklenburg-Strelitz. The series comprises a View of the Yachts at Harwich, the Embarkation of Queen Charlotte at Stade, and the above scene in which the Yacht Mary was laid on her beam ends during a storm.

Adrien Manglard (1695-1760)
French
View of the Bay of Naples with Mt Vesuvius in the distance
Oil on canvas
41½ x 82¾in (105.4 x 210.2cm)
£80,000-90,000 *S(NY)*

Circle of Thomas Luny (1759-1837)
British
Shipping in Rough Seas off the Rocks
Oil on canvas
9 x 13in (22.8 x 33cm)
£650-750 *CSK*

Thomas Mellish (active 1760-78)
British
A Two Decker and other Shipping off Dover
Signed, oil on canvas
14¼ x 22½in (36.5 x 57cm)
£14,500-15,500 *S*

Thomas Whitcombe (1763-1824)
British
HMS Brunswick and HMS George and other Shipping in Plymouth Sound
Indistinctly inscribed on the stretcher with the identity of the ships, oil on canvas
16½ x 23¼in (42 x 59cm)
£6,100-6,600 *S*

HMS Brunswick, a two-deck of 74 guns, was in commission from 1790 to 1826. In 1794, in the Battle of the Glorious First of June, she was engaged in the famous combat with the French Vengeur when the ships were so close together that she had to blow her gun-ports off. In this action, her Captain, John Harvey, and 43 others were killed, and 114 wounded. Her two other battle honours were the Cornwallis Retreat in 1795 under the command of Captain Lord Charles Fitzgerald, and the Baltic in 1807-8. HMS George, the fourth of that name, was a three-deck of 100 guns in commission from 1788-1822. She was also at the Glorious First of June, flying the flag of Vice Admiral Hood (later Lord Bridport). In this engagement she lost 20 killed and 72 wounded. She was Bridport's flagship at the Groix action on 1795, when 9 British ships fought 12 French ships and captured 3. The 1797 Spithead Mutiny started in her and she was also in the Dardanelles Action in 1807.

William Payne (c1760-c1830)
British
A View on a River near Plymouth, Devon
Signed and inscribed on backboard: 'Plymouth Sound taken near the battery at Mount Edgecumbe', pen and grey ink and watercolour over traces of pencil on laid paper
11¾ x 15¾in (30 x 40cm)
£2,300-2,600 *S*

19th Century

Frederick James Aldridge (1850-1933)
British
Venetian Fishing Boats
Signed, watercolour
14¼ x 11in (36.8 x 28cm)
£1,800-1,950 *SCG*

Charles Bentley (1806-1854)
British
Fishermen with their catch north of Scarborough
Signed, watercolour
10 x 14in (25 x 35cm)
£3,500-4,500 *JML*

Anglo-Chinese School (c1890)
The Four-masted Barque 'Lyndhurst' calling for a Pilot
Oil on canvas
18 x 23½in (45.7 x 59.7cm)
£2,000-2,500 *Bon*

The Lyndhurst was a steel four-masted barque weighing 2,311 tons that was built by MacMillan & Son in 1886. In 1898 she was sold to J. MacDonald and became one of the Anglo-American oil sailers, sailing from Sumatra to the Cape with naptha and paraffin oil. On 21st August 1911, an explosion ripped through the Lyndhurst, and a fire ensued. Survivors were picked up by the Clan Maclean, which was 35 miles away when the explosion occurred and the Lyndhurst was finally sunk by HMS Pandora, which fired 13 shells into her.

William Edward Atkins
(1842-1910)
British
The British Man-o'-War, St Vincent with other Men-o'-War in an Estuary Scene
Signed, pencil and watercolour
13½ x 21½in
(34.3 x 54.6cm)
£750-850 *Bon*

Stuart Henry Bell (1823-96) British
A Race for Life Signed and dated 1880
7½ x 11½in (19 x 29cm)
£600-700 *A*

Eugène Boudin (1824-98) French
Port en Bretagne
Signed and dated 73, oil on canvas
13 x 18in (33 x 46cm)
£35,000-40,000 *S*

William H. Borrow (active 1863-93)
British
Stormy Weather, Hastings
Signed, oil on canvas
16 x 26in (40.6 x 66cm)
£1,250-1,750 *CSK*

Hector Caffieri (1847-1932)
British
Shrimping off Boulogne
Signed, watercolour
14 x 20in (35.5 x 25.4cm)
£1,000-1,100 *EH*

Sam Bough (1822-78) British
The Old Man of Hoy
Signed and dated 1875, watercolour heightened with white
14¾ x 21½in (37.5 x 54.5cm)
£1,800-2,000 *S(SC)*

John F. Branegan (active 1871-75)
British
'Nr. Dover', a Beach Scene; and a companion, 'Noon', a pair
Signed and inscribed, watercolour
6¾ x 10in (17.2 x 26.7cm)
£300-350 *Bon*

John Callow (1822-78)
British
Shipping in the Harbour, Whitby
Signed and dated 1855, pencil and watercolour
heightened with white
21¼ x 31in (54 x 78.7cm)
£1,600-2,000 *C*

Thomas Buttersworth Junior (19thC?)
British
British Men-o'War and a Hulk in a Swell, a
Sailing Boat in the foreground
Signed with initials, oil on canvas
10 x 12¼in (25.5 x 31cm)
£2,800-3,000 *Bon*

William Callow (1812-1908) British Shipping in a French Port
Signed, watercolour over pencil heightened with bodycolour,
gum arabic and scratching out 7 x 10¼in (17.5 x 26cm)
£7,500-8,000 *S*

John Wilson Carmichael
(1800-68)
British
Hartlepool
Signed and dated 1850,
oil on canvas
20 x 29¼in (50 x 74.2cm)
£22,000-25,000 *BuP*

John Newington Carter (1835-71)
British
Small Craft off the Needles
Signed and dated '66,
watercolour and scratching out
9½ x 13¼in (24.2 x 33.6cm)
£750-850 *Bon*

Edmund Thornton Crawford (1806-85)
British
Loch Fyne
Signed, oil on canvas
21 x 33in (53 x 84cm)
£850-950 *S(SC)*

William Raymond Dommersen (active 1870-1900)
British
Meden Blyk, on the Zuider Zee
Signed, inscribed on the reverse, oil on millboard
8 x 16in (20.3 x 40.6cm)
£4,600-5,000 *BuP*

Charles Dixon (1872-1934)
British
'The Pool', shipping in the Pool of London
Signed, inscribed and dated '99, watercolour
21 x 14¾in (53.3 x 37.5cm)
£2,200-2,500 *Bon*

Nicholas Matthew Condy (1818-51)
British
A Cutter of the Royal Yacht Squadron in a Squall off the South West Coast
Signed, oil on board
12 x 16in
(30.5 x 40.5cm)
£9,500-10,000 *BB*

Pieter Christian Dommersen (1834-1908)
Dutch
Off Monnikkedam, Holland; and Blokzyl, Holland: a pair
Both signed and one dated 1901, oil on panel
11¾ x 16in (30 x 40.7cm)
£7,000-7,500 *C*

Reuben Chappell (1870-1940)
British
Amis Réunis of Falmouth
Signed, watercolour and bodycolour
14 x 20in (35.5 x 25.4cm)
£400-500 *L*

Myles Birket Foster (1825-99)
British
Ischia, the Bay of Naples
Signed with monogram, oil on canvas
30 x 43¾in (76 x 110cm)
£24,000-25,000 *O*

Miller's is a price GUIDE not a price LIST

English School (19thC)
An extensive Seascape with Various Shipping, a Coastline beyond and a Small Sailing Vessel in the foreground
Oil on canvas, unframed
24¾ x 29⅝in (62.8 x 75.3cm)
£550-650 *Bon*

Jules Dupré (1811-89)
French
A Seascape
Signed, oil on panel
11½ x 18¾in (29 x 47.5cm)
£3,900-4,300 *S*

English School (19thC)
A Fishing Boat and a Lifeboat off the Goodwin Lightship
Oil on canvas
24¼ x 35½in (61.6 x 90.2cm)
£1,200-1,400 *Bon*

Frederick R. Fitzgerald
(active late 19thC)
British
Cowes
Signed and inscribed verso, watercolour
5 x 9in (12.7 x 22.9cm)
£200-250 *Bon*

Arthur Wellington Fowles (1815-1883)
British
The Battle of Texel, 11th August 1673
Signed and dated 1881, oil on canvas
20 x 32in (50.8 x 81.3cm)
£4,000-4,500 *Bon*

Henry George Hine (1811-95) British
Fishermen and Beached Vessels on the Shore; a Windmill by a River
Both signed, watercolour
One 9¼ x 13½in (23.5 x 34cm) the other 6¾ x 13¾in (17 x 35cm)
£700-900 *S*

Thomas Bush Hardy (1842-97) British
Entrance to Portsmouth Harbour
Signed and inscribed, watercolour heightened with white
7¼ x 14½in (18.4 x 36.8cm)
£650-750 *P(S)*

British
A Schooner off Dover Signed and dated 1834, oil on canvas 33 x 49½in (85.5 x 126cm)
£4,500-5,000 *S*

Norman Hirst (19thC) British
Rowing Out
Signed with initials and dated '92, oil on canvas
15½ x 19¾in (39.5 x 50cm)
£650-750 *S(S)*

F. Horner (19thC)
British(?)
Royal Albert Yacht Club 20-ton Match, 1882; and a companion, a pair
Signed with initials, watercolour
9¼ x 14½in (23.5 x 36.8cm)
£1,300-1,500 *Bon*

The Royal Albert Yacht Club, established in 1865 and based in Southsea, was host to a 20-ton match between the yachts 'Buttercup', 'Katie', 'Freja' and 'Amethea' in 1882.

Abraham Hulk Snr (1813-97)
Dutch
Fisherfolk and Ships by the Coast
Signed, oil on panel
13 x 19¾in (33 x 50cm)
£12,200-13,000 *S*

Miller's is a price GUIDE not a price LIST

Eugène Isabey (1803-86)
French
Bringing the Boat Ashore
Signed and dated 1823, watercolour
6 x 8½in (15 x 21.5cm)
£1,150-1,300 *Bon*

John Cantiloe Joy (1806-66)
British
The Hull of the Barque 'Alliance' beached at Yarmouth Pier
Pencil and watercolour
6⅞ x 10⅛in (17.4 x 25.7cm)
£900-1,000 *C*

W. and J. C. Joy (1803-67 and 1806-66 respectively)
British
Men-of-War at Anchor off Portsmouth
Signed and dated 1858, watercolour
8¾ x 14¾in (21.9 x 36.9cm)
£6,500-7,500 *JML*

Johannes Hermanus Barend Koekkoek (1840-1912) Dutch
Dutch Fishing Boats and other Vessels offshore in a Strong Breeze
Signed, oil on canvas laid down on board
14⅝ x 21⅝in (37.2 x 55cm)
£5,800-6,200 *C*

Hermanus Koekkoek Snr (1815-1882)
Dutch
Shipping on a Rough Sea
Signed and dated '56, oil on canvas
15 x 22¾in (38 x 58cm)
£7,000-7,500 *Bon*

J.*** Lochert (?) (19thC)
British
The 'Zodiac' of Whitby (Captain W. Mansell)
Signed, inscribed and dated 1866
19 x 29¼in (48.2 x 74.2cm)
£800-900 *Bea*

William Callcott Knell
(active 1848-71)
British
Shipping off the Dutch Coast
Indistinctly signed, oil on canvas
18 x 32in (46 x 81cm)
£2,800-3,000 *PaHG*

Robert Malcolm Lloyd
(active 1879-1900)
British
Squally Weather on the Channel
Signed, watercolour
14 x 20in (37 x 51cm)
£2,000-2,500 *JML*

Arthur Joseph Meadows (1843-1907)
British
Fishing Boats on the River Rhône at Avignon
Signed and dated 1891, oil on canvas
23 x 35in (60 x 90cm)
£1,800-2,000 *EH*

Henry Mahrmann (?)
The Barque Kilmeny under Sail
Signed
23 x 38¼in (58.4 x 97cm)
£1,800-2,000 *Bea*

Edouardo de Martino (1838-1912)
Italian
A Man-o'-War Drying her Hammocks in the Mediterranean
Signed, oil on board
9¾ x 18in (25.2 x 45.7cm)
£1,700-2,000 *Bon*

Henry Redmore (1820-87)
British
On the Scheldt
Signed and dated 1871, oil on canvas
25½ x 40in (65 x 101.5cm)
£17,000-18,000 *O*

Jules Achilles Noël (1815-81) French
French Vessels moored outside a Town
Signed, oil on canvas
15¼ x 21½in (38.8 x 54.6cm)
£8,000-8,500 *C*

George Morland (1762-1804)
British
Wreck of an Indiaman off the Isle of Wight
Oil on canvas
35 x 54¼in (89 x 138cm)
£31,000-40,000 *S*

The painting shows a storm off Black Gang Chine, with sailors beaching a row-boat and salvaging bales from the wreck, and the Indiaman foundering on the rocks beyond.

Samuel Owen (1768-1857)
British
Shipping off Dover
Signed 'S. OWEN 28', watercolour over pencil heightened with bodycolour
5 x 9¼in (12.5 x 23.5cm)
£3,500-3,800 *S*

William Purser (1790-1852)
British
Shipping on a Calm Sea
Signed, watercolour with scratching out
6½ x 5in (16.5 x 12.5cm)
£1,100-1,400 *C*

Samuel Owen (1768-1857)
British
Dover
Watercolour
6 x 9in (15.2 x 22.8cm)
£1,400-1,500 *MS*

Thomas Sewell Robins (1814-80)
British
Fishing Boats across the Wind
Signed and dated 1865, watercolour
£3,800-3,950 *HAR*

Robert Taylor Pritchett (1828-1907) British
The Review of the Fleet at Spithead
Signed with monogram, inscribed 'Final Salute, 6.30pm' and dated Augt 21st 1891
Watercolour heightened with white
6¼ x 9½in (15.9 x 24.2cm)
£380-430 *Bon*

Charles Henry Seaforth (1801-after 1853) British
The Admiral's Barge returning to Shore
Signed on the buoy 'CHS', oil on canvas
29½ x 41½in (75 x 105cm)
£9,500-10,500 *S*

***Serritelli (19thC)
Italian
Figures on a Beach near Naples
Signed, oil on canvas
14½ x 25½in (37 x 65cm)
£6,100-6,400 *S*

Giovanni Signorini (1808-58)
Italian
Marina del Porto
Signed, oil on canvas
32 x 52½in (82 x 133cm)
£8,300-8,800 *S*

This is after a famous composition by Salvator Rosa, now in the Palazzo Pitti, Florence.

William A. Thornley (2nd half 19thC) British
Fisherfolk on the Shore in a Calm Estuary at Daybreak; and a companion, Unloading the Catch at Dawn
Signed, oil on canvas 17¾ x 29¾in (45 x 76cm)
£16,000-17,000 *BB*

Charles Thornely (active 1858-98)
British
On the North-East Coast
Oil on canvas
14 x 12in (36 x 31cm)
£2,250-2,450 *JN*

Ralph Todd (1856-1932)
British
A Calm Anchorage
Watercolour
11 x 15in (28 x 38cm)
£1,250-1,450 *WrG*

Theodore Weber (1838-1907)
British
Fishing Vessels at the Harbour Entrance
Signed, watercolour
9½ x 14½in (24 x 37cm)
£2,000-2,500 *JML*

William Lionel Wyllie (1851-1931)
British
Unloading Oysters at Concage
Signed, artist's proof drypoint etching
8 x 6in (20 x 15cm)
£260-280 *WyG*

William Lionel Wyllie (1851-1931)
British
Light Cruiser passing through
Black Rock Gate
Signed and inscribed, watercolour
12½ x 18in (31.7 x 45.7cm)
£400-500 *Bon*

Reproduced in More Sea Fights of the Great War, *by W. L. Wyllie, C. Owen and W. D. Kirkpatrick, pub 1919.*

William Henry Williamson (active 2nd half 19thC)
British
Off Scarborough
Signed, inscribed and dated 1865
11½ x 19½in (29.5 x 49.5cm)
£800-900 *S(S)*

20th Century

William Thomas Nichols Boyce (1858-1911)
British
North Shields Herring Boats and a Tramp Steamer
Signed and dated 1908
14½ x 21¼in (36.5 x 54cm)
£1,000-1,200 *AG*

English Naive School (c1901)
Shamrock 2 in the America Cup Race 1901; and another, similar, by the same hand
Inscribed, oil on board
14¼ x 19in (36.2 x 48.2cm)
£900-1,100 *Bon*

William Minshall Birchall (b1884) British
Warrior and Windjammer
Signed, watercolour
10 x 14in (25.4 x 35.5cm)
£600-680 *Dr*

Francis Russell Flint (b1915)
British
Shipbuilding
Signed, watercolour and bodycolour
21½ x 30in (54.5 x 76cm)
£1,200-1,400 *C*

Robert E. Groves (d c1944, active 1885-1920)
British
Sennen Cove
Signed, inscribed and dated 1901, watercolour and gouache
14 x 20¾in (35.5 x 52.7cm)
£850-950 *FL*

Salvatore Colacicco (20thC) The Sailing Ship Fidelia leaving Malta
Signed, oil on board 25½ x 42in (64.7 x 106.7cm)
£850-1,000 *Bon*

John Steven Dews (b1949) British
J. Class Yachts racing in the Solent, 1932
Signed, oil on canvas
30 x 60in (77 x 152cm)
£45,000-47,000 *JSD*

Karl Hagedorn (20thC)
British
Portuguese Sailing Boats
Signed, oil on canvas
18 x 22in (46 x 56cm)
£350-450 *Bon*

William Miller Fraser (1864-1961)
British
Summer, a West Coast Haven
Signed, painted c1910, oil on canvas
12 x 14in (30.5 x 35.5cm)
£1,500-1,650 *PaHG*

George Leslie Hunter (1877-1931) British The Quayside, Fife
Signed, watercolour and bodycolour 17¼ x 22in (44 x 56cm)
£5,600-6,100 *S(SC)*

Mary Krishna (1909-68)
Houseboats at Chelsea Reach
Signed, oil on canvas
30 x 24in (76.2 x 61cm)
£450-480 *SCG*

Stephen Goddard (20thC)
British
Tower Bridge Wharf
Mixed media
15 x 37½in (39 x 95cm)
£1,600-1,750 *PHG*

Laurence Stephen Lowry (1887-1976) British
Old House Boat at Aldeburgh
Signed and dated 1954, oil on canvas
12⅛ x 16in (30.8 x 40.6cm)
£11,200-12,200 *C*

Herbert Menzies Marshall (1841-1913) British
Waiting for the Ferry
Signed and dated 1907, watercolour heightened with white 13¾ x 20in (35 x 51cm)
£1,300-1,400 *S*

John Nash (1893-1977)
British
Yarmouth Docks
Signed, oil on canvas
36 x 25in (91.5 x 63.5cm)
£30,000-34,000 *C*

John Nash's interest in the industrial landscape was stimulated after visits to Bristol in 1925 and 1937. He greatly enjoyed the docks and paddle-steamers and these he wrote 'were the inspirations of many works'.

John Anthony Park (1888-1962) British
Fishing Boats in a Cornish Cove
Signed, oil 12 x 15in (30.5 x 38.1cm)
£3,000-3,250 *Dr*

Anne Redpath (1895-1965) British
Storm at Cambrils Signed, oil on panel
19¾ x 23½in (50 x 60cm)
£9,000-9,300 *C*

Stephen J. Renard (b1947) British
New York Yacht Club Cruise 1937 including Yankee, Ranger, Endeavour and Endeavour II
Signed and dated '89, oil on canvas
24 x 36in (61 x 91.4cm)
£1,200-1,500 *Bon*

R. Borlase Smart (1881-1947) British
Three Masted Sailing Ship unloading in RiverPlym
Signed, inscribed on reverse, watercolour and pastel
16 x 23in (41 x 58cm)
£700-800 *LH*

R. W. Usher (20thC) British Laying the Nets
Signed and dated 1927 **£350-450** *BWe*

Anthony E Skuse British
The Ship 'The West Australian' off a Lighthouse
Signed with initials and inscribed, oil on board
17¼ x 24½in (43.8 x 62.3cm)
£500-550 *Bon*

Edward Seago (1910-1974)
British
Tall Ships in Harbour
Signed, oil on board
12 x 16in (30.5 x 40.5cm)
£6,200-7,000 *S*

Bryan Pearce (20thC)
British
Smeaton's Pier from Promenade
Signed, oil on canvas
24 x 32in (61 x 81.5cm)
£1,500-1,700 *OLG*

Harold Wyllie (1880-1973)
British
'HMS Implacable' late duquay Trouin of 74 guns, sailing into Plymouth Sound, with a gold cock at the main truck in 1842, to pay off for the last time as sea going ship, the gold cock signified that she was the smartest ship at evolution in the Mediterranean Fleet
Signed, watercolour
10¼ x 14½in (26 x 36.9cm)
£800-1,000 *Bon*

Edward Wadsworth (1889-1949) British The Cattewater, Plymouth Sound
Signed, tempera on board
25 x 35in (63.5 x 89cm)
£160,000-180,000 *S*

Conceived in 1920 and completed 3 years later, The Cattewater, Plymouth Sound is the first in a series of Ports of England, the idea for which was inspired by a walk in the summer of 1921 along the south coast from Newlyn to London. Ports and docksides had been a favourite subject for Wadsworth, and in the first issue of 'Blast' Wyndham Lewis had listed them as an approved subject in the Vorticist repertoire. The Cattewater, Plymouth Sound, however, transcends his wartime interest in the workings of the dockside and the startling patterns of the dazzle-ships. In its departure from Vorticism it heralds a phase which is crucial both in Wadsworth's painting and to British art of this period. The preoccupation here is with landscape and the painting establishes Wadsworth as one of the leaders of the avant-garde artists who turned to landscape as a subject for both formal experiment and psychological escape after the harshness of war.

William Strang (1859-1921)
British
Boy Reading on a Harbour's Edge
Oil on canvas
18 x 21in (46 x 53.5cm)
£5,000-5,500 *C*

Jacob Adriaensz. Bellevois
(1621-1675)
Dutch
A Dutch Ship floundering
on Rocks in Coastal Waters
Signed, oil on panel
23¾ x 33in (60.3 x 83.8cm)
£12,600-13,500 *S(NY)*

Hendrick van Minderhout
(1632-1696)
Dutch
Aerial view of the Fort Saint
Philippe with Shipping on the
Slijkens Sluice, the Port of
Ostend in the distance
Signed, oil on canvas
64½ x 91in (163.8 x 231.1cm)
£28,000-35,000 *S(NY)*

Philippe Jacques de
Loutherbourg (1740-1812)
French
The Battle of Ushant, The
Glorious First of June, 1794,
showing Lord Howe's flagship,
the Queen Charlotte, closing
up on the starboard quarter
of Admiral Villaret-Joyeux's
flagship, the Montague
Oil on canvas, laid down
on panel
31½ x 41½in (80 x 105.5cm)
£16,000-18,000 *Bon*

John Wilson Carmichael (1800-1868)
British
Fishermen laying their nets and other shipping off the North Foreland and Shipping off the shore in a choppy sea
A pair, signed and dated 1845, oil on canvas
9¾ x 14in (24.7 x 35.5cm)
£12,500-13,000 *Pol*

Nicholas Matthew Condy (1816-1851) British
A British Frigate off the Coast at Mount Edgecumbe, Plymouth
Signed, oil on panel
8¾ x 11½in (22 x 29cm)
£5,300-5,600 *S*

Abraham Hulk (1855-1910)
Dutch
A Calm Evening in Harbour
A pair of oils on panel
6¼ x 9¾in (15.8 x 24.7cm)
£23,000-25,000 *BuP*

Jacobus Hendricus Johannes Nooteboom (1811-1878)
Dutch
A Ferry leaving the Shore
Signed and dated 1852,
oil on canvas
38 x 56in (96.5 x 142.2cm)
£28,000-30,000 *Pol*

Above right:
Henry Redmore (1820-1887)
British
A Calm on the Humber
Signed and dated 1859, oil on canvas $12^{1}/_{4}$ x $18^{1}/_{4}$in
(31.1 x 46.3cm)
£16,000-16,500 *BuP*

Anton Schranz (1769-1839)
Born in Ochsenhausen, active in Minorca
The Grand Harbour, Valetta, Malta, with H.M.S. Britannia, flying the flag of Vice Admiral Sir Pulteney Malcolm (1768-1838)
Oil on canvas
$11^{1}/_{2}$ x $17^{3}/_{4}$in (29 x 45cm)
£9,000-9,500 *S*

George Webster
(active 1797-1832)
British
Vessels off the Dutch coast
Signed, oil on canvas
25 x 30in (63.5 x 76.2cm)
£4,500-4,700 *Bon*

Louis Verboeckhoven (1802-1889)
Belgian
Fishing vessels by the shore
Signed and dated 1830, oil on canvas
$36^{1}/_{2}$ x $50^{1}/_{2}$in (93 x 128cm)
£11,700-12,500 *S*

Stanhope Alexander Forbes (1857-1947) British
The Harbour at Mousehole Signed and dated 1911, oil on canvas
20 x 24in (50.8 x 60.9cm) **£45,000-50,000** *DM*

Charles Cundall (1896-1971)
British
Dockland Ferry
Oil
9 x 12in (22.8 x 30.5cm)
£1,000-1,100 *Dr*

Maxime Maufra (1861-1918)
French
La Rentrée des Bateaux de Pêche
Signed, oil on canvas
23¾ x 28½in (60.3 x 72.4cm)
£15,000-16,000 *S(NY)*

Sir John Lavery (1856 - 1941)
British
On the Thames at Remenham
Oil on canvas
27 x 39in (68.6 x 99.1cm)
£72,000-77,000 *DM*

Edward Seago (1910-1974)
British
Upton Dyke, Norfolk
Signed, oil on board
14 x 20in (36 x 51cm)
£8,400-9,000 *Bon*

James Brereton (b.1954)
British
The Great Tea Race 1866
Aerial and Taeping
Signed, oil on canvas
28 x 42in (72 x 107cm)
£2,800-3,000 *JSG*

Harry Clarke (1890-1931)
British
From Poe's 'Tales of Mystery and Imagination'
Watercolour
14½ x 10½in (36.8 x 26.6cm)
£9,600-9,900 *EJ*

Stephen J. Renard (b.1947)
British
Jockeying for Position
Signed, oil on canvas
40 x 50in (102 x 128cm)
£5,500-6,000 *JSG*

David Napp (20thC)
British
Juanita
Chalk pastel
12 x 19in (31 x 48cm)
£800-850 *WG*

Sidney F. Honed (b.1912)
British
Boats at Polperro
Signed, oil
17 x 23in (43 x 58.4cm)
£400-450 *Dr*

Malcolm Morley (b.1931)
British
Loveboat
Oil on canvas
50 x 80in (127 x 203.2cm)
£23,000-25,000 *S(NY)*

Tristram Hillier (1905-1983)
British
Shipbuilding at Peniche
Signed and dated 1947, oil on canvas
24 x 32in (61 x 81.5cm)
£40,000-45,000 *S*

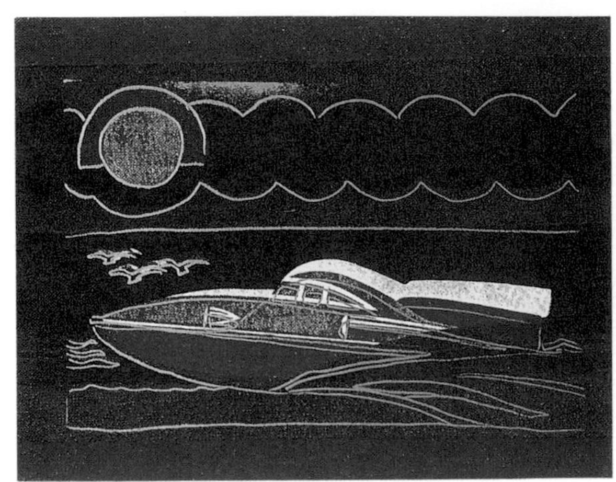

Andy Warhol (1930-1987)
American
Speedboat
Signed and dated '83 on the reverse,
polymer silk screen on canvas
8 x 10in (20.3 x 25cm)
£5,600-6,000 *S*

Lucas Cranach I (1472-1553)
German
Portrait of a young Lady, seated three-quarter length, wearing a red and orange dress and a wide-brimmed plumed hat and holding a flower
Signed with the serpent device, oil on panel
33⅞ x 21⅞in (86 x 55.6cm)
£470,000-550,000 *C*

Sir Peter Lely (1618-1680)
British
Portrait of Barbara Villiers, Countess of Castlemaine and Duchess of Cleveland (1640-1709)
83¾ x 51½in (213 x 131cm)
£58,000-70,000 *S*

Gainsborough Dupont (1754-1797)
British
Portrait of Charlotte Brydges (1766-1849)
Oil on canvas
91¼ x 59¼in (252 x 151cm)
£9,000-9,500 *S*

Anton von Maron (1733-1808)
Austrian
Portrait of Elizabeth Davers,
Countess of Bristol (1733-1800)
Signed c.l.: *Maron f. Romae 1779*,
oil on canvas
37½ x 27¾ (95 x 70.5cm)
£15,500-18,500 *S*

Eugène Delacroix (1798-1863)
French
Tête d'étude d'une Indienne
Signed, oil on canvas
23½ x 19¼in (60 x 49cm)
£795,000-850,000 *S*

François Henri Mulard (1769-1850)
French
Portrait of a Lady in elegant dress
Signed, oil on canvas
39 x 31¾in (99.1 x 80.6cm)
£95,000-105,000 *S(NY)*
Painted c1810

Eugène Delacroix (1798-1863)
Tete d'une Vielle Femme (Mme Bornot?)
Oil on canvas, bears the artist's *cachet de vente* seal on the stretcher
16 x 12¾in (40.5 x 32.3cm)
£95,000-110,000 *S*

Claude Marie Dubufe (1790-1864)
French
Portrait of a Lady on a Terrace
Signed, oil on canvas
82 x 56cm (208 x 142cm)
£14,000-15,000 *S*

Charles S. Lidderdale (1831-1895)
British
Country Charm
Signed, oil
22 x 17in (55.8 x 43.1cm)
£2,500-2,750 *Dr*

Thomas Millie Dow (1848-1919)
British
Spring
Signed with monogram and dated
86 and inscribed, oil on canvas
53 x 39in (134.6 x 99cm)
£4,000-4,500 *C(S)*

Edward Thompson Davis
(1833-1867) British
Sweet Solitude
Signed with initials 1860, oil, dated
9 x 54in (22.8 x 137.1cm)
£2,200-2,400 *Dr*

Abbey Altson (late 19thC)
British
Portrait of a Woman in Shakesperian
Costume; and Portrait of a Maiden (a pair)
Both signed, oil on canvas
28 x 18in (71.2 x 45.7cm)
£4,500-5,000 *C(S)*

Emma Sandys (active 2nd half 19thC)
A Medieval Beauty
Signed with monogram and dated 1866, oil on panel
12 x 10in (30.5 x 25cm)
£2,300-2,800 *S*

George Weiss (b.1861)
French
Seamstresses at work
Signed and dated 1902, oil on canvas
38 x 31in (96.5 x 80cm)
£14,500-15,000 *Pol*

Alfred Stevens (1823-1906)
Belgian
La Douloureuse Certitude
Signed, oil on canvas
31 x 23½in (80 x 60cm)
£30,000-35,000 *S*

Gustave de Jonghe (1829-1893)
Belgian
The Secret Drawer
Signed, oil on panel
28¾ x 21¼in (73 x 54cm)
£12,200-13,500 *S*

Wilhelm Schütze (1840-1898)
German
The New Kittens
Signed, oil on canvas
30 x 24in (76.2 x 61cm)
£40,000-46,900 *HFA*

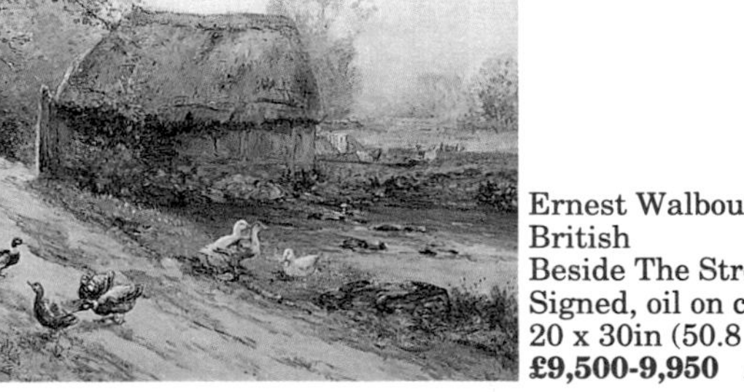

Ernest Walbourn (active 1895-1920)
British
Beside The Stream
Signed, oil on canvas
20 x 30in (50.8 x 76.2cm)
£9,500-9,950 *HFA*

Albert Goguet Mantelet (b.1858)
French
Promenade au bord de la Riviere
Oil on canvas
20 x 13in (51 x 33cm)
£4,600-4,950 *JN*

John Strevens (b.1902)
British
Monique
Oil on canvas
18 x 14in (46 x 35.5cm)
£3,500-3,750 *JN*

Endre Röder (b.1933)
Hungary
Friends
Signed, oil on board
28 x 23¾in (71.1 x 60.3cm)
£800-1,000 *FL*

Robert H Barnes (1899-1983)
British
Joan
Signed and dated 1953, oil on canvas
48½ x 32½in (123.1 x 82.5cm)
£2,250-2,500 *SCG*
Exhibited: Royal Academy 1953

Marie Laurencin (1885-1956)
French
Les Deux Amies
Signed, oil on canvas
13¾ x 10¾in (35 x 27.3cm)
£39,000-45,000 *C*
Painted circa 1935

John Singer Sargent (1856-1925)
British
The Green Parasol
Pencil, watercolour and bodycolour
18¾ x 13¾in (47.5 x 35cm)
£290,000-320,000 *C*
Executed circa 1910

Harold Harvey (1874-1941)
British
The Girl, Zennor
Signed and dated '26, inscribed on the stretcher *'The Girl' Zennor*, oil on canvas
18 x 18in (46 x 46cm)
£6,200-7,000 *C*

Duncan Grant (1885-1978)
British
Portrait of Vanessa Bell, recto;
A Corner of the Inn, Kings Lynn, verso
Signed, oil on canvas
19½ x 15¾in (49.5 x 40cm)
£35,500-40,500 *C*

Martial Raysse (20thC)
French (?)
Brigitte Bardot I
Signed and dated '65, acrylic and 'flocage' on card laid down on canvas
64 x 38in (163 x 97cm)
£53,000-60,000 *S*

Shabner (active 1940s-1950s)
American
Original gouache for a lipstick advertisement
18¼ x 16⅜in (46 x 43cm)
£425-450 *JD*

Léon de Smet (1881-1966)
Belgian
Buste de Femme, une Rose à la Main
Signed and dated 1925, oil on canvas
27⅜ x 22in (69.5 x 56cm)
£9,500-10,500 *C*

John Duncan Fergusson (1874-1961)
British
Corinthian Kathleen
Signed and dated 1916 and labelled on the reverse by Margaret Morris *Corinthian Kathleen,*
oil on board
13⅞ x 10¼in (35.3 x 26cm)
£5,000-5,500 *C(S)*

Edmund Adler (1871-1957)
Austrian
Posies for Mother
Signed, oil on canvas
27 x 22in (68.5 x 55.8cm)
£9,250-9,500 *HFA*

François Kinson (1771-1839)
French
A Portrait of Duchess MacMahon and her son
Signed and dated 1827 l.l., oil on canvas, unframed
95¼ x 65in (242 x 165cm)
£20,000-25,000 *S*

Marguerite Gérard (1761-1837)
French
La Correspondance Familiale
Signed, oil on canvas
25½ x 21¼in (64.8 x 54cm)
£82,000-95,000 *S(NY)*

Sir Thomas Lawrence (1769-1830)
British
Portrait of Mrs. Ayscoghe Boucherett with her two eldest Children Emilia and Ayscoghe, and her half sister Juliana Angerstein, later Madame Sabloukoff, in a garden.
Signed with initials and dated 1794, an extensive inscription on a label attached to the reverse of the frame reads 'Pastel by Sir Thomas Lawwrence, P.R.A./*'Madame Sabloukoff and Family'.* / Formerly from the Collection of William Angerstein Esq./of Weeting Hall, Norfolk- and more recently/ from the Count de Castellane of Paris'; pastel in an English 18th century carved and gilded Carlo Maratta frame
20 x 16¼in (50.7 x 41.2cm)
£83,000-95,000 *C*

Carlton Alfred Smith (1853-1946)
British
A Stitch in Time
Signed and dated 1905, watercolour
19 x 27½in (48 x 70cm)
£7,200-8,000 *S*

Irene Wolburn (b.1911)
British
Young Mothers
Signed, oil
32 x 22in (81.2 x 55.8cm)
£400-450 *Dr*

George Harcourt (1869-1947)
British
A Tangled Skein
Signed and dated 1917, titled and inscribed with the artist's address, oil on canvas, unframed
76 x 100in (193 x 254cm)
£42,000-50,000 *S*

Thomas Benjamin Kennington (1856-1916)
British
Maternity
Oil on canvas
54 x 72in (137 x 183cm)
£24,000-30,000 *S*

PORTRAITS AND PICTURES OF THE HUMAN FIGURE

16th-20th Century

'There is a very strong demand for interesting historical portraits', notes David Moore-Gwyn of Sotheby's British Paintings Department. 'Because prices didn't rise so dramatically as they did for the Impressionists, the field has not been badly hit by the recession and the market is good.'

In Sotheby's April 1992 Sale, a portrait of King James V of Scotland far exceeded its estimate of £30,000-40,000, as did Lely's portrait of Barbara Villiers, famous beauty and mistress of Charles II (see colour sections).

Both pictures epitomise the qualities of a desirable portrait, summarised by Moore-Gwyn as 'historical importance and physical good-looks'. 'In this field,' he adds, 'the appearance and identity of the sitter can easily outweigh the name of the artist; however good the painter, if the subject is ugly and unimportant then you've got problems.'

Auction houses will devote time to researching the history of individual sitters both because it makes a picture more generally desirable, and because it can help them to target specific potential buyers such as family descendants, or people otherwise connected with the subject. Conversely if doubts are raised about the identity of a sitter, as sometimes happens, that can stop a picture from selling.

Up until the turn of the 18thC, the auction houses offer a wide selection of portraits. 'There are some very good opportunities for the collector and you can still buy decent 18thC pictures without breaking the bank,' states Moore-Gwyn. '19thC portraits appear far less frequently and tend not to be worth a great deal unless they are by someone well known,' explains Moore-Gwyn. 'Generally speaking they are more standardised, their quality is less good and their frames less decorative.'

The section of the Picture Price Guide devoted to 19thC pictures of women, for example, shows how portraits of specific individuals have largely been replaced by general and idealised portrayals of womanhood: elegant and anonymous society beauties, miscellaneous Victorian maidens, rosy cheeked milkmaids, cheeky servants, devoted mothers – some pictures telling a story and most expressing a sentiment. 'This type of genre picture – pretty people in pretty settings – was painted purely as decoration for the masses,' notes Martin Beisly, head of the 19thC Picture Department at Christie's. 'The pictures are easy to look at and easy to value – if you think they're pretty, then other people will think they're pretty and they'll make money. But in the current climate, they won't make as much money as they once did, although there are specific collectors,' explains Beisly. 'Pictures like these tend to appeal to the popular taste and the more frivolous purchaser often buys on impulse. As such they run with the economy – when times are good, prices soar and in today's contracted market, when your average purchaser doesn't have a spare £3 or £4,000 in the bank – values have certainly dropped.'

The same is also true for the 20thC and contemporary markets, one of the areas to be most profoundly affected by the recession and many of the 20thC pictures appearing in the following sections and throughout the Guide as a whole, either sold below or at the bottom end of their estimates.

WOMEN

16th & 17th Century

English School (16thC)
Portrait of Margaret Russell, Countess of Cumberland (1560-1616)
Inscribed Margaret/Countess of Cumberland, oil on panel, unframed
14 x 12in (35.5 x 30.5cm)
£3,400-3,700 *S*

The sitter married the celebrated mathematician, navigator and adventurer George Clifford, Earl of Cumberland in 1577. 'The union was unhappy, Clifford, a great favourite of the Queen was handsome, faithless and a terrible spendthrift; Margaret who was "endowed with a large share of moral virtues" separated from him and spent much of her later years trying to obtain for their only daughter the family estates dissipated by her reckless husband.'

Manner of Hans Holbein (1497-1593)
German
Portrait of Anne of Cleves (1515-57)
Oil on panel, in a fine illusionistic architectural frame with a tesselated ground
17¾ x 14¾in (45 x 37.5cm)
£6,200-6,500 *S*

Manner of Nicholas Hilliard (1547-1619)
British
Portrait of Elizabeth I
Oil on panel
15 x 12in (38.1 x 30.5cm)
£750-850 *CSK*

Kings and Queens abound in portrait sales, and however mediocre the picture, there is usually a buyer for a royal face.

Circle of Sir Antonio More (c1517-76)
Dutch
Portrait of Mary Tudor
Oil on panel
27 x 17½in (68.5 x 44.5cm)
£12,200-13,000 *S*

Master MZ (Mattheus Zaisinger?) (16thC)
The Woman with the Owl (B21; L19)
Engraving, 1500
6¼ x 4¾in (15.9 x 12.2cm)
£4,900-5,400 *S(NY)*

Circle of Cornelis Ketel (1548-1616)
Dutch
Portrait of a Lady, dated 1588
Oil on panel
13⅜in diam (34cm diam)
£3,900-4,200 *C*

Pierfrancesco Cittadini (1616-81)
Italian
Portrait of a Lady
Oil on canvas
26 x 20⅜in (66 x 51.7cm)
£9,300-9,700 *C*

Follower of Van Dyck (1599-1641)
Portrait of a Lady
Oil on panel
15½ x 12⅛in (39.4 x 20.8cm)
£2,400-2,800 *Bon*

French School, circa 1630
The Head of a Young Woman
Red and white chalk, watermark bunch of grapes (cf Briquet 1307)
10½ x 9in (26.8 x 23.5cm)
£2,700-3,000 *C*

Attributed to Giovanni Francesco Barbieri, Il Guercino (1591-1666)
Italian
A Young Woman
Inscriptions on the mount 'guercino No. 370' and 'N6', pen and brown ink
8⅞ x 6⅞in (22.7 x 17.4cm)
£3,500-3,800 *S(NY)*

Follower of Sir Peter Lely (1618-80)
British
Portrait of a Lady, said to be Venetia Stanley
Oil on canvas
24 x 21in (61 x 53cm)
£2,000-2,200 *S*

Follower of Kneller (1646-1723)
British
Portrait of a Lady
Oil on canvas, unframed
30 x 26in (76.2 x 66cm)
£600-700 *Bon*

Sir Peter Lely (1618-80)
British
Portrait of Elizabeth Hamilton, Comtesse de Grammont (1641-1708)
Signed with monogram, oil on canvas
50 x 40in (127 x 101.5cm)
£10,000-11,000 *S*

The Comtesse de Grammont 'La Belle Hamilton', was one of the greatest beauties of the Restoration Court. Charles II described her as being 'as good a creature as ever lived'. She refused many offers of marriage from the highest-born suitors until, after an ardent and famous courtship, she married Philibert, Comte de Grammont, and went to live with him in France. Her wedding and its somewhat unusual circumstances were said to have been the basis for Moliere's play 'La Mariage Forcée'.

Nicolaes Maes (1634-93)
Dutch
Portrait of a Lady said to be Barbara Beerning, daughter of Willem Elsevier
Bears inscription on the reverse: Berbera Beerning. tr./Willem Elsevier
Oil on panel,
16 x 12¼in (40.7 x 31.1cm)
£3,600-3,900 *S*

Follower of Paulus Moreelse (1571-1638)
Dutch
A Shepherdess
Oil on panel
21⅛ x 16⅝in
(53.6 x 42.2cm)
£11,200-11,600 *C*

Theodore Russell (1614-88)
British
Anne Villiers, Countess of Morton, c1640
Oil on panel
15½ x 12in (39.5 x 30.5cm)
£3,700-3,800 *WWG*

Rembrandt Harmensz. van Rijn (1606-69)
Dutch
The Great Jewish Bride (B. Holl. 340; H. 127; BB 35-C)
Etching and drypoint, 1635
8⅝ x 6½in (21.9 x 16.6cm)
£7,500- 8,000 *S(NY)*

John Scougall (c1645-1730)
British
Portrait of Lady Susanna Hamilton, 3rd daughter of John, 4th Earl of Hadinton, and portrait of Margaret, Countess of Rothes, wife of Charles, 5th Earl of Hadinton
Inscribed, oil
13¼ x 11¼in (33.6 x 28.6cm)
13¾ x 11¼in (35 x 28.6cm)
£3,900-4,300 *C*

Circle of Robert Walker (active 1641-58)
British
Portrait of a Lady
Oil on canvas
29¼ x 24½in (74.5 x 62cm)
£3,800-4,100 *S*

Michael Dahl (1659-1743)
Swedish
Portrait of Mrs Haire
Inscribed on the reverse: Mrs Mary Haire/By Mr Doll 1711, oil on canvas, in a painted oval, in a carved wood frame
29¼ x 24¼in (74.5 x 62cm)
£6,100-6,500 *S*

18th Century

Attributed to Edme Bouchardon (1698-1762)
French
A Servant Woman Holding a Steaming Pot
With inscription 'ch', red chalk, watermark cross above an encircled six-pointed star
14¾ x 8½in (37.4 x 21.6cm)
£2,300-2,600 *S(NY)*

Circle of Richard Cosway (1742-1821)
British
Portrait of Lady Caroline Damer (1742-1821), daughter of the 1st Earl of Dorchester
11¾ x 9¾in (29.8 x 24.8cm)
£1,050-1,250 *C(S)*

Condition is a major factor in a picture's price

Samuel Cotes (1734-1818) British
Portrait of Miss Williams of Penpont
Signed and dated 1790, pastel, oval
23½ x 18in (59.5 x 45.5cm)
£2,500-2,700 *S*

The sitter is probably Anne, daughter of Philip Williams and his wife Osborne Yeats.

Studio of Nathaniel Dance (1735-1811) British
Portrait of Charlotte, Countess of Abingdon
Oil on canvas
50 x 40in (127 x 101.5cm)
£2,100-2,400 *S*

Christian Wilhelm Ernst Dietrich, called Dietricy (1712-74) German
A Young Woman Reading a Letter
Signed and dated D.1762, oil on panel
11 x 9½in (27.7 x 23.9cm)
£3,100-3,400 *S*

François-Xavier Fabre (1766-1837) French
Portrait of Jeanne-Robertine, Marquise d'Orvillier, nee Rillet (1772-1862) Oil on canvas
29⅛ x 24¼in (74 x 61.6cm) **£6,100-6,600** *C*

English School, 18thC
Portrait of Catherine of Aragon
Oil on canvas
29 x 24in (73.5 x 61cm)
£1,200-1,500 *S*

Daniel Gardner (1750-1805)
British
Portrait of Miss Hopkins
Pencil, pastel and bodycolour
10½ x 8½in (27 x 21.5cm)
£4,500-4,800 *C*

Enoch Seeman (1694-1745) Polish
Portrait of a Lady, probably Mary Fermor (d1729), wife of Sir John Wodehouse, 4th Bt
Later inscribed: Lady Lempster/1685, oil on canvas
49 x 39in (124.5 x 99cm)
£6,100-6,400 *S*

As demonstrated by the present work, inscriptions are often added subsequently to a picture and can easily be incorrect. Always beware of making assumptions about a painting purely from what has been written on the canvas and when in doubt, consult specialist advice.

John Lewis (active 1739-69)
British
Portrait of Jane Magendie
Signed and dated 1769
31 x 23in (78.5 x 58.3cm)
£3,000-3,300 *C(S)*

The last known signed example by the artist. It is possible that the sitter was a Dublin actress.

Charles Jervas (c1675-1739)
Irish
Portrait of Lady Bacon
Inscribed: Lady Bacon, 1712, oil on canvas
49¼ x 39½in (125 x 100.5cm)
£5,000-5,300 *S*

Frans van der Mijn (c1719-83) Dutch
Portrait of a Lady as a Shepherdess Signed 1746, oil on canvas
29 x 24¼in (73.5 x 61.5cm) **£5,600-6,000** *S*

Attributed to Henry Pickering
(active 1740-71) British
Portrait of a Lady
Oil on canvas
49 x 39in (124 x 100cm)
£7,200-7,500 *S*

Circle of Jean Frederic
Schall (1752-1825)
French
A Girl Watering Roses in
a Garden Setting
Oil on canvas
15½ x 12in (39.4 x 30.5cm)
£10,500-11,500 *S(NY)*

John Opie (1761-1807) British
Portrait of the Hon Caroline Sackville
Oil on canvas
29¼ x 24¼in (74 x 61.5cm)
£6,700-7,000 *S*

The son of a Cornish village carpenter, Opie was to become one of the most successful portrait painters of his period. His talent and intelligence combined with a complete lack of the usual social graces made him a source of some fascination amongst his peers. 'I have been introduced to Mr Opie, who is in manners and appearance as great a clown and as stupid looking fellow as ever I set my eyes on,' wrote fellow-artist Martin Archer Shee. 'Nothing but incontrovertible proof of the fact would force me to think him capable of anything above the sphere of a journeyman carpenter . . . I intend calling upon him occasionally; for I know him to be a good painter, and though appearances are so much against him, he is, I am told, a most sensible and learned man.'

Lewis Vaslet (1742-1808)
British
Portrait of Elizabeth Maria Chevalier
Oil on canvas
16½ x 13¼in (42 x 33.5cm)
£5,600-6,000 *S*

Jean-Antoine Watteau (1684-1721) French
Studies of Two Girls' Heads Black, red and white chalk
5⅛ x 7⅝in (13.2 x 19.4cm)
£140,000-160,000 *S(NY)*

Circle of Francis Wheatley (1747-1801)
British Portrait of a Lady with St Michael's Mount in the distance
Oil on canvas 28 x 23in (71 x 58.5cm)
£2,800-3,200 *C(S)*

19th Century

William Affleck (active 1890-1915) British
In a Flower Garden
Signed, watercolour
16 x 11in (41 x 28cm)
£1,700-2,000 *S*

Attributed to George Beechey (1798-1852) British
Portrait of an Indian Girl Oil on canvas
20¾ x 16½in (52.5 x 42cm) **£6,700-7,200** *S*

Arturo Marion Colavini (late 19thC) Italian(?)
A Young Woman Reclining in an Opulent Interior
Signed and indistinctly inscribed, watercolour
11¾ x 18¼in (29.8 x 46.3cm) **£900-1,000** *Bon*

The Parisien and European artists of the late 19thC developed a new vision of female beauty: luxurious and metropolitan women reclining sensuously in opulent interiors, crammed full with objects and swathed in silks, satins and furs. Whilst English painters were often more at home portraying country lasses and Victorian maidens, these visions of fin de siècle decadent glamour find their British and literary counterpart in the novels of Elinor Glyn, the famous creator of sex on a tiger skin rug.

Jules Frederic Ballovoine (19thC) French
A Young Beauty
Signed, oil on panel
8⅝ x 6¼in (22 x 16cm)
£1,400-1,600 *CSK*

A classic example of the anonymous and fashionable 19thC 'Beauty'.

Bernardus Johannes Blommers (1845-1914)
Dutch
Preparing a Frugal Meal
Signed, oil on panel
8¼ x 6¼in (21 x 16cm)
£5,300-5,600 *S*

John Constable (1776-1837) British
Portrait of Lady Croft, half length, in a white dress in a wooded landscape, painted in 1807
30¼ x 25in (76.9 x 63.5cm)
£23,000-26,000 *C*

Sir Edward Coley Burne-Jones (1833-98)
British
Study for 'The Wine of Circe'
Sanguine
12 x 11½in (30.5 x 29cm)
£20,000-25,000 *S*

A study for the 1863-69 gouache exhibited at the Old Watercolour Society, 1869, No 197.
The sitter is Maria Zambaco, neé Cassevetti, grand-daughter of Constantine Ionides. In 1866 she returned to London having left her husband, Demetrius Zambaco, doctor to the Greek community in Paris. Here she soon began moving in artistic circles and was introduced to Burne-Jones by Alphonse Legros. Burne-Jones became totally mesmerised by the beautiful Greek girl who personified the ideals of pre-Raphaelite beauty and who was to become his model, pupil and mistress.

E. Davids (late 19thC)
British(?)
At the Fountain
Signed and dated '81, oil on canvas
30 x 17½in (76.2 x 44.5cm)
£2,700-3,000 *C*

Jan Jac Matthys Damschroeder (1825-1905)
German
A Lady Knitting by a Window
Signed, oil on panel
18½ x 13½in (47 x 34.5cm)
£1,500-1,700 *S*

Condition is a major factor in a picture's price

William Charles Thomas Dobson (1817-98)
British
Gathering Flowers
Watercolour over pencil heightened with gouache
21 x 16½in (53.5 x 42cm)
£1,200-1,500 *S(S)*

Another archetypal Victorian 'Beauty', this time portrayed in the countryside and gathering flowers in a manner that is certainly more decorative than practical.

English School (19thC)
A Lady wearing a Lace Trimmed Lilac Coloured Dress, in a Landscape
30 x 25in (76 x 64cm)
£900-1,000 *HSS*

William Eadie (late 19thC)
The Farmer's Wife
Signed and dated 1871
19½ x 16½in (49.5 x 42cm)
£600-700 *S(S)*

Mary Ellen Edwards (active 1862-1908)
British
A Simple Story
Signed with initials and dated 1889, oil on board
7½ x 11¼in (19 x 28.5cm)
£2,500-2,800 *S*

English School (19thC)
A half-length Portrait of a Girl
Indistinctly signed, oil on canvas
25 x 20in (64 x 50.8cm)
£900-1,000 *Bon*

Paul Gauguin (1848-1903)
French
Tahitiennes
Charcoal
16⅛ x 12¼in (41 x 31cm)
£475,000-500,000 *S*

English School (19thC)
A Lady Turning in a Doorway with her Dog at her Skirt
Oil on canvas
55 x 44in (139.7 x 111.76cm)
£1,450-1,650 *Bon*

Belisario Gioja (1829-1906)
Italian
An Importunate Friend
Signed and inscribed Roma, watercolour
19½ x 13½in (49 x 34cm)
£1,250-1,450 *S*

Ferdinand Heilbuth (1826-89) French
A Lady walking by a lake Signed, oil on cradled panel
8 x 12½in (20.5 x 32cm)
£7,800-8,200 *S*

Edwin Harris
(1855-1906)
British
Under the Blossom
Signed, oil on canvas
20 x 16in (51 x 40.5cm)
£800-900 *S*

Gerald E. Harrison (active late 19th/early 20thC)
British
A Portrait of a Lady standing in an interior
Signed and dated '02, oil on canvas
49¾ x 29¾in (126.3 x 75.7cm)
£400-500 *Bon*

Hugh de Twenebrokes Glazebrook (1855-1937)
British
Portrait of a Lady, said to be Mrs Robertson Ewing
Signed, oil on canvas
55¼ x 43¼in (140 x 109cm)
£800-900 *C*

George Elgar Hicks (1824-1914) British
Alone
Signed and dated 1880, oil on board
16½ x 12½in (42 x 32cm)
£4,500-5,000 *S*

This is a smaller and later version of the artist's 1878 Royal Academy exhibit, No 325.

Paul César Helleu (1859-1927)
French
Madame Letellier Reading
Signed, coloured chalk
29½ x 20¾in (74 x 53cm)
£17,000-18,000 *S*

According to Helleu, Madame Letellier was one of the two most beautiful women in Paris. The other was Madame Georges Menier.

Charles M. Horsfall (active 1893-1914)
British
Portrait of a Lady, wearing a blue dress
Signed, oil on canvas
77 x 57½in (196 x 146cm)
£6,100-6,400 *C*

Charles Sillem Lidderdale (1831-95)
Serving Refreshment
Signed with monogram and dated 1891, oil on canvas
30 x 20in (76 x 51cm)
£5,500-6,000 *O*

Léon Lhermitte (1844-1925) French
A Portrait of an Old Woman Signed, charcoal
23½ x 17in (59 x 43cm) **£2,000-2,300** *S*

Frederick, Lord Leighton (1830-98) British
Type of Beauty
Inscribed, oil on canvas
17 x 12in (43 x 30.5cm)
£18,000-20,000 *C(S)*

Attributed to James John Hill (1811-82)
British Contentment
Bears title on the frame, oil on canvas
19 x 16in (48 x 41cm) **£1,700-2,000** *S*

George Goodwin Kilburne (1839-1924)
British
Far Away Thoughts, Seated Lady and Cat at a Cottage Door Signed, watercolour 10 x 14in (25.4 x 35.6cm)
£3,000-3,200 *DG*

Aristide de Lannoy (late 19th/early 20thC)
French
A Portrait of a Lady, wearing a Feather Boa
Signed, pastel 31 x 23in (78.8 x 58.3cm)
£450-550 *Bon*

Edith Martineau (1842-1909) British
The Wheelbarrow
Signed and dated 1884, watercolour heightened with bodycolour
10¼ x 13¼in (26 x 34cm)
£1,900-2,200 *S*

William Oliver (1804-53)
British
A Young Beauty
Signed, oil on panel
11½ x 8½in (29.3 x 21.6cm)
£1,600-1,800 *CSK*

William Osborne (1823-1901)
British
Portrait of Mrs Thomas Conolly of Castletown
44 x 52¼in (112 x 132.7cm)
£17,800-19,000 *C*

Edoardo Navone (19thC)
Italian
The Swing
Signed and inscribed Roma, pencil and watercolour
19 x 9in (48.2 x 22.8cm)
£1,100-1,400 *CSK*

Laslett John Pott (1837-98) British
On the Bridge
Signed with initials, oil on canvas
13½ x 18in (34.3 x 45.7cm)
£800-900 *Bon*

Charles Pyne (b1842)
British
The Sailors Farewell
Signed, watercolour
19¾ x 13½in (50.1 x 34.3cm)
£450-550 *Bon*

Theodore Jacques Ralli (1852-1909) Greek
A Portrait of a Greek Woman, Helen from Megara
Signed and inscribed in Greek, oil on panel
8½ x 6in (21.5 x 15.5cm) **£29,000-32,000** *S*

Ralli's portrait tripled its estimate at Sotheby's sale of 19thC European pictures in March '92, going to a Greek collector. Continental pictures often return to their country of origin in the salerooms.

Rudolph Svoboda (1859-1914)
Austrian
A Young Lady in Japanese Costume
Signed and dated 1894, oil on cardboard
11¾ x 7in (30 x 18cm)
£2,800-3,100 *S*

Carlton Alfred Smith (1853-1946)
British
Leisure Moments
Signed, watercolour
14¼ x 10¼in (36.5 x 26cm)
£3,600-3,800 *S*

Sir Robert Ponsonby Staples Bt (1853-1943) British
A Society Lady Coloured chalks
14 x 10in (35.5 x 25.4cm)
£2,800-2,900 *DM*

The voque for spotted veils came in towards the end of the 90s and this is possibly a portrait of Baroness Burdett-Coutts whom Staples had met at her home, Holly Lodge, in Highgate in September 1892. Staples subsequently painted her husband's portrait and she frequently visited his studio with or without an entourage of friends. Staples later commented that he had got used to painting amidst constant distractions.

David Woodlock (1842-1929) British
Amidst the Blossoms Signed and dated '97, watercolour 28 x 19in (71 x 48cm)
£1,800-2,200 *S*

Hans Schlimarski (b1859)
Austrian
Portrait of a Lady
Signed, pastel on cardboard
24¾ x 19in (63 x 48cm)
£1,500-1,700 *S*

Julian Alden Weir (1852-1919)
American
Anna, the Artist's Wife c1891
Oil on board
13¾ x 19in (35 x 48cm)
£47,000-50,000 *DM*

Weir's wife, Anna, who had been an inspiration to his work, died shortly after the birth of the couple's third child in 1892.

Henri de Toulouse-Lautrec (1864-1901)
French
La Revue Blanche (D. 355; A. 115; W. P16; Adr. 130)
Lithograph printed in colours, 1895
49¾ x 36⅛in (126.5 x 91.8cm)
£6,300-6,600 *S(NY)*

20th Century

John Aubrey (active 1938-65)
British
The Barmaid
Signed and dated 1952, canvas
17 x 15in (43.1 x 38.1cm)
£650-750 *SCG*

Giacomo Balla (1871-1958)
Italian
Ritratto della Signora Emma Calabria
Inscribed, signed and dated 1937, pastel
20¾ x 15¾in (53 x 40cm)
£13,500-14,500 *C(R)*

Alfred Broge (b1870)
Danish
A Lady Crocheting by the Window
Signed and dated 1918, oil on canvas
24½ x 19¾in (62 x 50.5cm)
£2,200-2,700 *S*

John Cooke (late 19th-early 20thC)
British
Miss Constable in Fancy Dress
Signed and dated 1912, oil on canvas
84 x 36in (213.5 x 91.5cm)
£2,000-2,200 *S*

Lucian Davis (1860-1941)
British
In the Conservatory
Watercolour, signed
40 x 30in (101 x 76cm)
£8,250-8,500 *Bne*

Miguel Covarrubias (20thC)
Mexican?
Mestiza
Signed, India ink and pencil on paper
11 x 8⅜in (27.9 x 21.3cm)
£1,600-1,800 *S(NY)*

Jean Gabriel Domergue (1889-1962)
French
Portrait of 'Chichi'
Signed, inscribed on the reverse, on masonite
9½ x 7½in (24 x 19cm)
£1,600-1,800 *CSK*

Sir Jacob Espstein (1880-1959)
British
Woman's Head
Signed, black crayon heightened with white on a green wash ground
18 x 12½in (45.7 x 31.7cm)
£600-700 *L*

Whether in sculpture or in drawing, Epstein was renowned for his brutal portrayals of his sitters. 'When Sir Hugh Lane saw my bust of Lady Gregory for the first time' he recalled, 'he threw up his hands in horror and exclaimed, "Poor Aunt Augusta. She looks as if she could eat her own children". Epstein's death provoked the following anonymous couplet which unintentionally sums up his genius:
'From life's grim nightmare he is now released who saw in every face the lurking beast.'

Edward Reginald Frampton (1872-1923)
British
Elaine
Signed and painted in 1921, oil on canvas
25 x 15in (63.5 x 38.1cm)
£5,600-6,000 *C*

Painted and exhibited at the Royal Academy in 1921, three years before Frampton's death. The picture illustrates the well-known opening lines of Tennyson's 'Lancelot and Elaine' from the Idylls of the King.
Elaine the fair, Elaine the lovable,
Elaine the lily maid of Astolat,
High in a chamber up a tower to the east
Guarded the sacred shield of Lancelot.

Otto Heichert (b1868) German
A Portrait of Frau Freundlich
Signed and dated Berlin 1919, oil on canvas
56 x 67¼in (142 x 171cm)
£2,900-3,200 *S*

Augustus John (1878-1961)
Poppet in a Yellow Hat
Signed, oil on canvas
22 x 15in (56 x 38cm)
£19,500-24,000 *S*

Painted c1926 during one of the John family's trips to the South of France. Poppet (Elizabeth John) was the artist's daughter and was born in 1912.

Childe Hassam (1859-1935)
American
Virginia and a New York Winter Window
Etching, signed in pencil with the cypher and inscribed 'imp', 1934
10⅜ x 12⅞in (26.3 x 32.8cm)
£8,600-9,000 *S(NY)*

Wilfrid de Glehn (1871-1951)
British
Jane de Glehn by the Stream
Purtud, Val D'Aosta, c1907, oil on canvas
23 x 30in (59 x 76cm)
£90,000-100,000 *DM*

Painted while the de Glehns were staying with Sargent in Switzerland during August 1907.

George Henry (1858-1943)
British
A Geisha
Signed, watercolour heightened with bodycolour
13⅝ x 9¼in (34.6 x 23.5cm)
£4,800-5,200 *C(S)*

David Hockney (b1937)
British
An Image of Celia
Lithograph and silkscreen printed in colours, with collage, 1984-86, signed in pencil, dated and numbered 2/40
65¼ x 48in (165.6 x 122cm)
£50,000-60,000 *S(NY)*

Condition is a major factor in a picture's price

Gwen John (1876-1939)
British
Old Woman in a Black Shawl
Stamped signature, watercolour, bodycolour and black crayon on beige paper
6⅛ x 4⅝in (15.5 x 11.5cm)
£4,700-5,000 *C*

Oskar Kokoschka (1886-1980)
Austrian
Portrait of Niuta Kallin
Inscribed Malina, c1922, charcoal on paper, laid down on board
24¾ x 16¾in (62.9 x 42.5cm)
£8,600-9,000 *S(NY)*

In Spring 1921 Kokoschka met the Russian Jewess Niuta Kallin (called Anna) who was studying music in Dresden. She became his mistress until 1925 and remained a close friend and correspondent until the mid-30s. She posed for several of his works.

Kathe Kollwitz (1867-1945)
German
Gesenkter Frauenkopf
Soft ground printed in brown, 1905, signed in pencil, with the signature of the printer, Felsing on Japan paper
15 x 12½in (38.2 x 31.7cm)
£1,800-2,100 *S(NY)*

Yasuo Kuniyoshi (1893-1953)
American
Burlesque Queen
Inscribed in pencil '100 prints', lithograph
11¾ x 9⅝in (29.7 x 24.3cm)
£2,800-3,100 *S(NY)*

Jules Pascin (1885-1930)
American
La Blonde Marcelle
Signed, oil and pencil on canvas
29 x 23¼in (73.8 x 59.2cm)
£35,000-40,000 *S*

Painted in 1921 at the artist's studio in rue Caulaincourt, Montmartre.

Philip de Laszlo (1869-1937) British
Portrait of Dame Gwen Ffrangcon-Davies as Mary Queen of Scots
Signed, inscribed and dated 1934, oil on canvas
36 x 28in (91.5 x 71cm)
£17,500-20,000 *S*

In 1934 Dame Gwen appeared at the New Theatre, London, to play Mary Stuart in John Gielgud's production of Gordon Daviot's play 'Queen of Scots'.

Sir John Lavery (1856-1941)
British
Lady in Sables
Signed, oil on canvas
31½ x 26½in (80 x 67.5cm)
£13,000-15,000 *S*

Noel Laura Nisbet (1887-1956)
British
Dressing for the Carnival
Signed with initials, watercolour, and a similar
watercolour by the same artist
15¾ x 12½in (40 x 32cm)
£350-400 *Bon*

Henri Matisse (1869-1954)
French
Martiniquaise
Signed and dated aôut 47, black crayon
20⅜ x 15⅞in (51.8 x 40.3cm)
£51,000-56,000 *S*

Tamara de Lempicka (1898-1980)
Polish
La Femme au Turban Rouge
Oil on canvas
10½ x 8in (27 x 21cm)
£6,500-7,000 *C(R)*

Arthur Segal (1875-1944)
Romanian
Schlafende Frau
Signed and dated 1925, oil on board (in the artist's painted frame)
31⅛ x 38¾in (79.2 x 98.5cm)
£36,000-40,000 *S*

Pablo Picasso (1881-1974)
Spanish
Femme au Chignon
Signed in red crayon, numbered in pencil 47/50, lithograph, 1957
22 x 17⅝in (55.7 x 44cm)
£13,300-14,000 *S(NY)*

William Bruce Ellis Ranken (1881-1941)
British
Pygmalion
Signed, oil on canvas
43½ x 33½in (110.5 x 85cm)
£4,200-4,500 *C*

Miller's is a price GUIDE not a price LIST

Sarah Rigby (b1962)
British
Autumn
Signed
36½ x 52in (93 x 132cm)
£800-900 *Bon*

Alphonse Mucha (1860-1934) Czech
Leslie Carter
Lithograph printed in colours, on two joined sheets 79¾ x 29¼in (20.3 x 74.3cm)
£3,200-3,500 *S(NY)*

Linda Sutton (20thC) British Robot Cat in Silver
Mixed media 40 x 30in (101.5 x 76cm)
£2,800-3,000 *OLG*

Harry George Theaker (1873-1954) British
A Young Maiden with Pan and Cupid, in a wild Garden Signed, pencil and watercolour 21½ x 14⅜in (54.7 x 36.5cm)
£2,000-2,300 *C*

Edouard Vuillard (1868-1940) French
Portrait de Femme Signed, c1922, pastel
10¼ x 8¼in (26 x 21cm)
£17,000-20,000 *S*

David Wright (20thC) British
Vivien Leigh
Gouache
11½ x 11in (29 x 28cm)
£1,750-1,850 *JN*

Theo van Rysselberghe (1862-1926)
Belgian
Portrait de Femme
Signed with the monogram and dated Juin 1918,
oil on canvas laid down on board
17⅜ x 13⅝in (44 x 34.5cm)
£13,500-14,500 *S*

Franz von Stuck (1863-1928)
German
Portrait of a Lady, wearing a black dress and holding a book
Signed and dated 1918,
oil on canvas
36½ x 36½in
(92.7 x 92.7cm)
£6,200-6,600 *C*

Fernand Toussaint (1873-1955)
Belgian
The Artist's Favourite Model
Signed, oil on canvas
39 x 32in (100 x 80cm)
£38,000-40,000 *PaHG*

Andy Warhol (1930-87)
American
16 Jackies
Signed on the overlaps, synthetic polymer and ink silkscreened on canvas, in 16 panels
80½ x 64in (204.5 x 162.6cm)
£220,000-250,000 *S(NY)*

Painted in 1965, 16 Jackies belongs to the well-known series of portraits of the First Lady by Warhol following the assassination of President Kennedy.

MOTHERS & CHILDREN

Jean-Honoré Fragonard (1732-1806)
French
A Child's First Steps Towards his Mother
Black chalk heightened with white
6¾ x 8⅞in (17.2 x 22.5cm)
£11,500-12,500 *S(NY)*

After Sir Joshua Reynolds (1723-92)
British
The Duchess of Marlborough and Child, by James Watson
Mezzotint
17¾ x 12¾in (45 x 32.5cm)
and with a mezzotint by Thomas Watson after Sir Joshua Reynolds of Lady Whitmore
£200-250 *CSK*

Léon Caille (1836-1907)
French
The Reading Lesson
Signed and dated 1867, oil on panel
12¾ x 9½in (32.5 x 24cm)
£3,900-4,300 *S*

Edward Charles Barnes (active 1856-82)
British Poppies
Oil on canvas 35½ x 28¼in (90.5 x 72cm)
£2,000-2,200 *S*

George Sheridan Knowles (1863-1931)
British
Mother
Signed, watercolour
17¼ x 23in (44 x 58.4cm)
£4,000-4,250 *SCG*

Karl Adolf Gugel (1820-85)
German
The Harvesters
Signed and dated 1857, oil on canvas
39 x 34¾in (99 x 88.2cm)
£3,600-4,000 *C*

George Goodwin Kilburne (1839-1924)
British
The Master of the House
Signed and inscribed, pencil and watercolour heightened with white
16½ x 12¾in (42.3 x 32.5cm)
£2,100-2,500 *C*

L. Hunt (late 19thC) British
Watching over Baby
Signed, oil on canvas
28 x 36in (71 x 94.4cm)
£2,600-2,800 *CSK*

John Henry Henshall (1856-1928)
British
In the Springtime
Signed, pencil and watercolour
13½ x 9½in (34.5 x 24.5cm)
£1,500-1,800 *CSK*

The present work epitomises Henshall's taste for highly dramatic subjects brimming with pathos and sentiment.

William Henry Midwood (active 2nd half 19thC)
British
A Sailor's Farewell
Oil on canvas, arched top
18 x 14¾in (45.5 x 37.5cm)
£1,700-2,000 *S*

Alexander Leggitt (active 2nd half 19thC)
British
His Boat in Sight
Signed and inscribed
23½ x 17½in (60 x 44.5cm)
£1,300-1,500 *A*

Luigi Pastega (1858-1927)
Italian
Helping Hand
Signed and dated, oil on canvas
30 x 19¾in (76.2 x 50.2cm)
£6,700-7,500 *C*

Bernard Pothast (1882-1966)
Belgian
The Reading Lesson
Signed, oil on canvas
22¼ x 18¼in (56.5 x 46cm)
£9,800-10,500 *C*

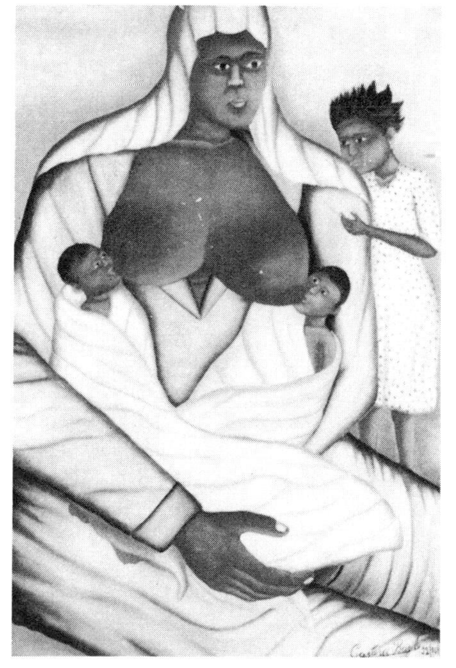

Castera Bazile (20thC)
Haitian
Caritas
Signed and dated 22/10/52, oil on masonite
24 x 16in (61 x 40.6cm)
£9,200-10,000 *S(NY)*

Reuben T. W. Sayers (1815-88) British
Maternal Love
Signed, inscribed and dated 1849 on reverse, oil on canvas
11¼ x 15¼in (29 x 39cm)
£800-1,000 *S(S)*

Carlton Alfred Smith (1853-1946)
British
New Friends
Signed and dated 1906, watercolour
19 x 27½in (48.2 x 68.9cm)
£10,500-11,500 *Bon*

Istvan Csok (1865-1961)
Hungarian
A Mother Pushing a Pram on the Bank of a River
Signed, oil on canvas
35¾ x 32in (91 x 81cm)
£2,000-2,300 *S*

William Lee-Hankey (1869-1952) British
The Kiss: Lizette et Pierre: Goose Girl
3 etchings, each signed in pencil
9¾ x 8in (25 x 20cm); 9¾ x 6¼in (24.5 x 16cm); 10½ x 7¾in (26.5 x 19.75cm)
£450-550 *S(S)*

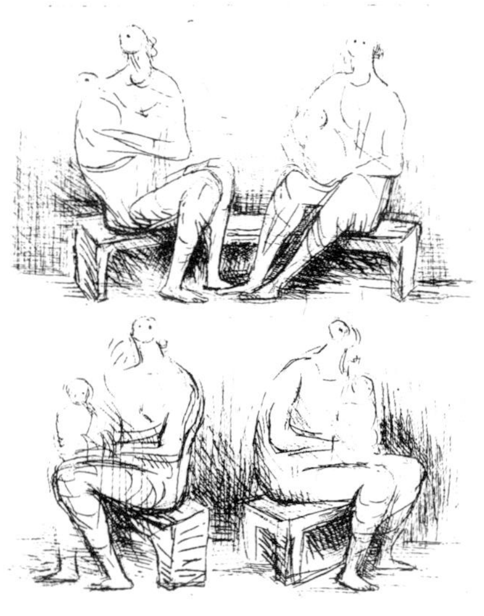

Henry Moore (1898-1986) British
Four Mothers (Cramer 189)
Etching, 1971-72, on wove, signed in pencil and numbered 33/100
12 x 9¼in (30.5 x 23.5cm)
£400-500 *S(S)*

Laurence Stephen Lowry (1887-1976) British
Figures on a Pier Signed and dated 1969, pencil
11¼ x 16in (28.5 x 41cm)
£2,500-3,000 *C*

MEN

16th Century

Attributed to the Master of the Countess of Warwick (16thC)
British
Sir Gabriel Poyntz, aged 36, the coat-of-arms inscribed 'Gabriel Poyntz/Ano Domini 1568
Oil on panel
38 x 28in (96.5 x 71cm)
£10,700-11,500 *B*

Albrecht Dürer (1471-1528) German
Erasmus of Rotterdam
Engraving, 1526
9⅞ x 7⅝in (25.2 x 19.4cm)
£9,500-10,000 *S(NY)*

Hanns Lautensack (1524-60)
German
Ferdinand I
Etching and engraving, 1556
14 x 10½in (35.5 x 26.8cm)
£3,200-3,600 *S(NY)*

Hendrick Goltzius (1558-1616)
Dutch
The Great Standard Bearer
Engraving
11⅛ x 7⅝in (28.3 x 19.3cm)
£8,300-8,800 *S(NY)*

Attributed to Giacomo Palma, called Palma il Giovane (1548-1628)
Italian
Portrait of a Bearded Man
Oil on canvas, in a carved and giltwood frame
26¾ x 20in (69 x 51cm)
£7,800-8,400 *S*

Follower of Hans Holbein II (1497-1593)
German
Portrait of King Henry VIII
Oil on panel
35 x 27¾in (89 x 70.5cm)
£4,000-4,400 *C*

The present picture is derived from the brush-drawing on canvas in the National Portrait Gallery, itself a cartoon for part of the Whitehall Palace mural.

Condition is a major factor in a picture's price

Attributed to Jacob Cornelisz van Oostsanen (c1470-1533)
Dutch
Portrait of Edward I, Count of East Friesland
Oil on panel
27¾ x 22in (71 x 56cm)
£9,000-9,500 *S(NY)*

Attributed to Paul Van Somer (c1577-1622)
Flemish
Portrait of Sir Thomas Peyton
Oil on canvas
41¼ x 35¼in (105 x 89.5cm)
£4,200-4,500 *S*

The Flemish born artist settled in England in 1616 and became a successful court portrait painter. According to records, he charged £30 for a full length Royal portrait.

17th Century

Attributed to Dirck van Baburen (active 1611-24)
Dutch
Heraclitus with a Globe
Inscribed lower right on globe T B fecit Ano 1622, oil on canvas
28 x 22½in (71.1 x 57.2cm)
£8,200-8,600 *S(NY)*

The Greek philosopher Heraclitus (active c500 B.C.) was a popular subject with artists of the Renaissance and Baroque periods. Known as the 'Crying Philosopher' because of his dark and melancholic pronouncements, he was generally portrayed with a grief stricken expression and in dark clothing and often accompanied by a companion portrait of his opposite, 'Democritus', the so-called 'laughing philosopher' (active 460-370 B.C.), who was perpetually amused by the follies of mankind.

Attributed to Maria Giovanni Battista Clementi, La Clementina (1690-1761)
Italian
Portrait of Carlo Emanuele III, King of Sardinia
Oil on canvas
89¼ x 55⅜in (226.6 x 140.6cm)
£4,200-4,500 *C*

Mary Beale (1633-99)
British
Portrait of Charles Beale, The Artist's Husband
Oil on canvas, in a carved wood frame
42 x 34¼in (106 x 87cm)
£5,600-6,000 *S*

Whereas many women's careers come to an end with marriage and children, Mary Beale's seems to have flourished after her marriage to Charles Beale, when she became one of the more prolific portrait painters of the period. According to some reports, Charles appears to have been a 17thC prototype of the New Man. Whilst his wife worked hard at painting, Charles 'managed their household affairs and the mechanics of her career, priming her canvases, mixing her colours, and eventually becoming an art dealer'. He kept painstakingly detailed records of her various commissions and daily activities, and many of his notebooks survive. The present portrait, painted c1666, is almost certainly the companion portrait to the artist's self-portrait in the National Portrait Gallery, London. See N. G. Heller – Woman Artists, Virago Press, 1987 (p.47).

Jacques Callot (1592-1635)
French
La Noblesse
Set of 12 plates, etchings, c1621, bound in modern boards
£1,800-2,000 *S(NY)*

Jan van Bijlert (1603-71)
Dutch
A shepherd, wearing a feathered cap and holding a houlette
Signed, oil on canvas
32 x 25in (83 x 64.5cm)
£290,000-320,000 *CAm*

Niccolò Cassana (1659-1714)
Italian
Portrait of an English Gentleman, wearing an ermine hat and ermine-lined cape
Oil on canvas
28⅜ x 21⅝in (72 x 55cm)
£5,000-5,500 *C*

Circle of Gerard Dou (1613-75)
Dutch
Portrait of an Elegant Young Man, possibly a Guild Member
Oil on panel
14¾ x 12¼in (37.5 x 31.1cm)
£11,500-12,000 *S(NY)*

Circle of William Dobson (1610-46)
British
Portrait of Colonel Francis Hammond
Inscribed with the identity of the sitter, oil on canvas
29½ x 24½in (75 x 62cm)
£3,400-3,700 *S*

The sitter, shown in armour (born c1584), took part in many conflicts including the Thirty Years' War in Germany, where he fought 14 single combats, and the Civil War when he commanded at the Battle of Edgehill in 1642.

Genoese School, 17thC
Portrait of a Gentleman Dressed in Black
Oil on canvas
42½ x 34½in (108 x 87.6cm)
£43,000-50,000 *S(NY)*

After Sir Anthony van Dyck (1599-1641)
Flemish
Portrait of Charles I with Prince Charles
Oil on canvas
48 x 38½in (122 x 98cm)
£4,200-4,500 *S*

After the group portrait of Charles I and Henrietta Maria with their two eldest children in the Royal Collection.

'In most sales there is always a portrait of Charles I, usually of modest quality', says David Moore-Gwyn of the British Paintings Department at Sotheby's. 'You can nearly always find a buyer for a good royal name.'

Follower of Sir Anthony van Dyck (1599-1641)
Flemish
Portrait of a Gentleman, called Inigo Jones (1573-1652) Oil on canvas
22¾ x 18in (58 x 46.5cm)
£5,600-6,000 *S*

Flemish School, 17thC
Head of a Bearded Man, and a subsidiary study of an ear
Numbered '40', red and white chalk, upper right corner cut
8 x 5⅞in (20.3 x 15cm)
£4,000-4,300 *S(NY)*

English School, 17thC
Portrait of Francis Bacon (1561-1626)
Inscribed with the identity of the sitter, oil on canvas
29½ x 24½in (74.5 x 62.5cm)
£8,300-8,700 *S*

Bacon certainly fulfils the requirements of an interesting sitter. Described by Alexander Pope as 'the wisest, brightest, meanest of mankind', he was a writer, philosopher and celebrated lawyer at the courts of both Elizabeth I and James I. He dealt with some of the major legal issues of the day including the prosecutions of the Earl of Essex and Sir Walter Raleigh and in 1618 was appointed Lord Chancellor. Found guilty of bribery and corruption three years later he was deprived of office and briefly sent to the Tower – he devoted his final years to his writings.

Jacob Jordaens (1593-1678)
Flemish
Head of a Bearded Man
Black, red and white chalk, pen and brown ink, on buff paper
10⅝ x 8in (27 x 20.3cm)
£13,000-14,000 *S(NY)*

After Sir Peter Lely (1618-80)
British
Portrait of Charles II, wearing armour
Oil on canvas in a painted oval cartouche, in a carved wood frame
28 x 24in (71 x 61cm)
£2,000-2,200 *S*

Circle of Richardson (17thC) British
Portrait of a Gentleman
Oil on canvas
50 x 40in (127 x 101.6cm)
£700-800 *Bon*

Thomas Pooley (1646-1722/23)
Irish
Portrait of Robert Percival
Inscribed Robert 2nd Son. To Sr. John Percival (5th of that name) Bar.t. Nat.AD 1657. Ob 1677/Aet. 20, oil on canvas
30 x 24¾in (76 x 63cm)
£2,100-2,400 *S*

Johann Kerseboom (active 1680-1708)
British
Portrait of an Officer
Oil on canvas
49¼in x 39¼in (125 x 100cm)
£6,400-6,800 *S*

Circle of Rembrandt Harmensz van Rijn (1606-69)
Dutch
Portrait of an Oriental, possibly a Portrait of King Uzziah
Oil on canvas
40 x 31½in (101.6 x 80cm)
£27,000-30,000 *S(NY)*

The present work repeats the composition of a painting by Rembrandt in the collection of the Duke of Devonshire, Chatsworth, Derbyshire.

Jonathan Richardson (c1664-98)
Portrait of Charles Hawtrey (1663-98)
Oil on canvas, in a carved wood frame
28¾ x 23in (73 x 61cm)
£1,400-1,600 *S*

Locate the source

The source of each illustration in Miller's can be found by checking the code letters below each caption

Salvator Rosa (1615-73) Italian
Portrait of the Artist
In the original carved and gilded 17thC Florentine pierced and swept frame
45½ x 37in (115.5 x 94cm)
£410,000-440,000 *C*

Circle of John Riley (1646-1791) British
Portrait of a Gentleman
Oil on canvas
47 x 37½in (119.5 x 95cm)
£3,100-3,400 *S*

Herman Saftleven (1605-85) Dutch
A Man Carrying a Sack
Signed with monogram 'HS', black chalk, grey and brown wash, with traces of red chalk, watermark crowned shield with Saint George and the dragon
11¾ x 7¼in (29.8 x 18.4cm)
£6,000-6,400 *S(NY)*

Robert Walker (active 1641-1658) British
Portrait of John Evelyn, the Diarist, wearing a white shirt and a blue wrap, at a table, leaning on a skull
Inscribed top centre in Greek (tr 'Repentance is the beginning of wisdom'); inscribed lower left in Latin (tr 'but when death comes to meet him, no one welcomes it cheerfully, except the man who has long since composed himself for death, Seneca Epistulae XXX')
34½ x 25¼in (87.9 x 64.1cm)
£240,000-260,000 *C*

On 1st July, 1648, this famous diarist recorded in his journal: '[I] sate for my Picture *(the same wherein is a* Death's Head*) to Mr* Walker *that excellent Painter'. The skull was traditionally used in portraits and still-lifes as a reminder of the transcience of earthly life.*

Circle of Daniel Mytens (1590-1648) Dutch
Portrait of Charles I
Oil on canvas, in a carved wood frame
25 x 19in (63.5 x 48.5cm)
£4,000-4,400 *S*

Adriaen Pietersz van de Venne (1589-1662) Dutch
A Cry; Isser Niet te Vegen!: A Chimney Sweep
Inscribed 'Isser niet te Vegen', oil on panel
11⅛ x 8¾in (28.2 x 22.2cm)
£7,500-7,800 *C*

18th Century

Andrea Casali (c1700-84) Italian
Portrait of the Hon Augustus Townshend (1716-45)
Inscribed Augs: Townshend Obt: 1745/2nd son to Charles Lord Vis/Townshend by his 2nd wife, oil on canvas
88 x 57in (224 x 146cm)
£13,300-14,000 *S*

Decorative period frames can add substantially to the appeal of historical portraits.

Nathaniel Dance (1735-1811) British
Portrait of a Gentleman
Oil on canvas in a carved wood frame
29½ x 24½in (75 x 62cm)
£8,000-8,500 *S*

Henri Pierre Danloux (1753-1809) French
Portrait of Richard Foster, wearing a blue coat
Oil on canvas
17¾ x 13¾in (44 x 35cm)
£2,300-2,500 *S*

Circle of Arthur William Devis (1762-1822)
British
Portrait of a Young Man
Oil on canvas
19¼ x 15½in (49 x 39.5cm)
£1,200-1,400 *S(S)*

Attributed to Gainsborough Dupont (1754-97) British
Portrait of Lord Frederick Campbell
Oil on canvas, in a painted oval
29 x 24¼in (74 x 61.5cm)
£950-1,000 *S*

Dupont was nephew, imitator and a devoted assistant to Thomas Gainsborough.

English School (18thC)
Portrait of officer in red coat with gold braid
Unsigned
30 x 23in (76 x 58.4cm)
£1,400-1,500 *ALL*

English School c1751
Portrait of the Rt Hon Ralph Howard, Viscount Wicklow, 1st Baron Clonmore (c1726-86)
Inscribed Painted by/Batoni? and with the identity of the sitter, oil on canvas
87 x 58¼in (221 x 148cm)
£25,500-30,000 *S*

The white patches on this painting look very alarming, but they are in fact merely pieces of tissue-like synthetic material placed on the surface of oil paintings by restorers to prevent paint loss should the canvas be in a delicate state. In this instance, David Moore-Gywn of Sotheby's points out that a potential buyer can see the auctioneers have not touched the picture in any way. It is not unusual to encounter lots treated in this way at auction.

English School (c1780)
George Daubeny (1742-1806)
Inscribed extensively 'George Daubeny Esq' Glorious Majority 372/ and 'Fixt gainst/the Envy of/less Happier/Climes/blest/Liberty/and on/a Rock/Religion's/Purest Flame/thy law', pencil and pen and ink
9¾ x 6¾in (24.8 x 17.2cm)
£250-300 *C*

George Daubeny MP, Bristol 1781-84 spoke 'with great heat' in the House of Commons on 27 November 1781 in favour of continuing the American War and declared that the Citizens of Bristol 'were willing to sacrifice half their fortune in the prosecution of it'.

Daniel Gardner (1750-1805) British
Portrait of the Hon Hamilton Douglas Halyburton (1763-84), as a midshipman in a blue naval uniform
An inscription on the reverse of the frame reads 'The Hon Hamilton/Douglas Hadley Burton/ brother of Lord Morton', pencil, pastel and bodycolour, in a Louis XVI carved and gilded frame
£3,100-3,300 *C*

Having joined the Royal Navy as a youth, at 20 he met a tragic fate. During the evacuation of New York in December 1783, he volunteered to pursue a long boat of mutineers and commanding a barge, led '12 young gentlemen and 1 mariner, it not being judged prudent to trust more of the common sailors on such service'. All were found dead on the first day of January 1784, lying in the mud on the Jersey shore.

Giles Hussey (1710-88)
British
Portrait of Prince Charles Edward Stuart
Grey wash
9¾ x 7¼in (24.5 x 18.2cm)
£1,000-1,200 *C*

Sir Henry Raeburn (1756-1823) British
Portrait of Colonel Alex Creighton
Unsigned, oil on canvas
29 x 24in (73.6 x 61cm)
£1,800-2,000 *ALL*

John Hoppner (1758-1810)
British
Portrait of Sir Henry Goodricke, Bart
Oil on canvas
35 x 27in (88.9 x 68.6cm)
£9,500-10,000 *S(NY)*

Thomas Gainsborough (1727-88)
British
Portrait of Sir William Stanhope
(1702-72)
Inscribed S. W Stanhope/Aetat
62.1764, oil on canvas,
in a painted oval
29 x 24¾in (74 x 63cm)
£9,700-10,200 *S*

Circle of Robert Hunter
(active 1752-1803)
British
Portrait of a Gentleman
Oil on canvas in a carved wood frame
50¼ x 38¼in (128 x 97cm)
£950-1,050 *S*

After Thomas Barker of Bath (1769-1847)
British
The Woodcutter
Oil on canvas
21 x 16in (53.3 x 40.6cm)
£300-350 *CSK*

Follower of Antoine Pesne (1683-1757) French
Portrait of François P. J. Cravau, wearing a lawyer's red gown, holding a book and a letter
Inscribed 'A Monsieur Cravau, premier juré de la Ville de Nivelle &c', oil on canvas
24¾ x 28in (62.8 x 71.1cm)
£500-550 *Bon*

Attributed to Sir Henry Raeburn (1756-1823)
British
Portrait of Archibald Skirving (1749-1819)
18¼ x 13¾in (46.5 x 35cm)
£2,800-3,000 *S*

Raeburn was renowned for his skilful likenesses, and his disregard for the feelings of the sitters led to portraits which could be unflattering in their frankness.

Allan Ramsay (1713-84)
British
Portrait of Brigadier General Sir John Mordaunt K.B. (1697-1780)
Signed A Ramsay/1746, and inscribed on a label on the reverse Brig Gen John Mordaunt 1746/7, oil on canvas, in a painted oval, in a carved wood frame
30 x 25in (76 x 63.5cm)
£12,200-13,000 *S*

Attributed to Petrus Johannes van Reyschoot (1702-72)
Flemish
Portrait of Sir Armine Wodehouse, 5th BT (1714-77)
Oil on canvas in a carved wood frame
30¼ x 24in (77 x 61cm)
£2,100-2,400 *S*

Attributed to Sir Martin Archer Shee (1769-1850)
British
Portrait of a Gentleman, said to be Gawen William Rowan Hamilton-Rowan
Oil on canvas
30 x 25in (76 x 63.5cm)
£9,400-10,000 *S*

Sir Thomas Lawrence (1769-1830)
British
Portrait of a Gentleman, probably the Hon William Lamb, 2nd Viscount Melbourne
(1779-1848)
Oil on canvas
30 x 25in (76.5 x 63.5cm)
£11,200-12,000 *S*

In 1805, William Lamb married Lady Caroline Ponsonby. Vastly different in temperament, their marriage soon went disastrously wrong and in 1812 she began her notorious liaison with Lord Byron, resulting in another unhappy failure. 'She is a villainous intriguante', wrote Byron in 1815, 'mad and malignant – capable of all and every mischief'. The Lambs separated in the 1820s and Lady Caroline died in 1828. William (now Lord Melbourne), went on to hold a number of major political appointments and was Prime Minister in 1834 and again from 1835-41, during which time he successfully introduced the young Queen Victoria to her royal duties: '... the person who makes me feel safe and comfortable', noted Victoria in her diary, 4 July 1838.

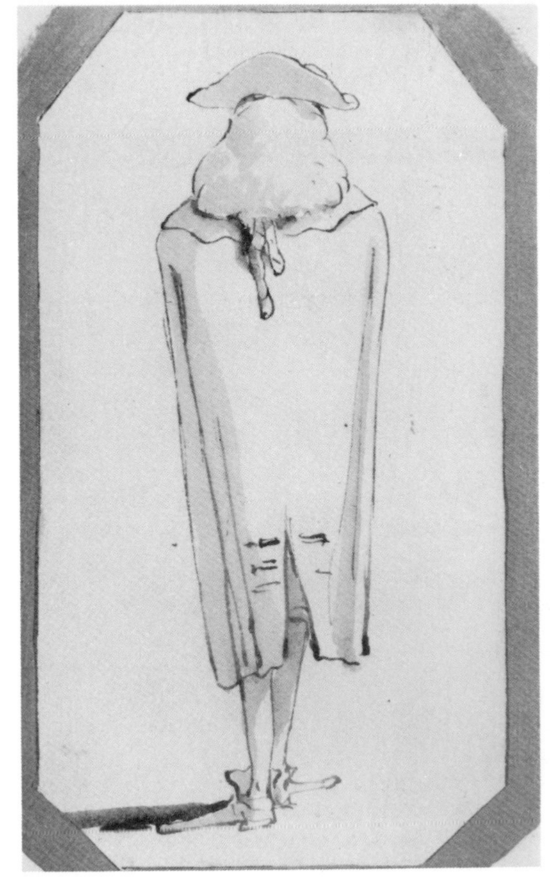

Giovanni Battista Tiepolo (1696-1770)
Italian
Caricature of a Man, in a coat and a tricorne
Pen and brown ink, brown wash
7 x 4in (18.9 x 10.3cm)
£8,300-8,600 *C*

Both caricatures doubled their estimates at auction.

Giovanni Battista Tiepolo (1696-1770) Italian
Caricature of a Gentleman, holding a tricorne
Pen and brown ink, brown wash, watermark flower 6 x 4½in (15.7 x 11.4cm)
£10,500-11,000 *C*

Condition is a major factor in a picture's price

Stephen Slaughter (1697-1765)
British
Portrait of Captain John Long Bateman
Signed and inscribed John Long Bateman Esq/Captn in Col Ponsonby's/independent/ Regiment/Stephn Slaughter/Pinx/1744, oil on canvas
49 x 39in (124 x 99cm)
£10,000-10,500 *S*

Jacob Van Stry (1756-1815) Dutch
A Seated Old Man
Signed, black chalk, brown and grey wash, watercolour, black ink framing lines
9¾ x 8¼in (24.8 x 20.9cm)
£1,200-1,500 *S(NY)*

Attributed to Gilbert Stuart (1755-1828)
British
Portrait of John Crone of Byblox (c1722-90)
Oil on canvas in a painted oval
28 x 23½in (71 x 59.6cm)
£2,300-2,500 *C(S)*

19th Century

Erwin Eichinger (late 19thC)
Austrian
A Good Drink:
A Good Smoke
A pair, both signed, oil on board
10 x 7¼in
(25.5 x 18.5cm) each
£2,500-2,800 *S(S)*

Ferdinando Cavalleri (1794-1865)
Italian
A Portrait of a Gentleman
Signed and indistinctly dated Roma 18, oil on canvas
50¼ x 38in (128 x 97cm)
£2,800-3,000 *S*

Modesto Brocos (late 19thC)
South American
Portrait of Jean-Léon Gérôme, holding a cigar
Signed and dated 1879 and indistinctly inscribed on the reverse, oil on canvas
13 x 9⅝in (33 x 24.4cm)
£600-650 *C*

Alfred Bryan (1852-99)
British
Caricature of Whistler
Signed with monogram, pen and Indian ink
3½ x 2½in (9 x 6.5cm)
£400-450 *Bon*

Georges Croegaert (b1848)
French
A Gentleman Waiting in an Interior
Signed and inscribed Paris, oil on panel
10¼ x 7½in (26 x 19cm)
£2,000-2,300 *S*

A typical 19thC example of 18thC genre painting.

George Fox (late 19thC)
British
A Gentleman Seated at His Desk Accounting
Signed and indistinctly dated, oil on canvas
7½ x 5⅜in (19.1 x 13.7cm)
£600-650 *Bon*

Richard Dighton (1795-1880)
British
Portrait of a Gentleman standing by his Dog
Signed and dated 1853, pencil and watercolour heightened with gum arabic
9⅞ x 7½in (25.2 x 19cm)
£900-950 *C*

English School (19thC)
Half-length portrait of a Gentleman
Oil on canvas
35 x 27in (89 x 69cm)
£140-160 *ALL*

John Eyre (c1850-1927)
British
The Age of Romance
Signed and inscribed, pencil and watercolour heightened with white
9½ x 7in (24.2 x 17.7cm)
£850-950 *C*

Léon Herbo (1850-1907)
French
Portrait of the painter Julien Dillens, holding his Prix de Rome
Signed, inscribed and dated 'A mon/ami/ J Dillens/un souvenir/de son/Prix de Rome/1877/ Léon Herbo', also inscribed 'Vooruit', oil on canvas
39½ x 23in (100.2 x 58.4cm)
£4,500-5,000 *C*

Innocent-Louis Goubaud (1780-1847) French
Portrait of Napoleon Bonaparte, full-length, enthroned on a map of Europe, wearing a laurel wreath and Imperial Robes, holding a baton, inscribed 'J Goubaud de Rome professeur de dessin/aux licées Bonaparte et Charlemagne Paris 1811'
Black chalk
28 x 22½in (71.1 x 57.5cm)
£12,600-13,600 *S(NY)*

Exhibited Salon of 1812, No. 423 'Dessin allégorique à la gloire de S M l'Empereur'. This official portrait pleased Napoleon so much that he rewarded the artist with 6,000 francs and commissioned him to draw a pendant portrait of the Empress Marie-Louise in the same allegorical guise.
The iconography is close to David's imperial portrait of 1805, the main difference being the extended gesture of the hand in a sign of peace. The importance of this portrait lies in its technique. Goubaud was appointed professor at the Lycée Charlemagne in 1810, one of the new institutions opened by Napoleon throughout the country to promote higher education. Goubaud's principal aim in the present drawing was to display the advantages of the new technique of the synthetic drawing pencil called crayon conté, after its inventor Nicolas-Jacques Conté.

Alexander Fraser Snr (1786-1865) British
Searching for Coppers
Signed, oil on board
9¾ x 8in (25 x 20.5cm)
£950-1,000 *S(SC)*

Irish School (19thC) The Deer Hunter
Oil on canvas 24 x 20in (60.9 x 50.8cm)
£7,800-8,300 *CSK*

This striking portrait greatly exceeded its £600-800 estimate when auctioned at Christie's South Kensington in March 1992.

Irish School (c1820)
Portrait of Henry Samuel Close of Newton Park, County Dublin, in a blue coat and buff waistcoat
26 x 21½in (66 x 54.5cm)
£950-1,000 *C(S)*

Sir Francis Grant (1803-78)
British
Portrait of James Hunt
Oil on canvas
44 x 36in (112 x 91cm)
£2,000-2,200 *S*

Mortimer L. Menpes (1859-1938)
British
A Portrait of Whistler
Signed in pencil, etching with drypoint
6½ x 5¾in (16.5 x 14.5cm)
£200-250 *S(S)*

Carl Heuser (late 19thC)
German
A Pinch of Snuff: and A Good Smoke
Signed 'C Heuser', oil on panel
6⅝ x 4⅞in (16.2 x 12.4cm)
£3,100-3,300 *C*

Jean François Millet (1814-75)
French
A Study for Le Berger et la Mer
Stamped with the cachet de vente (Lugt 1460)
1.1, charcoal
8 x 5¼in (20.2 x 13.2cm)
£2,300-2,600 *S*

This is a study for Le Berger et la Mer, published in 1873 for Fables de la Fontaine (engraved by A. Salmon). There are similar studies in the Louvre.

Charles Hunt (late 19thC)
British
A Pat for the Donkey
Signed and dated '99, oil on canvas
16½ x 23in (42 x 58.5cm)
£3,800-4,200 *S*

Pieter Cornelis Kramer (19thC) German
A Huntsman
Signed and inscribed München, watercolour heightened with white
8½ x 6¾in (21.6 x 17.2cm)
£2,100-2,300 *Bon*

Adolf Friedrich Erdmann Menzel (1815-1905)
German
Contemplation
Signed and dated 'A Menzel/30 April 88', pencil on paper
12 x 8in (30.5 x 20.2cm)
£3,900-4,300 *C*

Did you know?

MILLER'S Picture Price Guide will build up year by year to form the most comprehensive photo-reference library available

Sir William Rothenstein (1872-1945) British
Portrait of Robbie
Signed, inscribed To Robbie's mother, from his affectionate friend and dated 1898, black and coloured chalks on brown paper
13½ x 9½in (34.5 x 24cm)
£9,000-9,500 *S*

The sitter was a close friend of Oscar Wilde. They were intimate companions from 1885 until Wilde met Lord Alfred Douglas in 1891. Ross supported Wilde throughout his notorious trial and rescued many of his manuscripts from the bankruptcy sale that followed his sentence: two years hard labour for homosexual practices. After his release, Wilde moved to France, and the present drawing was executed in 1898, in the first year of his exile. Ross became Wilde's literary executor and when his friend died in Paris, he commissioned a tomb from Jacob Epstein. Ross's own ashes were eventually moved to the memorial at Père Lachaise cemetery.

James Northcote (1746-1831) British
Portrait of the Artist
Signed James Northcote/Pinxt 1807, and inscribed on the reverse: The Portrait of James Northcote, Royal Academician of London, member of the Ancient Etruscan Academy at Cortona, Member of the Imperial Academy at Florence and Member of the Academy Dei Forti at Rome. Painted by himself in the year 1807 as a present to Lady Northcote. Oil on canvas
35½ x 29in (90 x 74cm)
£25,500-27,500 *S*

Though the present work is considered to be the finest of all Northcote's self-portraits, Sotheby's thought it might be 'too academic in style' for many buyers and gave it an estimate of £8,000-12,000 at their British sale in March '92. To their surprise, the work doubled its estimate, reflecting contemporary interest in good, historical portraits.

After Sir George Reid (1841-1914)
British
Tom Morris
Photogravure, published by the Committee of the R and A, St. Andrews, 1 of 20 before letterproof
19 x 13½in (48 x 34cm)
£1,900-2,200 *Bon*

Attributed to Tingqua
A Portrait of Wong Tye, Legendary Emperor of China
Gouache heightened with gold, companion of Wong Leung, Empress of China, one of a pair
6⅝ x 5¾in (17 x 14.5cm)
£750-850 *Bon*

James Sharples (1825-93)
British
Portrait of a Gentleman seated in a Chair, in a blue coat, yellow waistcoat and white cravat
Pastel
9¼ x 8½in (23.5 x 21.6cm)
£1,200-1,400 *C*

It has been suggested that the sitter could be Philip Hone of New York.

Henry Terry (active 1879-1920)
British
A Pillar of the Conventicle
Signed
15½ x 11in (39.5 x 28cm)
£450-500 *S(S)*

Vanity Fair (Publishers) (19thC)
British
Ancient Painting (Laurence Alma Tadema)
Lithograph, printed in colours by Vincent Brooks Day and Son, published 22 March 1879,
together with 124 others, mounted
12¼ x 7¼in (31.1 x 18.4cm)
£600-700 *Bon*

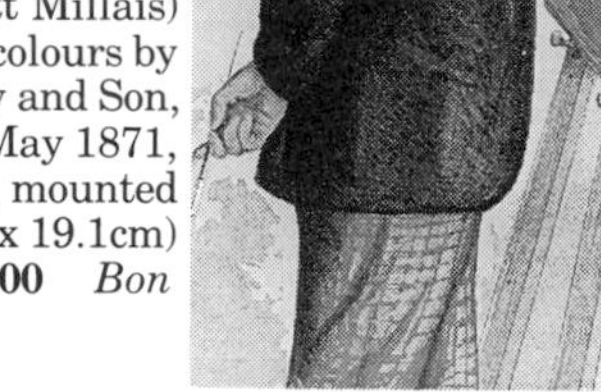

Vanity Fair (Publishers) (19thC)
British
A converted pre-Raphaelite
(Mr. John Everett Millais)
Lithograph, printed in colours by Vincent Brooks Day and Son,
published 13 May 1871,
together with 99 others, mounted
12¼ x 7½in (31.1 x 19.1cm)
£250-300 *Bon*

Vanity Fair (Publishers) (19thC)
British
A Great French Painter (Jean Louis Ernest Meissonier)
Lithograph, printed in colours by Vincent Brooks Day and Son, published 1 May 1880,
together with 99 others, mounted
12¼ x 7¼in (31.1 x 18.4cm)
£370-420 *Bon*

Vanity Fair (Publishers) (19thC)
British
The pre-Raphaelite of the World (William Holman Hunt)
Lithograph, printed in colours by Vincent Brooks Day and Son, published 19 July 1879,
together with 124 others, mounted
12⅛ x 7¼in (31 x 18.4cm)
£500-600 *Bon*

Vanity Fair (Publishers) (19thC)
British
Latin Literature
Lithograph, printed in colours by Vincent Brooks Day and Son, published 24 May 1894,
together with 31 others depicting various scholars
12½ x 7¼in (31.8 x 18.4cm)
£175-225 *Bon*

Vanity Fair (Publishers) (19thC)
British
Sensational Art (Paul Gustave Doré) Lithograph,
printed in colours by Vincent Brooks Day and Son, published 15 September 1877, together with 124 others, mounted
12⅛ x 7¼in (31 x 18.4cm)
£360-410 *Bon*

Vanity Fair (Publishers) (19thC)
British
Men of the Day, No. 33 – Natural Selection (Mr. Charles R. Darwin)
Lithograph, printed in colours by Vincent Brooks Day and Son, published 30 September 1871, together with 47 others depicting 'Men of the Day', mounted
12¼ x 7½in (31 x 19cm)
£160-200 *Bon*

Vanity Fair (Publishers) (19thC)
British
Statesmen, No. 114 – Tom Brown (Thomas Hughes)
Lithograph, printed in colours by Vincent Brooks Day and Son, published 8 June 1872, together with 122 others depicting 'Statesmen', mounted
12 x 7¼in (31 x 18.4cm)
£300-350 *Bon*

20th Century

Hans Bellmer (b1902-75)
French
Bildnis des Joe Bousquet
Signed and dated 1957, oil on board
19⅝ x 25⅝in (50 x 65cm)
£21,000-25,000 *S*

This is a portrait of the French poet Joe Bousquet (1897-1950). Bousquet devoted his life to writing after sustaining a wound to his spine that left him half paralysed at the end of World War I. He came into contact with the Surrealists André Breton, Paul Eluard and Max Ernst who introduced him to Hans Bellmer. Bousquet sat for Bellmer on several occasions and the present work, executed 7 years after the poet's death, is a posthumous tribute to his friend who through poetry, courage and imagination had triumphed over his crippled condition.

Georg Baselitz (b1938)
German
Orangenesser
Signed and dated 81, oil on canvas
79 x 63½in (200.7 x 161.3cm)
£126,000-145,000 *S(NY)*

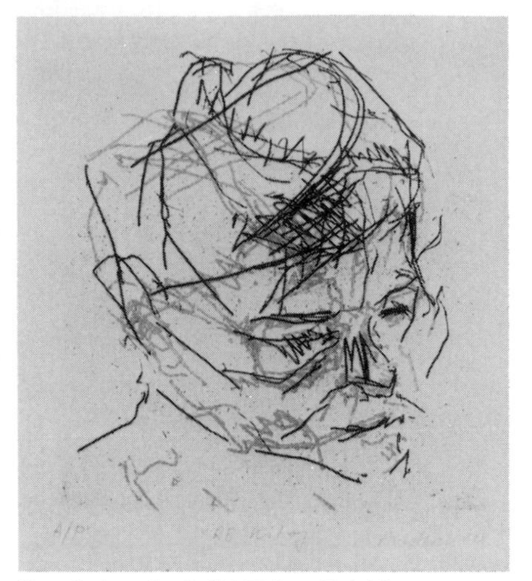

Frank Auerbach (b1931) British
R. B. Kitaj
Inscribed and dated '80 in pencil, etching with aquatint, artist's proof, edition of 50
6 x 5in (15 x 13cm)
£1,700-1,900 *Bon*

John Craxton (b1922)
British
Dancer in a Landscape, 1943
Pencil, charcoal, conté crayon and gouache
18 x 23in (45.5 x 58.5cm)
£29,000-30,000 *CH*

John Craxton is one of the very few artists who have broken the trend in prices since the recession hit, notes Christopher Hull Gallery, London. This is because he sold everything he did in the late '40s and '50s. Until the last two years none of his work had ever re-entered the market. His original collectors are now dying, and the first two pictures to come to auction fetched £27,000 and £55,000 – both to the trade.

Ronald Ossory Dunlop (1894-1973)
British
Self-portrait, c1930
Signed, oil on canvas
20 x 16in (50.8 x 40.6cm)
£1,400-1,500 *SCG*

David Bomberg (1890-1957) British
Head of Leo Koenig
Signed lower right Bomberg, inscribed lower left
Leo Koenig, pencil, pen and black ink
18½ x 13½in (47 x 34.5cm)
£1,500-1,700 *C*

Leo Koenig was the pseudonym of the Yiddish author, critic and journalist Leyb Yasse (1889- 1970). He studied art in Munich and Paris and was a close friend of Marc Chagall.

Veronica Burleigh (b1909)
British
Portrait of Sqd Ldr Peter Ellison
Signed and dated 1946, painted in Algiers
24 x 20in (61 x 50.8cm)
£900-950 *SCG*

John Bratby (b1928)
British
Self-Portrait
Signed and dated '85, oil on canvas
44 x 34in (112 x 85cm)
£750-850 *Bon*

Mary Fedden (b1915) British
Julian Trevelyan in a Cornish Village Street
Signed and dated 1988, oil on canvas
14 x 12in (35.5 x 30.5cm)
£2,200-2,400 *SCG*

Vera Cummings (1891-1949)
New Zealander
A Maori Chief
Signed and indistinctly inscribed, oil on canvas
12 x 10in (30.5 x 25.4cm)
£600-700 *Bon*

Jean Helion (b1904)
French
Portrait de Jean-Pierre Burgart
Signed with initial and dated H40, oil on canvas
23⅝ x 28¾in (60 x 73cm)
£10,000-10,500 *C*

Jean-Pierre Burgart was a writer and the son of Marcel Pagnol the author of Manon des Sources and other celebrated novels of the period.

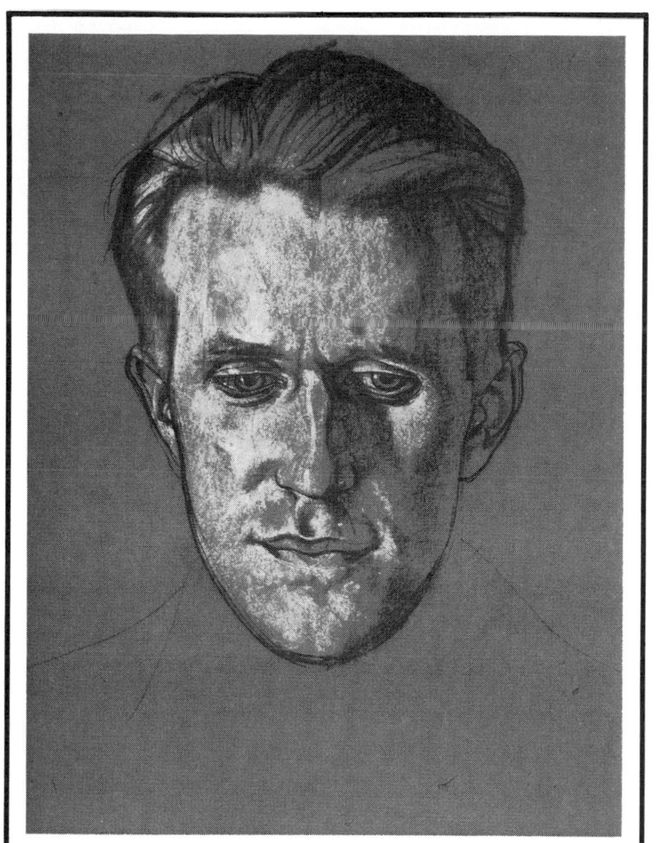

Eric Kennington (1888-1960)
British
Portrait of T. E. Lawrence
Black and white chalks on grey paper
17¾ x 13in (45 x 33cm)
£18,500-21,000 *S*

This work was executed in Cairo, when artist and subject met there for the opening of the Cairo conference on 12th March 1921. Lawrence was attending the talks to fulfill his wartime promises to his Arabian allies and his efforts were to secure the throne of Iraq for his friend Emir Feisal. Kennington was on his way to the Arabian peninsula to paint those allies for the book which Lawrence was engaged in writing, Seven Pillars of Wisdom. The men became friends and in a 1933 letter to his biographer Basil Liddell Hart, to whom he gave this drawing, Lawrence wrote of Kennington as 'a great man, and exceedingly fine draughtsman' and a good psychologist'.

Alexander Korolyov (1922-88) Russian
Stained glass design for the Museum of the Revolution "Vladimir Illyich Lenin", painted 1967, tempera on card
31 x 14in (78.7 x 35.5cm)
£2,000-3,000 *RMG*

Percy Wyndham Lewis (1882-1957)
British
Head of Ezra Pound
Signed with initials lower right WL, black crayon
12 x 9in (30.5 x 22.8cm)
£8,300-8,800 *C*

Executed in 1939.

George Grosz (1893-1959) German
Der Morgen Danach Signed and dated '37, stamped with the Nachlass mark on the reverse, pen and ink 22⅝ x 17⅞in (57.5 x 45.5cm)
£3,400-3,700 *S*

Sir Max Beerbohm (1872-1956)
British
Lord Randolph Churchill
Signed and dated lower right Max 1916, inscribed lower left Lord Randolph Churchill – a memory only but a very clear one, pencil, watercolour, brush and black ink
11 x 6½in (28 x 16.5cm)
£4,200-4,500 *C*

Cyril Mann (1911-80)
British
Portrait of the Artist, 1966
Oil on canvas
20 x 26in (50.8 x 66cm)
£7,800-8,000 *HG*

Jeanne Rij-Rousseau (1870-1956)
French
Le Lecteur
Signed and inscribed 'Paris' on the lining, painted c1920, oil on canvas
28⅜ x 20⅞in (72 x 53cm)
£11,600-12,200 *S*

Sir John Lavery (1868-1941)
Portrait of Patrick William Adam in his Studio
Signed, also signed, inscribed with sitter's name and dated 1918 on the reverse, oil on canvas
50 x 40in (127 x 101.5cm)
£33,000-40,000 *S*

The sitter was an Edinburgh painter and a friend of the artist. The portrait came into the possession of Winston Churchill, to whom Lavery gave painting lessons.

Eugene Fisk (b1938)
British
Portrait of Alex Williams
Oil on canvas
24 x 12in (61 x 31cm)
£900-1,000 *KG*

Nicol Laidlaw (20thC)
British
A Knight of the Revel
Signed and dated 1926
40 x 30in (101.5 x 76cm)
£650-750 *C(S)*

Jacques Villon (1875-1963)
French
Caliban
Signed and dated '39, oil on canvas
25½ x 21¼in (64.8 x 54cm)
£20,000-25,000 *C*

Ken Ferguson (20thC)
British
Newcastle Paperseller
Oil on board
12 x 8in (31 x 20cm)
£180-200 *VCG*

John Sloan (1871-1951)
American
Robert Henri, Painter
Signed in pencil and inscribed
'100 proofs', also inscribed by the artist
'Extra Fine proof JS',
etching, 1931
13½ x 11in (34.4 x 27.8cm)
£2,100-2,400 *S(NY)*

Pablo Picasso (1881-1974)
Spanish
Tête d'Homme
Signed and dated 10.5.70, dated 'Dimanche 10.5.70 Domingo' on the reverse, coloured crayon, felt-tip pen and pencil on card
6¼ x 4¾in (15.8 x 11.8cm)
£10,500-11,000 *S*

Charles Spencelayh (1865-1958)
British
Much Noise Little Music
Signed and inscribed, watercolour
10¼ x 14½in (26 x 37cm)
£10,000-10,500 *S*

Alice Neel (b1900)
American
Portrait of Edward Weiss
Signed and dated 76, oil on canvas
34 x 45in (86.4 x 114.3cm)
£9,000-9,500 *S(NY)*

Sir Stanley Spencer (1891-1959)
British
Self-portrait
Signed and dated 57, also signed and inscribed I don't usually sign my paintings but this I did by request, on the reverse, oil on panel
14 x 10in (35.5 x 25.5cm)
£37,000-45,000 *S*

In 1957, the vicar of Cookham, the Reverend Michael Westropp, invited the artist to open the village bazaar, instead of the cricketer Denis Compton who was ill with flu. He gladly agreed, and also donated this self-portrait which was auctioned among the locals and eventually sold for £11. A remarkable investment!

Miller's is a price GUIDE not a price LIST

Jack Butler Yeats (1871-1957)
British
The Minister
Signed, inscribed on the reverse The Minister, oil on panel, painted in 1913
14 x 9in (35.5 x 23cm)
£50,000-60,000 *C*

William Heath Robinson
(1872-1944)
British
Respectable Denizen of Pinner
Watercolour
4 x 6⅛in (10 x 15.5cm)
£850-950 *EJ*

Henry Spernon Tozer (active 1900-30)
British
A Keen Amateur
Signed 1926, watercolour
10 x 13in (25.4 x 33cm)
£1,550-1,650 *Dr*

Andy Warhol (1928-87) American Mao
Signed and dated 72 on the overlap, synthetic polymer paint silkscreened on canvas
26 x 22in (66 x 55.9cm)
£52,000-60,000 *S(NY)*

Edward Wolfe (1897-1982)
British
Portrait of a Soldier
Signed, oil on board
21½ x 18½in (54.5 x 47cm)
£1,000-1,200 *C*

Lombard School, early 16th century
Head of a Warrior
Tempera on pinewood panel
18¾ x 17½in (47.5 x 44.5cm)
£140,000-150,000 *S*

Garret Morphy (active 1680-1715)
British
Portrait of Brigadier General William Wolseley (1640-1697)
Signed and dated 1692, oil on canvas
51 x 40in (129.5 x 101.5cm)
£27,000-32,000 *S*

Attributed to Cornelius de Neve (c.1594-1664)
Flemish
Portrait of a Gentleman, possibly Sir Richard Weston (1591-1652)
Oil on canvas, in a painted oval
28½ x 23½in (72.5 x 59.5cm)
£8,300-9,000 *S*

Charles Jervas (c.1675-1739)
(After Sir Anthony van Dyck)
British
Portrait of Charles I and his Page, Lord Hamilton
Oil on canvas
87 x 75¼in (221 x 191cm)
£19,000-23,000 *S*

Hugh Douglas Hamilton (1736-1808)
British
Portrait of a Gentleman
Pastel with pencil
33½ x 25½in (85 x 65cm)
£25,000-30,000 *S*

Thomas Hudson (1701-1779)
British
Portrait of a Gentleman
Oil on canvas, in a carved wood frame
49¼ x 39½in (125 x 100.5cm)
£31,000-36,000 *S*

George Knapton (1698-1778)
British
Portrait of John Ross Mackye
Inscribed *John Ross Mackie. Esq,* oil on canvas
93¾ x 57in (238 x 145cm)
£21,000-25,000 *S*

Attributed to Jean Baptiste van Loo (1684-1745)
French
Portrait of the Hon. Sir James Campbell of Lawers
(1667-1745) oil on canvas
49 x 39in (19 x 99cm)
£9,000-9,500 *S*

Benjamin Hudson (19th C)
British
Portrait of Babu Rama Brasag Rai, half length, in a Dark Costume with Kashmir Shawl and Turban
30 x 24$^{3}/_{4}$in (76.2 x 62.8cm)
£14,000-16,000 *C(S)*

Walter Langley (1852-1922)
British
A Moment's Rest
Signed, watercolour and bodycolour
15$^{1}/_{4}$ x 15in (39 x 38cm)
£3,500-4,000 *C*

Charles Spencelayh
(1865-1958)
British
Once Too Often
Signed and inscribed, oil on panel
9 x 7in (23 x 17.5cm)
£5,300-6,000 *S*

Maximilien Luce (1858-1941)
Portrait of Charles Angrand seated at a Table
Signed and inscribed 'a l'ami gros souvenir d'Angrand Luce', oil on board
13 x 10$^{1}/_{4}$in (33 x 26cm)
£3,300-4,000 *C(S)* *Painted circa 1908*

Lucian Freud (b.1922)
British
Self Portrait
Oil on board
4$^{1}/_{2}$ x 3$^{1}/_{2}$in (11.5 x 8.8cm)
£90,000-100,000 *S*

Jack Butler Yeats
(1871-1957)
Irish
The Country Gentleman
Signed and inscribed, oil on panel
14 x 9in (35.5 x 23cm)
£24,000-30,000 *C*
Painted in 1913

Walter Richard Sickert
(1860-1942)
British
Ennui
Signed and dedicated
To Asselin / 1916,
oil on canvas
18 x 15in (46 x 38cm)
£115,000-135,000 *S*

Ennui is perhaps the most famous of all Sickert's subjects, best known from the large painting of the same title in the Tate Gallery, London.

Frank Auerbach (b.1931)
British
Head of Jym
Oil on board
22 x 20in (55.9 x 50.8cm)
£26,000-30,000 *S(NY)*
Painted in 1986

Sandro Chia (20th C)
Bumble Bee Hunter
Oil on canvas
66 x 59in (167.6 x 149.9cm)
£39,000-45,000 *S(NY)*
Painted in 1984

R.B. Kitaj (b.1932)
American
The Londonist
Oil on canvas
120 x 35⅞in (305 x 91.5cm)
£56,000-65,000 *S*

Nathan Oliveira (b.1928)
American
Seated Man
Signed and dated 60, oil on canvas
42 x 40in (106.7 x 101.6cm)
£36,000-40,000 *S(NY)*

Jan Anthonisz. van Ravesteyn (c.1570-1657)
Portrait of Joannes de Ruyter
Inscribed and signed lower left and dated 1632, oil on panel
47½ x 31in (120.7 x 78.7cm)
£98,000-115,000 *S(NY)*

After Sir Anthony van Dyck (1599-1641)
Flemish
The Three eldest Children of Charles I
Inscribed with the identity of the sitters, and inscribed on the reverse: *K Char: I Children / R.: Vandike...,*oil on canvas
50¾ x 58in (129 x 147.5cm)
£13,500-15,000 *Bon*

North Italian School, first half of the 18thC
Portrait of a Young Gentleman
Oil on canvas, octagonal
58¼ x 43¾in (148 x 111cm)
£26,000-30,000 *S*

Philip Mercier (1689-1760)
French
Three Children in a Garden
Indistinctly signed, oil on canvas
22 x 26½in (56 x 67.5cm)
£3,100-3,600 *S*

Joseph Wright of Derby (1734-1797)
British
Portrait of Master Curzon
Oil on canvas
20¼ x 16¾in (51.5 x 42.5cm)
£18,000-20,000 *S*

John Constable (1776-1837)
British
Portrait of the artist's eldest son, John Charles (1817-1841)
Head and shoulders, oil on canvas laid on board
14¼ x 11¼in (36.5 x 29cm)
£20,000-24,000 *S*

Follower of Sir Thomas Lawrence (1769-1830)
British
Portrait of William Hanbury, 2nd Baron Bateman (1826-1901) of Shobdon Court, when a Boy
Oil on canvas
60 x 48¼in (152.5 x 122.5cm)
£13,500-14,500 *S*

Alexis Harlamoff (b.1842)
Russian
The First Stitch
Signed and dated 1892, oil on canvas
41½ x 28½in (105.4 x 72.4cm)
£42,000-50,000 *C*

Joan Kathleen Eardley (1921-1963)
British
Little Glasgow Girl
Pastel
19½ x 14in (49.5 x 35.6cm)
£8,300-9,000 *C(S)*

Frederick William Macmonnies (1863-1937)
British
Berthe and Marjorie, the artist's daughters, sewing for "Tity-Dolly", 1903
Oil on canvas
19½ x 23½in (49 x 60cm) **£27,500-29,500** *DM*

Roderic O'Connor (1860-1940)
British
Head of a Breton Boy with Cap
Stamped with atelier mark on the reverse, oil on board
12 x 14in (30.5 x 35.5cm) **£21,000-23,000** *S*

Emma Magnus (active 1884-1906)
British
Portrait of a Girl
Signed and dated Nov 1906, oil on canvas
26 x 20in (66 x 50.8cm)
£5,500-5,800 *HLG*

Carl Fröschl
(1848-1934)
Austrian
A portrait of four Children
Signed, pastel
55 x 41¼in
(140 x 104cm)
£10,000-10,500 *S*

Caroline van Dewis
(1860-1932)
Danish
Children with Toys on a Red Sofa
Signed in mono 1918, oil
36 x 40in
(91.4 x 101.6cm)
£5,200-5,500 *Dr*

Harry Brooker (active 1876-1902)
British
Too Old to Play
Signed and dated 1888, oil on canvas
28 x 36in (71 x 91.5cm)
£11,100-12,100 *S*

Robert Thorburn Ross (1816-1876)
British
The Little Boat
Signed, oil on canvas
24 x 31in (60.9 x 78.7cm)
£12,000-12,500 *HFA*

William Stephen Coleman (1829-1904)
British
A New Pet
Signed, oil on canvas
16½ x 25½in (42 x 65cm)
£7,800-8,500 *S*

Antonio Rotta (1828-1903)
Italian
Nuovi Amichetti
Signed and dated Venezia 1879, oil on panel
16½ x 20½in (42 x 52cm)
£38,000-45,000 *C*

Charles-Bertrand D'Entraygues (b.1851)
French
Artillery Practice
Signed, oil on canvas
15 x 22in (38.1 x 55.9cm)
£8,300-9,000 *C*

Henry John Boddington (1811-1865)
British
A Path Through The Wood
Signed, oil on canvas
24 x 20in (66 x 50.8cm)
£9,000-9,500 *HFA*

Frans de Wilde (1840-1918)
Belgian
The Sleigh Ride
Signed and dated 1884, oil on canvas
41 x 28in (104.1 x 71.1cm)
£20,500-22,500 *HFA*

Arthur John Elsley (b.1861-active 1903)
The Tea Party
Signed and dated 1902, oil on canvas
29½ x 22½in (75 x 57.1cm)
£43,500-46,500 *HFA*

Robert Gemmell Hutchinson (1855-1936)
British
Dutch Tea Party
Signed, oil on canvas
20 x 27in (50.8 x 68.5cm)
£11,200-12,500 *C(S)*

Carl Hartmann (b.1861)
German
Autumn Day
Signed and dated 1903,
oil on canvas
$36^{1}/_{2}$ x $21^{1}/_{4}$in
(93 x 54cm)
£2,800-3,500 *S*

Edward Atkinson Hornel (1864-1933)
British
Silver Bells and Cockle Shells
Signed and dated 1906, oil on canvas
laid down on panel $26^{3}/_{4}$ x $47^{3}/_{4}$in
(68 x 123cm) **£16,600-18,600** *C(S)*

Rosina Emmet Sherwood
(1854-1948) British
Playing Amongst the Hay
Signed and dated 1900,
pastel on paper
£24,000-26,000 *DM*

Theophile Louis Deyrolle
(1844-1923) French
Springtime in Brittany
Signed, oil on canvas
$32^{1}/_{2}$ x $51^{1}/_{8}$in (82.5 x 130cm)
£30,000-32,000 *BuP*

William Henry Hunt (1790-1864) British
Girl in a Wood-House
Signed: *W. HUNT. 1837*, watercolour and bodycolour over pencil
21¼ x 16¼in (54 x 41cm)
£8,300-9,000 *S*

J. Henry Henshall (1856-1928)
British
The Lesson
Signed, watercolour
9 x 11in (22.8 x 27.9cm)
£3,400-3,600 *Dr*

Franz von Stuck
(1863-1928)
German
Knabe mit Trauben
Signed and dated 1903, oil on panel
30 x 27¼in
(76.2 x 69.2cm)
£10,500-11,500 *C*

Charles Edward Wilson
(active 1891-c.1936)
British
Bubbles
Signed, watercolour over traces of pencil
8in (20cm) circular
£4,700-5,500 *S(S)*

Augustus E. Mulready
(active 1863-1886)
British
A Penny, Please?
Signed and dated 1882 and signed, inscribed and dated "A Penny Please?" /Aug. E. Mulready/1882 on the reverse, oil on panel
15 x 11in (38.2 x 27.9cm)
£3,600-4,000 *C*

George Hillyard Swinstead (1860-1926)
British
April Showers
Signed, oil on canvas
24 x 20in (61 x 51cm)
£6,100-6,600 *S*

German School (19thC)
A Family Portrait
Oil on canvas
49½ x 66in (126 x 168cm)
£4,200-5,000 *S*

David Hosie (b.1962)
British
Family Portrait, 1991
Oil on canvas
72 x 56in (142 x 122cm)
£5,500-6,300 *JGG*

Gonzales Coques (1614-1684)
Flemish
Portrait of the De Meer Family in a River Landscape
Oil on canvas
26¼ x 32in (66.7 x 81.3cm)
£13,200-14,200 *S(NY)*

Francis Wheatley (1747-1801)
British
Portrait of Robert and Anne Campbell, with their Daughter Elizabeth Mary, under a Tree by the bank of the Thames at Greenwich
Oil on canvas
40 x 44¾in (101.6 x 113.7cm)
£63,000-75,000 *S(NY)*

Circle of Giuseppe de Gobbis
(c.1730-after 1775)
Italian
A masked Ball in a
palatial Interior
25⅜ x 30⅜in (64.5 x 77.2cm)
£18,500-20,500 *C*

Gerard Portielje (1856-1929)
Belgian
Not Wisely but too Well
Signed and dated Anvers 1879,
oil on panel
17 x 24½in (43 x 62.5cm)
£9,700-10,500 *S*

George Sheridan Knowles (1863-1931)
British
A Fishing Story
Signed, oil on canvas
18 x 24in (45.7 x 61cm)
£3,700-3,950 *HLG*

Sebastian-Jacques LeClerc, called LeClerc des Gobelins (1734-1784)
French
An Elegant Company Listening to a Hurdy Gurdy Player and Amorous Couples with Shepherds in a Landscape: a pair of paintings
Both oil on canvas
Each: 19 x 23¼in (48.3 x 59.1cm)
£76,000-90,000 *SN(Y)*

Attributed to Bonaventure de Bar (1700-1729)
French
A Fête Champêtre
Oil on canvas
31¼ x 25in (79.3 x 63.5cm)
£3,100-4,000 *C(S)*

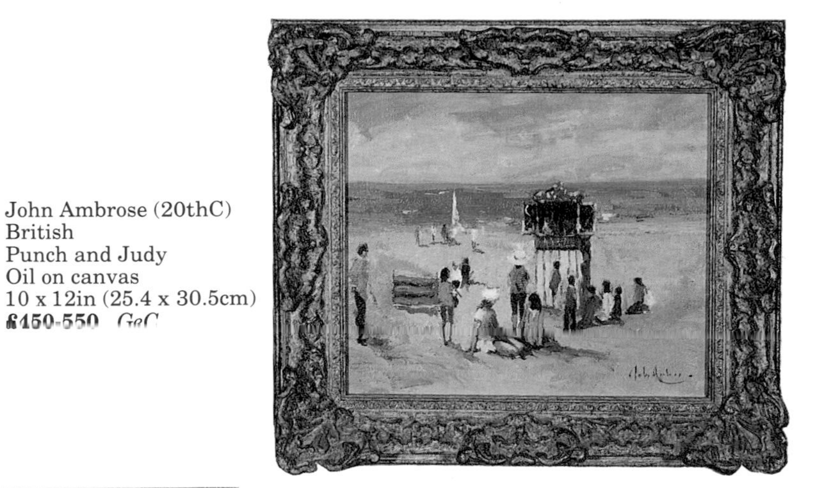

John Ambrose (20thC)
British
Punch and Judy
Oil on canvas
10 x 12in (25.4 x 30.5cm)
£150-550 *GeC*

Iosif Gurvich (b.1907)
Russian
The Bathers
Oil on canvas
58 x 36in (147.3 x 91.4cm)
£7,700-8,000 *CE*

Sidney F. Homer (b.1917)
British
Sunday Afternoon
Signed, oil
13 x 17in (33.2 x 43.1cm)
£300-350 *Dr*

Dorothea Sharp (1874-1955)
British
Children Bathing from the Rocks
Oil
18 x 24in (45.7 x 61cm)
£22,000-24,000 *Dr*

Jan Van Gool (1685-1765)
Dutch
A Farmer watching a Milkmaid at Work in a Meadow
Signed
$12^{1}/_{4}$ x $17^{3}/_{4}$in (31 x 45cm)
£4,000-5,000 *C*

Theobald Michau (1676-1765)
Flemish
A Vegetable Market near a Village
Signed T Michau, oil on canvas
$26^{1}/_{4}$ x $39^{1}/_{4}$in (66.6 x 99.5cm)
£11,500-12,500 *S*

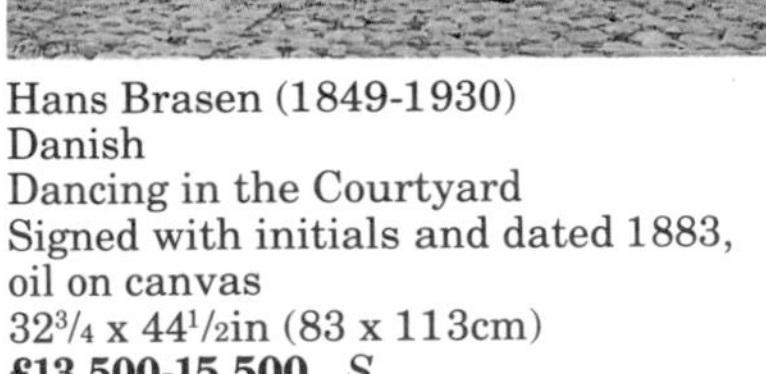

Hans Brasen (1849-1930)
Danish
Dancing in the Courtyard
Signed with initials and dated 1883, oil on canvas
$32^{3}/_{4}$ x $44^{1}/_{2}$in (83 x 113cm)
£13,500-15,500 *S*

Theophile Louis Deyrolle (1844-1923)
French
Picking Flowers
Signed, oil on canvas
28 x $39^{1}/_{4}$in (71 x 100cm)
£4,800-5,500 *S*

Cavaliere Giacomo di Chirico (1845-1884)
Italian
A Religious Procession in Winter
Signed, oil on panel
$28^{3}/_{4}$ x $22^{3}/_{4}$in (73 x 58cm)
£15,500-17,500 *S*

Charles Moreau (c.1830-1900)
French
The Proud Grandparents
Signed, oil on canvas
23½ x 28¾in (59.7 x 73cm)
£10,500-11,000 *Pol*

Pierre Edouard Frere (1819-1886)
French
The First Communion
Signed and dated 1867, oil on panel
23 x 28in (58.4 x 71.1cm)
£16,000-16,800 *HFA*

William Shayer Snr. (1787-1879)
British
A Rustic Family
Signed and dated '58, oil on canvas
24 x 20in (61 x 51cm)
£14,500-15,000 *Pol*

Robert McGregor (1847-1922)
British
Shrimping on the French Coast
Oil on canvas
26¼ x 33¼in (66.7 x 84.5cm)
£5,300-6,000 *C(S)*

George Smith (1829-1901)
British
The Last Scene in the Gambler's House
Signed and dated 1871, oil on canvas
20 x 30in (51 x 76.5cm)
£3,500-4,000 *S*

Alfons Walde (b.1891)
Austrian
Signed with monogram and dated 1912
Oil on board
11 x $10^{1}/_{4}$in (28 x 26cm)
£14,500-15,500 *S*

Sir Noël Coward (1900-1973)
British
Boy Peeling an Orange
Signed, oil on canvas-board
13 x 9in (33 x 23cm)
£2,300-3,000 *C*

Averil Burleigh (d.1949)
British
Harvesters
Oil on panel
20 x 24in (50.8 x 61cm)
£3,000-3,200 *SCG*

Boris Preobrazenski (b.1910)
Russian
Uganda, 1966
31 x $23^{1}/_{2}$in (79 x 59cm)
£750-800 *JD*

Gerbrand van den Eeckhout (1621-1674)
Dutch
Soldiers playing Tric-Trac in an Interior
Signed with initials and dated A 1651
17¼ x 14⅞in (43.8 x 37.8cm)
£350,000-400,000 *C*

David Teniers II (1610-1690)
Dutch
A Boor smoking in an Interior with an old Woman by a Brazier
Signed
11⅜ x 8¼in (29 x 21cm)
£11,200-12,000 *C*

Etienne Jeaurat (1699-1789)
French
Country Market scenes with Peasants drinking beside a Tavern and Women fighting over an overturned Basket of Eggs: a pair of paintings
Both oil on canvas
Each: 23¾ x 21in (60.3 x 53.3cm)
£13,000-14,000 *S(NY)*

Federico Andreotti (1847-1930)
Italian
Flirtation in the Wine Cellar
Signed, oil on canvas
25 x 18¼in (63 x 46.5cm)
£9,000-9,500 *S*

Robert Gemmell Hutchison (1855-1936)
British
The Village Carnival: Hi! Hi!! Hi!!!
Signed, oil on canvas
45 x 62in (114 x 157cm)
£31,000-35,000 *S(SC)*

Jean Dufy (1886-1964)
French
Scène de Cirque
Signed and dated '27, oil on canvas
$23^{5}/_{8}$ x $28^{3}/_{4}$in (60 x 73)
£12,200-13,000 *S*

Konstantin Lomikin (b.1924)
The Ballerina in Pink
Drawn 1986, pastel in board
25 x 20in (63.5 x 50.8cm)
£7,000-10,000 *RMG*

Dantè Gabriel Rossetti (1828-1882)
British
A Christmas Carol
Signed with monogram and dated 1867, red and white chalk
17¾ x 14¾in (45 x 37.5cm)
£35,000-40,000 *S*
This is a finished full-size drawing of the oil painting of the same title, also dated 1867, now in the Lady Lever Art Gallery, Port Sunlight. The model for the oil was Ellen Smith. The frame bore the inscription: "Here a maid, well-apparelled, sings a song of Christ's birth....'Jesus Christus hodie Natus est de Virgine'"

Paule Vezelay (1892-1984)
British
Eugene Goossens and Richard Tauber rehearsing at the Prince's Theatre, Bristol, 1925
Oil on canvas
31½ x 39in (80 x 99cm)
£9,500-10,000 *S*

Paul Sandby (1790-1803)
British
The Bagpiper with his Dancing Dog
Pen and black ink and watercolour over traces of pencil
8 x 6in (20 x 15.5cm)
£4,200-5,000 *S*

Léon-Marie Dansaert (1830-1909)
Belgian
Matinée Musicale
Signed, oil on panel
33¼ x 24¾in (84.5 x 63cm)
£12,200-13,000 *S*

Robert Alexander Hillingford (1825-1904)
British
The Duke's Musicians-
A Reminiscence of Hardwick Hall
Signed with monogram, oil on canvas
36 x 51in (91.5 x 130cm)
£23,000-25,000 *HFA*

Sebastian Vrancx (1573-1647)
Dutch
Landscape with a Cavalry Battle
Signed or bears signature: sv,
oil on panel
18 x 24½in (45.5 x 62cm)
£11,500-12,500 *S*

North Italian, 18th Century
Soldiers plundering a Convent
Oil on canvas
33½ x 45¾in (85.1 x 116.2cm)
£8,200-10,000 *S(NY)*

Niels Simonsen (1807-1885)
Danish
The Last Stand
Signed and dated 1867,
oil on canvas
30¾ x 43in (78 x 109cm)
£18,000-20,000 *S*

Marcel Brunery (19th/20thC) French
La Sonate
Signed, oil on canvas
$22^3/_4$ x $28^1/_4$in (58 x 72cm)
£9,000-9,500 *S*

Georges Croegaert (b.1848) French
The Connoisseur
Signed and inscribed 'Paris', oil on panel
$13^3/_4$ x $10^1/_2$in (33.6 x 26.6cm)
£7,200-7,500 *BuP*

François Brunery (late 19thC) Franco-Italian
Le petit Neveu de son Eminence
Signed, oil on canvas
$25^3/_4$ x $21^1/_2$in (65.5 x 54.6cm)
£11,200-12,000 *C*

Eduard von Grutzner (1846-1925) German
A Good Brew
Signed and dated '05', oil on panel
$10^1/_2$ x $8^1/_4$in (26.5 x 21cm)
£9,500-10,000 *C*

Arnaldo Tamburini (1853-1908) Italian
Tasting the Cream; The Cellarer
A pair, one signed and inscribed *Florence*, the other signed, oil on canvas
(30 x 24.5cm)
Each $11^3/_4$ x $9^3/_4$in
£2,300-2,600 *S*

Ettore Forti (19thC)
Italian
At the Antiquarians
Signed and inscribed *Roma*, oil on canvas
23¼ x 39¼in (59 x 100cm)
£25,000-30,000 *S*

Stephan Bakalowicz (b.1857)
Russian
The Letter
Signed, inscribed and dated 'St. Bakalowicz Romae/ MCMXIV', oil on panel
19 x 14½in (45.7 x 37cm)
£11,200-12,000 *C*

Anstey Dolland (late 19thC)
British
Roman Maidens on a Terrace
Signed, watercolour
19½ x 9½in (49.5 x 24.1cm)
£2,400-2,600 *Dr*

Jos. Suss (?)
A Classical Beauty
Signed 'Jos. Suss', oil on canvas
38½ x 19¼in (97.8 x 49.5cm)
£3,100-3,500 *CSK*

Ferencz Eisenhut (1857-1903)
Hungarian
The Armourer
Signed and dated *Munchen 87*, oil on canvas
28 x 21½in (71 x 54cm)
£12,200-13,000 *S*

Charles Wilda (1854-1907)
Austrian
At the Water's Edge
Signed and dated 1897,
oil on canvas
36 x 26½in (91.5 x 67.5cm)
£22,500-28,000 *C*

Peder Mønsted (1859-1941)
Danish
In the Outskirts of Cairo
Signed and dated 1893,
oil on canvas
15¾ x 21¾in (40 x 55cm)
£5,000-5,400 *S*

Frantz Charlet (1862-1928)
Belgian
Selim, the Street Singer of Algiers
Signed, oil on canvas
39¼ x 57in (99.5 x 144.5cm)
£3,900-4,400 *S*

Francis John Wyburd (1826-1893)
British
The Harem
Signed with initials and dated 1873, oil on canvas
28 x 36in (71 x 91.5cm)
£21,000-25,000 *S*

Rudolf Ernst (1854-1932)
Austrian
The Manicure
Signed, oil on panel
25¼ x 32½in (64 x 82.5cm)
£35,000-40,000 *S*

Benedetto Gennari (1633-1715)
Italian
Venus embracing Cupid
Oil on canvas, unframed
73½ x 53½in (186.7 x 135.9cm)
£42,500-50,000 *S(NY)*

After Rosalba Carriera (1675-1757)
Italian
Portrait of a young Lady as Ceres
26⅛ x 20⅞in (66.2 x 53cm)
£10,000-10,500 *C*

Edouard Kasparides (1858-1926)
Austrian
A Reclining Nude
Signed, oil on canvas
36¾ x 62¼in (93 x 158cm)
£10,000-10,500 *S*

Raffaele Giannetti (1832-1916)
Italian
An Odalisque
Signed, oil on panel
15 x 20½in (38.1 x 52cm)
£5,600-6,000 *C*

Paul Fischer (1860-1934)
Danish
The Three Bathers
Signed, oil on canvas
22 x 29in (55.5 x 73.5cm)
£21,000-25,000 *S*

F**** Walenn (19thC)
French
Nudes on a Beach
Signed and dated 1914, oil on canvas
45 x 37¼in (114.5 x 94.5cm)
£4,500-5,000 *S*

Charles Edouard Boutibonne (1816-1897)
Austrian
Mermaids Frolicking in the Sea
Signed and dated 1883, oil on canvas
59½ x 90½in (151 x 230cm)
£17,000-20,000 *S*

Peggy Somerville (1918-1975)
British
After the Bath
Pastel
11 x 8in (28 x 20cm)
£3,450-3,650 *DM*
Atelier Stamp No.1221

Duncan Grant (1885-1978)
British
Standing Male Nude
Oil on board
68 x 21in (173 x 53cm)
£7,200-8,000 *C*
Painted circa 1939

Alberto Burri (b.1915)
Italian
Adamo ed Eva,1946
Signed and dated, oil on canvas
19½ x 15½in (50 x 40cm)
£13,500-14,500 *C(R)*

Augustus John (1878-1961)
British
Female Nude
Oil on canvas
36¼ x 28in (92 x 71cm)
£37,000-45,000 *S*
Painted circa 1925-1930

Sir William Russell Flint
(1880-1969)
British
Jasmin
Signed, inscribed and framed
watercolour and tempera,
13 x 24¼in (33 x 61.6cm)
£18,000-20,000 *Bon*

Bernard Sleigh (b.1872)
British
Reclining Nude
Oil on board
25 x 10in (64 x 25cm)
£850-950 *GrG*

Lucien Henri Grandgerard
(1880-1970)
French
Standing Nude
Oil on board
30 x 24in (76 x 61cm)
£3,650-3,950 *JN*

Irene Welburn (b.1911)
British
Reclining Nude
Signed, oil
17 x 22in (43.1 x 55.8cm)
£325-375 *Dr*

Sir William Russell Flint
(1880-1969)
British
Miriam, Chloe and Jane
Signed, watercolour and
gouache
21 x 35in (53 x 89cm)
£24,500-30,000 *S*

André Lhote (1885-1962)
French
Nu à la Psyche
Signed, oil on canvas
28¼ x 23¼in (72 x 59cm)
£17,000-20,000 *S*

Le Corbusier (1887-1965)
French
Femme Nue
Signed with the initials and dated '33, signed and dated with the dedication *Pour Paul, 23 aout '33* on the reverse.
Oil on canvas
24¼ x 9in (31 x 23cm)
£6,800-7,500 *S*

George Condo (20thC)
Nude with Reflection
Signed and dated 89, oil on canvas
78¾ x 63in (200 x 160cm)
£34,500-38,000 *S(NY)*

Moïse Kisling (1891-1953)
Nu à la Draperie Rouge
Signed, oil on canvas
39⅜ x 28¾in (100 x 73cm)
£50,000-55,000 *S*
Painted circa 1918

CHILDREN – PORTRAITS & PICTURES

Roy Strong has noted that the earliest individual portrait of a child in British portraiture was Holbein's picture of the two year old Edward VI, presented to his father as a New Year's gift on 1 January 1539. Portraits of children began to appear from the 16thC, reflecting a new interest in childhood as a separate and important phase of life. Children were for the most part portrayed as miniature adults and dressed in the same formal fashions as their parents, until the second half of the 18thC when new ideas evolved about the education, upbringing and the clothes of children.

In 'Emile' published in 1762, the philosopher Jean-Jacques Rousseau criticised the idea of children wearing French fashions, which even adults found uncomfortable. 'The limbs of a growing child should be free to move easily in his clothing,' he insisted. 'Nothing should cramp their growth or movement . . . the best plan is to keep children in frocks as long as possible and then to provide them with loose clothing, without trying to define the shape which is only another way of deforming it. Their defects of mind and body may all be traced to the same source, the desire to make men of them before their time.' Rousseau's ideas were welcomed and to some extent anticipated in England. In the first half of the 18thC children of both sexes wore a loose fitting white muslin frock with a coloured sash until the ages of three or four. By the 1780s, girls were wearing this fashion until well into their teens, and even beyond, since the simple and free flowing style of girlhood dress was taken up by women during the Empire period, children's clothes for once being the precursor of adult fashions.

As the following pictures show it was not only ideas about children's dress that changed in the 18thC. By the late 1700s, artists were already beginning to adopt a more sentimental approach in their portrayals of children, an attitude that was to flourish in the following century. The bourgeois Victorian patron delighted in pictures of children, the more heart-tugging the better. The works illustrated on the following pages include conventionally pretty portraits, humorous pictures of infants at play or aping adult behaviour, and endless portrayals of rosy cheeked peasants gambolling in the fields. These idealised visions of childhood are still popular in today's salerooms and a sentimental stance remains constant in the work of many artists working in the 20thC.

In the contemporary field some of the most interesting portrayals of children are being produced by the illustrators of today's children's books such as Quentin Blake, Anthony Browne, Babette Cole and Tony Ross. Their lively, funny and frequently rude images conceal nothing of the baser, less than charming aspects of childhood, and provide a welcome relief from the treacly sweetness of so many 19thC painters.

Though works by these artists very rarely come up at auction and are not included in the present Picture Price Guide, such illustrators stand a good chance of being the collectable names of the future.

Attributed to Giovanni Battista Moroni (1529/30-78)
Italian
Portrait of Two Children
Oil on panel
36 x 45in (91.5 x 114cm)
£188,000-200,000 *S*

Giovanni Francesco Barbieri, il Guercino (1591-1666)
Italian
A Child, his left arm raised
Red chalk
7 x 5½in (17.1 x 13.9cm)
£14,500-15,500 *C*

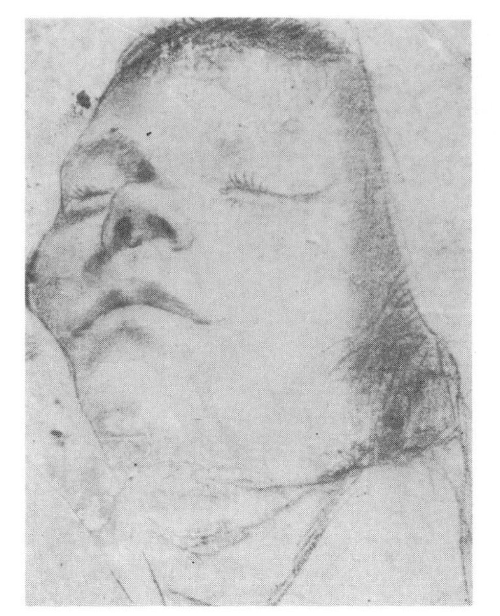

Attributed to Annibale Carracci (1560-1609)
Italian
Head of a Sleeping Child
Red chalk on light brown paper, bottom left corner made up
7 x 5½in (18.7 x 13.8cm)
£8,300-8,800 *C*

Pierre Mignard (1612-95)
French
Presumed Portrait of the artist's daughter, later Comtesse de Feuquière, looking down
Inscribed, red and white chalk, on light brown paper
4⅝ x 5¼in (11.7 x 13.4cm)
£2,200-2,500 *S(NY)*

After J. Kerseboon (active 1680s-1708)
British
Mr James Thynne, Son of the Lord Weymouth
3 years six months old
13 x 10½in (34.3 x 25.4cm)
£90-120 *C(S)*

It was customary to depict very young children nude, inspired by images of the classical putto or cherub, the drapery reflecting the fashion for the antique style.

Attributed to Robert Byng (active 1697-1729) British
Portrait of two young girls
Oil on canvas, unframed
51½ x 57¼in (131 x 145.5cm)
£4,900-5,400 *S*

The lamb, a traditional symbol of innocence, appears frequently in pictures of children.

Jacob Gerritsz. Cuyp (1594-1651/2)
Dutch
Double Portrait of a Girl aged 10 and a Boy aged 4, as Shepherds, in a wooded landscape, Dordrecht beyond
Signed, inscribed and dated 'Aeta.4./Aeta, 10 JG Cüyp.fecit/ . . . . 1646' (JG in monogram), oil on panel
35 x 35¾in (88.8 x 90.8cm)
£4,000-4,400 *C*

North Italian School, c1700
Portrait of a Young Man in a Red Coat
Inscribed on the reverse of the stretcher 'Ritratto del Cavaliere del ****re Sig Giovan Antonio Michelorzi/Fatto di mano del Sige Pietro Dandini,
oil on canvas
57 x 40¼in (144.5 x 102cm)
£6,700-8,200 *S*

Giles Hussey (1710-88) British
Portrait of a Boy, probably John Wolffe (1743-58)
Oil on canvas 31½ x 24in (80 x 61cm)
£21,000-24,000 *S*

Attributed to Thomas Bardwell (1704-67)
British
Portrait of Two Brothers, possibly members of the Fitzgerald family
Oil on canvas
46½ x 36in (118 x 92cm)
£5,300-5,800 *S*

Circle of Bartholomew Dandridge (1691-c1755)
British
A Group Portrait of a Boy and Girl, the former holding a bow and taking an arrow from a quiver, the latter holding a whip, a dog beside her, in the courtyard of a house
Inscribed 'Aet 3-5 MS' and 'Aet 1.2', in a contemporary giltwood frame carved and pierced with rocailles
44½ x 49in (113 x 124.5cm)
£15,500-16,500 *C*

Mason Chamberlain (1727-87)
British
Boy with Hoop
Oil on canvas
30 x 25in (76 x 63.5cm)
£11,500-12,000 *DC*

Attributed to Robert Davy (active 1760-63)
British
A portrait of Master Parker and his sister Theresa
Oil on panel
7⅞ x 6⅜in (20 x 16.2cm)
£500-600 *C(S)*

English School, c1770
Portrait of a Young Boy, probably Sir Joseph Lock
Oil on canvas
48 x 39½in (122 x 100.3cm)
£5,500-6,000 *Bon*

Sir Joseph Lock was knighted by the Prince Regent in Oxford High Street in 1813/14, when he was Mayor of Oxford City.

After Greuze (1725-1805)
French
A Boy with a Dog
Oil on panel
9½ x 7½in (24.3 x 18.8cm)
£3,600-4,000 *S*

After Greuze's famous canvas in the Wallace Collection, an oval composition which the copyist has expanded to rectangular format.

Greuze's sentimental portrayals of children set a prototype for the work of many artists in the following century. In their monograph on Greuze, the Goncourt brothers, the great 19thC novelists, art critics and collectors, noted the 'virginal voluptuousness' of his work. Although seduced by his portraits of children, in particular his portrayals of little girls with their pouting lips and pre-pubescent breasts, they were suspicious of his approach: 'his art suffers from something worse than a defect,' they wrote. 'It has a vice: it hides a kind of corruption, it is essentially sensual.'

Italian School, c1700, after Caravaggio
A Boy Peeling a Fruit
Oil on canvas
26 x 21in (66 x 53.3cm)
£11,200-12,000 *S*

A copy after an early composition by Caravaggio known through a number of copies. The original may not survive but claims have been made for some of the surviving pictures, most notably the one now in an Italian private collection.

Follower of James Latham (1696-1747) Irish
Portrait of Elizabeth Kettle (1730-1800)
Oil on canvas
47½ x 38in (121 x 96.5cm)
£1,500-1,800 *S*

Circle of Sir Peter Lely (1618-80) British
Portrait of a Young Child
Oil on canvas
28¼ x 24in (72 x 61cm)
£5,100-5,500 *S*

The young child is shown grasping a coral charm. Coral has always been regarded as a powerful charm for children. The Romans hung beads of red coral on babies' cradles to ward off all forms of illness and Sir Hugh Platt writing in 1594 recommended that coral should be hung round children's necks 'to preserve them from the falling sickness'. 'It also has some peculiar sympathy with nature,' he adds. 'For the best coral . . . will turn pale and wan if the party that wears it be sick, and it comes to its former colour again as they recover.' Coral was traditionally used for teething rings (believed to make the passage of the teeth easier) and the bells, often added to an infant's coral, were supposed to frighten away the evil spirits.

William Merritt Chase (1849-1916)
American
Alice Dieudonné Chase, c1899
Signed, oil on panel
17½ x 15½in (44 x 39cm)
£145,000-150,000 *DM*

Alice Dieudonné, seen here aged 12, was Chase's oldest daughter and a favourite model, often posing for him in costume.

Circle of Jacques Laurant Agasse (1767-1849)
Swiss
A Group Portrait of Two Boys and a Girl, standing half length, wearing red, black and green respectively
Oil on canvas, unframed
25½ x 29½in (64.8 x 75cm)
£1,700-2,000 *Bon*

Sophie Anderson (1823-1903)
A Little Charmer
Signed, oil on canvas
14 x 12in (35.5 x 30.5cm)
£6,250-6,500 *HFA*

George Chinnery (1774-1852)
British
Portrait of a young girl, possibly Mrs. M. Williams, née Nina Daniell
Oil on canvas
15½ x 13in (39.5 x 33cm)
£19,500-24,500 *S*

William Jabez Muckley (1837-1905)
British
Golden Days
Signed and dated 1864
16 x 19¾in (42 x 50cm)
£2,600-2,750 *HAR*

Louis Gratia (1815-1911)
French
Portrait of a little girl with a bouquet of Christmas Flowers
Signed and dated 1852, pastel
23½ x 19½in (59.5 x 49.5cm)
£1,200-1,500 *S(S)*

Gustav Igler (1842-1908)
German
The Picture Book
Signed and inscribed, oil on canvas
18¼ x 14in (46.4 x 35.5cm)
£5,800-6,300 *C*

Robinson Elliott (1814-94)
British
The Entomologist; The Ornithologist
Signed and dated 1866, a pair, oil on board
Each 12 x 10in (30.5 x 25.5cm)
£1,200-1,500 *S*

Alexei Alexeivich Harlamoff (1840-1915)
Russian
A Portrait of a Young Girl
Signed, oil on canvas
15¼ x 12in (39 x 31cm)
£3,400-3,700 *S*

Sir Robert Ponsonby Staples Bt (1853-1943)
British
Nora Painting
Signed and inscribed, watercolour over traces of pencil
10 x 18in (25.4 x 45.7cm)
£5,700-5,900 *DM*

Ludwig Adam Kunz (1857-1929)
Austrian
Children masquerading as Putti and Musicians amidst a Garland of Flowers with a Puppy at their feet
Signed, oil on canvas
39½ x 75in (100 x 190cm)
£2,700-3,200 *CSK*

Dante Gabriel Charles Rossetti (1828-82)
British
Calliope Coronio
Signed with monogram, dated 1869, coloured chalks on two joined sheets
28¼ x 19½in (71.7 x 49.5cm)
£90,000-100,000 *C*

Born in 1856, Calliope Coronio belonged to the Anglo-Greek Ionides family, who were important personalities and patrons in the late 19thC art world. Her mother, a woman of strong character and high intelligence, was friends with a number of painters including William Morris, Burne-Jones and Rossetti. The present portrait was drawn by the latter in 1869 when Calliope was 13 and shows her wearing Greek national costume. According to family memoirs, 'the little gypsy' as Rossetti called her was a lively and jolly child always full of fun. Her later life however seems not to have been very happy, marred by financial troubles and illness. She died of angina in 1906, and the day after her death her grief-stricken mother committed suicide by stabbing herself with scissors, creating a modern day Greek tragedy.

John Livingston (active 1827-34)
British
A group portrait of three children, thought to be of the McGillycuddy family, with a dog cart in a landscape
Signed and dated 1832
44½ x 35¾in (113 x 90.5cm)
£6,100-6,500 *C*

Attributed to Sir Martin Archer Shee (1769-1850)
British
Portrait of a boy
Oil on canvas
49½ x 39½in (126 x 100cm)
£11,200-12,000 *S*

Alexander M. Rossi (active 1870-1903)
British
The Little Neapolitan
Signed, watercolour heightened with bodycolour, paper laid down on canvas
21½ x 17in (54.6 x 43.2cm)
£2,300-2,500 *C(S)*

Gerald E. Harrison (active late 19th/early 20thC)
British
A Portrait of a Young Boy Standing at a Gate
Signed and dated '03, oil on panel
9⅝ x 5¾in (24.4 x 14.6cm)
£900-1,100 *Bon*

Samuel West (1810-65)
British
The Daisy Chain – portrait of the children of James K. Brown Esq.
Signed and inscribed, oil on canvas
55 x 41¼in (140 x 105cm)
£5,600-6,000 *S(S)*

Gerald Leslie Brockhurst (1891-1979)
British
The Basque Boy
Signed in pencil, etching
15 x 13in (38 x 33cm)
£800-900 *OEG*

Edmund Brock (1870-1938)
British
Portrait of Alexander Bullen
Signed, oil on canvas
35 x 44½in (89 x 112cm)
£2,800-3,000 *BAR*

Dame Laura Knight (1877-1970)
British
Friends
Signed, oil on canvas board
14 x 10in (35.5 x 25.5cm)
£11,700-12,500 *S*

W. H. Townsend (19thC)
British
The Good Companions
Signed and dated 1844, oil on board
20 x 16in (30.8 x 40.6cm)
£1,000-1,200 *LB*

Xavier Bueno (1915-)
Spanish
Young Girl carrying a Hen
Signed and dated '60
21½ x 19½in (54.5 x 49.5cm)
£1,000-1,200 *CSK*

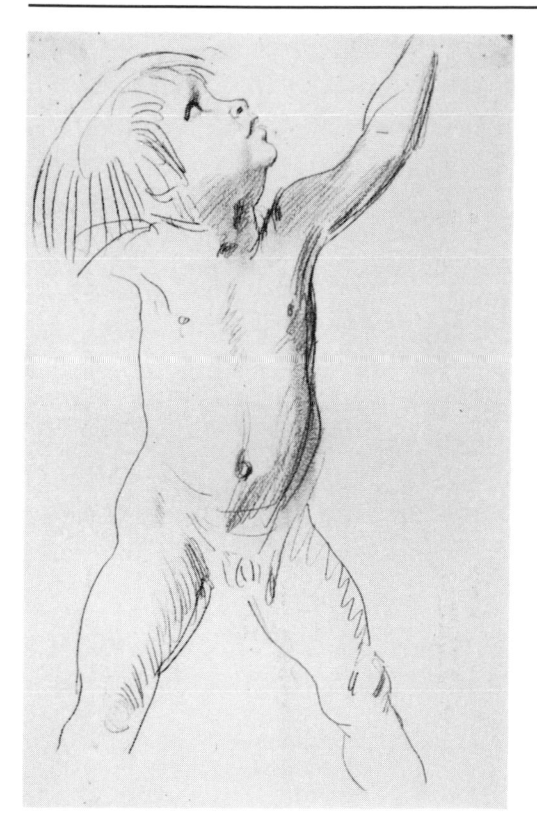

Augustus John (1878-1961)
British
Study for the Child, Forze e Amore, c1909
Pencil
15¼ x 9in (38.5 x 23cm)
£2,000-2,200 *C*

The child is probably John's son Edwin, born in 1905.

Sir John Lavery (1856-1941)
British
Portrait of Stella Donner
Signed, c1912, oil on canvas board
14 x 10in (35.5 x 25.5cm)
£13,300-14,300 *S*

René Legrand (1953-)
Swiss
Helen by a Lake
Oil on canvas
22 x 20in (55.8 x 50.8cm)
£2,700-2,850 *Tho*

Margaret Isobel Wright (1884-1957)
British
The Little Bluebell Girl
Signed, watercolour
14½ x 12½in (36.8 x 31.7cm)
£1,650-1,850 *FL*

Frank Taylor (20thC)
British
Oscar rides the Monster (Budapest)
Watercolour
18 x 24in (46 x 62cm)
£850-950 *PHG*

J. Patrick (19thC)
British
A portrait of Mary Greswolde Wilson, aged Three
Signed, inscribed and dated 1823, oil on canvas
35½ x 28¼in (90.3 x 71.8cm)
£1,000-1,200 *Bon*

Locate the source

The source of each illustration in Miller's can be found by checking the code letters below each caption with the list

Peter Rasmussen (20thC)
British
Time for Bed
Signed, pastels
14 x 9½in (35.5 x 24cm)
£450-500 *JN*

CHILDREN AT PLAY

Luigi Bechi (1830-1919)
Italian
Reading the News in the Artist's Studio
Signed, oil on canvas
56¼ x 40½in (143 x 103cm)
£32,000-36,000 *S*

C. Huskinson (19thC)
British
Tory versus Radical, 1845
Signed, oil on canvas
24 x 32in (61 x 81cm)
£3,600-4,000 *S*

Charles Hunt Jnr. (1829-1900)
British
In Front of the Teacher; The Dunce: a pair
One signed and dated '87, both oil on canvas
Each 16 x 20in (40.5 x 51cm)
£7,200-7,700 *S*

Sir Edward Coley Burne-Jones (1833-98)
British
Signed, inscribed and dated 'March. X/to L from ebj', black chalk
11 x 15⅝in (27.9 x 39.7cm)
£4,500-4,800 *C*

Burne-Jones produced similar humorous and whimsical drawings throughout his career, often for specific children such as his grand-daughter, 'but really,' as his wife observed, 'for the child that was always in himself.'

George Bernard O'Neill (1828-1917)
British
Forfeits
Signed and dated 1869, oil
16 x 21in (40.6 x 53.3cm)
£18,500-19,000 *Dr*

Edouard Frere (1819-86)
French
School's Out
Signed and dated 1872, watercolour
14¼ x 19½in (36.1 x 49.5cm)
£5,800-6,000 *HF*

Suzanne Eisendieck (b1908) German
Les Beaux Dimanches Signed, oil on canvas
29 x 23¾in (73.7 x 60.3cm)
£2,100-2,300 *S(NY)*

Hunt and his son (also Charles Hunt) specialised in pictures of children at play. Hunt Sen. created a vogue for theatrical subjects. The present work showing the 'play scene' in Hamlet (Act III, Scene 2) was obviously something of a triumph since he repeated the same composition on several occasions. Other theatrical subjects included 'The Banquet Scene: Macbeth' and 'The Trial Scene: Merchant of Venice', Hunt clearly relishing the comic potential of combining children and tragedy.

Charles Hunt (1803-77) British
The Young Volunteers Signed and dated 1861, oil on canvas 24 x 36in (61 x 91.4cm)
£5,300-5,700 *DN*

Harold Harvey (1874-1941) British
Boys Bathing
Signed and inscribed, oil on canvas
20 x 18¼in (51 x 46.5cm)
£6,400-7,000 *C*

William Frederick Gore (19th/20thC)
British
A Full Portfolio
Signed, oil on canvas
18 x 24in (46 x 61cm)
£2,300-2,500 *S*

George Bernard O'Neill (1828-1917) British
The Story Signed and dated 1900, oil on panel
20½ x 15¾in (52 x 40cm)
£15,500-16,000 *S*

Percy Tarrant (active 1883-1904) British
Oh! What a Lovely Surprise Signed, oil on board
14½ x 10½in (37 x 27cm)
£4,800-5,000 *BB*

William Marshall Brown (1863-1936) British
A Motor Boat Signed, oil on canvas
10 x 14in (25.4 x 35.5cm)
£11,300-11,500 *BuP*

Ann Walke (c1888-1965) British
Children Playing Signed, oil on canvas
24 x 29in (61 x 73.6cm)
£1,100-1,300 *L*

Harry Wingfield (b1910) British
Fishing in the Stream
Original illustration in gouache, signed
11 x 8in (28 x 20.3cm)
£350-375 *Dr*
Produced in the 1960s for the Ladybird 'Jane and Peter Books', such idealised visions of well-brought up, well-scrubbed, jolly decent children, have to a large extent disappeared from contemporary children's literature to be replaced by a less pristine and more realistic view of children. Hence the nostalgic appeal of the present work.

CHILDREN, PEASANTS & COUNTRY LIFE

English School (19thC)
Woodland Scene with two young girls
Oil on canvas
16 x 13in (40.6 x 33cm)
£1,300-1,500 *BWe*

Carl von Bergen (b1853)
German
Feeding the Ducklings
Signed, oil on canvas
29¼ x 33¼in (74 x 84cm)
£4,700-5,200 *S*

George Eliot expressed an ambiguous response to childish charms. 'It is a beauty like that of kittens, or very small downy ducks making rippling noises with their soft bills . . . a beauty with which you can never be angry but that you feel ready to crush for inability to comprehend the state of mind into which it throws you.' Most of her picture-buying contemporaries had no such doubts, paintings of children were infinitely desirable and all the more so if they also included playful kittens, faithful hounds, (or as with the present example) 'downy ducks'.

Charles Bertrand d'Entraygues (b1851)
French
Grandma's Puppet Show
Signed and dated 1883, oil on canvas
12 x 16in (30.5 x 40.6cm)
£14,500-15,000 *HFA*

Myles Birket Foster (1825-99) British Expectation
Signed with monogram, watercolour heightened with bodycolour
13 x 28in (33 x 71cm)
£21,000-25,000 *S*

Antonio Paoletti (1834-1912)
Italian
The Young Greengrocer
Signed and inscribed 'Venezia', oil on panel
13¼ x 21in (33.5 x 53cm)
£15,500-16,000 *S*

As the Picture Price Guide has already shown, Venice was an endlessly popular subject with artists. Interest was expressed not only in its canals and famous sights, but also in its more picturesque inhabitants: gondoliers, raven-haired Venetian beauties and lively peasant children (see Philip Hook and Mark Poltimore – Popular 19th Century Painting, 1986 – p594-602).

Antonio Paoletti (1834-1912)
Italian
Fishing in the Lagoon, Venice
Signed, oil on canvas
26 x 38in (66 x 96.5cm)
£30,000-32,000 *JN*

Laurence Duncan (active late 19thC)
British
Gathering Rushes
Signed with monogram and dated 1869, watercolour
11 x 9in (28 x 22.8cm)
£1,450-1,650 *Dr*

Edith Hume (active 1862-92) British
On the Dutch Coast; A Stitch in Time: a pair
Each signed, oil on panel
Each 9½ x 12in (24 x 30.5cm)
£12,500-13,000 *Pol*

James Hardy, Jun. (1832-89)
British
The Reproof
Signed and dated 1857, oil on panel
10 x 8in (25.4 x 20.3cm)
£9,250-9,450 *HFA*

Myles Birket Foster (1825-99) British
Out of School
Bears monogram, watercolour
12 x 16in (30 x 40cm)
£10,500-11,500 *HSS*

Niels Christian Hansen (b1834)
Danish
A Walk in the Forest
Signed and dated 1897, oil on canvas
19¾ x 26in (50 x 66cm)
£4,000-4,400 *S*

James Hardy, Jun. (1832-89)
British
Children Flying a Kite
Signed and dated 1869, watercolour heightened with white
21⅛ x 31¾in (53.7 x 80.7cm)
£2,700-3,200 *C*

William Marshall Brown (1863-1936)
British
Daydreams
Signed, oil on canvas
16 x 20in (40.6 x 50.8cm)
£26,000-28,000 *BuP*

Thomas Kent Pelham (active 1860-91)
British
The Peasant Girl
Signed, oil on canvas
30 x 22in (76.2 x 55.8cm)
£5,500-5,750 *HLG*

Johann Till (1827-94)
Austrian
Summer
Signed and inscribed 'Rom', oil on canvas
26¾ x 37in (68 x 94cm)
£3,900-4,300 *S*

Thomas Mackay (19th/20thC) British
Children Fishing by a Stream
Signed and dated 1902, watercolour
6 x 9in (15 x 22.5cm)
£1,700-1,900 *Dr*

William Lee Hankey (1869-1952) British
By the Stile
Signed and dated '02, watercolour and bodycolour heightened with gum arabic
11½ x 8½in (29 x 21.5cm) **£7,800-8,500** *S(S)*

Giulio del Torre (1856-1932)
Italian
Un Pasto Frugale
Signed and dated 1893,
oil on canvas
8¼ x 6¼in (21 x 16cm)
£2,900-3,200 *C*

Johannes Mari Ten Kate
(1831-1910)
Dutch
Flying the Kite
Signed, watercolour
17 x 22¾in (43 x 58cm)
£3,800-4,200 *S*

Friedrich Miess (b1854)
German
Children in the Forest
Signed, oil on canvas
27½ x 39½in (70 x 100cm)
£13,300-14,000 *S*

Sir James Lawton Wingate (1846-1924)
British
Wanderers
Signed and dated '78, oil on canvas
22½ x 30½in (57.2 x 77.5cm)
£7,800-8,500 *C(S)*

Dorothea Sharp (1874-1955) British
The Market Place, Cassis
Signed, oil on board
15 x 18in (38 x 46cm)
£14,500-15,000 *JN*

Edward Atkinson Hornel (1864-1933)
British
Paddling in the Burn, Kirkcudbrightshire
Signed and dated 1919, oil on canvas
19 x 23½in (48 x 59cm)
£6,700-7,200 *S(SC)*

Egon Schiele (1890-1918)
Austrian
Zwei Gassenbuben
Signed with the initial and dated '10', gouache and watercolour over pencil
15½ x 12⅝in (39.1 x 32.1cm)
£155,000-170,000 *S*

This watercolour is one of a series of watercolours depicting ragged peasant boys executed by Schiele during the summer of 1910. In 'Egon Schiele's Portraits', Berkeley, 1974, A. Comini describes how: "Both Schiele and Kokoschka roamed Vienna in their early years searching for models in the working-class children of the streets. Some of the most compassionate works of both artists are their quick pencil sketches of the big city's gamins. Kathe Kollwitz's stark and tragic graphics were also influential. The tendency of both Schiele and Kokoschka to heighten the realism of their child studies by an austere, selective line that bordered at times on caricature was reinforced by observation of the work of Toulouse-Lautrec . . . shown in good quantity . . . by the Miethke Gallery (in 1909)."

Dame Laura Knight (1877-1970)
British At the Hop-Bin
Signed, inscribed and dated 1963, oil on canvas
30 x 25in (76 x 63.5cm)
£7,800-8,300 *C*

Mabel A. Royds (active 1899-1940) British
Summer
Signed, colour woodcut
5½ x 9in (14 x 23cm)
£130-140 *HHG*

COUPLES: MEN & WOMEN

Filippo Falciatore (by 1718-68)
Italian
Elegant Figures Dancing, Strolling, in a Garden and Conversing: a set of 4 paintings
Oil on canvas, one laid down on board
25¼ x 19¼in (64.1 x 48.9cm)
£95,000-105,000 *S(NY)*

Condition is a major factor in a picture's price

Attributed to Jacob van Campen (1595-1657)
Dutch
Portrait of Constantijn Huygens and his wife Susanna van Baerle, holding a musical score
37⅜ x 30⅞in (95 x 78.5cm)
£115,000-130,000 *C*

Huygens (1596-1687), secretary to the Prince of Orange, was a man of considerable importance in Dutch 17thC political and cultural life. He was renowned as a poet, composer and astronomer, and was a friend of many of the artists of his time, including Rembrandt and Jan Lievens.

Huygens was painted on several occasions and it seems possible that the present portrait was commissioned from van Campen when the artist and renowned architect was assisting his patron in the construction of his stately home.

Dutch School (17thC) Portraits of a Lady and a Gentleman: a pair
Oil on canvas
31¾ x 25½in (80.5 x 64.5cm)
£3,500-4,000 *S*

Charles Melchior Descourtis (1753-1820)
French
L'Amant Surpris
Mixed method engraving and etching, printed in colours, one of a pair, after J. F. Schall, c1800
21⅞ x 17⅛in (55.7 x 43.5cm)
£1,050-1,250 *S(NY)*

Paolo Bedini (c1844-1900)
Italian
Deliberation
Signed and dated 1887, oil on canvas
14¾ x 20½in (37 x 52cm)
£8,250-8,500 *Pol*

Eugène Delacroix (1798-1863)
French
Adelaide Donnant le Poison au Jeune Page (Act V, Sc. VIII)
Lithograph, 1836-43
9⅞ x 7⅝in (25.1 x 19.5cm)
£3,900-4,400 *S(NY)*

Only a very few impressions exist of this subject because the stone was destroyed before an edition could be printed.

Pierre Edouard Frère (1819-86)
French
The Meal
Signed and dated 1875, oil on canvas
16 x 13in (40.6 x 33cm)
£9,000-9,400 *HFA*

Thomas James Lloyd (1849-1910)
British
An Evening Stroll
Signed and dated 1906, watercolour and bodycolour
15 x 27¼in (38.5 x 69cm)
£2,500-2,800 *S(S)*

Francis Stephen Cary (1808-80) British
Consolation Signed, oil on canvas
34 x 43⅞in (86.4 x 111.6cm)
£3,900-4,400 *C*

Gerrit Zegelaar (1719-94) Dutch
A Haymaker and his Wife resting outside a Farmhouse
Both signed, oil on panel: a pair
9⅝ x 7⅝in (24.3 x 19.4cm)
£4,200-5,000 *C*

Edith Martineau (1842-1909) British
Rustic Courtship
Signed and dated 1888, watercolour
11 x 14½in (28 x 37cm)
£2,500-2,900 *S*

Mario Sironi (1885-1961) Italian
Colloquio Signed, oil on canvas
8¾ x 11in (22.2 x 27.9cm)
£5,800-6,300 *S(NY)*

Charles Edward Hallé (1846-1919)
British
Paolo and Francesca
Oil on canvas
73½ x 48¾in (186.7 x 123.8cm)
£115,000-130,000 *C*

The picture illustrates the well-known story of Francesca da Rimini and Paolo Malatesta, the brother and sister-in-law, both married, who fell in love whilst reading a romance about Sir Lancelot. They became lovers, Francesca's husband caught them together and stabbed them both to death c1285. Dante knew the family, and introduced the couple into the Divine Comedy, where with other tragic lovers they are condemned to be forever swept along on the wind in the second circle of hell, the punishment for carnal sin. The subject was popular with romantic 19thC painters and Hallé portrays the pair at the moment of their falling in love, clasped in each other's arms, the book lying forgotten at their feet. The work made an auction record for the artist when sold at Christie's in March 1992.

Robert Colquhoun (1914-62) British Couple
Signed, painted in 1947, oil on canvas
40 x 28in (102 x 71cm)
£4,500-5,000 *S*

John Bratby (b1928-92) British
Brian Rix and Elspeth Gray
Signed, inscribed and dated: 'Bratby Brian Rix and Elspeth Gray June July 1967', oil on canvas
63 x 36in (160 x 91.5cm)
£1,300-1,600 *C*

Edward Reginald Frampton (1872-1923) British
Stone walls do not a prison make, Nor iron bars a cage
Signed, oil on canvas
35½ x 21¾in (90.1 x 55.2cm)
£35,000-45,000 *C*

The present picture illustrates a verse from Richard Lovelace's poem 'To Althea from Prison':

Stone walls do not a prison make,
Nor iron bars a cage;
Minds innocent and quiet take
That for an hermitage;
If I have freedom in my love,
And in my soul am free,
Angels alone that soar above
Enjoy such liberty.

The work was exhibited at the Institute of Oil Painters in 1908, where it sold for £65.

Frederick Walker (1840-75)
British
A Cosy Couple
Signed and inscribed, pen and black ink
3⅛ x 3⅞in (7.9 x 9.9cm)
£450-550 *C*

Malcolm Morley (b1931)
British
Vermeer, Portrait of the Artist in his Studio
Painted in 1968, acrylic on canvas
105 x 87in (266.7 x 221cm)
£326,000-350,000 *S(NY)*

Vermeer, Portrait of the Artist in his Studio is a literal recreation of a poster of an Old Master painting which is in the Kunsthistoriches Museum, Vienna.

Jacques Villon (1875-1963) French
Le Negre en bonne Fortune
Signed, executed c1899, gouache, ink wash and pencil on brown paper, backed with another sheet
12 x 14¼in (30.5 x 36.2cm)
£8,000-8,500 *S(NY)*

Amedeo Modigliani (1884-1920)
Italian (?)
Les Amoureux, 1917
Signed and inscribed 'Je t'aime', pencil on paper
13½ x 10in (35 x 25.5cm)
£32,000-35,000 *C(R)*

Condition is a major factor in a picture's price

Sir Eduardo Paolozzi (b1924)
British
A New Brand of Brilliance, Bunk Series
Signed, collage on pink paper
13½ x 10½in (34.3 x 26.7cm)
£9,500-10,000 *Wa*

From 1947 Paolozzi made collages embodying Surrealist ideas, juxtaposing incongruous images and modifying and combining existing reality and existing picture material. He used cuttings from old American magazines, advertising prospectuses, technological journals, etc. for his series of collages and scrapbooks. Paolozzi regarded these collages as "ready-made metaphors" and through these he was recognised as one of the leaders in the first generation of British Pop Art. This collage is one of a series executed in 1949 under the collective title "Bunk", that accompanied a lecture on The Independent Group at the Institute of Contemporary Arts given the same year.

Charles Spencelayh (1865-1958) British
She Stoops to Conquer Signed, oil on canvas
25 x 30in (63.5 x 76.2cm)
£31,000-35,000 *C*

Though the subject matter of this picture could be described as either humorous or downright tasteless depending on personal morals, no one could argue about its technical proficiency and the work had no difficulty selling at the upper end of its estimate when auctioned by Christie's in March '92.

Lilian J. Pocock (active 1908-41)
British
The Red Cross
Signed, watercolour
9¼ x 9¼in (23.5 x 23.5cm)
£600-700 *C(S)*

Hugh Thomson (1860-1920)
British
'What do you follow me for?'
Signed and dated '12, ink, pencil and wash
11 x 8¼in (27.5 x 20cm)
£650-750 *S(S)*

An illustration from 'The Lady's Not For Burning' by Christopher Fry.

THE FAMILY PORTRAIT

After Hugh Barron (1747-91)
British
Portrait of Charles Edwin Wyndham, in the uniform of the Ranger of the Forest of Dean, and his son, Thomas, wearing a blue jacket and breeches with silver buttons, standing on the terrace of a mansion
100 x 57½in (254 x 146cm)
£900-1,000 *C(S)*

After the picture previously in the Collection at Adare Manor.

Attributed to Philip Hussey (1713-82)
British
The Hore Family Conversation Piece
Oil on canvas
41 x 49¼in (104 x 125cm)
£27,000-35,000 *S*

English Provincial School (19thC)
A Family Group Before a House
Oil on canvas, unframed
28 x 42in (71.1 x 106.7cm)
£900-1,000 *Bon*

In very poor condition, this work was estimated at only £100-200 when it came up for auction at Bonhams in November 1991, but it succeeded in more than quadrupling its estimate.

Circle of Ramsay Richard Reinagle (1749-1833)
British
A Family Group in a River Landscape
Oil on canvas, unframed
34 x 27in (86.5 x 68.5cm)
£3,400-3,700 *S*

Orovida Pissarro (1893-1968)
British
The Young Family
Signed and dated 1949, oil on canvas
24 x 18in (61.5 x 45.5cm)
£1,400-1,600
GG

FIGURES & GROUPS – MISCELLANEOUS

Follower of Bernardo Strozzi (1581-1644)
Italian An Allegory of Vanity
Oil on canvas
62½ x 50½in (159.4 x 128cm)
£12,200-13,000 *S*

Attributed to Domenicus van Wijnen, called Ascanius (1661) (17thC)
Dutch
A Scene of Sorcery
Oil on canvas
28¾ x 22½in (73 x 57.5cm)
£27,000-32,000 *S(NY)*

Little is known about Domenicus van Wijnen other than his participation in the Schildersbent, an association of Netherlandish artists in Rome where the artist lived from 1680-90. Of the dozen or so paintings currently identified as being by the artist, many depict scenes of wild cosmic imagery, mythological allegories or witchcraft.

After John Opie (1761-1807)
British
The Discovery: and The Love Sick Maiden
Coloured mezzotints by William Ward in contemporary gilt and stucco frame, prints cut down to edge of image
26½ x 19½in (67.3 x 49.6cm)
£250-300 *C(S)*

Henry William Bunbury (1750-1811)
British
The City Refrigerium
Inscribed 'The City Refrigerium', black chalk, pen and black ink, grey wash
10 x 7¾in (25.4 x 19.7cm)
£260-300 *S(NY)*

Flouest (active 1789-91) French
The Tennis Court Oath
Signed 'Dessine sur les lieux . . . Flouest' and inscribed 'Serment Prêté dans lejeu. de paume à Versailles/le 20. juin 1789', black chalk, pen and brown ink, grey wash 14 x 5⅛in (35.6 x 13.1cm)
£20,000-25,000 *S(NY)*
A picture showing history in the making, and according to its inscriptions, drawn on the spot on 20 June 1789, in the Tennis Court at Versailles where the Third Estate (the Commons) met after having been excluded from their Assembly Hall by Louis XVI. Though the Third Estate represented 98% of the population, all power rested with the other two Estates: the Nobility and the Clergy – a challenge had to be made. To the great acclamation of the crowd, the Third Estate declared itself a national assembly, swearing to remain united and to meet until a new constitution had been drawn up for the country. This was a further and major step towards revolution.

George Henry Harlow (1787-1819) British
The Black Prince Mounted on his Charger with his Followers Oil on canvas
42¼ x 34¾in (107 x 88.5cm)
£4,000-4,400 *S*

After Henry Singleton (1766-1839)
British
Extravagance and Dissipation; and Industry and Economy by W. Ward (F.109 and 106)
Mezzotints, a pair, published by T. Simpson, London
25½ x 19in (65.3 x 48.7cm)
£350-400 *C(S)*

Thomas Rowlandson (1756-1827)
British
Bonaparte's Carriage Taken at Waterloo
Inscribed indistinctly with title, pen and grey and red ink and watercolour
6 x 9½in (15 x 24cm)
£5,600-6,000 *S*

After the battle of Waterloo in 1815, Napoleon's flamboyant travelling carriage was captured and presented to the Prince Regent, who immediately sold it to the showman William Bullock for £250. Bullock displayed it in London from January-August 1816, and then toured the country, over 800,000 visitors paying to see it. Bullock made a fortune before selling the carriage for £168 to a coachmaker, who in turn sold it to Madam Tussaud, who displayed it for over 75 years. In the foreground are other Napoleonic relics including the Emperor's travelling case and personal effects which Bullock displayed.

Thomas Brooks (1818-91)
British
Pets of our River
Signed and dated 1882; signed and inscribed with title on the reverse, oil on canvas
31½ x 48½in (80 x 123cm)
£7,800-8,500 *S*

Mariano Alonso-Perez (19th/20thC)
Spanish
Retrieving the Bonnet
Signed, oil on canvas
28½ x 23in (72 x 58.5cm)
£3,400-3,800 *S*

John Henry F. Bacon (1868-1914)
His Own Poems:
*"He, with kind intent,
One hot summer day
Aloud to them did read,
Poems of his own invent."*
Signed, oil on canvas
21 x 29in (53 x 73.5cm)
£3,400-3,700 *S*

John Edmund Buckley (1820-84) British
The Introduction: Elegant Figures in a Garden
Signed and dated 1870, watercolour and bodycolour
16 x 26⅝in (40.5 x 67.7cm) **£1,600-1,800** *C*

Margaret Dovaston (late 19th/early 20thC)
The New Venture Signed, oil on canvas
20 x 27in (51 x 69cm) **£6,100-6,500** *S*

Samuel Thomas George Evans
(1829-1904) British
Celebrating the Diamond Jubilee, 1897, Eton Signed, indistinctly inscribed, dated 7h 1897 and numbered 'I' on artist's label on reverse, pencil and watercolour
9 x 18¼in (22.8 x 46.3cm)
£950-1,050 *CSK*

Xaverio Della Gatta (late 18th/early 19thC) Italian
Veduta del Palazzo Reale, nel momento che vien tagliato l'albero della Libertà e la truppa in massa diretta dagli Inglesi
Signed and dated '1800 Neap', inscribed verso, gouache
22½ x 31in (57.2 x 78.7cm) **£75,000-85,000** *Bon*

Following the brief period of the French Parthenopean Republic in Naples during 1799, the Bourbon King Ferdinand IV was restored to power. This picture shows the pro-Royalist mob and Royalist troops destroying the symbols of the Republic in the Piazza del Plebiscito, Naples.

Della Gatta portrayed a number of political events during this turbulent period of European history.

Johann Hamza (1850-1927) German
The Christening
Signed, oil on canvas, unframed
14 x 10½in (36 x 26.5cm)
£4,700-5,000 *C*

Heywood Hardy (1843-1933) British
The Squire's Visit Signed, oil on canvas
18 x 24in (45.7 x 61cm)
£18,000-18,750 *HLG*

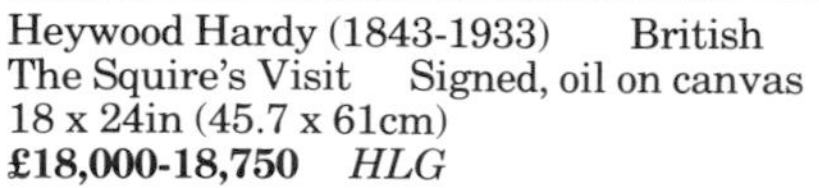

Joniel Hochmann (19thC) Austrian
Emperor Franz Josef at Gödölo Signed, oil on canvas 29 x 40½in (74 x 103cm)
£1,800-2,100 *S*

Fortunino Matania (b1881)
British/Italian
Taken Hostage
Signed, oil
12 x 16in (30.5 x 40.6cm)
£2,200-2,400 *Dr*

Costume pictures, such as the present work, were the pictorial equivalent of the historical novel, which emerged as a popular literary form in the 19thC. 'The public are attracted to costume subjects in the same way that they fall in love with the fancy dress of a masked ball,' explained sculptor Alfred Stevens. The typical nouveau-riche patron wanted a romantic and sentimental interpretation of the past with glamorous costumes, plenty of love interest and the minimum historical realism.

George Goodwin Kilburne (1839-1924)
British
An Important Critic
Signed, watercolour heightened with white
7¾ x 10¾in (19.5 x 27.5cm)
£1,700-2,000 *S*

Attributed to Bartolomeo Pinelli (1781-1835)
Italian
Bandits with a Girl on a Path
Pencil and watercolour
6 x 6¾in (15.2 x 17.2cm) **£450-550** *C(S)*

Claude A. Shepperson (1867-1921)
British
Moths
Signed, watercolour
20½ x 14½in (52 x 37cm)
£2,000-2,200 *BAR*

Charles Soubre (1821-93)
Belgian
A Violent Attack
Signed and dated 1847, oil on canvas
58½ x 43in (149 x 109cm)
£2,300-2,500 *S*

Heinrich Strehblow (b1862)
Austrian
Ladies Embroidering in a Workshop
Signed and dated 1892, oil on canvas
33½ x 49¼in (85 x 125cm)
£20,000-25,000 *S*

Harry George Theaker (1873-1954)
British
When a Queen, Long Dead, Was Young
Signed; signed and inscribed with title on a label on the frame, watercolour
17¾in (45cm) diam.
£6,000-6,500 *S*

Frank Moss Bennett (1874-1953)
British
Samuel Pepys in the Admiralty
Signed and dated 1950
16 x 20in (41 x 51cm)
£3,000-3,300 *S(S)*

Bennett's historical scenes were highly successful and many became well-known through calendars and other forms of popular reproduction.

Julian Bailey (b1963)
British
Friends in the Café at Lunchtime
Oil on board
24 x 26in (60 x 65cm)
£850-900 *NGG*

Auseklis Bauskenieks (b1910)
Russian
The Meeting in the Forest, 1965
Signed, oil on board
27 x 21in (68.5 x 53cm)
£4,500-5,000 *RM*

The present work was submitted by the Roy Miles Gallery in London. Roy Miles, a flamboyant example of capitalist success, was one of the first British gallery owners to bring contemporary Russian artists to the West. When he first visited the USSR in the 80s, the only Russian he knew was 'thank you' and 'how much?' which combined with a great deal of hard work and complex negotiation, proved sufficient to render him the major dealer of Russian art in the West.

Painted pre-Glasnost, Bauskenieks's 'Meeting in the Forest' appears to portray a peaceful sylvan scene, until one notices the figure with the Stalinesque moustache, lurking slyly behind the trees and keeping a watchful eye on the frozen figures.

David Bombert (1890-1951)
British
Men at Work
Signed and dated '19, pencil, pen, black ink, watercolour, recto; pencil, pen, brush black ink and grey wash, verso
10 x 7¾in (25.5 x 19.5cm)
£1,700-2,000 *C*

Gordon Close (20thC)
British
Reading Aloud
Mixed media
8½ x 12in (21 x 31cm)
£225-250 *VCG*

Maurice Denis (1870-1943)
French
Les Pelerins D'Emmaus (Cailler 84)
Signed in pencil and numbered 'no. 35/100', lithograph printed in colours, 1895
12¼ x 18⅛in (31 x 46.1cm)
£2,600-2,800 *S(NY)*

Lucien Dumser (active late 19th/early 20thC)
French
Les Epaves
Signed and titled, conté and bodycolour
18½ x 28in (47 x 71cm)
£1,500-1,600 *BAR*

Eve Disher (1894-1991)
British
Conversation Piece
Signed and dated, c1960s, gouache
30 x 21in (76 x 53.5cm)
£1,450-1,550 *G6*

L. Hilberth (early 20thC)
On the Terrace
Signed and dated 'L. Hilberth 1915', oil on canvas
38 x 43½in (96.5 x 110.5cm)
£4,500-4,800 *CSK*

Guy Noble (20thC)
British
The Suicide II 1991
Oil on paper
50 x 53in (127 x 134.6cm)
£4,100-4,250 *LG*

Maximilien Luce (1858-1941)
French
Les Travailleurs
Signed, oil on canvas
19¾ x 25½in (50.2 x 64.8cm)
£10,300-10,800 *S(NY)*

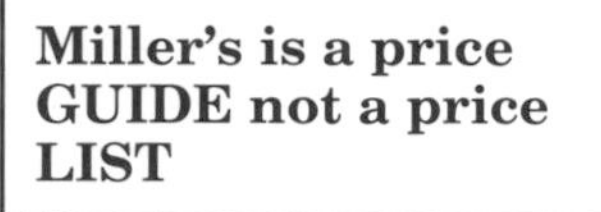

Miller's is a price GUIDE not a price LIST

Matthew Bradford (b1953) British
Which Way II, 1991 Oil on canvas
108 x 72½in (274 x 183cm)
£700-750 *Hou*

Paula Rego (20thC) Etching
Signed and numbered 5/50 in pencil
8½ x 12½in (21.5 x 32cm)
£400-450 *Bon*

William Roberts (1895-1980) British The Gutter
Signed, executed in 1934, pencil, watercolour and bodycolour 8½ x 15½in (21.5 x 39.5cm)
£10,000-10,500 *C*

John Sloan (1871-1951) American The Barber Shop (M.173) Etching and aquatint, printed in brown, 1915, signed and titled in pencil, inscribed '100 proofs' (only 35 were printed), on simili-Japan 9⅞ x 11⅞in (25 x 30.2cm)
£5,800-6,300 *S(NY)*

William Roberts (1895-1981) British
The Shoe-Shop Signed, painted in 1956, oil on canvas
36 x 24in (91.5 x 61cm)
£19,500-24,000 *S*

Ralph Steadman (20thC) British A cartoon inspired by the news that the stabilisers on the Queen Mary were not effective . . . Signed, unframed, brush and black ink with collage 19¼ x 24¼in (48.9 x 61.7cm)
£240-260 *Bon*

Albert Chevallier Tayler (1862-1925)
British
Sisters
Signed and dated 1905, oil on canvas
41¾ x 66½in (106.2 x 169cm)
£20,000-24,000 *C*

'Sisters', exhibited at the Royal Academy in 1905, is truly an Edwardian 'problem' painting: a virtuous, working wife and mother denounces her 'fallen' sister while their mother averts her eyes. Unlike the Victorians' depiction of the desperate, fallen woman, this prostitute is proud and her obvious wealth commands respect. While a groom carries her bag and helps her into a hackney coach, her sister tends a fish stall in virtual rags.

PEASANT FIGURES & COUNTRY LIFE

From the earliest times artists have recorded and celebrated agricultural life and labour. The present selection of works runs from 16thC portrayals of Flemish village festivals, to 20thC rural depictions of Russian farmworkers and includes every archetype from the country bumpkin to the noble peasant. The sheer volume of pictures sold emphasises the timeless appeal of pictures of country life.

Pieter Brueghel II (1564-1637) Flemish
The Seven Acts of Mercy
Oil on panel 17 x 23in (42.5 x 57.5cm)
£130,000-150,000 *C(Am)*

Bonifazio di Pitati, called Bonifazio Veronese (1438-1553) Italian
A Pastoral Landscape, possibly depicting the Infancy of Jupiter
Oil on panel
11¾ x 17½in
(29.5 x 44.5cm)
£5,600-6,000 *S*

Hans van Wechlen (b1537-?)
Flemish
A Wedding Scene
Signed with monogram on tree at centre: VW, oil on panel
15 x 20¾in (38 x 52.6cm)
£83,000-90,000 *S*

Circle of Nicolaes Berchem (1620-83)
Dutch
A Group of Shepherds passing by the ruins of a classical Temple, with inscription 'NB[interlaced]ercham'
Black chalk, pen and brown ink, grey wash framing lines
8⅛ x 7⅝in (20.6 x 19.5cm)
£650-750 *S(NY)*

Follower of Adriaen Frans Boudewyns (1644-1711)
Flemish
A River Landscape with a Ferry
Oil on canvas
9 x 12¼in (23 x 31cm)
£2,400-2,600 *S*

Pieter de Bloot (c1601-58)
Dutch
Peasants Standing at the Entrance to an Inn Listening to a Man Playing a Hurdy-Gurdy
Oil on panel
10¼ x 9¾in (26 x 24.8cm)
£10,700-11,500 *S(NY)*

North Italian School, c1700
Summer and Autumn, a pair
Oil on canvas
28¾ x 36¾in (73 x 93.3cm)
£4,000-4,500 *S*

Attributed to Barent Gael (c1635-after 1681)
Dutch
Travellers with Peasants outside a Farmhouse
Signed (?) B. Gael
Oil on panel
16⅝ x 23⅛in (42.2 x 58.7cm)
£1,900-2,200 *C*

Cornelis Dusart (1660-1704)
Dutch
A Village Kermesse
Signed and dated in the centre 'A van Ostade 1668', oil on canvas
34½ x 54¼in (86.5 x 135.6cm)
£48,000-55,000 *C(Am)*

After George Morland (1763-1804)
British
The Happy Cottagers
Mezzotint by Joseph Grozer, printed in colours, published by B. B. Evans, 1793
18¼ x 21½in (46.3 x 54.6cm)
and The Cottagers
Mezzotint after the same artist, framed
£200-250 *Bon*

Adriaen van Ostade (1610-84)
Dutch
The Cobbler (Godefroy, Holl. 27)
Etching, 1671
3½ x 5¾in (8.8 x 14.5cm)
£2,100-2,500 *S(NY)*

Attributed to Antonio Diziani (18thC) Italian
Peasants beating a Walnut Tree
21⅜ x 15⅛in (54.3 x 38.5cm) **£2,500-2,800** *C*

Thomas Rowlandson (1756-1827)
British
Sunday Morning
Signed, watercolour and pen and red and grey ink on original wash line mount inscribed: Sunday Morning
6¾ x 9½in (16 x 23.5cm)
£2,400-2,800 *S*

Follower of Francis Wheatley (1747-1801)
British
The Village Dance
Oil on canvas
17½ x 23¼in (44.5 x 59cm)
£380-450 *Bon*

W. Atway (19thC)
British
The Toilette
Signed, oil on canvas
19 x 22in (48 x 56cm)
£500-550 *QAG*

William Marshall Brown (1863-1936)
British
Fieldworkers Hoeing
Signed, oil on canvas
14 x 12in (35.5 x 30.5cm)
£3,800-4,200 *C(S)*

Joseph Clark (1834-1926)
British
An Apple from Grandmother
Signed and dated 1866, oil on canvas
16 x 12in (40.5 x 30.5cm)
£2,500-2,800 *S*

Bernardus Johannes Blommers (1845-1914)
Dutch
A Frugal Meal
Signed, watercolour
14½ x 20¼in (37 x 51.5cm)
£5,200-5,500 *S*

Georges Claude (1854-1921)
French
The Sacrament in the Mountains
Signed, oil on canvas
26½ x 40½in (67.5 x 104cm)
£1,900-2,300 *C*

Julius von Blaas (1845-1922)
Austrian
The Market
Signed and dated 1889, oil on panel
11½ x 20in (29.3 x 50.9cm)
£12,200-13,000 *C*

Francesco Bergamini (1815-83)
Italian
At the Fête Champêtre
Signed and inscribed 'Roma'
21½ x 33in (55 x 84cm)
£3,700-4,200 *S(S)*

Thomas Clater (1789-1867)
British
The Fish Seller
Signed and dated 1850, oil on canvas
36¼ x 53½in (92.1 x 135.2cm)
£5,600-6,000 *C(S)*

Bauer (19thC)
German ?
Interior of a tavern with figures watching a small dog smoking a pipe inscribed on frame, oil
24 x 30in (60 x 79cm)
£350-450 *HSS*

Continental School (19thC)
Kitchen interior with seated man playing a Jew's harp to two children
Oil on panel
15 x 12in (38.5 x 31cm)
£630-680 *P(S)*

Emile Claus (1849-1924)
Belgian
Les Marguerites
Signed and titled, c1890, oil on canvas
19¼ x 28½in (49 x 72.5cm)
£64,000-74,000 *S*

Sir Luke Fildes (1843-1927)
British
Study for 'The Widower'
Oil on canvas
21½ x 15in (54.6 x 38.1cm)
£6,300-6,700 *C*

Joseph Yelverton Dawbarn (active 1890-1930)
British
Children by a Dutch Canal
Signed, oil on board
29½ x 20in (75 x 51cm)
£480-560 *Bon*

Charles Hunt (1803-77)
British
At the Crossing
Signed, oil on canvas
40 x 60in (101.6 x 152.4cm)
£24,000-24,900 *HFA*

Robert Jobling (1841-1923)
British
Guiding Them In
Signed, oil on canvas
24 x 20in (61 x 50.8cm)
£4,300-4,500 *WG*

Charles Richards Havell (active 2nd half 19thC)
British
The Gleaners
Signed and inscribed, oil on canvas
20 x 24½in (51 x 63cm)
£2,800-3,200 *S*

A typically idyllic view of rural life, guaranteed to appeal to an urban patron.

Frederick Gerald Kinnaird (active 2nd half 19thC)
British
The Fern Gatherers
Signed, oil on canvas
28 x 40in (71.2 x 101.7cm)
£1,700-2,100 *CSK*

William Henry Midwood (active 1867-80) British
Come to Daddy Signed and dated 1876, oil on canvas 27 x 36in (68.5 x 91.4cm)
£15,500-16,000 *HFA*

Mark William Langlois (active 2nd half 19thC)
British The Spectacle Stall at the Market
Signed with initials, oil on canvas
11½ x 15¾in (29 x 39.5cm)
£650-700 *S(S)*

John Henry Mole (1814-86)
British
Gypsy Children
Watercolour
20 x 30in (50.8 x 76.2cm)
£3,900-4,000 *MS*

Jean François Millet (1814-79) French
Les Oies Sauvages
Signed, drawn in winter 1865, pastel and black crayon
23½ x 17in (60 x 43cm)
£58,000-65,000 *S*

'There are those who say that I deny the charms of the countryside,' wrote Millet in a letter to his friend and agent Alfred Sensier c1863. 'I find much more than mere charm – I find infinite glory.'

Adolph Müller (b1853-?)
German
Harvest Time on the Estate
Signed, oil on canvas
30 x 40in (76.2 x 101.6cm)
£14,500-15,000 *HFA*

Jean François Millet (1814-79)
L'Enfant Malade
Signed, executed c1858, black crayon and pastel
15 x 12¼in (38 x 31cm)
£243,000-260,000 *S*

Antonio Paoletti (1834-1912)
Italian
Selling Oranges on the Riva degli Schiavoni, Venice
Signed and inscribed 'Venezia', oil on panel
13¼ x 9¼in (33.5 x 23.5cm)
£4,500-4,800 *S*

Follower of Henry James Richter (1772-1857)
British
A Family Meal
Bears another signature, oil on canvas
20 x 16in (51 x 41cm)
£1,400-1,600 *S(S)*

John Thomas Serres (1759-1825)
British
Fishermen with a Cart by the Shore
Signed and dated 1808, black and white chalk on brown paper
8 x 11⅛in (20.3 x 28.3cm)
£850-950 *S(NY)*

Samuel Palmer (1805-81)
British
Old England's Sunday Evening
Signed SAMUEL PALMER, watercolour and bodycolour with scratching out and gum arabic
12 x 27½in (30 x 70cm)
£111,000-120,000 *S*

Exhibited at the Old Water-Colour Society in 1874. This work records a moment on a summer Sunday evening as country folk make their way to church across a cornfield. Palmer was working on illustrations for Milton and Virgil during this period and this picture shares the lush poetic atmosphere and the verdant landscape of many of his Milton watercolours.

Herman Ten Kate (1822-91)
Dutch
A Visitor
Signed, oil on panel
10¼ x 13½in (26 x 34cm)
£2,500-2,800 *S(S)*

William Shayer (1788-1879)
British
Harvest Time
Oil on canvas
20 x 30in (51 x 76cm)
£14,500-15,000 *JN*

Jan Jacob Lodewijks Ten Kate (1850-1929)
Dutch
Fisherfolk gathered on a Beach with a Boat Landing in a Gale
Signed and inscribed 'Amsterdam Opus 49', oil on canvas
39 x 89in (99 x 226cm)
£6,700-7,100 *C*

Johann Mari Ten Kate (1831-1910)
Dutch
An Artist at Rest by his Easel
Signed, oil on panel
13¼ x 17¼in (33.5 x 44cm)
£12,200-13,000 *S*

Circle of Andreas Franciscus Vermeulen (1821-84)
Dutch
A Candlelit Market
Oil on panel
27 x 21¼in (68.6 x 54cm)
£1,300-1,500 *Bon*

English School, 19thC, after Thomas Webster (1800-86)
Two Young Girls Dancing to the Music of an Organ Grinder
Oil on canvas
23½ x 35½in (59.7 x 90.3cm)
£680-780 *Bon*

Theodor Leopold Weller (1802-80)
German
The Festival
Signed and dated Rom. 1845, oil on canvas
32¼ x 26½in (82 x 67.5cm)
£16,800-17,400 *C*

Alfons Spring (1843-1908)
German At Church
Signed and inscribed, oil on panel
20½ x 12¾in (52 x 32.4cm)
£5,000-5,400 *C*

Friedrich August Zimmerman (19thC)
German
A Visit to the Fortune Teller
Signed and dated 'Fr. Zimmerman 1851', oil on canvas
30 x 26in (76.2 x 66.1cm)
£1,700-2,000 *CSK*

Bernard Batchelor (b1924)
British
French Fish Quay
Watercolour
4¾ x 11in (12 x 28cm)
£160-175 *HHG*

Die Brücke School(?) (20thC)
German
Figures Resting on a Track in Alpine Landscape
Oil on canvas
25½ x 31½in (65 x 80cm)
£1,100-1,400 *ALL*

Thomas Hart Benton (20thC)
American
I got a Gal on Sourwood Mountain (F.19)
Lithograph, 1938, signed in pencil, from the edition of 250, published by Associated American Artists
12½ x 9⅛in (31.8 x 23.3cm)
£1,500-1,800 *S(NY)*

Philip Connard (1875-1958)
British
Windswept
Signed, oil on canvas
30 x 40in (76 x 102cm)
£7,100-7,500 *S*

Josef Herman (b1911)
British
Mending Nets, c1978/9
Coloured inkwash
8 x 15½in (20 x 40cm)
£650-700 *BG*

Odette Dumaret (b1913) French
La Cueillette, 1989 Signed, oil on canvas
25⅝ x 32in (66 x 81.2cm)
£2,550-2,750 *CE*

Carlton Alfred Smith (1853-1946)
British
Time to Spare
Signed and dated 1901, watercolour
30 x 46in (76 x 116.5cm)
£27,000-28,000 *Bne*

Grant Wood (1892-1942) American
Approaching Storm
Lithograph, 1941, signed in pencil, from the edition of 250, published by Associated American Artists
11⅞ x 9in (30.2 x 22.8cm)
£2,600-2,800 *S(NY)*

Nikolai Obriynba (20thC)
Russian Harvest Break
Oil on canvas
40 x 60in (100 x 150cm)
£11,700-12,000 *CE*

Alexander Korolyov (1922-88)
Russian
Land to the Peasants, 1967
Tempera on card
31 x 14in (78.7 x 35.5cm)
£2,000-3,000 *RMG*

DRINKING, TAVERN AND CAFÉ SCENES

Follower of Bartholomeus Molenaer (17thC)
Dutch
A Tavern Interior
Oil on panel
31½ x 27½in (80.4 x 69.6cm)
£13,300-14,000 *S*

Jan Miense Molenaer (1610-68)
Dutch
A Tavern Interior with a Boor carousing with a Wench and others looking on
Signed, oil on panel
14¼ x 18⅜in (32.6 x 46.7cm)
£9,100-10,000 *C*

After Jan Miense Molenaer (1610-68)
Dutch
The Card Players
Bears signature, oil on panel
10 x 7½in (25.5 x 19cm)
£1,900-2,200 *S*

Pieter Verelst (1618-after 1671)
Dutch
Elegant Couples Drinking in an Interior
Signed, oil on canvas
17¾ x 14¼in (44.5 x 36.5cm)
£126,000-140,000 *S(NY)*

The subject of the present work may represent the feast of Cleopatra, where the luxurious queen drank pearls dissolved in wine to prove her wealth to the fascinated Anthony.

Follower of David Teniers the Younger (18thC)
Peasants Gambling in an Interior
Oil on panel
17 x 23¼in (43 x 59.4cm)
£2,500-2,800 *S*

Isaack van Ostade (1621-49)
Dutch
A Tavern with Peasants dancing, a Piper standing on a barrel
Signed with initials, black lead, pen and brown ink, brown wash
6 x 12¼in (15.3 x 31.2cm)
£23,000-28,000 *S(NY)*

Honoré Daumier (1808-79)
French
La Chanson à Boire
Signed, coloured crayons, pen and ink and watercolour
9⅞ x 13¾in (25 x 35cm)
£355,000-400,000 *S*

Circle of Alexander Nasmyth (1758-1840) British The Toast
Oil on canvas 25 x 30in (63.5 x 76.2cm) **£5,600-6,000** *C*

J*** D*** Aylward (early 20thC)
British
A Game of Cards
Signed and dated 1908, bears fragmented, signed and inscribed label on reverse of frame, oil on panel
9½ x 6½in (24 x 16.5cm)
£950-980 *S(S)*

Cavaliers were a popular subject of late 19th and turn of the century painting, reflecting the contemporary fascination with a glamorous past. The pictures we have received for the Picture Price Guide suggest that only rarely did the Cavaliers get down to the serious business of fighting, most of the time they were far too busy courting ladies or propping up the tavern bar. Like the majority of historical genre pictures of the period, Cavalier pictures present a domesticated version of the past, concentrating on scenes from everyday life rather than historical events.

A*** Appart (late 19th/early 20thC)
Cavaliers watching a Cock Fight
Signed, oil on canvas, framed
19½ x 23½in (50 x 60cm)
£400-450 *ALL*

Innes Fripp (active late 19th/early 20thC)
British
Cavaliers at the Village Inn
Signed, watercolour
11 x 14½ in (27.9 x 36.8cm)
£400-450 *Bon*

Lajos Kolozsvary (b1871)
Hungarian
Flirtation in the Inn
Signed, oil on canvas
16 x 20in (40 x 51cm)
£2,700-3,000 *S*

Wilhelm Löwith (1861-1932)
German
Smoking with some Friends; Tasting the Wine; a pair
Both signed and dated 1884, oil on panel
6¼ x 8½in (16.5 x 21.5cm)
£3,900-4,300 *S*

Erskine Nicol (1825-1904)
British
The Ryans and Dwyers, Calumniated Men
Signed and dated 'E. Nicol A.R.S.A./56' and signed and inscribed 'The Ryans and Dwyers. Calumniated Men/There is a story told of a rude and rather severe Irish judge of the/last century, named Robinson, that at the opening of his com/mission at an assize at Clonmel, he directed the gaoler to set/"the Ryans and the Dwyers at the bar"; upon which the Sheriff ex-/plained that there were none of those names in the dock./ "If they are not there," replied the angry judge, "they ought to/be there."/"Standard" of March 1856.' and 'No. 1. "The Ryans and Dwyers." Calumniated (Men)/Vide "Standard" March/56/ Painted for Jno. Knowles Esq. Manchester' on two old labels attached to the stretcher, oil on canvas
13 x 17⅛ in (33 x 43.5cm)
£7,500-8,000 *C*

Josef Herman (b1911)
British
The Drinkers
Oil on canvas
20 x 26in (51 x 66cm)
£3,900-4,300 *C*

Edmund Blampied (1886-1966)
French
Ici On Boit Bien
Inscribed, black crayon
7 x 8¾in (17.5 x 22cm)
£620-660 *C*

Adrian Allinson (1890-1959)
British
The Café
Signed, signed and inscribed on reverse, oil on board
13 x 16in (33 x 40.6cm)
£14,500-15,000 *Wa*

Jules Pascin (1885-1930)
American
Scène de Café
Pen and ink and watercolour
6¼ x 7⅞ in (15.9 x 20cm)
£3,900-4,200 *S*

Doris Zinkeisen (20thC)
British
Café in the Champs Elysée, signed
25 x 30in (63.5 x 76cm)
£725-825 *CSK*

ON THE BEACH

Robert Gemmell Hutchison (1855-1936)
British
Children Shrimping
Signed, oil on canvas board
9½ x 13½in (24 x 34cm)
£7,800-8,300 *S(SC)*

Alfred Godchaux (b1860)
Austrian
A la Plage
Signed, oil on canvas
25½ x 35½in (64 x 90cm)
£2,900-3,200 *S(S)*

Condition is a major factor in a picture's price

Pauline Brown (20thC)
British
Call of the Sea
Signed, watercolour
6 x 5in (15 x 12.5cm)
£255-295 *JN*

Charles de Belle (19thC)
Belgian
Children playing on Beach
Signed, oil on canvas
29 x 39in (72.5 x 97.5cm)
£1,100-1,250 *EH*

Mary Fedden (b1915)
British
Siren by the Sea
Signed and dated 1988, watercolour
7½ x 9in (19 x 23cm)
£500-700 *GG*

William Stewart MacGeorge (1861-1931)
British
Playing on a Beach
Signed, oil on canvas
12 x 16in (30.5 x 40.5cm)
£4,500-4,800 *S(SC)*

Sir Robert Ponsonby-Staples, Bt. (1853-1943)
British
Lillie Langtry on the Beach
Signed with monogram and inscribed 'Broadstairs', pencil and coloured crayon
9¾ x 13¾in (24.7 x 35cm)
£3,400-3,600 *DM*

In 1881, when Lillie Langtry's much publicised affair with the Prince of Wales was over, she trained to be a professional actress, amazing society with her genuine talent and her indefatigable energy. She toured extensively in America and Oscar Wilde wrote "Lady Windermere's Fan" specially for her although she never played in it. She was extraordinarily lucky, being the first lady to win the Cesarewitch and to enter the Jockey Club, while later she broke the bank at Monte Carlo. Inevitably Staples was a fan, scrawling in one sketchbook: "Will you come and see Mrs. Langtry if I can get seats at the Comedy? I will go now and see, then we can have a dish at The Monaco."

Mary Fedden (b1915)
British
Julian Trevelyan on the Beach
Signed and dated 1991, watercolour and bodycolour
9½ x 5¾in (24 x 15cm)
£450-500 *Bon*

William Burns (20thC)
British
High Summer – Scarborough Beach
Signed, oil
12 x 16in (30.5 x 41cm)
£650-750 *JN*

Sir William Russell Flint (1880-1969)
British
Sandpools and Rocks, Playmates, Bamburgh 1919
Signed and dated 1919, watercolour and bodycolour
12¾ x 19in (32.5 x 48cm)
£5,000-5,400 *C*

Sheree Valentine-Daines (b1956)
British
On the Beach
Signed, oil on board
6 x 9in (15.2 x 22.8cm)
£365-385 *Tho*

Martin Hardie (1875-1952)
British
The Bathing Corner
Signed, inscribed 'Boulogne' and dated 1917, pencil, blue crayon and watercolour
8½ x 11in (21.5 x 28cm)
£470-550 *Bon*

Together with a lithograph and an etching of Boulogne by the same hand and a book.

This watercolour was censored from publication in England as it was deemed frivolous to show French women enjoying themselves at the height of the bloodshed of the Great War.
As well as being a painter, Hardie wrote many books including Watercolour Painting in Britain, a classic work in its field (see Biblio).

Paul Cadmus (b1904)
American
Coney Island (Johnson 81)
Etching, 1935, signed in pencil, from the edition of 50, an inscription below the platemark at lower left erased, on laid paper
9⅛ x 10⅛in (23.2 x 25.7cm)
£2,600-3,000 *S(NY)*

Lawson Wood (b1878) British
The Tiff
Signed and dated '20, signed and inscribed on reverse, watercolour
8 x 5¾in (20.3 x 14.6cm)
£700-750 *Bon*

Robert Hagan (20thC)
Australian
Nature's Delights
Signed, oil on canvas
16 x 20in (40.6 x 50.8cm)
£1,400-1,500 *Tho*

Edward Steel Harper (1878-1951)
British
The Shell Seekers
Signed, oil
11½ x 15in (29 x 38cm)
£1,150-1,250 *AC*

Lucien Jonas (1880-1947)
French
Deux Personnages à la Plage
Signed, oil on board
11⅛ x 15¼in (28.2 x 38.7cm)
£2,500-2,800 *C*

Did you know?
MILLER'S Picture Price Guide will build up year by year to form the most comprehensive photo-reference library available

Roy Petley (b1950)
British
Summer's Day on Cromer Beach
Signed, oil on board
15¾ x 23¾in (40 x 60.2cm)
£1,850-2,000 *CSK*

Campbell A. Mellon (1876-1955)
British
On the Beach, Gorleston
Signed, oil on canvas
10 x 14in (25.5 x 35.5cm)
£920-1,000 *C*

Andrew Macara (b1944)
British
Croyde Bay, Devon
Signed, inscribed and dated 1989, oil on canvas
12 x 16in (30.5 x 40.5cm)
£400-450 *C*

Ben Tobias, St. Ives School (1901-85)
British
Cornwall: figures on the beach, bathing tents and boats offshore
Signed and dated 1957 and inscribed, oil on canvas
15½ x 19½in (39.3 x 49.5cm)
£750-850 *L*

Peggy Sommerville (1918-75)
British
Beach Scene
Atelier stamp No. 1362, pastel
15 x 20in (38 x 51cm)
£2,200-2,300 *DM*

Families holidaying on the beach at Aldeburgh were a constant source of delight for this artist.

Sheila Tiffin (20thC)
British
Children playing on a beach before St. Michael's Mount, Cornwall
Signed, oil on canvas
40 x 50in (101.5 x 127cm)
£1,550-1,700 *Bon*

Peggy Sommerville (1918-75)
British
Boating by the Deben
Atelier stamp No. 1683, board
12 x 20in (31 x 51cm)
£7,400-7,600 *DM*

Norman Wilkinson (1878-1971)
British
The Beach at Littlestone
Signed and inscribed on reverse, oil on canvas
18 x 14in (45.7 x 35.6cm)
£6,800-7,000 *Wa*

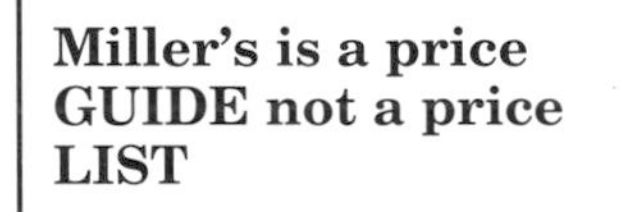

John Maclauchlan Milne (1885-1957)
British
On the Beach
Signed and indistinctly dated '3-, pastel
14½ x 20¼in (37 x 51.5cm)
£4,200-4,500 *S(SC)*

Dorothea Sharp (1874-1955)
British
At the Seaside
Signed, oil on canvas
16 x 19in (40.5 x 48cm)
£10,000-10,400 *C*

Nicholas St. John Rosse (b1945)
Card Trick
Signed, oil on canvas
18 x 24in (46 x 62cm)
£625-650 *PHG*

Jan Griffier, Snr. (1645-1718)
Dutch
Waterfowl in a River Landscape
Signed, oil on canvas
22¼ x 48½in (56.5 x 123cm)
£11,200-11,500 *S*

Follower of Melchior d'Hondecoeter (17thC)
Dutch
A Peacock, a Turkey and other Fowl by a Stream
26½ x 46⅝in
(67.3 x 118.5cm)
£7,800-8,000 *C*

Stephen Elmer (c1720-1796)
British
Blackgame in a mountainous Landscape
Oil on canvas
24¼ x 29½in (61.7 x 74.9cm)
£4,500-4,700 *C*

Winifred Marie Louise Austen (1876-1964)
British
House Martins
Signed with monogram, pencil and watercolour with touches of white
8¾ x 11in (22.2 x 27.9cm)
£1,400-1,500 *C*

Neil Cox (b.1955)
English
Winter Ptarmigan
Signed, watercolour
13 x 21in (33.2 x 53.3cm)
£700-750 *PBG*

Karl Franz Gruber (1803-1845)
Austrian
A Ring-necked Parakeet
Signed, watercolour with bodycolour
15¾ x 12¼in (39.8 x 31.3cm)
£2,800-3,000 *C*

John Cyril Harrison (1898-1985)
British
Goshawks
Signed, pencil and watercolour with touches of white heightening
20¼ x 15in (51.5 x 38.1cm)
£2,300-2,500 *C*

David Morrison Reid Henry (1919-1977)
British
A Hawk-headed Parrot
Signed, pencil, watercolour and bodycolour
14½in x 10½in (36.9 x 26.6cm)
£1,800-1,900 *C*

George Edward Lodge (1860-1954)
British
Red Grouse on Heathland
Signed, bodycolour
11¼ x 19¾in (28.6 x 50.2cm)
£6,400-6,500 *C*

George Edward Lodge (1860-1954)
British
A Slender-billed Nutcracker
Signed, pencil and watercolour heightened with white
11 x 8¾ (28 x 22.3cm)
£1,900-1,950 *C*

George Edward Lodge (1860-1954)
British
A Peregrine Falcon on a rocky Outcrop
Signed, oil on canvas-board
15¼ x 23¼in (38.7 x 59cm)
£2,300-2,400 *C*

Philip Rickman (1891-1982)
British
Eider Ducks at Sea
Signed and dated 1966, watercolour and bodycolour
22½ x 32½in (57.1 x 82.5cm)
£4,500-4,700 *C*

Edwin Penny (b.1930)
British
A Hobby
Signed, watercolour and bodycolour
14¼ x 9¾in (35.6 x 50.2cm)
£3,900-4,100 *C*

Richard Robjent (b.1937)
British
Blackgame at the Lek
Signed, watercolour and bodycolour
12 x 16⅛in (30.5 x 40.9cm)
£2,500-2,700 *C*

Sir Peter Scott (1909-1989)
British
Mallards Jumping
Signed and dated 1952, oil on canvas
25 x 36in (63.5 x 91.5cm)
£4,200-4,400 *S(SC)*

Frank Southgate
(1872-1916)
British
Cock Pheasants under a Beech Tree
Pencil, watercolour and bodycolour
15½ x 22½in
(39.4 x 57.2cm)
£3,100-3,300 *C*

Archibald Thorburn
(1860-1935)
British
Black Game
Signed and dated 1928, pencil, watercolour and bodycolour
14 x 21½in (35.6 x 54.6cm
£28,000-30,000 *C*

Charles Tunnicliffe
(1901-1979)
British
A Short-eared Owl
Signed, pencil and watercolour
with scratching out
15½ x 22½in (39.4 x 57.2c
£3,400-3,600 *C*

Alexandre-François Desportes (1661-1743)
French
Hunting Dogs chasing a Hare uphill, other Hares hiding in foliage below
Signed and dated 1723, oil on canvas
$42^{1}/_{2}$ x $46^{3}/_{4}$in (108 x 118.7cm)
£52,000-60,000 *S(NY)*

Philip Reinagle (1749-1833)
British
A Water Dog carrying a stick, a rowing boat on a river beyond
Oil on canvas
$14^{1}/_{2}$ x $19^{1}/_{2}$in
£34,000-38,000 *S*
The water dog was probably the earliest breed used for working in the water and for wild-fowling.
They were much used in coastal regions to retrieve gannets and large gulls from the sea.

Sir Edwin Henry Landseer (1802-1873)
British
Dash
Signed and dated 1825, pencil, pastel and gouache
10 x $9^{3}/_{4}$in (25.5 x 25cm)
£9,500-10,500 *S*

Basil Bradley (1842-1904)
British
Two Gun dogs
Signed and dated 1879, watercolour
13 x 19in (33.2 x 48.2cm)
£3,200-3,500 *HLG*

Francis Fairman (c.1863-1923)
British
English Setters
Signed, oil on canvas
6 x 9in (15.2 x 22.8cm)
£1,400-1,600 *Dr*

Filippo Palizzi (1818-1899)
Italian
A Dog on a Cliff
Signed and dated 1849, oil on canvas
$12\frac{1}{2}$ x 18in (32 x 46cm)
£6,100-6,400 *S*

John Berry (b.1920)
British
King Charles Cavaliers
Signed and dated 1988, oil on canvas
£2,000-2,200 *Dr*

A. Roland Knight (19thC)
British
A Breach of Promise
Seven in one frame, all signed with initials, inscribed with title on the overlap, oil on canvas
Two $9\frac{1}{2}$ x $11\frac{1}{2}$in (24 x 29cm),
five $9\frac{1}{2}$ x $7\frac{1}{2}$in (24 x 19cm)
£4,800-5,000 *S*

Karel Appel (b.1921)
Dutch
Creeping Cat
Signed and dated *53*, gouache and ink on paper
19 x $26\frac{1}{4}$in (48.3 x 66.7cm)
£9,200-9,500 *S(NY)*

Andrei Gennadiev (b.1947)
Russian
Cat
Signed, etching with watercolour on paper
£2,000-3,000 *RMG*

Pieter Casteels (1684-1749)
Flemish
Waterfowl in a river landscape, and a Fox and Poultry in a landscape
Both signed and dated 1729, oil on canvas
One 23½ x 35in (59 x 89cm), the other 24 x 35¼in (61 x 89.5cm)
£68,000-£80,000 *S*

M*** Vervoort (18th/19thC)
Dutch
Two Cockerels
Signed and dated 1821, oil on canvas
31 x 35in (78.5 x 89cm)
£4,200-4,500 *S*

Dutch School
(early 18thC)
An assembly of Fowl and a Dog in a kennel
Oil on canvas in a carved wood frame
57 x 41in (145 x 104cm)
£8,600-8,800 *S*

Follower of Melchior d'Hondecoeter (17thC)
Dutch
An assembly of Fowl
Oil on canvas, in a carved wood frame
32 x 43in (81.5 x 109cm)
£9,500-10,000 *S*

Richard Ansdell (1815-1885)
British
A Ewe with Lambs and a Heron beside a loch Signed and dated 1867, oil on canvas
32¼ x 44in (82 x 112cm)
£5,700-5,900 *S(SC)*

Thomas Sidney Cooper (1803-1902)
British
Snowed Up
Signed and dated 1867, oil on canvas
17½ x 13¼in (44.5 x 33.5cm)
£8,400-8,800 *S*

Charles Jones (1836-1892)
British
Summer Pastures
Monogrammed and dated (18)88, oil on canvas
24 x 40in (61 x 101.6cm)
£8,200-8,500 *Dr*

Thomas Sidney Cooper (1803-1902)
British
An approaching storm, summer skies
A pair, both signed and dated 1879, both oil on panel
12 x 10in (30.5 x 25.5cm)
£11,000-11,500 *S*

William Sidney Cooper (active 1871-1908)
British
Cool Waters
Signed and dated 1906, oil on canvas
14 x 20in (30.5 x 50cm)
£1,400-1,600 *Dr*

John Frederick Herring, Jnr. (c.1815-d.1907)
British
Stable Companions
Signed with initials, oil on panel
15 x 20in (38 x 51cm)
£5,000-5,200 *S*

Edgar Hunt (1876-1953)
British
Calves and Piglets
Signed and dated 1948, oil on canvas board
11 x 15in (28 x 38cm)
£5,300-5,500 *S*

Walter Hunt (1861-1941)
British
Feeding the Calves
Signed and dated 1931 twice, oil on canvas
24 x 36in (61 x 91.5cm)
£10,000-10,300 *S*

George Leon Little (1862-1941)
British
The Shepherd's Hut
Signed, oil on panel
9½ x 13½in (24 x 35cm)
£1,450-1,650 *SCG*

Tom Vallance (active 1897-1929)
British
Feeding the Calves
Signed, oil on canvas
18 x 23in (45.7 x 58.4cm)
£3,500-3,750 *HLG*

Herbert William Weekes
(active 1864-1904)
British
Farmyard Gossip
Signed, oil on canvas
17 x 13in (43 x 33cm)
£4,000-4,200 *S*

Attributed to Théodore-Jean-Louis Géricault (1791-1824)
French
Head of a Piebald Horse
Oil on canvas
$21^{1}/_{4}$ x $17^{3}/_{4}$in (54 x 45cm)
£18,000-19,000 *C*

John Ferneley, Snr. (1782-1860)
British
A Bay Hunter in a Stable
Signed *J Ferneley / Melton Mowbray 1854,* oil on canvas
33 x 43in (85 x 109cm)
£14,500-15,000 *S*

William H. Hopkins (fl.1853-90-d.1892)
British
King Monmouth
Signed and inscribed, oil on canvas
30 x 40in (75 x 100cm)
£4,100-4,500 *Bd*
Trained by Joe Enoch (seen holding the reins) for the Marquis of Zetland, King Monmouth is shown by the Rubbing-down House at Newmarket Heath, with his jockey Jack Watts looking on. The painting was sold at auction by the great-grandson of the trainer.

Charles Jones (1836-1892)
British
Feeding Time
Signed with monogram and dated 1899, oil on canvas
$35^{3}/_{4}$ x $56^{1}/_{4}$in (91 x 143cm)
£9,000-9,200 *S*

Edwin Bottomley (1865-1929)
British
A Shared Meal
Signed and dated 1928, watercolour
12 x 18in (30.4 x 45.7cm)
£1,600-1,750 *SCG*

Harry Fidler (d.1935)
British
White Plough Team
Signed, oil on canvas
10 x 13in (25.4 x 33cm)
£2,100-2,275 *Dr*

James Lynwood Palmer (d.1941)
British
Portrait of a Lady on a Hunter
Signed and dated 1917,
oil on canvas
40 x 50in (102 x 127cm)
£11,500-12,000 *S*

Coplestone Warre Bampfylde and
Richard Phelps (18thC)
British
Portrait of Col John Bampfylde M.P. (d.1750), of
Hestercombe Near Taunton.
Signed and dated 1746, oil on canvas
154 x 142in (390 x 360cm)
£72,000-77,000 *L*
The present picture was found rolled up and rotting in the stables of a South Dorset family, they nearly put it on a bonfire until at the last moment they included it with a batch of items to be sent for auction at Lawrences, Crewkerne. In spite of its poor condition, the picture specialist recognised the quality of the painting: a collaboration between the sitter's son (an amateur artist), and Somerset painter Richard Phelps and the picture exceeded every estimate.

Sir Alfred Munnings (1878-1959)
British
Winter Morning
Signed, oil on canvas
25 x 30in (63.5 x 76cm)
£39,000-41,000 *S*

George Wright (1860-1940)
British
Returning from the Hunt
Signed, oil
20 x 26in (50.8 x 66cm)
£6,200-6,500 *Dr*

Follower of August Querfurt (1696-1761)
German
An elegant Hunting Party resting after Luncheon beneath an Outcrop
Oil on copper
$17^{1}/_{4}$ x $13^{1}/_{8}$in (43.8 x 33.3cm)
£7,900-8,100 *C*

J.Sanderson Wells (1872-1955)
British
The End of the Run
Signed, oil on canvas
16 x 24in (40.6 x 60.9cm)
£5,000-5,200 *Dr*

Emil Hünten (1827-1902) and Georg Oeder (1846-1931)
German
Taking a tumble in the hunting field
Signed by both artists, oil on canvas
$45^{1}/_{4}$ x $73^{3}/_{4}$in (115 x 187cm)
£9,000-9,200 *S*

André Brasilier (20thC)
French
Repos des Cavaliers
Signed, titled and dated *1969,* oil on canvas
29 x $21^{1}/_{4}$in (73.7 x 54cm)
£2,000-2,300 *S(NY)*

John Emms (1843-1912)
British
Gone to Ground
Signed, oil on canvas
30 x 60in (76 x 152.5cm)
£10,000-10,400 *S*

Thomas Duncan (1807-1845)
British
Portrait of Robert and Thomas George Barclay out stalking
Signed with monogram, oil on canvas, in its original frame
39½ x 49½in (100.5 x 126cm)
£30,000-33,000 *S*

James Seymour (c.1702-1752)
British
The Hon. John Smith Barry out hunting with his Hounds
Signed with initials: *J.S. / 1749,* oil on canvas
24¾ x 39¾in (62 x 101cm)
£22,500-24,500 *S*

Henry Alken Jnr. (1810-1894)
British
The start and finish of the 1865 Derby
A pair, both signed, oil on paper
laid on canvas
Each 9½ x 13½in (24 x 34cm)
£11,200-11,500 *S*
The 1865 Derby was won by Count de Lagrange's "Gladiateur" ridden by Harry Grimshaw. Gladiateur, the only horse to have won the English Triple Crown and French Grand Prix, was without doubt one of the greatest horses of the nineteenth century, and his statue stands in the paddock at Longchamps, commemorating the most outstanding performer in French racing history.

Miguel Canals (20thC)
Spanish
After John Frederick Herring
Jockeys on Mounts Preparing for a Race, with Packed Stands in the Background
Oil on canvas
26 x 43in (66 x 110cm)
£850-900 *Bon*

Harrington Bird (active late 19thC)
British
Carriage Racing
Four, all signed, three dated 1891, all oil on canvas
Each 18 x 35in (46 x 89cm)
£18,000-20,000 *S*

Sir Alfred Munnings (1878-1959)
British
Study no.2 for
"Cheltenham Race Meeting"
Signed, oil on panel
12 x 22in (30.5 x 56cm)
£75,000-80,000 *S*
Painted in 1947, this work is a study for "Cheltenham Saddling Paddock, the March Meeting", which was, as the artist recalled in his autobiography "the one picture I had always desired to do". The finished work was exhibited at the Royal Academy in 1947 (no.18).

Late 18th Century Company School Study of a Casuary
Gouache and gum arabic
14¾ x 9½in (37.5 x 24.2cm),
and a Study of a Coypu (2)
£3,000-3,200 *Bon*

Rosa Bonheur (1822-1899)
French
A Wounded Chamois
Signed, oil on canvas
19 x 25¼in (48 x 64cm)
£3,300-3,500 *S*

Juris Jurans (b.1944)
Russian
Butterflies
Oil on canvas
59 x 43½in (150 x 110.5cm)
£7,000-8,000 *RM*

Eileen Soper (1905-1990)
British
Hind and Fawn leaping in long Grass
Watercolour
22 x 30in (56 x 76.2cm)
£420-470 *Bon*

Andrei Gennadiev (b.1947)
Russian
Lion's Roaring, 1980
Etching with watercolour
12 x 8in (30.4 x 20.3cm)
£2,000-3,000 *RMG*

Arthur Wardle (1864-1949)
British
Jaguar and Macaw
Signed, bears title on a label on the stretcher, oil on canvas, unframed
20 x 30in (51 x 76cm)
£4,500-4,700 *S*

Marc Chagall (1887-1985)
French
Le Loup et L'agneau
Signed, gouache and watercolour
$19\frac{3}{4}$ x $16\frac{3}{4}$in (50 x 42.5cm)
£60,000-65,000 *S*

CIRCUS AND FAIRGROUND SCENES

James Stephanoff (c1786-1874)
British
The Fair, held on the 1st August, in Hyde Park
Signed and dated 1815, pencil and watercolour with touches of white heightening
16⅝ x 23½in (42 x 59cm)
£7,800-8,300 *C*

Hyde Park Fair was held on 1st August 1814, to celebrate the centenary of the House of Brunswick (or Hanover, as it is now better known). The Gentleman's Magazine reported that there were 'booths and shows in profusion' whilst on 'the wide peopled magnificence of the Serpentine' a Naval engagement was enacted between English and American forces, followed by fireworks.

Honoré Daumier (1810-79)
French
La Parade
Signed with initials, charcoal, pen and ink, pastel and watercolour on paper laid down on board
17¼ x 13in (44 x 33.4cm)
£390,000-450,000 *S*

'If you were to show Raphael a Daumier he would admire it,' claimed Dégas.

Alexander Calder (1898-1976)
American
Untitled (Circus Series)
Signed and dated '74, gouache on paper
43¼ x 29¼in (109.9 x 74.3cm)
£16,200-17,000 *S(NY)*

Gabriel Dauchot (b1927)
French
The Clown
Signed, oil on canvas
39¼ x 19¾in (99.7 x 50.2cm)
£1,000-1,200 *S(NY)*

Marc Chagall (1887-1985)
French
Circus Girl Rider (M.419)
Signed in pencil, dated 1964, and inscribed 'épreuve d'artiste XIII/XXV', lithograph printed in colours
24½ x 20½in (62.5 x 52cm)
£6,300-6,600 *S(NY)*

Yasuo Kuniyoshi (1893-1953)
Japanese/American
Trapeze Girl (D.L71)
Signed, dated 1936, titled in pencil, lithograph
12¾ x 9¾in (32.5 x 24.6cm)
£3,500-3,800 *S(NY)*

Alexander Calder (1898-1976)
American
Tightrope Walkers: A Double-Sided Drawing
Signed and dated 1932, Indian ink on paper
21⅝ x 29¾in (54.9 x 75.6cm)
£8,600-9,000 *S(NY)*

Did you know?

MILLER'S Picture Price Guide will build up year by year to form the most comprehensive photo-reference library available

Michael Coulter (b1937)
British
Girls and a Waltzer
Watercolour
15 x 20in (38.5 x 51cm)
£850-900 *PHG*

Richard Geiger (1870-?)
Austrian
Pierrot and Columbine
Signed 'Geiger R', oil on canvas
31 x 23½in (78.8 x 59.6cm)
£750-850 *CSK*

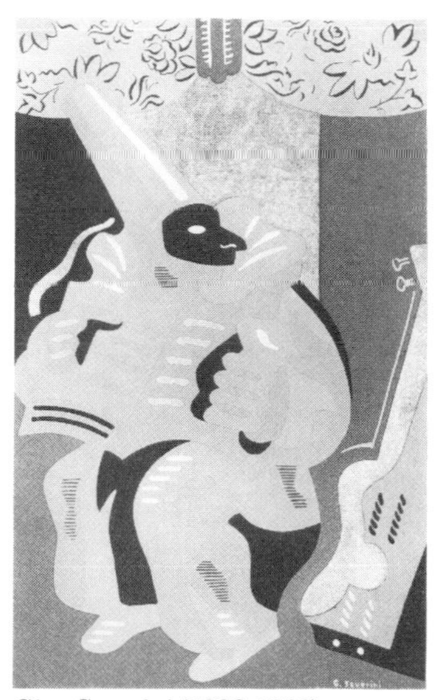

Gino Severini (1883-1966)
Italian
Policinelle au Livre
Signed, pochoir on paper
From 'Fleurs et Masque', London,
Fetchell McDonald, 1930
13¾ x 8½in (35 x 21.5cm)
£1,500-1,700 *C(R)*

Jean Dufy (1888-1964)
French
L'Orchestre
Signed, oil on canvas
13¾ x 10¾in (34.9 x 27.3cm)
£11,500-12,000 *S(NY)*

Georges Rouault (1871-1958)
French
Clown a la Grosse Caisse
1930, aquatint printed in colours
12¼ x 8⅜in (31.2 x 21.4cm)
£1,500-1,700 *S(NY)*

Dame Laura Knight (1877-1970)
British
Chinese Acrobats
Signed and dated 1960, watercolour, charcoal and pencil
22 x 15in (56 x 38cm)
£3,100-3,300 *C*

From childhood, Laura Knight was always fascinated by the circus. Alfred Munnings introduced her to the great circus impressario Bertram Mills, who allowed her to go where she liked during rehearsals and she made endless studies of clowns, acrobats, animals and all the characters of the circus world throughout her life.

A. Moliner (20thC)
Spanish
Study of Two Clowns
Signed, oil
9½ x 8in (25 x 20cm)
£360-380 *LH*

Marc Chagall (1887-1985)
French
Clown (M.468)
1966, lithograph in colours
10 x 7½in (25.5 x 19cm)
£400-425 *WO*

Jack Noel Kilgour (20thC)
Acrobats Exercising at Worth's Circus, Sydney, 1945
Signed, oil on board
24 x 29in (61 x 74cm)
£1,900-2,200 *Bon*

Fernand Léger (1881-1955)
French
Personnage de la Grande Parade, Le Clown au Banjo
Signed with initials and dated, F.L. 53, gouache on paper
17¼ x 12¾in (45 x 32.4cm)
£13,300-13,700 *C*

Edward Smith (1923-1988)
British
Three Clowns, 1951
8½ x 16¼in (47 x 41.5cm)
£450-500 *JDG*

MUSIC AND DANCE

Willem Buytewech (c1585-1626)
Dutch
The Flute Player
Engraving, 1606
5⅝in (14.3cm) diam
£4,300-4,500 *S(NY)*

The inscription on the print 'I stick to the swan's neck and to the good beer; as long as the pitcher is full I enjoy myself', refers to The Swan's Neck, an inn on the River Rotte near Rotterdam, Buytewech's birthplace.

Rembrandt Harmensz. van Rijn (1606-1669) Dutch
The Strolling Musicians
Etching, c1635
5⅜ x 4½in (13.8 x 11.4cm)
£2,100-2,300 *S(NY)*

After Caspar Netscher (1639-84)
Dutch
Ladies Making Music in a Garden
16¾ x 13¾in (42.5 x 35cm)
£750-850 *S(S)*

Dutch School (early 18thC)
The Music Party
Oil on canvas
35 x 32¼in (88.8 x 81.8cm)
£3,700-3,900 *Bon*

George Logan (20thC)
British
A Woodland Recital
Signed, pencil and watercolour heightened with white
12 x 18½in (30.5 x 47cm)
£850-950 *C(S)*

Follower of Theodor Rombouts (1597-1637)
Flemish
The Five Senses: An Elegant Company in a Wooded Landscape
22⅜ x 30¼in (57 x 77cm)
£9,000-9,500 *C*

Allegorical portrayals of the five senses were a popular theme with Flemish genre painters of the 17thC. In tavern scenes, drinkers represented Taste, pipe smokers Smell, and singers or musicians Hearing. In this work, Sight is presumably symbolised by the young woman reading and Touch by the old lady clasping the gourd.

George Goodwin Kilburne Snr (1839-1924)
British
The Trio
Signed, watercolour
14 x 20½in (35.5 x 52cm)
£7,750-7,950 *FL*

Hermann Seeger (b1857)
German
On the Beach
Signed, oil on canvas
35½ x 28¼in (90.2 x 71.7cm)
£3,800-4,000 *C*

Giacomo Mantegazza (1853-1920)
Italian
The Entertainer
Signed and dated 1884, oil on canvas
32¾ x 47¼in (83 x 120cm)
£11,100-11,500 *S*

Jean Carolus (19thC)
Belgian
The Music Lesson
Signed and dated 1858, oil on panel
23¼ x 19in (59 x 48cm)
£5,000-5,400 *S*

William Lomas (active late 19thC) British
Music Signed and dated '82, oil on canvas
44 x 32in (112 x 81cm)
£3,900-4,200 *S*

Raoul Dufy (1877-1953)
French
L'Orchestre
Signed, watercolour on paper
19⅝ x 25⅜in (49.8 x 64.4cm)
£22,500-25,000 *C*

Executed in 1941, this work is part of a series of 'orchestra' paintings and watercolours which Dufy produced at that period. He made sketches during rehearsals of the Paris Conservatory Orchestra where, according to the conductor, his favourite seat was under the organ and next to Passerone, the famous percussion player. Dufy sought to convey the sound of the music and to translate melody and the tone of an instrument into pictorial form. The great cellist Pablo Cassals, looking at one of Dufy's works, claimed that whilst he could not name the piece the orchestra were playing, he could tell the key in which it was written.

Rigby Graham (b1931)
British
Glen Nephin Cuckoo
Woodcut with 7 colours
21 x 30in (53.3 x 76.2cm)
£525-575 *GO*

Sherree Valentine Davies (20thC)
British
A Rest Rehearsal
Signed, oil
16 x 21in (41 x 53cm)
£1,000-1,200 *Bne*

Italian School (late 18thC)
A Dancer
Black chalk, pen and brown ink, grey wash
12½ x 7¾in (31.1 x 19.5cm)
£720-820 *C*

John Melville (1902-86)
British
Lady with Mandolin, 1945
Oil on board
24 x 20in (61 x 51cm)
£4,300-4,500 *JB*

Konstantin Lomikin (b1924)
Russian
Prima Ballerina
Oil on canvas, 1979
38 x 32in (96.5 x 81.2cm)
£14,000-16,000 *RMG*

Pierre-Paul Prud'hon (1758-1823) French
A Woman Dancing Playing a Tambour
Charcoal and white chalk, on grey-blue paper
18 x 9in (45.4 x 22.7cm)
£15,500-16,000 *C*

A design for one of the statuettes of a surtout de table *commissioned by the Préfet de la Seine, Nicolas-Thérèse-Benoist Frochot as part of the furniture presented by the city of Paris as a gift to the Empress Marie-Louise to celebrate her wedding in 1810, and later the birth of the King of Rome in 1811.*
Although the table centrepiece was never completed, the great sculptor and bronze-maker Thomire did cast the bronze of the figure studied in the present drawing.
Two studies for the same commission, of dancing women playing a triangle and cymbals, are in the Louvre and at Bayonne respectively.

Sir Robert Ponsonby Staples (1853-1943) British
A Black and White Minstrel Black chalk
14 x 10in (35.5 x 25.4cm)
£1,400-1,500 *DM*

Black faced minstrels, based on ideas of the American plantation negro, were popular with music hall audiences from the turn of the century, and all-black shows such as 'In Dahomey' at the Shaftesbury Theatre in 1903 introduced 'shocking' dances such as the cakewalk to the British public.

Henri Matisse (1869-1954)
French
Danseuse Couchée
Signed in pencil
numbered 47/130,
lithograph, 1927
11⅛ x 18⅛in (28.4 x 46cm)
£6,000-6,500 *S(NY)*

Vyacheslav Tokarev (b1910)
Russian
Russian Dance, 1954
Oil on canvas on board
23 x 29in (58.5 x 73.5cm)
£3,300-3,500 *RMG*

MILITARY SUBJECTS

Lucas Cranach The Elder (1472-1553)
German
St George on Horseback
Woodcut, c1507
9⅛ x 6½in (23.1 x 16.5cm)
£3,000-3,300 *S(NY)*

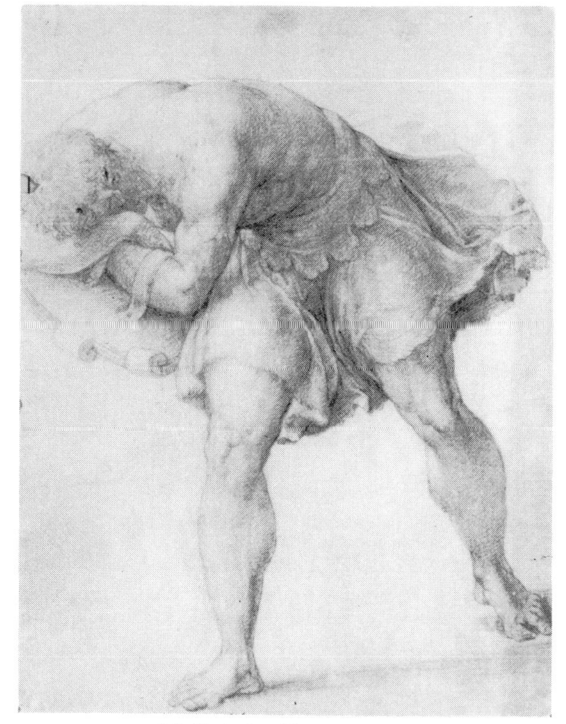

Attributed to Francesco Salviati (1510-63)
Italian
A Soldier Shielding his Eyes: Study for a Resurrection (?)
Black chalk
13⅝ x 10¼in (34.6 x 26.1cm)
£7,800-8,200 *S(NY)*

Antonio Tempesta (1555-1630)
Italian
A Battle Scene
Black chalk, pen and brown ink, brown wash heightened with white, on blue paper
14¼ x 20¾in (36.3 x 52.5cm)
£5,600-6,000 *C*

Attributed to Palamedes Palamedesz, called Stevaerts (17thC)
Dutch
A Military Encampment with Mounted Soldiers in the Foreground
Oil on panel
15½ x 28in (39.5 x 71cm)
£5,800-6,200 *S*

Pieter Meulener (1602-54)
Dutch
A Cavalry Battle
Signed and dated 1647, oil on canvas
28 x 40¼in (71.3 x 102.3cm)
£8,300-8,800 *S*

Thomas Rowlandson (1756-1827)
British
An English Hussar and a French Cuirassier
Pencil, pen and red and grey ink and watercolour
8¼ x 10¾in (21 x 27.3cm)
£2,700-3,000 *C*

Paul Sandby (1730-1809)
British
St George's Gate, Canterbury
Pencil, pen and grey ink and watercolour
12⅝ x 20in (32.2 x 50.8cm)
£21,000-25,000 *C*

The subject represents a recruiting party outside St George's Gate, Canterbury. Canterbury at this time was a large garrison city, where fresh recruits were always in demand. The recruiting party in the foreground shows an officer handing out the 'Royal Shilling' to an interested party.

Russian School (c1780)
Hussars cavorting with Women in a Stable
Watercolour
14⅜ x 19½in (36.5 x 49.5cm)
£550-650 *C(S)*

Carle Vernet (1758-1836)
French
A Battle Scene by an Italian Port
Signed, pencil, pen and ink and grey wash, heightened with white bodycolour
9 x 13¾in (23 x 35cm)
£4,500-4,800 *S*

E.H. (19thC)
A Hussar with his Charger Resting
Signed with initials, inscribed and dated 1886, watercolour
11¾ x 9in (29.8 x 22.8cm)
£800-900 *C(S)*

John Mulcaster Carrick (active 1854-78)
British
The Recruiting Sergeant
Signed with monogram and dated 1862, oil on canvas
40 x 50in (101.6 x 127cm)
£26,000-30,000 *S(NY)*

English School (1817)
His Royal Highness The Prince Regent and the Duke of Wellington's Visit to Waterloo Bridge, on the 18th June 1817
Watercolour over pencil heightened with white
7 x 11¾in (18 x 30cm)
£1,700-2,000 *S*

The bridge, originally known as the Strand Bridge, was designed by John Rennie and built between 1811 and 1817 by the contractors Joliffe and Banks. It was opened by the Prince Regent on 18th June 1817, the second anniversary of the Battle of Waterloo.

Bertalan de Karlovszky (1858-1938)
Austrian
Taking a Prisoner
Signed and inscribed Paris, oil on panel
30½ x 39½in (77 x 100cm)
£2,500-2,800 *S*

Hermanus Willem Koekkoek (1867-1929) Dutch
Cavalry Officers and Horses Signed, oil on canvas
16¾ x 23in (42.5 x 58.5cm) **£5,000-5,400** *S*

Edouard Manet (1832-1883) French
L'Execution de Maximilien
Lithograph, 1868
13⅛ x 17⅛in (33.2 x 43.4cm)
£7,500-8,000 *S(NY)*

Manet was fascinated by the execution in 1867 of Maximilien, Emperor of Mexico and Napoleon III's protégé. He produced three pictures of the execution and one lithograph, basing his work on newspaper reports and photographs. The subject was controversial and politically sensitive, the French Government was displeased and the Ministry of the Interior wrote to the artists, banning the pictures from the Salon and forbidding the publication or printing of the lithograph. This work was never published during Manet's lifetime and the stone itself narrowly missed being effaced by the printer.

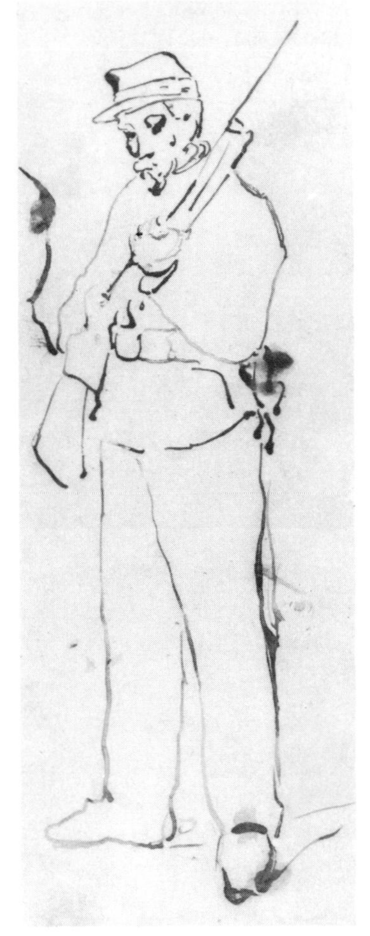

Edouard Manet (1832-83)
French
Soldat Examinant son Fusil
Pen and sepia ink on tracing paper laid down on card
10⅜ x 3⅜in (26.5 x 9.7cm)
£25,000-30,000 *S*

Executed c1867-68, this work relates to the soldier on the right hand side of the painting L'Execution de Maximilien, of which there are three versions in Kunsthalle, Mannheim, the National Gallery, London and the Ny Carlsberg Glyptotek, Copenhagen.

George Housman Thomas (1824-68)
British
Cavalry
Signed, inscribed and dated Maidstone 1861,
watercolour
12¼ x 18½in
(31 x 47cm)
£600-700 *Bea*

Edward Burra (1905-76)
British
War in the Sun
Watercolour
42 x 62½in (106.5 x 157.5cm)
£185,000-210,000 *S*

Painted c1938, War in the Sun is among the largest of the series of pictures relating to the Spanish Civil War which the artist painted between 1935 and 1939. Burra never chose a side. Loving Spain, which he had visited on several occasions, he saw in the war only the death of the country he had known. Partisanship was irrelevant for him, the victims and aggressors of the Civil War series are unidentified, universal and timeless in spite of their modern weaponry.

Wilhelm Velten (1847-1929) Russian The Refreshment
Signed, oil on panel
14¼ x 18¼in (36 x 46.3cm)
£8,900-9,400 *C*

Sir William Orpen (1878-1931)
British
Major A. N. Lee, DSO, OBE, TD, in his Hut Office at Beaumerie-sur-Mer, France
Signed and inscribed, dated 1918, oil on canvas
30 x 25in (76 x 63.5cm)
£35,000-40,000 *Bon*

Orpen was an official war artist, receiving a major's pay, and Major Lee was responsible for censoring the work of the painters at the front. The two men clashed in 1918 on the occasion of Orpen's exhibition of war pictures at Agnews. Orpen submitted for his approval two portraits of his French mistress Yvonne Aubicq, justifying their unwarlike qualities by entitling them 'The Spy' and concocting an elaborate story of how this beautiful German agent, shot by a French firing squad, had at the last minute let fall her greatcoat to stand in glorious nudity before her executioners. Lee was not impressed by his powers of invention and refused to pass the majority of the pictures submitted for the show, a decision that was later reversed by Orpen's more influential contacts. In spite of this incident, the two men became friends.

Christopher Richard Wynne Nevinson (1889-1946)
Battlefields of Britain; Opus V 'Amongst the Clouds'
Signed, oil on panel
16 x 11¾in (40.5 x 30cm)
£4,200-4,600 *C*

This picture was purchased by John Major and hangs on the walls of No 10 Downing Street.

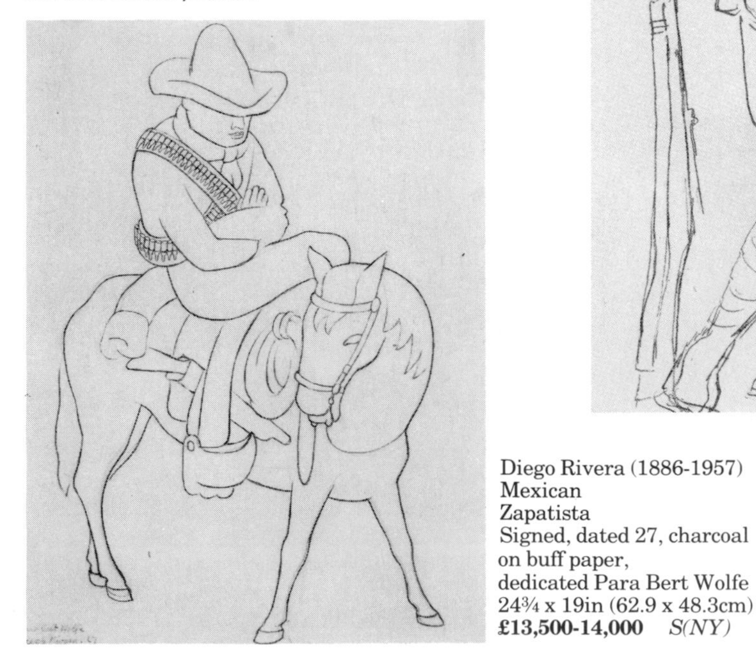

Diego Rivera (1886-1957)
Mexican
Zapatista
Signed, dated 27, charcoal on buff paper,
dedicated Para Bert Wolfe
24¾ x 19in (62.9 x 48.3cm)
£13,500-14,000 *S(NY)*

Augustus John (1878-1961)
British
A Canadian Soldier holding a Rifle
Pen and black ink on beige paper, c1917
13¾ x 9in (35 x 23cm)
£2,100-2,400 *C*

LAWYERS

Lawyers are a frequently recurring theme in pictures, and are unsurprisingly popular with satirists. Perhaps the greatest of these was Daumier whose political cartoons brought him into conflict with the law (he was imprisoned for six months) and he was renowned for his grotesque and brilliant portrayals of Parisian lawyers. 'Every little meanness, every absurdity, every quirk of the intellect, every vice of the heart can be clearly seen and read in these animalised faces,' wrote Baudelaire feelingly, having himself suffered at legal hands when he was tried for obscenity on account of his poems.

Robert Dighton (1752-1814)
British
A Lawyer and his Agent
Signed, pen and ink and watercolour
12⅝ x 10in (32.1 x 25.3cm)
£1,400-1,700 *C*

Thierry Poncelet (20thC)
Belgian
The Family Lawyer
Oil
38½ x 32½in (98 x 82.5cm)
£3,300-3,500 *HOP*

Honoré Daumier (1808-79)
French
Avant L'Audience
Signed with initials, charcoal, pen and brush and Indian ink, pastel and watercolour on paper laid down on card
15 x 11in (38 x 28.5cm)
£135,000-150,000 *S*

Honoré Daumier (1808-79)
French
Après L'Audience
Signed, charcoal, pen and ink and watercolour on paper laid down on paper
11⅜ x 14⅛in (29 x 35.8cm)
£375,000-400,000 *S*

MONKS AND CARDINALS

Monks and cardinals were a popular subject with 19thC genre painters. Almost invariably these men of the spirit are shown heartily involved in the pleasures of the flesh: eating, drinking or otherwise enjoying themselves. Whilst cardinals inhabit apartments of opulent gilt and splendour, bursting with pictures and costly objects, monks are shown in the monastery kitchen or in simple chambers – yet both are united in their single-minded pursuit of pleasure and their apparently total disinterest in religious duty.

Frank Moss Bennett (1874-1953) British
Under Suspicion Signed, oil on canvas
24 x 36in (61 x 91.5cm) **£12,700-13,500** *C*

François Brunery (19thC)
French
A Wrong Note
Signed, oil on canvas
32 x 39¼in (81 x 100cm)
£38,000-45,000 *S*

Victor Marais Milton (1872-?) French
La Sieste
Signed, watercolour
13½ x 10½in (34 x 26cm)
£1,600-1,800 *S*

Salvatore Marchesi (1852-1926)
Italian
In the Sacristy
Signed, oil on canvas
41 x 26½in (104 x 67cm)
£13,300-14,000 *S*

Marc Thedy (1858-1924) German
The Solo Performance Signed, oil on panel
15¼ x 19¼in (38.5 x 49cm)
£1,200-1,500 *S(S)*

VICTORIAN ROMANS AND THE CLASSICAL GENRE PAINTERS

For many 19th and early 20thC artists, portraying history was more a question of dressing up the present than recreating the past. The classical genre painter popularised antiquity, making it accessible and anecdotal. Pictures are filled with Victorians in togas: creamy skinned beauties and curly headed infants. Roman matrons lounge in their living rooms and shop in the High Street (see Colour Review), mirroring the daily lives of their Victorian counterparts with all the glistening of marble and lovingly reproduced archaeological details.

John William Godward (1861-1922) British
The Tambourine Girl
Signed and dated 1906, oil on canvas
45 x 30in (114.5 x 76cm)
£45,000-50,000 *S*

Clemens von Pausinger (1855-1936)
Austrian
The Tambourine Girl
Signed and dated Vindobona '91, pastel on panel
27½ x 21¼in (70 x 54cm)
£4,200-4,500 *S*

Stephan Bakalowicz (1857-?)
Russian
A Roman Garden
Signed and dated MCMXIX, oil on canvas
25 x 18in (63.5 x 45.7cm)
£4,500-5,000 *C*

After Frederic Lord Leighton (1830-96)
British
Fatidica
Photogravure, signed in pencil, published by Thomas Agnew & Sons, 1895
22 x 15¾in (55.8 x 40cm)
£380-450 *Bon*

ORIENTALIST PAINTERS AND PICTURES

The Arab world exercised a powerful fascination for 19thC western artists, and the majority of works in this section belong to this period. The pioneer Orientalists who visited the Near and Middle East in the first part of the century were followed by a stream of European painters in search of new and exotic subjects. 'The journey to Algeria has become as indispensable to painters as the pilgrimage to Italy,' wrote the French critic Theophile Gautier. 'There they will learn about the sun, study the light, find original characters, customs and primitive Biblical attitudes.'
It was not only daily life in the souks and deserts that attracted artists and their patrons, but the hidden world of the harem. Since this was by its very nature unpenetrable, artistic imagination ran riot to create decorative and erotic visions of Oriental delight. As writers Philip Hook and Mark Poltimore note (see Biblio), Muslim women were forbidden to sit for artists – most of the exotic ladies portrayed were European models disguised in Eastern accessories, and many artists were happy to portray these popular and sensationalised scenes of Oriental life without ever leaving their studios in London, Paris or Munich.

In the manner of Carle van Loo (1705-65) French
A Sultan and his Harem being entertained by a Dancer on a Garden Terrace 18¾ x 22¼in (47.6 x 56.5cm)
£5,600-6,000 *C*

18thC Follower of Antonio Tempesta (1555-1630) Italian
Turks Hunting Lions; Moors Hunting Leopards
Oil on canvas, a pair
38¼ x 52½in (97.5 x 133.5cm)
£28,000-33,000 *S*

Hercules Brabazon Brabazon (1821-1906) French
The Vegetable Market at Kaironomi
Signed with initials, watercolour and bodycolour over pencil on grey paper
6¾ x 9½in (17 x 24cm)
£1,200-1,500 *S*

Frederic Goupil (19thC) French
The Sultan's Favourites
Signed, pencil and watercolour
10¼ x 14¼in (26 x 36cm)
£1,100-1,300 *CSK*

Elisabeth Jerichau-Baumann (1819-81) Polish
An Oriental Beauty
Signed, oil on canvas
38½ x 28½in (97 x 72.5cm)
£3,000-3,300 *S(Am)*

Joseph Austin Benwell (active 2nd half 19thC)
An Arab Caravan
Signed and dated 1873, watercolour
10½ x 19in (26.5 x 48cm)
£650-750 *Bon*

James Shaw Crompton (1853-1916)
British
An Arab Warrior
Signed and dated 1885
13¾ x 9¼in (35 x 23.5cm)
£900-1,000
S(S)

George Spencer Cautley (1807-80)
British
Grass Boats on the Nile
Watercolour
5 x 7in (12.7 x 17.7cm)
£275-300 *MS*

Almost by accident, the dealer Mark Senior purchased an album of Oriental watercolours by this long forgotten 19thC artist, ignored by most of the standard reference books. In looking into his past, Senior uncovered a fascinating story. Cautley was a dwarf and a hunchback and chaplain to the Marquis of Northampton, who sent him to the East in order to prepare the ground for his own grand tour. Cautley was a remarkable character – a member both ot the clergy and of the Rosicrucians (a society of mystics, alchemists and occultists). He was, amongst many other things, an artist, a scholar, a renowned expert on symbology and a mentor of the Pre-Raphaelites, coming into contact with many of the leading artists and personages of the period. Cautley's life merits a book rather than a paragraph and demonstrates the value of research.

Attributed to Benjamin Constant (1845-1902)
French
A Harem Beauty
Bears signature, oil on canvas
38 x 45¼in (96.5 x 114.9cm)
£8,000-8,500 *S(NY)*

Alfred Choubrac (1853-1902)
French
Mourning the Deceased
Signed and dated 1879, oil on canvas
50¾ x 35¾in (129 x 91cm)
£4,500-5,000 *S*

An example of one of the more ridiculous Oriental fantasies – a bare bottom scarcely being a traditional way of presenting one's respects to the dead.

Cyril Hardy (active 1900-20)
British
An Old Mosque, Morocco, and Mosques of Arabia
Signed, a pair
10¾ x 7¼in (27 x 18cm)
£400-500 *AG*

Frederick William Jackson (1859-1918)
British
Tangier
Signed, watercolour
10¼ x 14¼in (26 x 36cm)
£1,050-1,250 *S*

Jean-Baptiste-Paul Lazerges (1845-1902) French
An Arab Encampment by Moonlight
Signed, oil on canvas
32 x 39¼in (81.3 x 99.7cm)
£3,900-4,300 *C*

Alexander-Louis Leloir (1843-84) French
La Belle Exotique
Signed and dated 76, pencil and watercolour heightened with white on card
10 x 13in (25.3 x 33cm)
£3,600-4,000 *C*

The fashion for the Orient spilled over into portrayals of Parisian demi-mondaines in the later half of the 19thC. Ladies recline in luxurious boudoirs filled with Persian carpets and rich textiles, Turkish slippers dangling from provocatively naked feet, their languorous bodies draped in soft and revealing silks. Feminine, decorative and sensuous, these pictures presented their purchasers with a Western version of the harem.

H*** Pinggera (19th/20thC)
Continental
In a Babylonian Court
Signed indistinctly, oil on canvas
37¾ x 55½in (96 x 141cm)
£3,600-3,900 *S*

Ettore Simonetti (19thC)
Italian
Trying on Shoes
Signed and inscribed Roma, watercolour on paper
30 x 21½in (76.2 x 54.6cm)
£10,300-11,000 *S(NY)*

Count Preziosi Amadeo (1816-82)
Italian
Turkish Warriors
Signed and dated 1854, pencil and watercolour heightened with white on paper,
20½ x 17¼in (52 x 43.8cm)
£4,700-5,000 *C*

Dennis Syrett (20thC)
British
Wadi Feran
Oil
38 x 26in (96.5 x 66cm)
£1,300-1,500 *PHG*

Geoffrey Squire (20thC)
British
Sheherazade
Signed, oil on canvas, 1991
£4,800-5,000 *OEG*

NUDES

Throughout history, artists painting the nude have 'dressed up' their chosen subject in a variety of different guises. In a moral climate where a straight nude was rude, a naked Classical nymph was considered perfectly acceptable. Mythology provided an extensive cast list of gods and goddesses and endless story lines from rape to Bacchic revelry; the Bible was an equally rich source of sanctified nude scenes (Adam and Eve, Susanna and the Elders), whilst generalised allegorical themes such as 'Time Revealed by Truth' (see p443) gave a serious cover to a saucy subject.

For Victorian artists, pictures of the antique past or the mysterious East provided further opportunities to portray scantily clad women lounging in Oriental harems and splashing in Roman baths. Nudes were acceptable so long as they were distanced either geographically or historically from everyday life, and provided that their bodies maintained the smooth and perfect hairlessness of Classical statues. It was only in the late 19thC that portrayals of nudes in contemporary surroundings began to be more commonplace.

After Titian, Italian School (17thC)
Venus and an Organist
Oil on canvas
40¾ x 58½in (103.5 x 148.5cm)
£2,200-2,500 *Bon*

Circle of Michelangelo Buonarroti (1475-1564) Italian
Two Nudes, after the central section of the Battle of Cascina
Pen and brown ink, on vellum
11¾ x 7½in (30.1 x 19.8cm)
£7,800-8,300 *C*

Emilian School (c1520)
Italian
Bacchus
With inscription '44' partly erased, pen and brown ink
5½ x 5in (13.4 x 12.4cm)
£3,400-3,700 *C*

Circle of Joseph van Aken (1709-49)
A Musical Soirée
Oil on canvas
24½ x 29½in (62 x 74cm)
£2,600-2,900 *S*

Girolamo Francesco Maria Mazzola, il Parmigianino (1503-40) Italian
Two Lovers
With inscriptions in a 16thC hand of a draft of a letter (verso), pen and brown ink
5½ x 6in (13.1 x 15.2cm)
£35,500-40,500 *C*

A number of drawings by Parmigianino dating from this period, after his return to his native Parma, reveal a similar taste for amorous subject matter: it certainly appealed to patrons such as the Cavaliere Baiardo, for whom he painted his Cupid, now in the Kunsthistorisches Museum, Vienna. The picture boasts an impressive provenance having belonged to artists Sir Peter Lely, Richard Cosway and Sir Thomas Lawrence.

Giacinto Calandrucci (1646-1707) Italian
Studies of a Female Nude
10½ x 16½in (27 x 42.1cm)
£2,100-2,400 *C*

Red and white chalk on blue paper

Circle of Giovanni Antonio Pellegrini (1675-1741)
Italian
Eve (?)
20⅝ x 16½in (52.4 x 41.9cm)
£1,400-1,600 *C*

Johann Heinrich Füssli, Henry Fuseli (1741-1825)
Swiss
Haman, after Michelangelo
Signed, pen and grey ink
14½ x 9½in (37 x 24.4cm)
£12,200-13,000 *C*

In January 1992, a man walked into Christie's with an album containing 58 hitherto unknown drawings by Henry Fuseli, the collection covering nearly every aspect of the artist's career and subject matter. The man, a civil engineer in his sixties, was no art historian but had purchased the book some 15 years previously from a coin dealer without knowing what it was, because he liked the drawings and recognised their quality. It proved a wise purchase since the sale of the drawings at Christie's on 14th April 1992 made a total sum of £748,440.

Pieter van der Werff (1665-1722)
Dutch
Adam and Eve in the Garden of Eden
Oil on panel
18½ x 16in (46.8 x 40.5cm)
£3,900-4,200 *S*

The subject of Adam and Eve was tailor-made for the study of the nude.

French School (18thC)
Naked Female Bathers Cavorting Around a Swing
Gouache
11¾ x 8¾in (30.4 x 22.2cm)
£450-550 *S*

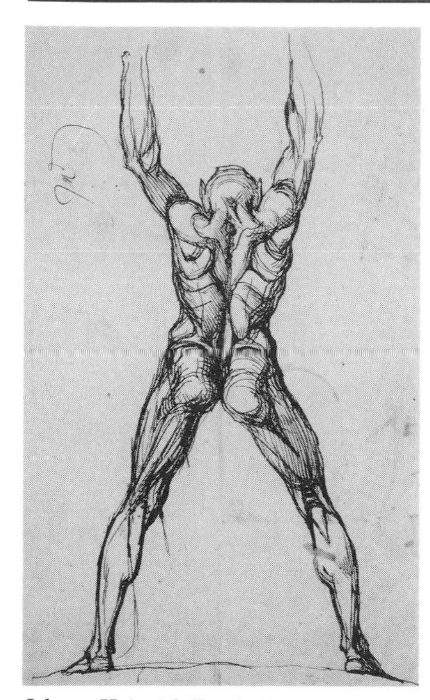

Johann Heinrich Füssli, Henry Fuseli (1741- 1825)
Swiss
A Nude with Raised Arms seen from behind
Inscribed 'In'd', pen and brown ink
12½ x 7½in (31.4 x 19cm)
£7,200-7,600 *C*

Mattias Terwesten (1670-1757)
Dutch
Time Revealing Truth
Oil on canvas
49¼ x 39½in (125 x 100cm)
£6,300-6,700 *S(NY)*

19th Century

Frank Bramley (1857-1915)
British
Boys Bathing by a Fire
Inscribed on label attached to reverse 'Study of boys by Frank Bramley, RA, 1896, to Launce Armstrong from Katherine Bramley, March 1927,' on unstretched canvas
14 x 12¾in (35.5 x 32.5cm)
£2,700-3,000 *S(S)*

William Stephen Coleman (1829-1904)
British
The Young Bather
Watercolour
8 x 6in (20 x 15cm)
£1,800-2,000 *MS*

Paul Cézanne (1839-1906)
French
The Small Bathers (Venturi 1156, Druick III, Johnson 22)
Lithograph printed in colours, 1896-97
8¾ x 10⅝in (22.2 x 27.1cm)
£7,500-8,000 *S(NY)*

Delphin Enjolras (1857-?)
French
A Nude by Firelight
Signed, pastel
28 x 20in (71 x 51cm)
£4,200-4,500 *S*

Louis Welden Hawkins (1849-1910)
English/French
Les Aureoles
Signed, oil on canvas
24 x 19¾in (61 x 50cm)
£13,300-14,000 *S*

Continental School (19thC)
Touché
Oil on canvas, a pair
10¾ x 15¾in (27.3 x 39.7cm)
£850-950 *Bon*

William Etty (1787-1849)
British
The Bathers
24 x 20in (60.9 x 50.8cm)
£2,000-2,300 *C*

Franz Bohumil Doubek (1865-?)
Czech
Sleeping Cupid Discovered by Nymphs
Signed, oil on canvas
19 x 27¾in (48.2 x 70.5cm)
£3,900-4,300 *CSK*

French School (19thC)
Leda and the Swan
Lithograph with original hand colouring
Published France 1859
£300-350 *Lan*

L. ** Faille (19th/20thC)
Continental
Too Hot to Handle
Oil on canvas
22 x 35½in (55.8 x 90.2cm)
£1,300-1,500 *Bon*

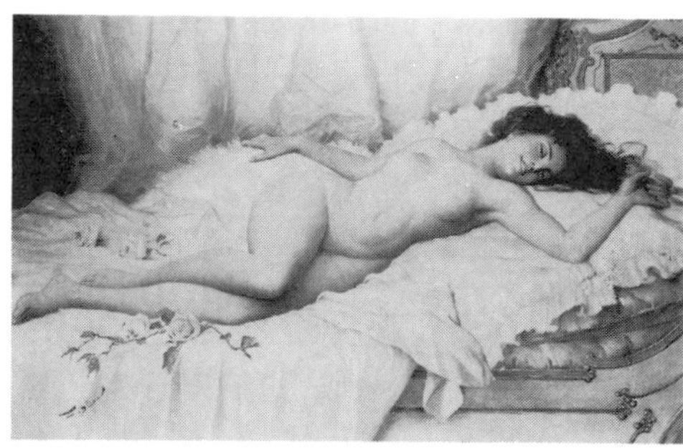

F. Olivoe (19thC)
Spanish?
A Young Beauty Reclining on a Bed
Signed, oil on canvas
27 x 41½in (68.6 x 105.4cm)
£4,100-4,500 *CSK*

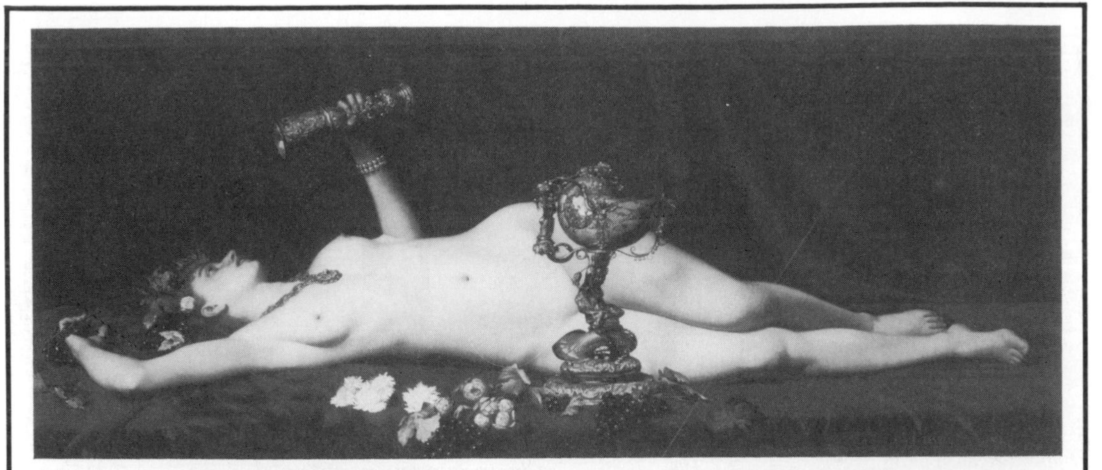

Adolphe Alexandre Lesrel (1839-90)
French
Bacchante Enivrée
Signed and dated 1882, oil on canvas
34½ x 78¾in (87 x 200cm)
£14,300-15,000 *S(NY)*

Classical and Oriental subjects and genre pictures provided a convenient excuse for the portrayal of the nude. Here the artist makes the most of his props. The nautilus shell cup adds an element of opulent luxury and scene setting, offering a certain amount of concealment (albeit somewhat inadequate), while at the same time drawing the eye to the centre of the canvas.

Jean-Baptiste Mallet (1795-1835)
French
Une Nymphe au Bain, Environnée d'Amours
Oil on canvas
15 x 18in (38.1 x 45.7cm)
£15,000-16,000 *S(NY)*

Charles Lucien Moulin (19thC)
French
Baigneuses à la Tresse
Signed, oil on canvas
67¾ x 28in (172 x 71.1cm)
£4,600-5,000 *S(NY)*

Sir Edward John Poynter (1836-1919)
British
A Study for the 'Cave of the Storm Nymphs'
Signed with initials, dated 1901, black and white chalk on grey paper
11¼ x 18⅛in (28.6 x 46cm)
£1,300-1,600 *C*

Pierre-Auguste Renoir (1841-1919) French
Les Baigneuses
Signed, oil on canvas
13⅜ x 18⅛in (34 x 46cm)
£170,000-200,000 *S*

'My aim has always been to paint people as if they were luscious fruits,' claimed Renoir. For the artist the nude was a key subject – he produced many paintings of nudes and bathers, taking a sensual delight in the powerful female body ('I always caress the buttocks for days and days before finishing a canvas,' he reportedly told Modigliani, and appreciating texture and colour as much as form. 'I have a horror of the word flesh . . . what I love is skin; a young girl's skin that is pink and shows that she has a good circulation.'

Martinez Tudela (late 19thC) Spanish?
A Reclining Nude
Signed and inscribed, oil on board
7¼ x 10in (19.7 x 25.4cm)
£2,700-3,000 . *C*

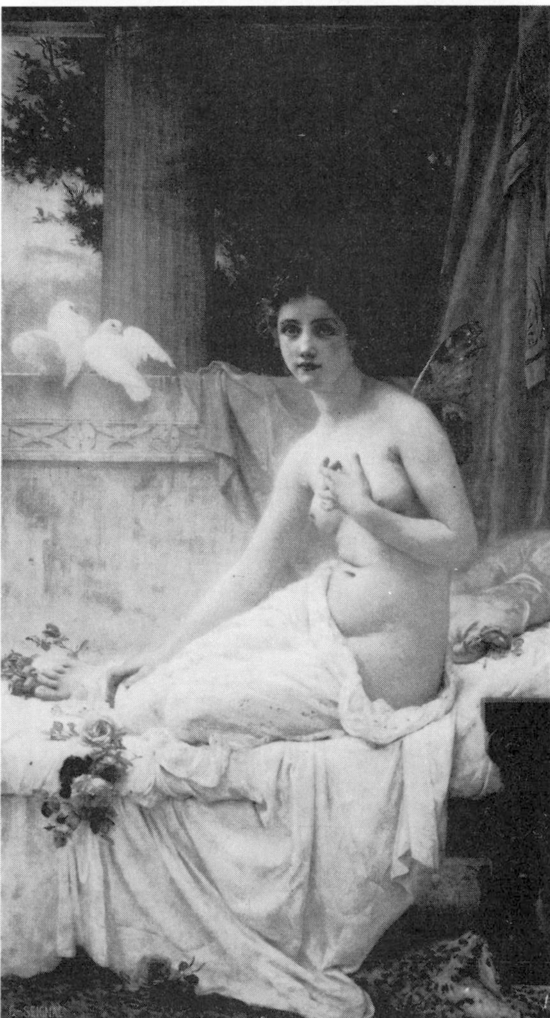

Guillaume Seignac (1870-1924)
French
Psyche
Signed, oil on canvas
69¼ x 38in (175.9 x 96.5cm)
£58,000-70,000 *S(NY)*

Pierre-Auguste Renoir (1841-1919)
French
Baigneuses dans La Forêt
Signed, pencil on buff paper laid down on paper
24¾ x 38⅜in (63 x 97.5cm)
£80,000-90,000 *S*

Executed c1895-97, this drawing relates closely to the painting of the same title dated 1897, in the Barnes Collection, Philadelphia.

20th Century

Alexander Archipenko (1887-1964)
Russian
Two Female Nudes (Karshan 25)
Lithograph, 1921-22, signed in pencil and numbered 42/110
14⅛ x 11⅛in (36 x 28.3cm)
£1,300-1,500 *S(NY)*

Condition is a major factor in a picture's price

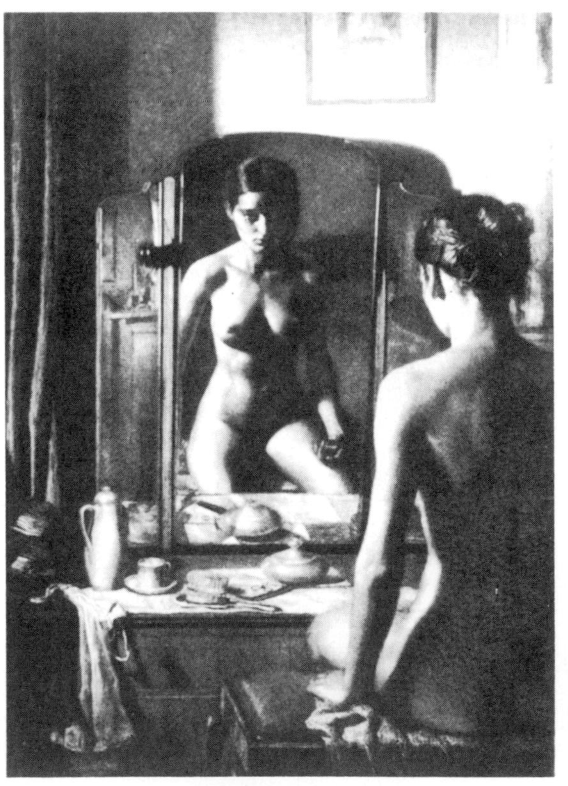

Gerald Leslie Brockhurst (1890-1978)
British
Adolescence (Fletcher 75)
Etching, 1932
14⅜ x 10⅜in (36.6 x 26.4cm)
£5,100-5,500 *S(NY)*

Edmund Blampied (1886-1966)
French
He's Married Six Times
Inscribed, pen and black ink; and two further drawings
4¾ x 7¼in (12 x 18.5cm)
£450-550 *C*

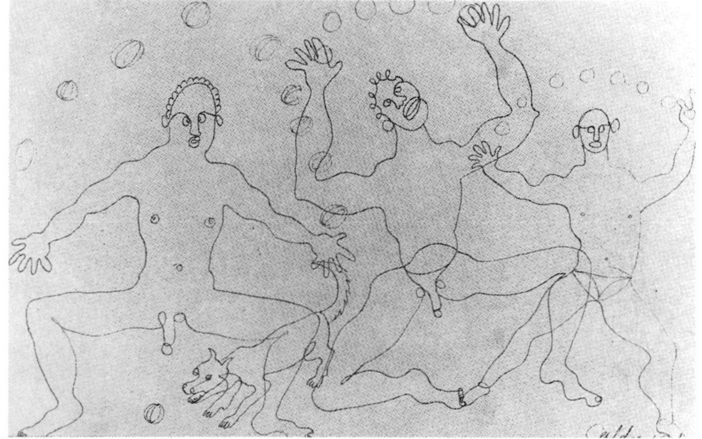

Alexander Calder (1898-1976)
American
Jugglers
Signed and dated '31,
pen and ink on buff paper
11 x 17in (28 x 43cm)
£2,400-2,800 *Bon*

Joannès B. Chaleye (1878-?)
French
Nude Standing by River
Signed, oil on canvas
15 x 21½in (38.5 x 54cm)
£650-750 *Cae*

Giorgio de Chirico (1888-1978)
Italian
Ninfa che Riposa (c1958)
Signed and inscribed, oil on canvas
19½ x 23½in (50 x 60cm)
£22,000-26,000 *C(R)*

Salvador Dali (1904-89) Spanish
Femme Nue Allongée
Brush with grey and brown washes on paper
14½ x 20¾in (36.8 x 52.7cm)
£4,600-5,000 *S(NY)*

Paul Delvaux (1897-?)
Belgian
The Garden (J.47)
Lithograph 1971, signed in pencil and numbered 5/50
22 x 30in (56 x 76cm)
£2,400-2,700 *S(NY)*

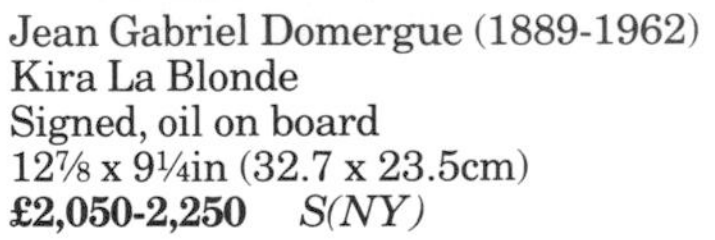

Jean Gabriel Domergue (1889-1962)
Kira La Blonde
Signed, oil on board
12⅞ x 9¼in (32.7 x 23.5cm)
£2,050-2,250 *S(NY)*

Ludwig Fahrenkrog (1867-1915)
German
Die Heilige Stunde (The Holy Hour)
Signed and dated 1911, oil on canvas
66 x 103¾in (167.6 x 263.5cm)
£5,000-5,400 *C*

Eric Fischl (20thC)
Study for Sleepwalker, 1979
Oil on three sheets of overlapping glassine
75 x 73¾in (190.5 x 187.3cm)
£40,000-45,000 *S(NY*

The only one of the artist's early glassine drawings to evolve into a major painting, Sleepwalker foreshadows many of Fischl's most important themes such as the child coming of age, the exploration of sexual taboos, and the psychological tension among family members. In Sleepwalker, the masturbating boy becomes a symbol for the nakedness and vulnerability of the artist and his public exploration of heretofore forbidden ideas. 'I wanted to make a painting that would deal with the taboo and be quasipornographic,' Fischl explained. 'I painted this sympathetic image of a profound moment in a child's psychological and sexual life.'

John Duncan Fergusson (1874-1961)
British
Female Nude, and another, Seated Female Nude
Watercolours
6⅞ x 4⅜in (17 x 11cm) and 7¼ x 5¼in (18.5 x 13.5cm)
£1,500-1,800 *C(S)*

Odette Dumaret (1913)
French
La Toilette, 1987
28 x 23in (71.1 x 58.4cm)
£3,400-3,500 *CE*

Jacob Epstein (1880-1959)
British
Seated Nude
Pencil drawing, c 1929
26 x 22in (66 x 56cm)
£3,700-3,800 *BOU*

RUSSELL FLINT

'Russell Flint is so universally popular, he will always sell,' explains Caroline Oliphant, who pioneered the specialist Russell Flint sales at Bonhams in 1989. 'In a bull market, he will make exorbitant prices and even in a recession, though there are fewer people in the running for more expensive pictures, pieces under £10,000 are selling like hot cakes.' Flint sales always inspire strong interest from private buyers. The high price of watercolours has increased the demand for sketches and prints. Prints are available from only a few hundred pounds, though as Oliphant advises, it is important not to buy indiscriminately. 'Beware of faded prints and the more commonplace reproductions,' she warns.

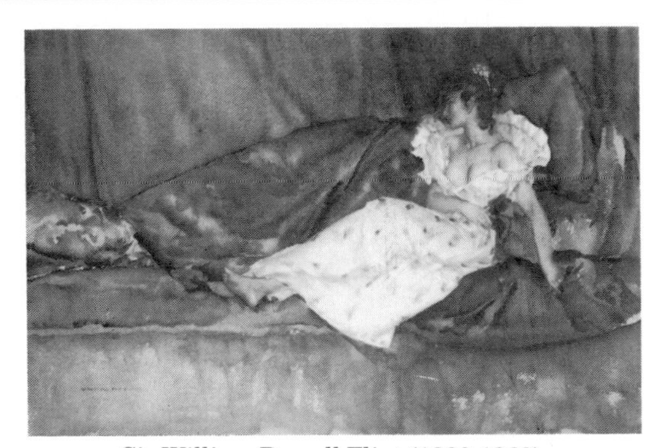

Sir William Russell Flint (1880-1969)
British
Alexia
Signed, inscribed and dated 1958, watercolour
13½ x 20in (34.2 x 50.8cm)
£16,500-18,500 *Bon*

Sir William Russell Flint (1880-1969) British
The Sentimental Blonde Signed, watercolour
19½ x 26½in (50 x 67cm)
£14,600-15,600 *S*

Sir William Russell Flint (1880-1969)
British
Study of Reclining Nude
Signed, coloured chalks
7⅜ x 12½in (18.7 x 31.8cm)
£2,700-3,000 *Bon*

Sir William Russell Flint (1880-1969)
British
Ray
Signed, red chalk on grey paper
11½ x 17in (29 x 43cm)
£5,300-5,800 *S*

Sir William Russell Flint (1880-1969)
British
Reclining Nude III
Reproduction in colours, 146/850
15¼ x 23¾in (38.7 x 60.3cm)
£950-1,100 *Bon*

Colin Hutcheon Gibson (1907-?)
British
Life Study, the Artist's Wife
Signed and inscribed, sangurine heightened
14 x 11in (35.5 x 28cm)
£260-280 *SCG*

Jean Souverbie (1891-)
French
Repose by the Sea
Signed, oil on canvas
19¾ x 24in (50.2 x 61cm)
£5,400-6,000 *S(NY)*

Duncan Grant (1885-1978) British
Seated Nude, c1934
Pastel and watercolour
18½ x 23½in (47 x 60cm)
£3,800-4,200 *S*

Gottfried Hofer (1858-1932)
German
Male Nudes by a River in an Alpine Landscape
Signed and dated 1902, oil on canvas
94½ x 75in (240 x 190.5cm)
£3,500-4,000 *C*

George Grosz (1893-1959)
German
Nudo (1935-40)
Signed, oil on paper
24 x 18¾in (64 x 48cm)
£4,500-5,000 *C(R)*

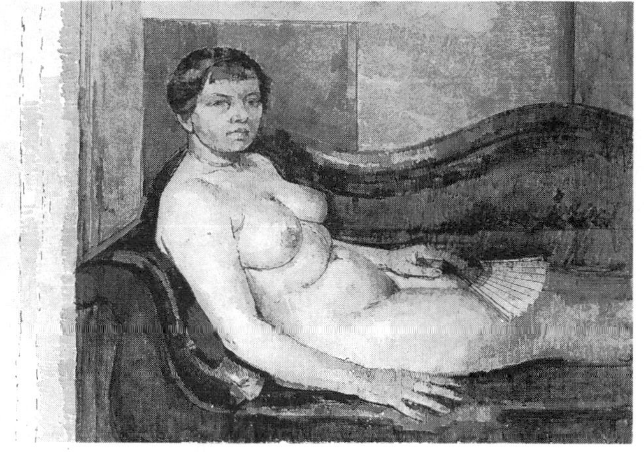

Sir Roger de Grey (1918-) British
Girl with a Fan Signed, oil on canvas
30 x 42in (76 x 107cm) **£950-1,050** *C*

Johfra (1919-1936)
Dutch
Mythological Figure
Signed, oil on panel
26¾ x 19½in (67.9 x 49.5cm)
£1,500-1,800 *S(NY)*

Ethelbert White (1891-1972)
British
The Artist's Wife
Signed, oil on canvas
21 x 25in (53.5 x 63.8cm)
£1,400-1,600 *GG*

Mark Gertler (1891-1939)
British
Adolescence
Signed and dated 1922, oil on canvas
30 x 20in (76 x 51cm)
£7,100-7,600 *S*

Robert King (1936-) British
Morning Sunlight
Signed, gouache
31¾ x 24¾in (80.6 x 62.8cm)
£3,000-3,250 *BuP*

Dora Holzhandler (20thC)
The Lovers
Signed, coloured pencil on paper
12 x 16in (31 x 41cm)
£350-400 *HG*

Phyllis Mahon (20thC)
In the Pursuit of Passion (detail)
Linoprint, 1989
20 x 60in (51 x 152cm)
£230-250 *LG*

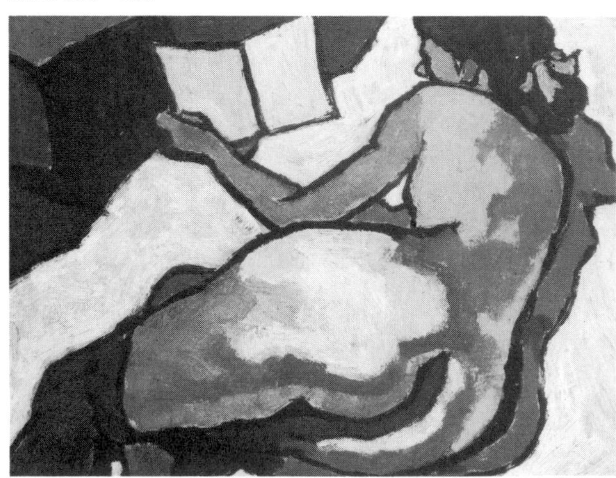

Cyril Mann (1911-1980)
British
Nude Reading, c1952
Oil on canvas
16 x 12in (40.5 x 30.5cm)
£5,300-5,600 *HG*

Yves Klein (1928-62)
French
Venus Bleue
Synthetic resin on plaster, numbered 13/300, 1982
27⅞in (68.2cm) high
£13,500-15,000 *S(NY)*
This blue Venus demonstrates Klein's fascination with monochrome works. His preferred colour was blue; 'blue has no dimensions, it is beyond dimensions,' he explained. 'All colours arouse specific associative ideas, psychologically material or tangible, while blue suggests at most the sea and sky, and they, after all, are in actual visible nature what is most abstract.' Klein, one of the leaders of the European Neo-Dada movement, was a gifted showman and performance artist. In 1960, he created a sensation with his first public exhibition of Anthropometries (imprints of the human body) in which girls smeared with blue pigment were dragged over canvas laid on the floor to the accompaniment of his Symphonie monotone, a composition in which a single note, played for ten minutes, alternated with ten minutes silence.

Ken Howard (1932)
British
Seated Nude in the Studio
Signed, oil on canvas
24 x 20in (61 x 51cm)
£3,900-4,300 *C*

Alexander Kreapin (20thC)
Maiden with Llama and Flowering Cactus
Pastel on paper
42¼ x 27⅛in (107.3 x 68.9cm)
£1,300-1,500 *S(NY)*

John Matthews (1920-)
British
Reclining Nude
Charcoal
£300-350 *A*

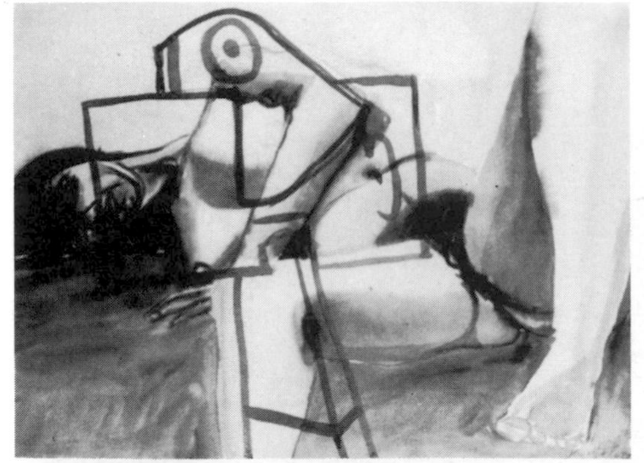

David Salle (20thC) Untitled
Signed and dated 84, watercolour on paper
18 x 24in (45.7 x 61cm)
£4,000-5,000 *S(NY)*

Willy Schlobach (1865-1951) Belgian
Les Eléments en Mouvement
Signed with monogram and dated 1900, oil on canvas
56 x 73in (142.3 x 185.5cm)
£5,000-5,500 *C*

George Sheridan (20thC)
British
Two Graces
Gouache
25¼ x 33in (64 x 84cm)
£2,800-3,000 *HOP*

Julian Schnabel (1951-)
American
Bob's Worlds
Oil, wax, bondo, and horns on wood and canvas
97½ x 146 x 12in
(247 x 370.8 x 30.5cm)
£166,000-180,000 *S(NY)*

Painted in 1980, Bob's Worlds boldly represents Schnabel's concern with a painting's surface to create a more physical view of the images. Through the artist's use of a three-dimensional support upon which he adheres objects such as broken plates and horns, he creates a 'surface aggression' more intensely than any previous artist. Bob's Worlds exhibits all the elements of the artist's famous plate paintings which captured the attention of the art world in the early 1980s.

Sir Matthew Smith (1879-1959)
British
Draped Nude
Oil on canvas
24 x 29in (61 x 73.5cm)
£13,300-14,500 *S*

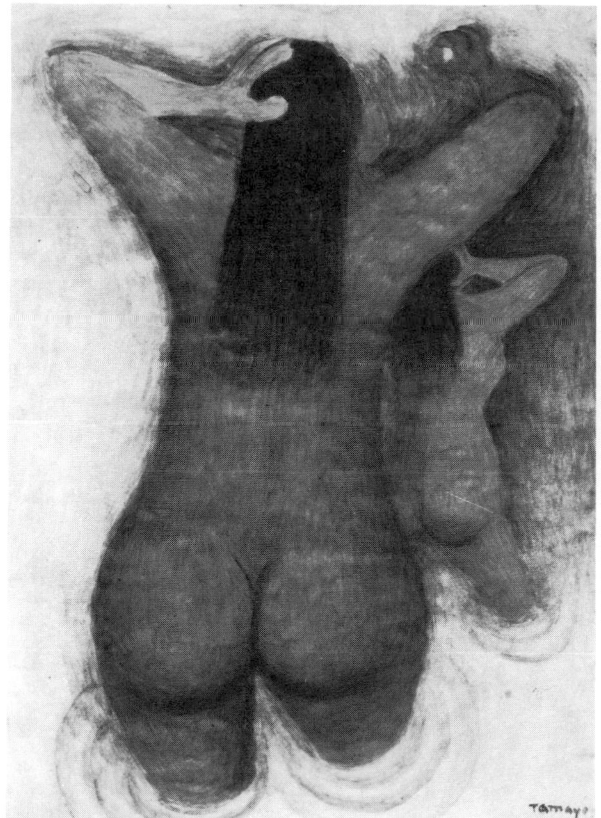

Rufino Tamayo (1899-) Mexican
Bañistas
Signed, gouache on paper, c1935, mounted on board
24¾ x 18½in (62.9 x 47cm)
£35,000-40,000 *S(NY)*

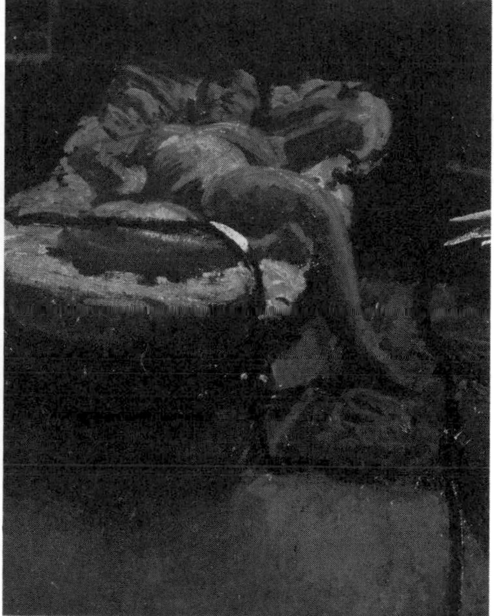

Walter Richard Sickert (1860-1942) British
Nuit d'Eté Oil on canvas, c1906
20 x 16in (51 x 41cm)
£42,000-50,000 *S*

The present work relates to a series of nudes painted by Sickert in the early 1900s. Reacting against the tradition of posed figures in elegant settings ('Taste is the death of a painter,' declared Sickert), his nudes are laid out in dingy bedrooms, their foreshortened bodies sprawling casually on rumpled draperies. Paint is grainy and sensuous colours muted and dull and the lighting subtly dramatic, revealing the nude in the words of Degas, Sickert's great mentor, 'as though seen through a keyhole'.

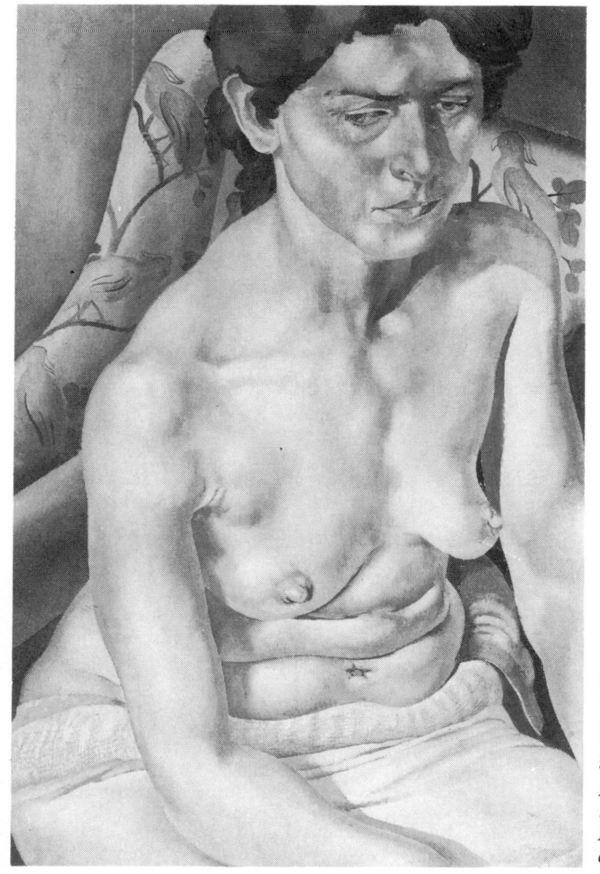

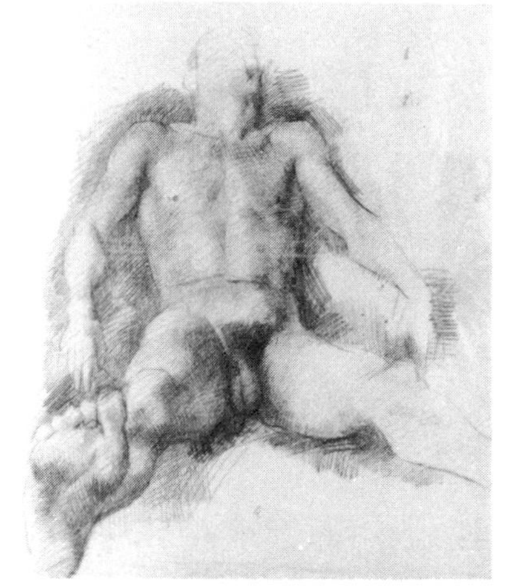

Pavel Tchelitchew (1898-1957)
Russian
Study of a Male Nude
Stamped with signature verso, pencil and crayon on tissue
22 x 17¼in (55.9 x 43.8cm)
£2,100-2,500 *S(NY)*

Sir Stanley Spencer (1891-1959)
British
Seated Nude
Oil on canvas, 30 x 20in (76 x 51cm)
£225,000-250,000 *S*

Painted in the last few months of 1936, this work is Spencer's only nude portrait of his first wife, Hilda, painted when they were already living apart.

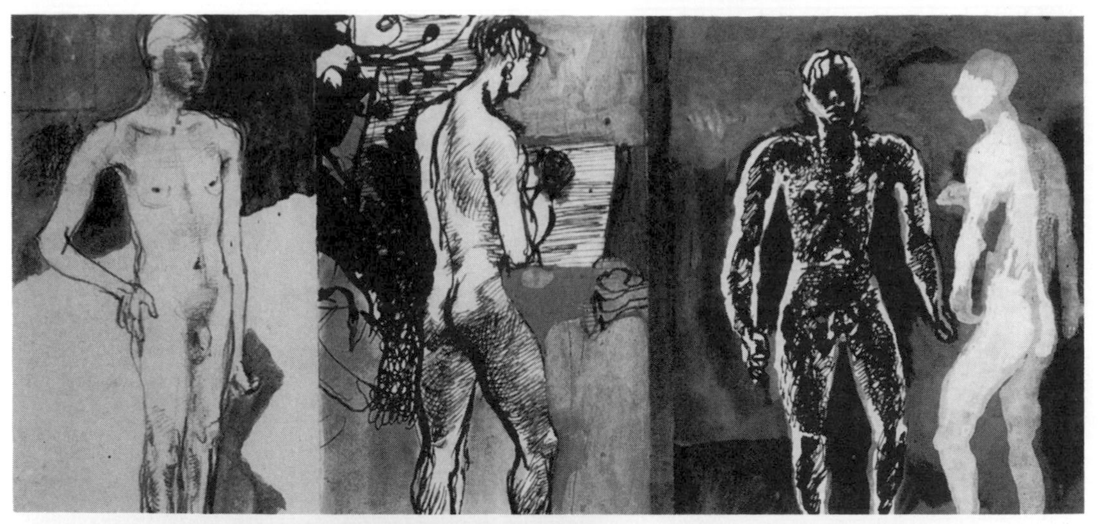

Keith Vaughn (1912-77)
British
Triptych of Figure Studies
Pencil, pen and black ink, watercolour and gouache
5 x 11in (13 x 28cm)
£2,400-2,700 *S*

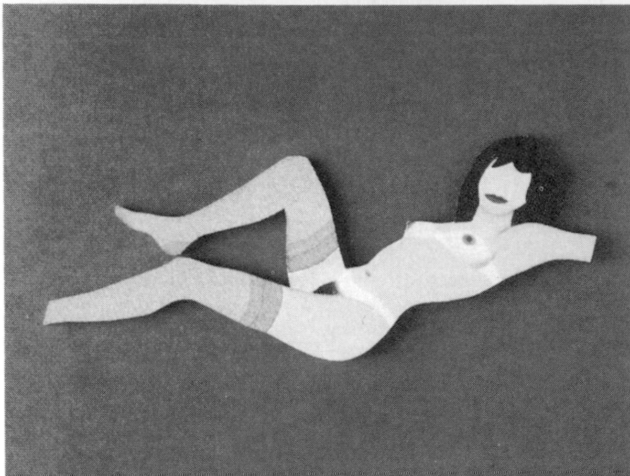

Tom Wesselmann (1931-)
Study for Reclining Stockinged Nude
Signed, titled and dated 81 on reverse, oil on canvas laid down on board
6½ x 15¼in (16.5 x 38.7cm)
£8,000-8,500 *S(NY)*

Pavel Tchelitchew (1898-1957)
Russian
Study for the One Who Fell
Signed on the reverse, gouache on paper
25½ x 19¾in (64.8 x 50.2cm)
£4,500-4,800 *S(NY)*

Edward Wolfe (1877-1981) British
Two Mexican Boys
Signed, pastel
33 x 24in (84 x 63.5cm)
£1,000-1,200 *C*

RELIGIOUS AND MYTHOLOGICAL WORKS

As John Somerville, Sotheby's Director, notes: 'With Old Master pictures, be they mythological or religious, it is not the subject that is so important so much as artist, quality, rarity and condition. These factors and, of course, whether or not the work is fresh to the market are what determine the price. A gory and brutal religious scene such as Judith holding the severed head of Holofernes by a tenth rate artist will be difficult to sell, whereas the same subject by a great painter can easily go way over its estimate – generally speaking, subject is not the important issue.'

Perhaps one of the reasons for this is that many of us no longer possess the cultural vocabulary that allows us to recognise the stories and decode the symbols of much mythological and religious painting. If one looks up the tales behind the pictures, they can make gripping reading: classical soap operas bubbling over with sex and violence, the life of even the obscurest saint being often filled with so much horror and excitement as to make the adventures of today's popular icons, Rambo, Terminator and their ilk, seem positively gentle by comparison. Many of the pictures themselves were meant to be read like stories, and probably the best book to help one do this today is James Hall's Dictionary of Subjects and Symbols in Art (John Murray), a clear and user friendly guide to the classical myths, religious stories and secular themes that form the subject of so much Western art.

Flemish School (17thC)
Cupid (recto); Studies of a Basket and Drapery (verso)
Red and white chalk, on light brown paper
10 x 7⅜in (25.3 x 18.2cm)
£3,200-3,500 *S(NY)*

Circle of Giovanni Battista Piazzetta (1683-1754)
Italian
A Seated Faun
Black and white chalk, on light brown paper
21½ x 15½in (54.4 x 40cm)
£2,300-2,600 *C*

Alessandro Marchesini (1664-1738)
Italian
Phaethon Approaching his Father Apollo
Oil on canvas
34 x 43¼in (86.4 x 109.9cm)
£17,300-18,000 *S(NY)*

The subject is described in detail in Ovid's Metamorphoses. Phaethon, insulted by a friend who doubted his divine parentage, asks his father Apollo to be allowed to drive the Chariot of the Sun for one day, in order to prove his heritage to the world. Apollo reluctantly agrees and disaster ensues: Phaethon sets the world on fire, is sent hurtling to his death in a ball of flame, and his sisters weeping over his grave are turned into poplar trees. Phaethon himself became the symbol of all those who aspire to what they are incapable of achieving.

Circle of Abraham Bloemaert (1564-1651)
Dutch
Vertumnus and Pomona
Black chalk, pen and brown ink, brown wash heightened with white, on light grey paper
6¾ x 9in (17 x 22.8cm)
£450-550 *S(NY)*

Studio of Sebastiano Ricci (1659-1734)
Italian
The Childhood of Castor and Pollux
42⅞ x 37¾in (109 x 96cm)
£21,000-26,000 *C*

This picture derives from The Childhood of Romulus and Remus in the Hermitage Museum, datable to 1706-08. The most significant difference being the addition of the serving girl on the right carrying a dish with two eggs, symbolic of their birth, since the twins had hatched from the eggs laid by Leda after Jupiter, in the shape of a swan, had lain with her.

Herman van Swanevelt (1600-55) Dutch
A River Landscape with Venus and Adonis
Signed with monogram HVS, black chalk, grey wash, on vellum
7⅜ x 9in (20.1 x 22.8cm)
£2,900-3,200 *S(NY)*

Mariano Rossi (1731-1807) Italian
Cephalus and Procris
9 x 11⅝in (23 x 29.5cm)
£3,800-4,200 *C*

Pierre-Jean David d'Angers (1789-1856)
French
Venus and Cupid with Nymphs, after an antique bas relief
Inscribed twice on mount, black chalk, pen and grey ink, grey and green wash
3 x 11¾in (7.8 x 30cm)
£700-800 *C*

Circle of Pieter Coecke van Aelst (1502-50)
Dutch
January: Janus on a Chariot drawn by Owls and Ravens, accompanied by an Old Woman riding a Boar, Cripples and Peasants, Figures on a Frozen Lake and a Shipwreck Beyond
Inscribed Hans Holbein on the mount, pen and brown ink, grey wash
11½ x 11¼in (29.5 x 28.9cm)
£2,700-3,000 *C*

Bernadino Campi (1522-91)
Italian
Bacchus in a Niche
Black and red chalk, pen and brown ink, brown wash heightened with white
10 x 4½in (24.9 x 11.3cm)
£9,000-9,500 *C*

Circle of Jean Jacques Bachelier (1724-1806)
French
A trompe l'oeil of a Cat bursting through a picture of Putti at a Pond
19½ x 23½in (49.5 x 59.6cm)
£4,200-4,600 *C*

Giovanni Domenico Tiepolo (1727-1804)
Italian
A Centaur with a Nymph
Signed Dom Tiepolo f, black chalk, pen and brown ink, brown and grey wash
9¾ x 12in (25 x 31.2cm)
£7,800-8,300 *C*

Circle of Ignaz Stern, called Stella (1680-1748)
German
Glaucus and Scylla
50⅛ x 40½in (127.3 x 102.8cm)
£8,500-9,000 *C*

Flemish School (18thC)
A pair of Bacchic Scenes
One inscribed on verso, both gouache on vellum, laid down on board
8 x 12½in (20.5 x 32cm)
£1,900-2,300 *S*

Bacchic scenes were a popular subject because they sanctioned a liberal display of female flesh.

Circle of Jean-Auguste-Dominique Ingres (1780-1867)
French A Study after the Lapiths and the Centaurs from the Parthenon Inscribed, black lead
5 x 8in (12.5 x 20.7cm)
£800-900 *C*

Italian School (early 19thC)
A Mythological scene with the figure of Justice; and another with a figure of Mercury in front of Cybele
Oil on canvas, a pair
18½ x 48in (47 x 123cm)
£950-1,050 *S*

Florian Grospietsch (1789-1830)
German
Orpheus Charming the Animals
Signed with monogram, dated 1821, oil on canvas
18 x 22½in (46 x 57cm)
£6,700-7,200 *S*

Paul Falconer Poole (1810-79)
British
The Escape of Glaucus and Ione, with the blind girl Nydia, from Pompeii
Signed with monogram, dated 1860, oil on canvas
43 x 60½in (109.1 x 153.6cm)
£3,600-4,000 *C*

This painting illustrates the closing chapters of Bulwer-Lytton's novel The Last Days of Pompeii (1834). Glaucus, the Athenian hero, and his lover Ione, together with the blind Thessalian flower girl Nydia, whose extra-sensory perception has enabled them to escape the cataclysm, sail to safety over a moonlit sea. Nydia plays her harp; she loves Glaucus herself, but, aware that she has no chance of winning his heart, will soon plunge quietly to her death as the others sleep.

Frederick Richard Pickersgill (1820-1900) British
Flight of the Pagan Deities Signed with initials and dated 1856, oil on canvas 44¼ x 77¼in (112.4 x 196.2cm)
£12,600-13,400 *S(NY)*

Published by Mariage (c1800)
French
Psiche dans le Temple de Cerès
Stipple engraving printed in colour, after Raphael, c1800
£350-400 *Lan*

Odilon Redon (1840-1916)
French
La Chute d'Icare
Signed with initials, oil on paper laid down on board
7¾ x 9⅞in (19.7 x 25.2cm)
£23,000-26,000 *S*

Jean-Pierre Norblin de la Gourdaine (1745-1830)
French
Paris and Helen
Signed and dated f.:N:/1822, black lead, grey wash heightened with white, on grey paper
6⅛ x 6¾in (15.8 x 17.2cm)
£1,100-1,400 *S(NY)*

Eduard Veith (1856-1925)
Austrian
An Allegory of Plenty
Signed and inscribed WIEN, oil on canvas
55 x 66½in (140 x 169cm)
£2,500-2,800 *S*

Ernst Novak (1853-1919)
Selene Visiting the Sleeping Endymion
Signed, oil on canvas
50¾ x 70½in (129 x 179cm)
£6,700-7,200 *S*

Carel Weight (b1908-)
British
Pygmalion
Signed and inscribed, oil on canvas
28 x 36in (71 x 91.5cm)
£9,000-9,500 *C*

Pygmalion was a sculptor from Cyprus who fell in love with a marble statue that he had carved. The goddess Venus changed the statue into a woman whom Pygmalion married and they had a son named Paphus.

Hans Zatzka (1859-?)
Austrian
The Nymphs' Garden
Signed, oil on canvas
30½ x 22½in (77.5 x 57cm)
£4,500-5,000 *S*

David Kirk (20thC)
British
Bridge in Prior Park, Bath with Classical Figures
Acrylic on canvas
48 x 25in (122 x 64cm)
£950-1,100 *SJG*

RELIGIOUS PICTURES

14th, 15th and 16th Century

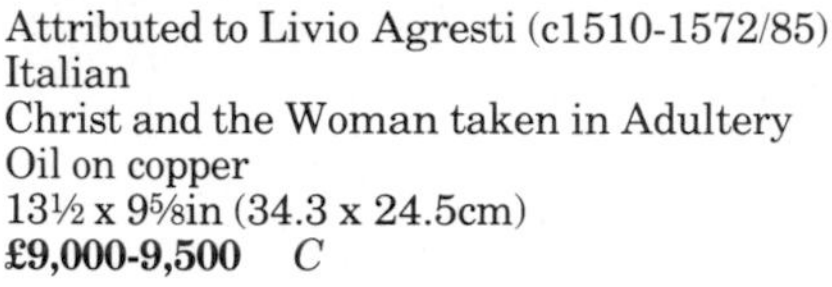

Attributed to Livio Agresti (c1510-1572/85)
Italian
Christ and the Woman taken in Adultery
Oil on copper
13½ x 9⅝in (34.3 x 24.5cm)
£9,000-9,500 *C*

Jacopo di Cione (active c1355-98) Italian
A Triptych: The Madonna and Child enthroned with Saints Lucy, Nicholas, Anthony Abbot and Catherine; on the wings the Nativity and the Crucifixion, with the Annunciation above
Tempera on gold ground panel
20¼ x 20in (51.5 x 51cm)
£190,000-230,000 *C*

Basel School (c1490)
Scenes from the Life of Christ
Black chalk, pen and black ink, grey wash, on two joined sheets
16 x 11½in (40.4 x 29.2cm)
£4,200-4,600 *C*

In the foreground of the drawing is the Resurrection, with the Calling of Saint Peter, Noli Me Tangere and the Harrowing of Hell in the background.

Circle of Jean Bourdichon (c1479-1521)
French
Ecce Homo
Black chalk, body colour, gold leaf, on vellum
3½ x 2½in (9.4 x 6.8cm)
£950-1,050 *C*

The name given to many pictures of Christ, crowned with thorns, bound with ropes, bearing a cloak and reed sceptre, as he was shown to the people by Pontius Pilate. 'Ecce Homo!' (Behold the Man!), said Pilate. 'Crucify! Crucify!' responded the onlookers. (John 19: 4-6)

Baccio Bandinelli (1493-1560) Italian
Blind Lamech Slays his Great-Grandfather
Inscribed, black chalk, pen and brown ink
11½ x 10¾in (29.6 x 27.2cm)
£9,000-9,400 *C*

Catalan School
(c1470)
Saint Blaise; and
Saint Ermengou
Parts of a retable
Inscribed, on gold
ground panel
24¼ x 11⅞in
(61.5 x 30.2cm)
£3,900-4,300 *C*

Circle of Baccio della Porta, Fra Bartolommeo
(1472-1517)
Italian
God the Father supported by Angels (recto);
Studies of Angels Blowing Trumpets (verso)
Inscribed, pen and brown ink
8¼ x 9¾in (20.8 x 24.8cm)
£1,300-1,600 *S(NY)*

Neri di Bicci (c1491)
Christ on the Road to Calvary with Saint Veronica Offering her Veil, the City of Jerusalem beyond
Tempera on panel
21¾ x 15¼in (55.2 x 38.7cm)
£20,000-25,000 *S(NY)*

Francesco Bonsignori (c1455-1519)
Italian
Saint Sebastian
Black chalk, pen and brown ink
8¾ x 6in (22.7 x 15.9cm)
£3,400-3,800 *C*

Luis de Morales, called el Divino (active 1546-86)
Spanish
Christ Carrying the Cross
Oil on slate
31¾ x 22in (80.5 x 56cm)
£35,000-40,000 *S*

Studio of Mariotto Albertinelli (1474-1515)
Italian
The Mystic Marriage of Saint Catherine with Saint Mary Magdalen and Angels in Attendance
Inscribed, tempera, oil and gilt on panel
24½ x 19in (62.2 x 48.3cm)
£17,500-18,500 *S(NY)*

After Pieter Bruegel the Elder (1528-69) Flemish
The Seven Vices (Bastelaer, Holl. 125-131; Lebeer 18-24)
Set of 7 engravings, 1558
£8,000-8,500 *S(NY)*

Circle of Raffaellino Motta da Reggio (1550-78) Italian
The Madonna and Child appearing to the Parents of a sick child
Black chalk, pen and brown ink, brown wash
9¼ x 9¾in (23.5 x 24.5cm)
£600-700 *C*

Bernardo Rosselli (1450-1526)
Italian
The Virgin with the Infant Saint John the Baptist Adoring the Christ Child in an Extensive River Landscape
Tempera on panel
31½ x 17¼in (80 x 44cm)
£35,000-40,000 *S(NY)*

Monogrammist I.K.
(active early 16thC)
A Scriptorium with the Four Evangelists
Signed with monogram, dated 1539/IK, inscribed, red chalk, pen and brown ink, brown wash heightened with white
10¾ x 14¾in (27.4 x 37.5cm)
£21,000-25,000 *S(NY)*

Andrea Schiavone (1522-63) Italian
The Madonna and Child with the Infant Saint John and Saint Anne
Oil on canvas
38½ x 44in (97.5 x 111.5cm)
£18,200-19,000 *S*

Martin de Soria (active 1475) Spanish
The Adoration of the Shepherds; and the Adoration of the Magi
Tempera on panel, a pair
58 x 28in (147.3 x 71.1cm)
£16,500-17,500 *S(NY)*

Giovanni Francesco Barbieri, Il Guercino (1591-1666)
Italian
Saint Francis holding the Infant Christ and kneeling before the Virgin, attended by two Angels
Inscribed Guarchin, black chalk, pen and brown ink, brown wash
10¾ x 8in (27.7 x 20.6cm)
£47,000-55,000 *C*

Attributed to Orazio Vecellio (1525-76)
Italian
The Madonna and Child with the Infant Saint John the Baptist in a Landscape
Oil on canvas
20½ x 28in (52 x 71cm)
£17,700-18,700 *C*

Spanish School (c1520)
Saints Roch, Vincent Ferrer, Nicholas and Peter Martyr
Two sections from a retable in one frame, oil on panel
22⅞ x 44in (58 x 111.8cm)
£5,000-5,500 *C*

Saints are traditionally identified by their symbols. Here, for example, St Roch the figure on the far left and the patron saint of plague sufferers pulls back his tunic to display the plague spot on his thigh, whilst his faithful dog stands at his feet. A good dictionary of Saints is an invaluable purchase for anyone interested in religious art.

Santi di Tito (1536-1603) Italian
The Execution of Saint John the Baptist
Inscribed, black chalk, pen and brown ink, brown and grey wash heightened with white, on light brown paper
13 x 8½in (33.2 x 22.2cm)
£14,500-15,500 *C*

This was one of the most popular and dramatic subjects for religious pictures.

Circle of Marten de Vos (1532-1603)
Flemish
The Prophet Habakkuk giving Sustenance to Daniel in the Lion's Den
Oil on panel
38¼ x 58¾in (97.2 x 149.3cm)
£3,600-4,000 *C*

Attributed to Francesco Guarino (1611-54)
Italian
The Annunciation
Inscribed, pen and brown ink, and another
7 x 8in (17.6 x 20cm)
£350-450 *C*

Giovanni Balducci, called Il Cosci (c1560-1631?)
Italian
The First Passover Seder, Preceding the Exodus from Egypt
Oil on copper
4¼ x 10in (10.8 x 25.4cm)
£19,000-20,000 *S(NY)*

The scene depicts the first Passover dinner, on the evening that Moses visits upon the Egyptians the tenth and final plague. Moses warned that on this night the firstborn son of every household would die. To protect the Israelites, and to make sure they were ready to flee as they must after Pharoah's resultant rage, Moses instructed them to prepare a meal of a roasted, unblemished lamb, retaining its blood in order to paint above the door of every home a tau-sign (T), so that the angel of death would pass over that home thus sparing the firstborn's life. The Israelites are gathered around the dinner table which holds the roasted lamb and unleavened bread (there being no time to allow dough to rise) carrying their staffs as instructed and dressed for travel. In the distance can be seen the Egyptians gathering in the streets and carrying the dead from their homes.
This subject is only rarely depicted and the work doubled its auction estimate at Sotheby's New York in January '92.

Battista Castello, called Il Genovese (c1545-1639)
Italian Adoration of the Kings
Inscribed and dated 1613, gouache and gold on vellum, laid down on board
18 x 14in (45.7 x 35.6cm)
£41,000-50,000 *S(NY)*

Gerbrandt van den Eeckhout (1621-74)
Dutch
Ruth and Boaz
Signed and dated 1663, oil on panel
13¾ x 14¼in (34.8 x 36.3cm)
£6,100-6,500 *S*

Antonio Molinari (1655-1734) Italian
David with the Head of Goliath before Saul
Oil on canvas
45 x 70in (114 x 178cm)
£16,000-17,600 *S*

Circle of Noël Coypel (1628-1707)
French
Lot and his Daughters
35 x 42½in (89 x 108cm)
£23,500-26,500 *C*

Believing after the destruction of Sodom and Gomorrah that they are the only people left on the earth, Lot's daughters are shown getting their father drunk so that they could sleep with him and thus perpetuate the human race. Both daughters bore their father a son.

Jocob de Gheyn II (1565-1629) Flemish
Saint Lucy
Inscribed, black chalk, pen and brown ink, grey wash
5⅛ x 6⅝in (13 x 16.8cm)
£22,000-27,000 *S(NY)*

Legend relates that a nobleman wanted to marry Lucy for the beauty of her eyes so she plucked them out and gave them to him so that he would leave her alone and pure for God. This self-inflicted suffering was as nothing compared to the tortures she faced later on in life which included molten lead being poured in her ears, having her breasts sheared off, and immersion in boiling urine. Lucy is the patron saint of those suffering from eye disease.

Jean Jouvenet (1644-1717)
French
Saint Paul in Meditation
Oil on canvas
30⅞ x 26⅛in (78.4 x 63.8cm)
£19,000-22,000 *S(NY)*

Pieter de Jode I (1570-1634) Flemish
Elijah in the Fiery Chariot, with Elisha Parting the Waters of the River Jordan
Black chalk, pen and brown ink, brown wash
7⅝ x 11in (19.4 x 28.2cm)
£3,100-3,500 *S(NY)*

Workshop of Bartolome Esteban Murillo (1618-82)
Spanish
The Martyrdom of Saint Andrew
Oil on canvas
51 x 66in (129.5 x 167.6cm)
£7,000-7,500 *S(NY)*

Andrew, patron saint of Greece and Scotland, was executed on an X-shaped cross by the Egeas, Roman Governor of Patras because he had converted the Governor's wife to Christianity and persuaded her to deny her husband conjugal rights for ever more.

School of Parma (c1600)
Madonna and Child with the Infant Saint John the Baptist, a Wooded Landscape beyond
Oil on canvas
40 x 36¼in (101.6 x 92.1cm)
£22,000-27,000 *S(NY)*

Circle of Juan de Valdés Leal (1622-90) Spanish
King David, David and Bathsheba beyond; Christ and Saint Peter with Zacchaeus up a tree beyond; Saint Longinus, Calvary beyond; and the Centurion of the Guard at the Resurrection, himself witnessing the Resurrection beyond
All four inscribed with monogram 74⅜ x 40⅛in (189 x 102cm)
£33,000-45,000 *C*

Attributed to Lucio Massari (1569-1633)
Italian
Saint Sebastian
Inscribed, black chalk heightened with white, on grey-brown preparation
10⅛ x 7½in (25.7 x 19.1cm)
£1,200-1,500 *S(NY)*

18th Century

Bolognese School (c1700)
The Sacrifice of Isaac
Oil on canvas
67 x 49¼in (170.5 x 125cm)
£8,000-8,500 *S*

François Boucher (1703-70) French
The Adoration of the Magi
Black chalk, grey and white bodycolour, on light brown paper
9 x 10½in (22.4 x 26.6cm)
£35,000-45,000 *C*

Benedetto Luti (1666-1724)
Italian
A Bearded Apostle Reading
Signed and dated, pastel
16 x 13in (41 x 33cm)
£11,100-12,000 *C*

Pietro Antonio Novelli (1729-1804) Italian
The Risen Christ, after Michelangelo; and another drawing
Black chalk, pen and brown ink
20½ x 10in (52.1 x 25.4cm)
£650-750 *S(NY)*

John White Abbott (1763-1851) British
Madonna and Child with the Infant St. John, after Paolo Farinati
Signed with initials and inscribed on mount, pen and brown ink
9¾ x 8⅝in (24.7 x 22cm)
£310-400 *C*

Richard van Orley (1663-1732) Susanna and the Elders
Signed and dated 1713, black chalk, bodycolour heightened with white and gold, on vellum
7¾ x 5¾in (19.7 x 14.6cm) **£3,200-3,500** *S(NY)*

Susanna, the beautiful and virtuous wife of a prosperous Jew, was assailed during her evening bathe by two village elders who swore that unless she slept with them, they would publicly accuse her of deceiving her husband with a young man. Susanna repulsed their advances, the men carried out their threat and Susanna was dragged before the court, found guilty of adultery and condemned to die. At the last possible minute she was saved by the prophet Daniel, who cross-examined the elders and proved them to be liars. The subject was popular with artists from the Renaissance onwards because it sanctified the portrayal of female nudity.

19th Century

Sir Edward Coley Burne-Jones (1833-98) British
The Annunciation (The Flower of God)
Signed, inscribed and numbered 1, watercolour and bodycolour
23¾ x 20¾in (60.3 x 52.7cm)
£83,000-95,000 *C*

Executed in 1863, this watercolour was produced for the wood engravers George and Edward Dalziel, who were currently commissioning designs from Burne-Jones, amongst others, for their Illustrated Bible. When it was exhibited the following year, with three of the artist's other pictures, critics were not impressed, '. . . the Virgin kneels in her nightdress. The Angel Gabriel in his flight appears to have been caught in an apple tree,' sneered the Art Journal, concluding that 'to those who believe . . . that truth is beauty and beauty is truth, forms such as these are absolutely abhorrent.'

Russian Icon (late 19thC) St George and the Dragon
12 x 10½in (30.5 x 26.5cm)
£300-700 *MG*

Josef Anton Koch (1768-1839)
German
Landscape with Ruth and Boaz
Signed, c1818-22, oil on canvas
33¼ x 43¼in (84.5 x 110cm)
£250,000-300,000 *S*

Russian Icon (late 19thC)
Resurrection and Descent into Hell with 12 Cardinal Feasts of the Church
7 x 5½in (18 x 14.5cm)
£500-1,200 *MG*

Simeon Solomon (1840-1905)
British
Quia Multum Amavit
Signed with monogram, dated 1892, inscribed, red chalk
14⅛ x 16in (35.8 x 40.7cm)
£3,100-3,500 *C*

The subject is Christ and Mary Magdalene, the title derived from St Luke's Gospel, Ch7, v.47: 'her sins which are many are forgiven; for she loved much'. The theme had a personal significance for Solomon who according to Christopher Wood (see Biblio) was affected by the 'corrupting influence' of Swinburne and 'in 1871 was arrested for homosexual offences'. Solomon became a social outlaw, rejected by both friends and family. He spent much of his remaining life in the workhouse and finally died of alcoholism.

John Roddam Spencer Stanhope (1829-1908) British The Song of Solomon
A triptych, eight compartments, gouache 42¼ x 102in (107.5 x 260cm) in total
£28,000-35,000 *S*

20th Century

Sir Stanley Spencer (1891-1959)
The Daughters of Jerusalem
Oil on canvas
21½ x 45½in (54.5 x 115.5cm)
£355,000-400,000 *S*

Daughters of Jerusalem was painted in early 1951, the picture and its companion piece Christ Delivered to the People, were the first in a series depicting Christ's Passion that was to be the final great pictorial cycle of the artist's life. The picture shows Christ, condemned by Pontius Pilate and handed over to the people of Jerusalem, being dragged and shoved by the men of the city towards the Hill of Calvary, the place of His crucifixion. In the foreground their womenfolk weep for Him, and his admonishment to them gives the picture its title: 'Daughters of Jerusalem, weep not for me, but weep for yourselves and your children'. As with many of his religious paintings, the episode is set in Cookham, and the parts are played by the villagers.

Fred Yates (1922-) British
The Heaven Boat
Oil
42 x 60in (106.6 x 152.4cm)
£2,400-2,500 *Tho*

Thompson's Gallery, who submitted this work, opened in the West End in April 1992, 'at a time (they note) when such a move seemed to border on the depths of daftness'. Nevertheless, signs from the first few months are encouraging, with the gallery concentrating in their own words on 'good quality pictures at relatively low prices'. 'Collectors have not lost their appetite for acquiring paintings,' explains partner John Martin. 'They are just rather nervous about spending too much.'

Attributed to Cornelis de Vos (c1585-1651)
Flemish
The Judgement of Paris
Oil on copper
$19^7/_8$ x $25^5/_8$in (50.5 x 65cm)
£4,700-5,000 *C*

Attributed to Simon Vouet (1590-1649)
French
Helen Presenting to Meneleus the Cup with the draught of Queen Polydamna
Oil on canvas
$39^1/_4$ x $31^3/_4$in (99.7 x 80.6cm)
£19,000-21,000 *S(NY)*

Gerard Hoet (1648-1733)
Dutch
Diana and Callisto
Signed, oil on copper
$13^3/_4$ x $17^1/_4$in (34.9 x 43.8cm)
£24,000-26,000 *S(NY)*

Domenico Piola (1627-1703)
Italian
An Allegory with a classically dressed Female Figure holding a Torch and Two Putti, possibly an Allegory of the element of Fire
Oil on canvas
$60^3/_4$ x $46^1/_2$in (154.3 x 118.1cm)
£76,000-78,000 *S(NY)*

Paolo de Matteis (1662-1728)
Italian
The Goddess Iris appearing to the Goddess Cybele
Oil on canvas
$50^1/_2$ x 60in (128.3 x 152.4cm)
£27,000-30,000 *S(NY)*

Attributed to Paul Amable Coutan (1792-1837)
French
Castor and Pollux delivering Helen
Oil on canvas
44 x 57in (112 x 145cm)
£16,000-18,000 *S*
Coutan painted this subject for the Prix de Rome of 1817 and was graded in twelfth position

Attributed to Pierre Narcisse Guérin (1774-1883)
French
Achilles' Quarrel with Agamemnon
Oil on canvas
44 x 57½in (112 x 146cm)
£16,000-17,000 *S*
Agamemnon, leader of the Greek armies, had won a priest's daughter as a prize of war. On the advice of the seer Calchas he gave her up, and to compensate for her loss, arrogantly laid claim to a slave-girl, Briseis, the property of Achilles. Athene (Minerva) who was on the side of the Greeks, intervenes just in time.

Jean-Jacques Lagrenée, le jeune (1739-1832)
French
Minerva and Apollo crowning the Arts:
A pair of paintings
Signed and dated 1773, oil on canvas
26½ x 53¼in (67.3 x 135.3cm)
£19,000-21,000 *S(NY)*

Jean Charles Pérrin (1754-1831)
French
La Generosité de Scipio
Oil on canvas
31¾ x 39in (81 x 99.5cm)
£11,500-12,000 *S*
Having won a beautiful maiden as a prize of war, Scipio restored her unharmed to her fiancé, whilst at the same time delivering a sermon on the moral probity of the Romans.

Theresa Georgina Sassoon, née Thorneycroft (1835-1947)
British
Flower Maidens
Oil on canvas
55 x 134in (140 x 340cm)
£3,800-4,000 *S*

Theresa Sassoon came from a remarkably artistic family. Her parents were both successful sculptors, and her father produced the bronze statue Bodicea and her Daughters at Westminster Bridge, London. Two of her sisters were artists and her younger brother was celebrated sculptor Hamo Thorneycroft. Theresa was the mother of the poet Siegfried Sassoon.

Attributed to Michelangelo Maestri (19th C)
Italian
Europa and the Bull; a Roman Sacrifice
A pair, both watercolour
$12^{1}/_{2}$ x $27^{1}/_{2}$in (31.5 x 70cm)
£2,300-2,500 *S*

Constantin Makovsky (1839-1915)
Russian
The Toilet of Venus
Oil on canvas
96 x 146in (244 x 372cm)
£34,000-37,000 *S*

The present work was commissioned in the 1890s as a ceiling decoration for the palace of V.Dervis in St. Petersburg. After World War I the palace was bought by Baron Anton Alftan, who asked Makovsky to add his signature to the picture. The artist demanded a fee of 100 roubles, the owner indignantly refused and the picture remains unsigned.

Master of Saint Ivo
(active c1400)
Italian
The Madonna and Child
enthroned flanked
by Saints Peter and Lawrence
Gold ground, tempera on panel
shaped top without engaged
frame
27 x 15in (68.6 x 38.1cm)
£38,000-40,000 *S(NY)*

Attributed to Jan Gossaert,
called Mabuse (c1478-c1536)
Flemish
Descent from the Cross
Oil on panel
22 x 16¾in (56 x 42.5cm)
£190,000-200,000 *S(NY)*

Riccardo Quartararo (late 15thC)
Italian
The Archangel Michael Triumphant over Satan
Oil on panel
36 x 25¾in (91.4 x 65.4cm)
£26,000-27,000 *S(NY)*

Master of 1310 (active 1310-c.1325)
Italian
Scenes from the Life of a Martyred Female
Saint, perhaps Margaret of Antioch
Gold ground, tempera on panel
35¾ x 50in (90.8 x 127cm)
£47,000-50,000 *S(NY)*

This 14th Century portrayal of female saints was purchased by the 20th Century's leading female icon: the pop star Madonna.

Attributed to
Ercole Banci
(early 16thC)
Italian
Madonna and Child
Oval, oil on panel
$19^{3}/_{4}$ x $15^{3}/_{4}$in
(50.2 x 40cm)
£12,000-13,000 *S(NY)*

Vittore Carpaccio (1450-1522)
Italian
Madonna and Child
Oil and tempera on panel
$23^{1}/_{4}$ x $19^{1}/_{4}$in (59.1 x 48.9cm)
£44,500-46,500 *S(NY)*

Francesco Zaganelli da Cotignola
(c1470-1532)
Italian
Madonna and Child
Tempera and oil on panel
20 x 16in (50.8 x 40.6cm)
£23,000-25,000 *S(NY)*

Vincent Sellaer (active from 1538)
Flemish
The Madonna and Child with
Saints Elizabeth and
other members of the Holy Family:
The Holy Kinship
Oil on panel
$37^{1}/_{4}$ x $42^{3}/_{4}$in (94.6 x 108.6cm)
£19,000-20,000 *S(NY)*

Giovanni Pietro Rizzo Pedrini,
called Gianpetrino
(active c1520-1540)
Italian
The Virgin and Child with the
Infant Saint John the Baptist
Oil on panel
$23^{3}/_{4}$ x 20in (60.3 x 50.8cm)
£32,000-34,000 *S(NY)*

Sebastiano Mainardi (died 1513)
Italian
The Madonna and Saint Joseph adoring the Christ Child,
the City of Florence in the distance
Tondo, tempera on panel
$31^{1}/_{2}$in (80cm) diameter
£67,000-70,000 *S(NY)*

Circle of Giovanni Francesco Barbieri, called Il Guercino (1591-1666)
Italian
Saint Matthias
Inscribed on the book Sous cecidit sapere Mattin.
Arched top, oil on canvas
41¼ x 43¼in (105 x 110cm)
St Matthias was chosen to replace Judas Escariot after Judas hanged himself. According to legend, he was martyred by being chopped to pieces, hence his symbol: the axe.
£48,000-50,000 *S(NY)*

Pier Francesco Mola (1612-1666)
Italian
Aaron, High Priest of the Israelites, Holding a Censer
Oil on canvas
37¼ x 27¾in (94.6 x 70.5cm)
£38,000-40,000 *S(NY)*

Antonio Molinari (1665-1728/34)
Italian
Saint Sebastian
Oil on canvas
41 x 38in (104.1 x 96.5cm)
£8,900-9,100 *S(NY)*

Giovanni Raggi (1712-1792/4)
Italian
Saint Grata showing her father Lupus the flowers of Saint Alexander
Oil on canvas
97¾ x 61½in (248.3 x 156.2cm)
£38,000-40,000 *S(NY)*
This painting initiated a major dispute when the nuns of Saint Grata Bergamo who had commissioned the work in the 1730s refused to pay Raggi the full price, claiming that it had in fact been painted by Tiepolo. Raggi eventually proved his authorship with a legal action.

After Raphael (19thC)
Italian
Madonna Della Sedia
Oil on Canvas, in an ornate carved wooden frame
28in (71cm) diameter
£7,200-7,500 *S*

This is one of the most copied of all Old Master paintings. The work was possibly used as an exercise in 19th century art schools, and copies frequently appear at auction, often in richly carved surrounds. The difference in price between two apparently identical works can reflect both the craftsmanship of the painting and the quality of the frame.

After Raphael (19thC)
Italian
Madonna Della Sedia
Oil on canvas, in an ornate carved wooden frame
28in (71cm) diameter
£5,000-5,200 *S*

Jean-Jacques Henner (1829-1905)
French
The Magdelene
Signed, oil on panel
13 x 8½in (33 x 21.5cm)
£3,600-3,800 *S*
A larger version of this picture is in the Petit Palais, Paris.

A*** de Rohden (19thC)
German
Madonna and Child
Signed and dated Roma 1878, oil on panel
22½ x 14½in (57 x 37cm)
£1,800-2,000 *S*

Johann-Nepomuk Ender (1793-1854)
Austrian
King David
Signed and dated '845, oil on panel
49¼ x 37½in (125 x 95cm)
£2,900-3,100 *S*

Edward Reginald Frampton (1872-1923)
British
St Joan of Arc Visited by St Catherine and St Margaret in Prison at Rouen
Signed, oil on canvas
46½ x 50in (118 x 127cm)
£3,900-4,100 *S*

Maurice William Greiffenhagen (1862-1931)
British
The Vision
Signed and dated 1921, oil on canvas
65 x 49½in (165 x 125.5cm)
£3,100-3,300 *S*

Greiffenhagen became a noted illustrator of the writings of H.Rider Haggard.

Xavier de Mellery (1845-1921)
Belgian
La Trinité
Signed, mixed media and gold paint
26¾ x 34¼in (68 x 87cm)
£7,200-7,500 *S*

Attributed to Master of the Hartford Still Life (17thC) British
Still Life of Flowers in an Armorial Majolica Vase
Oil on canvas
$29^{3}/_{4}$ x $34^{3}/_{4}$in
(75.6 x 88.3cm)
£49,000-52,000 *S(NY)*

Francesco Fieravino called Il Maltese (active 1650-1680)
Maltese
Still Life of Sweetmeats in a Gilt Dish on an Elaborately Draped Table
Oil on canvas
36 x $49^{1}/_{2}$in (91.4 x 125.7cm)
£25,000-27,000 *S(NY)*

Giuseppe Recco
(1634-1695)
Italian
Still Life of Fish and Lobsters
Oil on canvas
20 x 28in (50.8 x 71.1cm)
£8,000-8,500 *S(NY)*

Circle of Roloef Koets (17thC)
Dutch
Still Life of Fruit and Birds
Oil on panel
20¼ x 30¼in (51.4 x 78cm)
£7,500-8,000 *Bon*

Circle of Pieter de Putter (before 1600-1659)
Dutch
Cod, a Skate, Plaice and other fish on a shore
Indistinctly signed
53⅞ x 72¾in (136.8 x 184.7cm)
£3,100-3,300 *C*

Follower of Joris van Son (1658-1715)
Flemish
A Still Life of Fruit, with a Song Bird
Oil on canvas
9½ x 13in (24 x 33cm)
£6,000-6,500 *S*

Attributed to Simone del Tintore
(active 1630-1670)
Italian
Still Life with Fruit and Vegetables
Oil on canvas
25½ x 36in (65 x 91.5cm)
£18,500-20,000 *S(NY)*

Louis-Léopold Boilly (1761-1845)
French
Still Life of Flowers in a Glass Vase, two Birds, a branch of Blossoms and an Insect on a Table
Signed, oil on panel
12¾ x 10½in (32.4 x 26.7cm)
£145,000-150,000 *S(NY)*
Known predominantly as a genre and portrait painter, Boilly also produced a small number of still-lifes. This fine example reveals the influence of the Dutch masters of the 17th century in its careful execution and attention to detail.

Jakob Bogdani (died 1724)
Hungarian
Still Life of Fruit on a Ledge
Signed, oil on canvas
14½ x 15in (37 x 38cm)
£14,500-15,000 *S*

Pieter Hardimé (1667/8-c1758)
Dutch
Still Life of Flowers in a Basket
Oil on canvas
32¼ x 47¼in (81.9 x 120cm)
£22,500-23,500 *S(NY)*

William Jones of Bath
active 1744-1747)
British
Still Life of Fruit in a Basket with Bullfinch
Oil on canvas
20¼ x 26¾in (51.5 x 68cm)
£3,500-4,000 *S*

Roman School (18thC)
Still Life of Fruit and Flowers
Oil on canvas
50½ x 36½in (128 x 92.7cm)
£40,000-42,000 *S(NY)*

Tommaso Realfonso, called Masillo (c1677-1743) Italian
Still Life with Flowers in elaborate silver and gold Urns and Fruit
Signed in monogram on melon lower left, oil on canvas
36¼ x 36½in (92.1 x 92.7cm)
£16,000-17,000 *S(NY)*

Henri-Horace Roland de la Porte (1725-1793)
French
A set of four Still Lifes of Fruit and other subjects
Oil on canvas
14¼ x 17¼in (36.2 x 43.8cm)
£135,000-140,000 *S(NY)*

Jean Baptiste Simeon Chardin (1699-1779)
French
Still Life with a Glass Mug, three Walnuts, a Basket of Peaches and Pears
Signed, oil on canvas on the original stretcher
14½ x 17¾in (37 x 45cm)
£1,260,000-1,360,000 *S(NY)*

Chardin is acknowledged as one of the greatest still life painters of all time, transforming commonplace objects into the most sophisticated and serene works of art. 'He has proclaimed the divine equality of all things,' enthused his fellow countryman, the writer Marcel Proust, ...having understood the life of his paintings you will have conquered the beauty of life itself'. Chardin was highly successful in his own period.
'There is no collection in Europe, where his paintings are not placed among the ranks of the greatest masters', reported one newspaper in 1761, and the same is true today.

Thomas F. Collier (active 1856-1874)
British
Roses at Sundown
Signed, watercolour
15 x 11in (38 x 28cm)
£1,000-1,275 *Dr*

André Perrachon (1827-1909)
French
A Still Life of a vase of Summer Flowers
Signed and dated 1857, oil on canvas
45¼ x 34½in (115 x 87cm)
£10,500-11,000 *S*

Adriana-Johanna Haanen (1814-1895)
Dutch
A Still Life of Flowers and Peaches
Signed and dated 1850, oil on panel
11¾ x 10in (30 x 25cm)
£10,000-10,500 *S*

Johan Laurentz Jensen
(1800-1856)
Danish
A Garland of Roses
Signed and dated 1846,
oil on panel
11 x 15in (28 x 38cm)
£10,000-10,500 *S*

Henri Fantin-Latour
(1836-1904)
French
Pèches et Raisins
Signed and dated *96,*
oil on canvas
$11\frac{5}{8}$ x $16\frac{1}{2}$in
(29 x 42cm)
£72,000-75,000 *S*

Emilie Preyer (1849-1930)
German
Peaches, Plums and Grapes
on a draped Table
Signed, oil on canvas
$6\frac{3}{4}$ x $9\frac{1}{8}$in (17.2 x 23.2cm)
£12,000-12,500 *C*

Giovanni Sottocornola
(1855-1917)
Italian
A Still Life of Peaches
on Foliage
Signed and dated 1888,
oil on canvas
19 x $30\frac{3}{4}$in (48 x 78cm)
£12,000-12,500 *S*

Albert André (1869-1954)
French
Pommes dans une Coupe
Signed, painted in 1921, oil on panel
15 x 21⅞in (38 x 55.5cm)
£4,200-4,500 *S*

Dora Meeson (d.1955)
British/Australian
Flowers near a Window
Signed and dated '47, oil on canvas
22 x 17in (55.9 x 43.2cm)
£2,000-2,250 *Dr*

Duncan Grant (1885-1978)
British
Still Life- Jug, Bottle and Lemon
Signed and dated /*30,* oil on canvas
24 x 20in (61 x 51cm)
£5,800-6,000 *S*

Harold Gilman (1876-1919)
British
Still Life with Flowers in a Vase
Signed, painted c1911-1914
oil on canvas
10 x 12in (25.5 x 30.5cm)
£13,500-14,000 *C*

Pinchus Kremegne (b.1890)
Russian
Nature morte aux Fruits
Signed, oil on canvas
20 x 24in (50.8 x 61cm)
£8,200-8,500 *S(NY)*

André Bauchant (1873-1958)
French
Fleurs des Champs
Oil on canvas laid down on board
10¾ x 13¾in (27.3 x 34.9cm)
£4,500-4,800 *C*

Marevna (Maria Vorobieff) (1892-1984)
Russian
Vase de Fleurs des Champs
Signed, painted in 1932, oil on canvas
21⅝ x 15⅛in (55 x 38.5cm)
£6,200-6,500 *C*

Mark Gertler (1891-1939)
British
Fruit and everlasting Flowers
Signed and dated 1926, oil on canvas
25 x 21½in (63.5 x 54.5cm)
£20,000-22,000 *S*

Henri Manguin (1874-1949)
French
Fleurs dans une Vase
Stamped signature, oil on canvas
28¾ x 23¾in (73 x 60.3cm)
£15,500-16,500 *C*

Louis Valtat (1869-1952)
French
Vase de Tulipes
Signed, painted in 1941, oil on canvas,
23⅝ x 28¾in (60x 73cm)
£20,000-21,000 *S(NY)*

STILL LIFE

The Dutch and Flemish flower painters of the 17th and 18th centuries were amongst the best-paid artists of their time and many of their works are still fetching high prices today. A major Jan Van Huysum Flowerpiece (see p501) doubled its estimate of approx $2,000,000 when sold at Sotheby's New York in January 1992, and at the European Fine Art Fair in Maastricht, the Newhouse Gallery of New York offered another floral still life by the same artist for approx £2m. In the mid-1980s, you would not have expected to pay more than £200,000 for such a decorative work, yet whilst values have tumbled in the impressionist and modern picture fields, prices at the top end of the old master market could, in a number of instances, literally be described as blooming.

17th Century

Jan Brueghel the Younger (1601-78)
Flemish
Still Life of Flowers in a Vase
Oil on panel
21¾ x 16¼in (55.5 x 41cm)
£62,000-70,000 *S*

According to legend, the first flower still life was produced when a lady asked an artist to paint some rare blooms for her because she was unable to obtain them for her garden. Whatever the truth of this story the Dutch and Flemish merchants of the 17th and 18thC certainly had a passionate love for flowers and horticulture. They brought back rare plants from their travels, competed with each other in cultivating exotic and costly blooms often spending fortunes on a single bulb and commissioned the painters of the day to make permanent records of their favourite fugitive subject. For all their shining exactitude, 17thC flowerpieces were rarely painted wholly from life. Pictures often show blossoms which bloom at different times of year, they were composed from a series of different studies and artists often repeated the same elements in different pictures.

Balthasar van der Ast (c1593-1656)
Dutch
Still Life of Flowers, Fruit and Seashells
Signed, oil on panel
14¼ x 24½in (36.5 x 62cm)
£90,000-100,000 *S*

Abraham-Jansz Begeyn (1637-97)
Dutch
Still Life of Butterflies, Birds, Toadstools and Lizard
Signed, oil on canvas
22 x 26in (55.9 x 66cm)
£24,000-25,000 *HFA*

School of Bergamo (17thC)
Still Life of Fruit and Ceramics
Indistinctly signed with monogram AB, oil on canvas
21¾ x 26½in (55.2 x 67.3cm)
£9,500-10,500 *S(NY)*

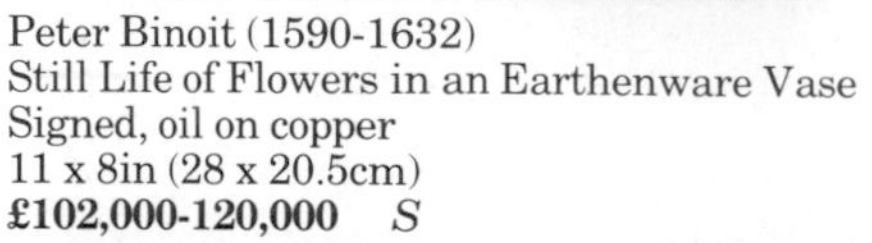

Peter Binoit (1590-1632)
Still Life of Flowers in an Earthenware Vase
Signed, oil on copper
11 x 8in (28 x 20.5cm)
£102,000-120,000 *S*

Monogrammist CL (17thC)
Flemish
Still Life of Game and Hunting Equipment
Oil on canvas
34¾ x 46¾in (88.5 x 118.5cm)
£28,000-35,000 *S*

Jan Pauwel Gillemans (17thC) Flemish
A Pair of Still Lifes of Fruit on a Stone Ledge
Oil on canvas
11¼ x 9½in (28.5 x 24cm)
£17,500-20,000 *Bon*

J* van Kessel (active 1661)
Flemish
A Swag of Roses suspended from Blue Ribbon
Oil on canvas
23¾ x 19½in (60.5 x 49.5cm)
£21,000-24,000 *S*

Circle of Cristoforo Munari (1648-1730)
Italian
Still Life of Fruit and Funghi
Oil on canvas
22½ x 32in (57 x 81.3cm)
£17,000-18,000 *S(NY)*

Did you know?
MILLER'S Picture Price Guide will build up year by year to form the most comprehensive photo-reference library available

Attributed to Pietro Navarra (1631-c1690)
Italian
Still Life of Fruit and Game in a Landscape with Roosters and a Guinea Pig
Oil on canvas
28¾ x 38½in (73 x 97.8cm)
£9,500-10,000 *S(NY)*

Still life painters often concentrated on certain themes: there were specialists in flowers and fruit; in fish and dead game; in simple breakfast scenes and opulent banquet settings. Some artists were even more specific in their preferred subject matter: choosing to portray shells, fungi, armour and even oysters.

Barend Van Der Meer (b.1659)
Dutch
Still Life with Fruit in a Colonade Landscape
Signed and dated 1695, oil on canvas
29 x 24in (73.6 x 61cm)
£40,000-42,500 *HFA*

Follower of Pieter Gerritsz van Roestraten (1630-1700)
Dutch
Still Life of a Yixing Teapot, Chinese Export Cups and Saucers and Other Objects on a Ledge Bears initials on the spoon l.l.; ET, oil on canvas
30 x 24½in (76 x 62.3cm)
£5,800-6,500 *S*

Attributed to Giovanni Battista Ruoppolo
(1620-85) Italian
Still Life with Fruit
Oil on canvas
28½ x 38in (72.4 x 96.5cm)
£15,800-17,000 *S(NY)*

Spanish School (17thC)
Still Life of Fruit
Oil on canvas
21 x 26in (53.3 x 66cm)
£1,700-2,000 *Bon*

Follower of Simon Pietersz. Verelst (1644-1721) Dutch
Flowers in an Urn, with Peaches and a Watch 38⅝ x 29⅞in (98 x 76cm)
£9,400-10,000 *C*

The watch or timepiece was a traditional vanitas element – a reminder of the transcience of earthly life.

18th Century

Anon – Late 18thC School
Still Life of Fish
Oil
24 x 27in (60 x 68cm)
£1,500-1,700 *HSS*

English School (late 18thC)
Basket of Flowers
Gouache on vellum
11½ x 8½in (29.2 x 21.6cm)
and a companion piece (a pair)
£1,000-1,300 *Bon*

Attributed to Giacomo Ceruti, called il Pitocchetto (1698-1767) Italian
Still Life of Oysters, Bread and a Wine Bottle
Oil on canvas
18 x 15¼ (45.7 x 38.4cm)
£8,000-8,400 *S*

Flemish School (c1700)
Still Life with Fruit
Oil on canvas
23½ x 39in (59.7 x 99.1cm)
£10,700-11,500 *S(NY)*

Jan van Huysum (1682-1749) Dutch
Flowers in a Terracotta Vase on a Marble Plinth with Orange Blossoms and a Bird's Nest, a Garden Beyond Signed, painted c1730, oil on panel
31½ x 24in (80 x 61cm) **£2,011,500-2,500,000** *S(NY)*

Huysum was called by his contemporaries 'the phoenix of all flower painters', his still lifes were avidly collected in his own day and fetched enormous sums. He guarded the secrets of his trade with extreme caution and his one pupil, a woman, was the only person ever to be allowed into his studio. Unusually, Huysam appears to have worked very closely from nature, waiting to complete his canvases until the actual flowers or fruits he needed were available, possibly a reason why his still lifes sometimes bear two dates.

Follower of Carel de Moor (b.1695) Dutch
Still Life of Military Equipment Accompanied by Two Soldiers in a Landscape Oil on panel 22¼ x 31¾in (56.5 x 80.5cm)
£12,200-13,000 *S*

William Sartorius (18thC)
British
Still Life of Fruit, Ewer and Basket
Oil on canvas
18¾ x 22¾ (47.5 x 57.5cm)
£2,100-2,500 *S*

Tommaso Realfonso, called Masillo (c1677-1743)
Italian
Still Life of a Basket with Knitting, a Basket of Hazelnuts, a Blue and White Jar and two Game Birds
Signed, oil on canvas
15½ x 25¾in (39.4 x 65.4cm)
£11,500-12,000 *S(NY)*

19th Century

C. T. Bale (active late 19thC)
British
Basket of Fruit with Pitcher
Signed, oil
24 x 20in (61 x 50.8cm)
£2,200-2,400 *Dr*

Vincent Clare (c1855-1930)
British
Still Life of Summer Flowers
Signed and dated 1898, oil on canvas
9 x 13in (22.5 x 33cm
£2,300-2,600 *S*

Giovanni Barbaro
Italian
Still Life of Fruit
Signed, watercolour
26¼ x 59¼in (66.7 x 151.1cm)
£1,100-1,400 *Bon*

Oliver Clare (c1853-1927) British Primroses, Blossoms and Bird's Nest
Signed, oil 9 x 12in (22.5 x 30.5cm)
£1,700-1,900 *Dr*

Vincent Clare (c1855-1930)
British
Violets, Blossom and a Bird's Nest
Signed, oil on canvas
12¼ x 10¼in (31 x 26cm)
£1,700-2,000 *S*

Vincent Clare (c1855-1930)
British
Pair of Still Lifes depicting Fruit and a Bird's Nest on a Mossy Bank
Signed, oil on canvas
6 x 8in (15.2 x 20.3cm)
£1,800-2,000 *BWe*

Oliver Clare (c1853-1927)
British
Grapes, Plums and Strawberries
Signed, oil on board
6¼ x 9¾in (16 x 25cm)
£1,250-1,450 *S*

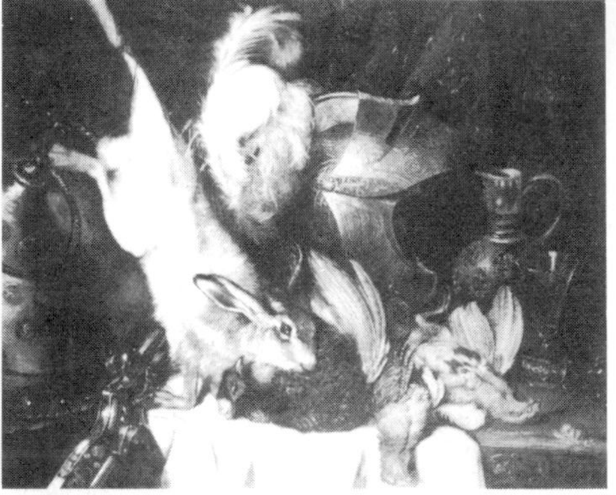

Follower of William Duffield (1816-63) British
Still Life of Dead Game and Armour
30¼ x 35¼in (77 x 90.5cm)
£1,600-1,800 *S(S)*

A specialist in still lifes of dead game, William Duffield literally died for his art. According to the Redgrave brothers (the great chroniclers of 19thC painting), he was working on a slain stag which remained in his studio so long that it became extremely decayed. From a previous illness, Duffield had lost his sense of smell; unable to scent the danger, he inhaled the poisonous miasma over a certain period, contracted an infection and died in 'the earnest pursuit of his profession'.

James Hardy Jnr (1832-89) British
Still Life of Game Birds in a Kitchen
Signed, oil on canvas
13in (33cm) diam
£2,400-2,600 *I*

Henri Fantin-Latour (1836-1904) French Nature Morte – Roses, Raisins et Peches Signed and dated '74, oil on canvas 11¾ x 22¾in (30 x 58cm) **£390,000-420,000** *S*

William Henry Hunt (1790-1864)
British
Still Life of Fruit in a Basket
Signed, watercolour with bodycolour
9 x 10¼in (22.5 x 26cm)
£1,800-2,000 *S*

Known as '"Hedgerow" or "Birdsnest Hunt" the artist's career began as a result of a deformity in his legs. Since he could only walk with difficulty, it was decided that he should train as an artist and his parents placed him with the painter John Varley. In the late 1820s he began to paint fruit and flowers and using bodycolour, he developed an individual method of hatching and stippling over a white ground. His charming and decorative watercolours were extremely successful and Ruskin compared him to the greatest Dutch masters (see Christopher Wood – ***The Dictionary of Victorian Painters****– 2nd edition, Antique Collector's Club, 1987).*

Italian School (19thC)
A Trompe L'Oeil with Prints
Oil on canvas
19 x 24½in (48.5 x 62cm)
£5,600-6,000 *S*

Edward Ladell (1821-86)
British
Still Life of Fruit and Flowers in a Basket
Signed with monogram, oil on panel
8 x 10½in (20 x 26cm)
£3,400-3,800 *S*

French School (late 19thC)
Baskets of Fish on a Shoreline
Indistinctly signed, oil on canvas
36¼ x 59in (92.1 x 149.9cm)
£800-1,000 *CSK*

Johan Laurentz Jensen (1800-56)
Danish
Still Life with Flowers in an Earthenware Vase
Signed and dated 1836, oil on canvas
13½ x 10½in (35 x 27cm)
£11,100-12,100 *S*

Ellen Ladell (19thC)
British
Still Life of Birds, Fruit, Roses and a Bird's Nest
Signed, oil on canvas
18 x 14in (46 x 35.5cm)
£2,900-3,200 *S*

This husband and wife team collaborated on many works, repeatedly using the same objects in their compositions.

G* Sturm (1855-1923)
Austrian
Still Life Studies of Game on a Table (a set of three)
Signed
7½ x 9½in (19 x 24cm)
£1,300-1,500 *S(S)*

Harry Sutton Palmer (1854-1933)
British
Still Life of a Jay and Beech Nuts on a Mossy Bank
Signed and dated 1812, pencil and watercolour – heightened with white
10¾ x 15in (27.9 x 38.1cm)
£350-450 *CSK*

Harry Sutton Palmer (1854-1933)
British
Still Life with Apples, Blackberries and Nuts
Signed and dated '68, watercolour heightened with white
7½ x 10¼in (19 x 26cm)
with another still life (a pair)
£1,400-1,600 *S*

Condition is a major factor in a picture's price

Eloise Harriet Stannard (active 1852-93)
British
Still Life of Grapes, Peaches and Raspberries on a Marble Ledge
Signed and dated 1886, oil on canvas
17 x 14in (43 x 35.5cm)
£5,000-5,500 *S*

Pierre-Auguste Renoir (1841-1919) French Sucrier et Citron
Signed, oil on canvas
6¼ x 12⅝in (16 x 32in)
£27,000-35,000 *S*

Emma Walter (active 1885-91) British Still Life of Fruit and Flowers Signed, watercolour 21 x 26½in (53.3 x 67.3cm)
£1,700-2,000 *Bon*

F. Faulkner White (19thC) British
Still Life of a Wine Vase, Fruit and Flowers
Signed and dated 1885, oil on canvas
30 x 22in (76.2 x 55.8cm)
and a companion piece (a pair)
£1,000-1,250 *Bon*

Thomas Worsey (1829-75)
British
Still Life of Primulas, Pansies and a Bird's Nest
Signed and dated 1861, oil on canvas
11 x 9in (28 x 23cm)
£1,600-1,900 *S*

Johann Wilhelm Volcker (1812-73) German
Still Life of Flowers on a Marble Ledge
Signed, oil on canvas
17¼ x 13½in (44 x 34cm)
£6,100-6,500 *S*

20th Century

John Armstrong (1893-1973)
British
Still Life with Vases and Fruit
Signed and dated '60, oil on canvas
16 x 12in (41 x 30.5cm)
£3,400-3,700 *C*

Edward le Bas (1904-66)
British
Still Life with Roses on a Checked Cloth
Signed, oil on canvas
14 x 12in (35.5 x 30.5cm)
£4,200-4,400 *S*

John Armstrong (1893-1973) British Falling Tulips
Signed and dated '51 16 x 20in (40.6 x 50.8cm)
£6,100-6,400 *CSK*

Henry Charles Brewer (1866-1950)
British
Roses and Sweet Peas in an Oriental Vase
Signed, pencil and watercolour heightened with white
14 x 10in (33.6 x 25.4cm)
£360-400 *CSK*

William Boissevain (b.1927)
Australian
White Flowers in a Vase
Signed and dated '76
35½ x 39¼in (90 x 101cm)
£1,800-2,000 *S(S)*

Angel Botello (20thC)
Signed and numbered 2059, oil on masonite
33 x 48in (83.8 x 121.9cm)
£6,700-7,000 *S(NY)*

Marc Chagall (1887-1985) French Bouquet de Bleuets
Signed, painted c1930, oil on canvas
18½ x 14¾in (47. x 37.5cm) **£150,000-160,000** *S(NY)*

'You might say that in my mother's womb I had already noticed the colour of the flowers,' Chagall once claimed with typical imaginitive passion. 'I don't know if colour chose me or I chose colour, but since childhood I've been married to colour in its pure state.'

Chagall is one of those artists who has suffered from the collapse of the Modern market, the present work selling considerably under its estimate of $300,000-400,000, when auctioned at Sotheby's New York in February 1992.

Miguel Canals (20thC)
Spanish
Still Life after Menendez
Oil on canvas
31⅞ x 27⅛in (81 x 69cm)
£400-450 *Bon*

Emily Beatrice Bland (1864-1951)
British
Still Life with Flowers in a Jug
Signed – verso: a study of a house and garden, oil on board
10½ x 14in (26.5 x 35.5cm)
£300-400 *Bon*

John Bratby (b.1928)
British
Sunflower
Signed, oil on canvas
48 x 36in (122 x 96.5cm)
£1,000-1,200 *C*

Harold Clayton (1896-1979) British
Midsummer
Signed, oil on canvas
20 x 24in (51 x 61cm)
£7,200-7,500 *S*

Marcel Dyf (20thC) French Vase de Fleurs
Signed, oil on canvas 21⅜ x 25⅝in
£5,000-5,300 *S*

Charles E. J. Le Corbusier (1887-1965)
Swiss
Nature Morte à Bouteille et Verre
Signed, red crayon on paper
10¼ x 7⅞in (26 x 20cm)
£5,600-6,000 *C*

André Derain (1880-1954)
French
Deux Pommes
Signed, painted in 1928, oil on canvas
6¼ x 9½in (15.8 x 24.1cm)
£10,300-11,300 *S(NY)*

Odette Dumaret (b.1913)
French
Still Life with Yellow Bottle
17 x 21in (43.1 x 53.3cm)
£7,800-8,000 *Ce*

Emil Fila (1882-1953) Czech
Cubish Still Life
Signed, oil on canvas
39⅜ x 31⅞in (100 x 81cm)
£45,000-55,000 *C*

John Duncan Fergusson (1874-1961) British
Still Life with Coffee Cups
Black chalk
4¾ x 8in (12 x 20cm)
£800-1,000 *S(SC)*

Frederick Gore (b.1913) British
Provencal Flowers on a Kitchen Table
Signed, oil on canvas
32 x 38in (81 x 71cm)
£3,800-4,200 *C*

Duncan Grant (1885-1978) British Still Life with a portrait of Nijinsky Signed, oil on canvas 20 x 16in (51 x 40.5cm)
£5,600-6,000 *S*

Painted in 1972, this work shows the fireplace at Charleston (home to Duncan Grant and Vanessa Bell). In front of the picture of Nijinsky stands a pot by Grant on a gramophone cabinet decorated by Bell.

Pauline Glass (b.1908) British
Flowers in a Vase Signed, oil on canvas
30 x 24in (76.2 x 61cm)
£350-400 *G*

Alexander Goudie (20thC) Three Fish on a Table Signed, acrylic
13 x 22½in (33 x 57.1cm) **£700-800** *C(S)*

Emilio Greco (20thC)
Still Life of Flowers and Fruit
Oil on panel
21⅜ x 17⅜in (54.3 x 44.2cm)
£450-525 *Bon*

Konstantin Lomikin (b.1924) Russian Watermelons
Signed, painted in 1970, oil on canvas
£1,700-1,800 *RMG*

Rowland Henry Hill (1873-1952) British A Vase of Roses
Signed and dated 1928, watercolour
10 x 12in (25.4 x 30.5cm)
£900-1,100 *SCG*

Talbot Hughes (20thC) British
Sweet Peas
Signed and dated 1941, oil on canvas
23¾ x 17¾in (60 x 45cm)
£1,400-1,600 *S*

Robert Macbryde (1913-66)
British
Yellow Still Life
Signed, oil on canvas
20 x 24in (51 x 61cm)
£2,300-2,500 *S*

Charles Levier (20thC)
French
Méditeranée
Signed, oil on canvas
40 x 30in (101.6 x 76.2cm)
£630-730 *S(NY)*

Henri Matisse (1869-1954) French
Anemones dans une Vase à Godrons Signed and dated '43, painted in Venice, oil on canvas
18⅛ x 21⅝in (46 x 55cm)
£1,100,000-1,200,000 *S*

'To copy the objects in a still life is nothing,' claimed Matisse. A still life painter 'must render the emotion they awaken in him'. The present painting is another example of an important work by a major 20thC artist that fell below its lowest estimate when it came up for auction at the end of 1991.

Paul Maze (1887-1979) French
Flowers on a Red Tray
Signed, pastel
21½ x 29½in (53.75 x 73.75cm)
£21,500-23,000 *S(S)*

Paul Maze (1887-1979) French
Flowers
Signed, oil on canvas
28¼ x 36in (70 x 90cm)
£16,000-17,000 *S(S)*

Jean Metzinger (1883-1956) French
Nature Morte
Signed, oil on cradled panel
7⅞ x 9¾in (20 x 24.8cm)
£5,700-6,000 *S(NY)*

Lowell Nesbitt (b.1933) American
Parrot Tulip on White Signed and dated '79, oil on canvas 40 x 40in (101.6 x 101.6cm)
£1,900-2,100 *S(NY)*

S. J. Peploe (1871-1935)
British
Red and White Wallflowers and a Wine Glass
Signed
10 x 14in (25.4 x 35.5cm)
£1,800-1,850 *LB*

James Stuart Park (1862-1933) British
Pink Roses Signed, oil on canvas
20 x 20in (51 x 51cm) **£2,300-2,600** *S(SC)*

Edouard Pignon (b.1905) French
Nature Morte
Signed and dated '44, oil on canvas
28¾ x 23⅝in (73 x 60cm)
£10,300-11,000 *S(NY)*

Mary Potter (1900-81)
British
Magnolia Blossom
Signed
24 x 19¾in (61 x 50cm)
£720-820 *CSK*

Josef van de Roye (20thC)
Dutch Still Life of Fruit on a Table
Signed and dated 1928
25½ x 39½in
£2,600-3,000 *Bea*

William Scott (b.1913) British
Still Life with Flowers on a Table
Oil on canvas
20 x 24in (51 x 61cm)
£22,000-25,000 *Bon*

William Walker Telfer (20thC) British
Still Life of a Bottle, Fruit and a Pot Plant
Signed, oil on board 13 x 10in (33 x 25.5cm)
£950-1,050 *S(SC)*

Sir Matthew Smith (1879-1959)
British
Tulips in a Bowl
Painted c1932, oil on canvas
21¾ x 25½in (55 x 65cm)
£36,000-40,000 *S*

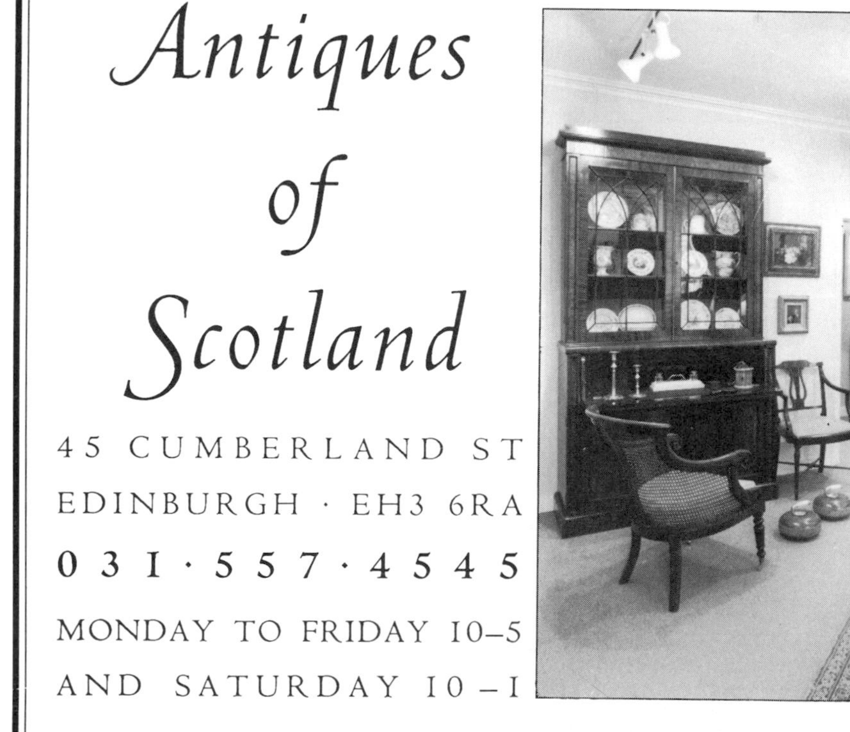

Fred Spencer
(active early 20thC)
British
Antiquarian Books
Signed, watercolour
6¾ x 10in (17 x 26cm)
£2,700-3,000 *S*

William E. Gladstone Solomon (active 1904-40) British
Spring Blossoms in a Vase
Signed, oil on canvas
23 x 29in (58.4 x 73.6cm)
£400-450 *L*

Rex Whistler (1905-44)
British
Dahlias in an Antique Urn
Oil on canvas
19 x 14in (48.5 x 35.5cm)
£5,100-5,300 *S*

The present work was painted in the summer of 1929 at No. 3 Foro Romano in Rome, the house owned by Lord Berners the composer, artist and writer. Whistler met Lord Berners in Rome in 1928 and they travelled Italy together.

Indulis Zarins (20thC)
Russian
The Mandolin
Signed and dated '90, oil on canvas
23 x 32in (58.4 x 81.2cm)
£4,250-4,500 *CE*

BIRDS

In spite of the recession, watercolours and pictures of birds have performed well over the past year. 'Collectors flock to birds sale to send prices soaring,' noted the Antiques Trade Gazette gleefully, reporting the success of Christie's specialist sale on 25th February 1992. Christie's first started this category in 1989 and this was their best sale so far attracting a large turnout, including many private collectors from Britain, the United States and the Continent, who heavily outnumbered the trade in the bidding. 'A buoyant market,' concluded the expert in charge, Harriet Drummond.

Circle of Pieter Casteels III (18thC)
Flemish
A Silver Pheasant and a Golden Pheasant
Oil on canvas
39¼ x 41¾in (99.7 x 106cm)
£3,500-4,000 *Bon*

18th Century

Jaques Barraband (1767/8-1809)
French
A Pied Currawong; and A Western Bird of Paradise
Both signed, watercolour
20½ x 15⅝in (52.1 x 39cm) and 20½ x 15¼in (52.3 x 38.7cm)
£4,500-4,800 *C*

Charles Collins (active 1720-60s)
British
Species of Grouse
Inscribed, signed and dated May 1742, watercolour and bodycolour on laid paper
21 x 15in (53.5 x 38cm)
£2,000-2,100 *S*

English School, early 18thC
A Consort of Birds
Inscribed on the book: *COMPOSED BY . . ./ SUNG BY . . .*, watercolour and bodycolour on vellum
7½ x 9½in (19 x 24cm)
£1,400-1,600 *S*

The music in the manuscript is birdsong. The late 17th and early 18thC saw an increased interest in birdsong, and attempts were made to transcribe their songs, for example in 'The Bird Fancier's Delight', published in 1717.

Charles Collins (active 1720-60s)
British Grouse
Inscribed, signed and dated March 1741, watercolour and bodycolour on laid paper
21¼ x 15in (54 x 38cm)
£1,900-2,000 *S*

Peter Paillou (active 1745-80) British Tar Tar Hens (a pair)
One signed and dated 1755, watercolour and bodycolour
19 x 15¼in (48.5 x 35cm) and 17¾ x 14½in (45 x 37cm)
£2,500-2,800 *S*

19th Century

Anglo-Chinese School (c1830)
Three Birds on a Branch
Inscribed No. 5, watercolour
18¼ x 23¼in (46.4 x 59cm)
With another watercolour of four birds on a branch by the same hand (a pair)
£5,300-5,600 *C*

Locate the source

The source of each illustration in Miller's can be found by checking the code letters below each caption

Johannes Gerardus Keulemans (1842-1912)
Bee-Eaters
Signed, pencil and watercolour with touches of white heightening
7½ x 6in (19 x 15.3cm)
£1,200-1,500 *C*

J. C. Bell (active 1857-68)
British
Black Game in the Highlands
Signed and dated 'J.C. Bell 1961', oil on canvas
22¼ x 38⅛in (56.5 x 76.7cm)
£5,000-5,500 *C*

German School (19thC) Studies of Various Birds
Watercolour on paper, unframed 9½ x 13¾in (24 x 33.7cm) and smaller; and two studies of moths
£2,800-3,000 *C*

Edward Neale (active 1858-81) British Blackgame
Signed and dated 1871, pencil and watercolour
14⅛ x 12⅜in (36 x 31.5cm)
£950-1,050 *C*

Mrs Augusta Innes Withers (active 1829-65)
British Canaries on a Ledge
Signed, watercolour
13¾ x 11¾in (35 x 29.8cm) **£750-800** *Bon*

Henry Stacey Marks (1829-98)
British Lears Macaw
Signed with initials, watercolour heightened with white
£450-550 *Bon*

Presumably like many ornithological painters, Marks claimed that he preferred 'birds to human sitters'. He studied the creatures at London Zoo. 'Some of the parrots', he recalled, 'resented having their portraits taken, and the moment that pencil and sketch-book appeared, became very restless and fidgety or indulged in shrieking remonstrances.' (See Jeremy Maas – Victorian Painters – Barrie and Jenkins, 1988.)

Johannes Gerardus Keulemans (1842-1912)
A Waxwing
Signed, pencil and watercolour with touches of white heightening
£1,300-1,500 *C*

20th Century

Winifred Marie Louise Austen (1876-1964)
British
Mallards Coming In
Pencil, watercolour and bodycolour
9 x 12in (22.9 x 20.5cm)
£1,200-1,400 *C*

Edward Julius Detmold (1883-1957)
British
Budgerigars
Watercolour
16 x 13in (40.5 x 33cm)
£450-500 *Bon*

Raymond Booth (b.1929)
British
Barn Owl at Dawn, Eccup
Signed and dated 1980, oil on board
29½ x 36in (75 x 91.5cm)
£6,400-7,000 *C*

Basil Ede (b.1931) British
Bullfinch
Signed, watercolour and bodycolour on grey paper
9 x 11⅜in (22.8 x 29cm)
£750-800 *C*

Basil Ede (b.1931)
Goldfinch
Signed, watercolour and bodycolour on grey paper
9 x 11⅜in (22.8 x 29cm)
£900-950 *C*

Mary Fedden (b.1915) British Nightjars
Signed and dated '58 Oil on canvas
15¼ x 19½in (38.5 x 49cm) **£800-850** *C*

David Morrison Reid Henry (1919-77)
British
Red-Cheeked Bulbul
Signed, pencil, watercolour and bodycolour
11⅜ x 8¾in (29 x 21.4cm)
£750-850 *C*

John Cyril Harrison (1898-1985) British
Demoiselle Cranes Preening
Signed, pencil and watercolour with touches of white heightening
14¾ x 21¾in (37.5 x 55.2cm)
£950-1,050 *C*

Philip Rickman (1891-1982) British
Mallard
Signed, pencil, watercolour and bodycolour on grey paper
8 x 12¼in (20.3 x 31cm)
£1,200-1,400 *C*

Philip Rickman (1891-1982)
A Study of a Woodcock in Flight
Signed, pencil, black chalk and grey wash heightened with white on grey paper
6 x 5¾in (15.2 x 14.7cm)
With two other studies
£1,200-1,500 *C*

Richard Robjent (b.1937)
British
Golden Eagles in the Highlands
Signed and dated 1981, pencil and watercolour heightened with white on grey paper
22 x 10¼in (55.9 x 76.5cm)
£1,200-1,350 *C*

Frank Southgate (1872-1916)
British
Pink-Footed Geese on the Shore
Signed, grisaille
15¼ x 23¼in (38.7 x 59cm)
£900-1,050 *C*

Southgate not only specialised in painting birds, but also enjoyed shooting them. An enthusiastic sportsman with the gun, he became a regular contributor to 'The Illustrated Sporting and Dramatic News' for which the present work was executed.

Frank Southgate (1872-1916) British
Canada Geese Flighting over an Estuary Signed, watercolour and bodycolour 14½ x 22½in (36.8 x 57.2cm)
£2,700-3,000 *C*

Sir Peter Scott (1909-89) British
Widgeon Displaying
Signed and dated 1932, oil on canvas
14½ x 17⅝in (36.8 x 44.7cm)
£3,100-3,300 *C*

Archibald Thorburn (1860-1935)
British
Grouse Coming Down Wind
Signed and dated 1901, inscribed with title and the sum '34 guineas' on reverse, pencil and watercolour with touches of white heightening
14½ x 21¼in (36.8 x 53.9cm)
£6,800-7,300 *C*

Archibald Thorburn (1860-1935)
British
A Greenland or Gyr Falcon
Signed and dated 1899, watercolour heightened with white
29½ x 21¼in (75 x 54cm)
£23,000-25,000 *S(SC)*

Charles Frederick Tunnicliffe (1901-79)
British
A Swan and Cygnets
Oil on canvas
34¼ x 41½in (86.7 x 105.5cm)
£11,200-12,000 *C*

Archibald Thorburn (1860-1935) British
Robin in Winter
Signed and dated 1930, watercolour and bodycolour
10¾ x 7¼in (27.5 x 18.5cm)
£6,500-7,000 *C*

Archibald Thorburn (1860-1935)
British
Terns
Grisaille
Signed
13 x 9½in (33.2 x 24cm)
£1,600-1,800 *C*

Charles Frederick Tunnicliffe (1901-79)
British
A Racing Pigeon
Inscribed and stamped with artist's name and date 1980, pencil, black chalk, watercolour and bodycolour
11¾ x 9½in (29.8 x 24.2cm)
£1,250-1,300 *C*

Charles Frederick Tunnicliffe (1901-79)
British
Herring Gulls with their Young
Signed, stamped and dated 1980, pencil, black chalk and watercolour heightened with white
14 x 18¾in (35.6 x 47.6cm)
Along with a watercolour of collared doves
£1,050-1,250 *C*

CATS AND DOGS

Cats and dogs are always popular in the sale room – and it is an area where the appeal of the subject matter can carry more weight than the quality of the paintings.

The majority of pictures belong to the 19th and early 20thC, when many artists specialised in the genre. Typical works include portraits of favourite pets and hunting dogs, caricatures and comic drawings, and sentimental and anthropomorphised pictures of puppies and kittens at play in middle class domestic interiors reflecting both the home and ideals of their patrons.

CATS

18th Century

Thomas Rowlandson (1756-1827)
British
Cats' Chorus!
Pen and brown ink and watercolour over traces of pencil
5¼ x 8¼in (13 x 21cm)
£2,300-2,500 *S*

19th & 20th Century

Mary Fedden (b.1915) British
The Black Cat
Signed and dated 1991, oil on canvas
11¼ x 13in (28.5 x 33cm)
£800-850 *C*

English School (early 20thC)
The Performing Cats
Initials E.S.H., watercolour
8½ x 10in (21.6 x 25.4cm)
Together with a companion piece 'A Pony Taking Tea at a Table', a pair
£280-300 *Bon*

Bessie Bamber (late 19thC) British Four Kittens
Initialled, oil on mahogany panel
10½ x 22⅜in (26.7 x 56.8cm)
£800-900 *Bon*

There were many women cat-painters in the Victorian era. Along with still lifes, this is one of the few areas of 19thC art where women are strongly represented, suggesting that such subjects as flowers, fruit and kittens were considered eminently suitable for the female brush.

Johann Hartung (late 19thC) German
The Dressing Table; In the Kitchen A pair, both signed, oil on panel 6¾ x 8¾in (17 x 22cm)
£2,000-2,300 *S(S)*

Wilson Hepple (1854-1937) British
Tabby Kittens and a Chinese Bowl
Signed and dated '99 **£1,300-1,500** *A*

Arthur Heyer (1872-1931) German
A Persian Cat Jumping onto a Tea Table
Signed, oil on canvas
21 x 26in (53.3 x 66cm) **£830-950** *Bon*

Arthur Heyer (1872-1931)
German
Three Persian Cats
Signed, oil on canvas
21½ x 26½in (54.6 x 67.3cm)
£1,600-1,800 *Bon*

Arthur Heyer (1872-1931)
German
Playing with Mother – A Persian Cat and Kitten
Signed, oil on canvas
18½ x 27in (47 x 68.6cm)
£850-900 *Bon*

Winifred Humphrey (20thC) British
A Ginger Cat Amongst Irises Oil on canvas
15½ x 18in (39.4 x 45.7cm)
£340-380 *Bon*

Helena J. Maguire (1860-1909)
British
The Caught Rabbit
Signed and dated 1897, watercolour
12¾ x 18⅞in (32.4 x 48cm)
£850-900 *Bon*

Kathleen Irene Nixon (b.1894) Taken by Surprise
Signed, charcoal watercolour and gouache
14¼ x 21in (36.2 x 53.3cm)
£600-650 *Bon*

Anne Mortimer (20thC) British
Tosca Lives Here
Signed and dated '91, watercolour
6¾ x 4⅞in (17.2 x 12.4cm)
£280-300 *Bon*

Louis Wain (1860-1939) British
The Little Nipper
Signed, monochrome gouache
14 x 10½in (35.6 x 26.7cm)
£500-550 *Bon*

Louis Wain's cat pictures are well-established collectables. According to one London dealer, specialising in the work of British illustrators, in the summer months when the art market is dead and most galleries shut up shop, a Louis Wain show is always guaranteed to pull in the punters.

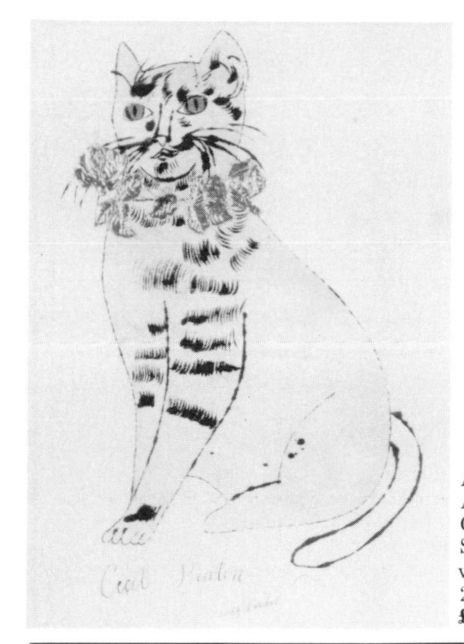

Andy Warhol (1930-87)
American
Cecil Beaton
Signed and titled, ink, watercolour and collage on paper
22 x 14¾in (56 x 36.5cm)
£5,300-5,500 *S*

Cornelis Raaphorst (1875-1954)
Dutch
Playful Kittens
Signed, oil on canvas
23½ x 31½in (60 x 80cm)
£2,900-3,200 *CAm*

CATS & DOGS

Henry William Carter (active 1867-93) British
Cat and Dog Life
Four in one mount – signed and dated 1882, oil on board
Each 4 x 5½in (10 x 14cm), overall 17 x 19½in (43 x 49.5cm) **£2,900-3,200** *S*

Bessie Bamber (late 19thC) British
'That's my Rug and Three's a Crowd' Signed, oil on white glass
6 x 8in (15.2 x 20.3cm) **£1,800-2,100** *C*

DOGS

17th & 18th Century

Adriaen Cornelisz Beeldemaker (1618-1709) Dutch
A Landscape with Hounds
Signed and dated 1690, oil on canvas
17½ x 20¾in (44.7 x 52.8cm)
£5,000-5,400 *S*

Francis Barlow (1626-1704)
British
The Fox, the Fowl and the Dog
Signed and dated 1695 and numbered 46, pen and brown ink and grey wash
6 x 8½in (15 x 22cm)
£2,100-2,400 *S*

Francis Barlow was the first British born artist to specialise in animals and sporting subjects – 'ye famous painter of fowls, birds and beasts', noted his equally renowned contemporary, the diarist John Evelyn. The powerful vitality of Barlow's drawings and prints had an important influence on the development of sporting painting in Britain. The price and the quality of the present work shows that drawings can offer real bargains to the discerning buyer.

Circle of Alexandre Francois Desportes (1661-1743)
French Stag Hunt
Oil on canvas
37¾ x 51in (95.9 x 129.5cm)
£16,000-17,000 *S(NY)*

Attributed to Sawrey Gilpin (1733-1807)
British
A Tibetan Spaniel, owned by Sir George Wombwell Bt
Oil on canvas
24½ x 30in (62 x 76cm)
£11,600-12,000 *S*

Gilpin was one of the most important animal artists of the 18thC, and though only attributed to his hand the present work nearly tripled its £2,000-4,000 estimate when sold at auction at the end of 1991.

Attributed to Sawrey Gilpin (1733-1807)
British
Sir George Wombwell's Pointer
Oil on canvas
28½ x 40¼in (72.5 x 102cm)
£4,200-4,500 *S*

19th & 20th Century

Cecil Charles Windsor Aldin (1870-1935)
British
The Soul's Awakening
Signed and inscribed, pencil and black chalk
6¾ x 7in (17 x 17.5cm)
£950-1,000 *S*

English School (19thC)
A King Charles Spaniel Seated on a Stool
Indistinctly signed, oil on panel
9¾ x 13¼in (24.8 x 33.6cm)
£2,300-2,600 *C*

Richard Ansdell (1815-85)
British
Meal Time
Signed and dated 1866, oil on canvas
44 x 33in (111.7 x 83.8cm)
£21,980-22,980 *HFA*

Born in Liverpool, Ansdell became one of the most successful sporting and animal painters of the day. Following the 19thC vogue for all things Scottish, he painted many highland scenes: stags in glens, moorland shooting parties, cattle in lochs, etc; he also produced a number of historical and Spanish genre pictures. Like his great rival Edwin Landseer, the ultimate Victorian animal painter, Ansdell was forgotten for many years and it was not until the 1960s/70s that his work was reassessed.

Robert Cleminson (active 1860s)
British
Gun Dogs at Rest (pair)
Signed, oil on canvas
27½ x 29½in (70 x 90cm)
£6,800-7,200 *S(SC)*

Eden Box (d.1988)
British
A Lonely Winter
Signed, oil on canvas
19½ x 23¼in (49.5 x 59cm)
£850-950 *C*

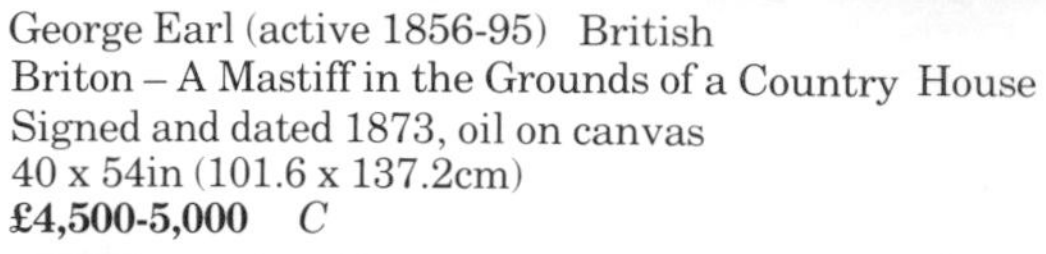

George Earl (active 1856-95) British
Briton – A Mastiff in the Grounds of a Country House
Signed and dated 1873, oil on canvas
40 x 54in (101.6 x 137.2cm)
£4,500-5,000 *C*

John Emms (1843-1912) British
Jim; Head of a Jack Russell (pair)
Both signed and one dated '93,
oil on canvas 10 x 8in (25.5 x 20.5cm)
£1,700-1,800 *S*

English School (19thC)
'A Bulldog' and seven other studies of different
dogs, all by different hands including Colin Graeme (Roe)
Various media and measurements
£5,000-5,300 *C*

W. J. Gibbon (mid-19thC) British
A King Charles Spaniel on a Blue Stool
Signed, oil on canvas
13¼ x 15¾in (33.6 x 40cm)
£1,000-1,200 *C*

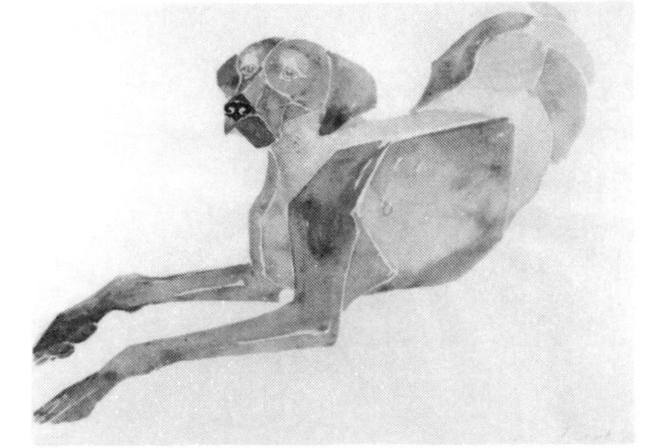

Elizabeth Frink (b.1930) British
A Great Dane
Signed and dated 1980, watercolour
22 x 30in (55.8 x 76cm)
£3,300-3,500 *SCG*

Charles Jones (1836-92) British
On the Moor
Signed and dated '87, pencil and watercolour
heightened with white on card
12 x 16in (30.5 x 40.6cm)
£600-700 *C*

Niels Aagard Lytzen (1826-90)
Danish
A Golden Retriever in a Landscape
Signed and dated 1853, oil on canvas
49 x 60in (124.4 x 152.3cm)
£2,300-2,500 *C*

Alan Parker (b.1965)
British
Green Jacket
Signed
43 x 50in (109 x 127cm)
£1,100-1,400 *Bon*

Moritz Muller (1841-99)
German
A Hound with a Fox
Signed, oil on canvas
7 x 9⅞in (17.8 x 25cm)
£850-900 *CSK*

Charles McRobb (early 19thC)
British
A Water Spaniel and Fox Terriers
Signed and dated 1821, oil on canvas
27 x 33⅛in (68.6 x 84.2cm)
£2,300-2,500 *C*

Frank Paton (1856-1909)
British
Midge
Signed and dated 1908, watercolour
10 x 13in (25.4 x 33.3cm)
£550-600 *DN*

Paton's works neatly encapsulate two classic examples of dog painting that regularly appear in the market place: the hunting dog with its prey, and the lapdog on its cushion.

Frank Paton (1856-1909)
British
Retriever and Partridge
Signed and dated 1895, watercolour and gouache
9 x 12¾in (23 x 32.5cm)
£750-850 *S(S)*

Condition is a major factor in a picture's price

George Soper (1870-1942)
British
The Weekend Luggage
Signed, etching (together with another signed etching)
5⅞ x 7⅞in (14.9 x 20cm)
£400-450 *Bon*

Philip Eustace Stretton (1884-1919)
British
'Jock' – a Favourite Jack Russell; Study of the Head of a Staffordshire Bull Terrier A pair, both signed and dated 1896 and 1898 respectively, oil on canvas laid down on board
11½ x 9in (29 x 23cm)
£2,600-3,000 *S(S)*

George Soper (1870-1942)
The Gollywog's Friend
Signed, etching (together with two other etchings)
£300-330 *Bon*

Frances E. Young (20thC)
British
Mouse and Nipper
Signed
Rectangular – 4in (10cm)
Sold at auction along with photographs of the dogs with members of the artist's family.
£300-330 *Bea*

Samuel Spode (19thC)
British
'Dido' and 'Fop' – Two Favourite Pointers
Inscribed with dogs' names, oil on canvas
17½ x 23in (44.5 x 58cm)
£1,450-1,550 *S*

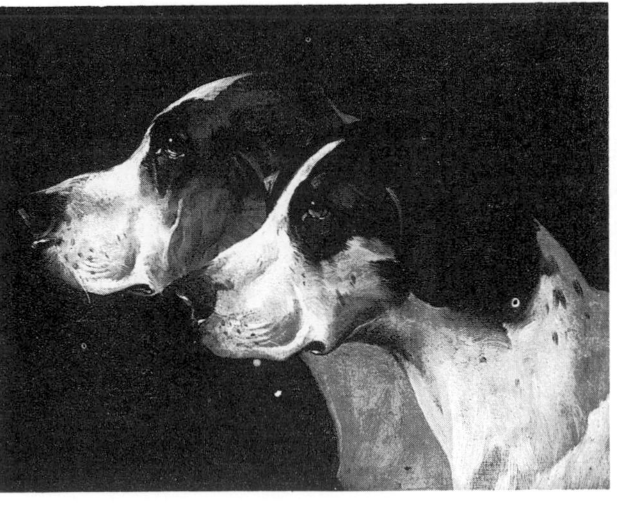

John Arnold Wheeler (1821-1904)
British
Fox Hounds
Oil on canvas
16 x 20¼in (40.6 x 51.4cm)
£1,800-2,100 *C*

FISH

Only a very few artists specialised in fish and Victorian pictures tend to fall into two main categories – the fish as sporting trophy and as still life subject. All the 19thC examples illustrated below fetched over their estimate at auction, reflecting both the rarity of pictures in the field and the appeal of the subject itself – fishing after all, being one of the most popular international pastimes.

A Roland-Knight (late 19thC)
British
A Prize Salmon; Landing a Perch; A Trout Jumping; Gaffing a Pike
Set of four, all signed, oil on board
5½ x 8½in (14 x 21.5cm)
£1,850-2,000 *S(S)*

Attributed to Henry Leonidas Rolfe (active 1847-81)
British
Coarse Fish on the River Bank
Oil on canvas
23½ x 28½in (59.9 x 72.5cm)
£2,500-2,700 *S*

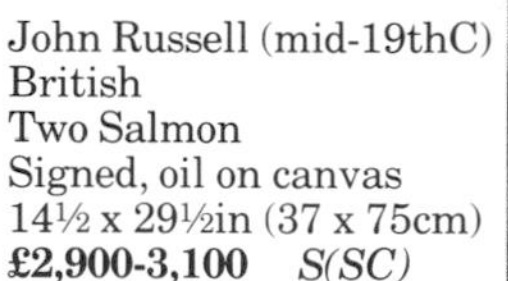

John Russell (mid-19thC)
British
Two Salmon
Signed, oil on canvas
14½ x 29½in (37 x 75cm)
£2,900-3,100 *S(SC)*

Frances E. Young (20thC) British
Golden Gleam Signed and dated 1935
Rectangular 3½in (8.8cm)
£75-100 *Bea*

Andrei Gennadiev (b.1947) Russian
'Danger'
Executed in 1978, etching with watercolour
12 x 12in (30.5 x 30.5cm)
£2,000-3,000 *RMG*

FARMYARD ANIMALS

An established subject matter of 17thC Dutch and Flemish painting, the portrayal of farm animals reached its zenith of popularity in the 19thC. As society became increasingly urbanised, so patrons demanded pictures of rural scenes: cattle grazing in the meadows, lambs gambolling in the fields, decorative and deoderised pictures of country life. Today, galleries and auction houses are still filled with these pictures, showing us not only that vast numbers of them were produced throughout Europe, but also suggesting that the taste of modern purchasers differs very little from that of their Victorian forebears.

Follower of Philipp Peter Roos, called Rosa da Tivoli (1657-1706)
German
Peasants Watering Cattle and Sheep
A pair
13½ x 15⅝in (34.2 x 29.5cm)
£2,800-3,000 *C*

17th & 18th Century

David de Conink (1636-99)
Flemish
Rabbits and Birds Surprised by a Cat in a Landscape, a Cockerel looking on
Oil on canvas
35½ x 49in (90 x 124cm)
£24,000-25,000 *WT*

'Though selective, the Old Master market is holding up well,' notes Bond Street dealer William Theuiller. 'Prices are as strong as ever for pictures of exceptional quality, in good condition and reasonably new to the market. This robust, colourful work is typical of De Coninck's animal landscapes and came from a private collection in Brussels.'

Marmaduke Cradock, c1660-1716/17
British
Poultry in a River Landscape
Oil on canvas
19 x 23in (48 x 58.5cm)
£2,500-2,800 *S*

Follower of Pieter Casteels (18thC) Flemish
Poultry in a Farmyard Oil on canvas
20 x 26½in (51 x 67.5cm) **£3,700-4,000** *S*

Dutch School, 18thC
A Shepherdess and Her Lover with Sheep and Cattle
Oil on canvas
13¾ x 16¼in (34.8 x 41.2cm)
£1,700-2,000 *Bon*

George Morland (1762/63-1804) British
Sheep in a Stable in Winter
Signed and dated 1799, oil on panel
13¼ x 17¾in (34 x 45.5cm)
£3,600-4,000 *S*

Morland 'was very precocious, naturally gifted and naturally dissolute' notes Ellis Waterhouse (Dictionary of British 18th Century Painters – Antique Collector's Club, 1981). He spent his apprenticeship producing gifted copies and forgeries of Dutch landscapes. His own work included genre pictures, landscapes and rural scenes. 'The best of them are remarkable in execution and wonderfully true in tone, and the total absence of any intellectual qualities have made them always very popular,' writes Waterhouse. Morland's pictures became extremely successful, and ironically ended up being copied, faked and falsely signed themselves in large numbers. According to reports, in his declining years Morland was rarely sober and spent much of his time hiding from creditors or in prison.

John Harris was a publisher who produced a number of Morland's drawings in sketchbook form.

George Morland (1762/63-1804) British
Study of Heads and Calves
Signed and inscribed for J. Harris Esq/Grower of Gardens Oil on canvas
9 x 10½in (23.5 x 26.5cm)
£1,800-2,000 *S*

19th & 20th Century

William Baptiste Baird (b.1847)
American
Chickens
Oil on board
9½ x 13in (24 x 33cm)
£1,200-1,500 *S*

David Bates 1840-1921
British
In Glen Mullan, Dumbartonshire
Signed, oil on canvas
43½ x 33½in (110 x 85cm)
£1,700-1,900 *A*

Anton Braith (1835-1905)
German
Goats Grazing
Signed and dated Munchen 1878, oil on panel
9¼ x 12½in (23.6 x 31.7cm)
£10,000-10,500 *C*

Miller's is a price GUIDE not a price LIST

Thomas Sidney Cooper RA (1803-1902)
British
Sheep in the Snow
Signed, inscribed and dated 1867, watercolour
8½ x 11in (21.5 x 28cm)
£2,550-3,000 *S*

Henry Charles Bryant (active 1860-80)
British
In the Farmyard
Signed, oil
20 x 24in (50.8 x 60.9cm)
£4,000-4,250 *Dr*

Thomas Sidney Cooper (1803-1902)
British
At The Ford
Signed and dated 1833, oil on canvas
17 x 21¼in (43 x 54cm)
£4,500-5,000 *S*

A hugely popular painter, both in the 19thC and today, Cooper specialised in studies of sheep and cattle in landscapes. He was extremely prolific and told fellow artist, Sir William Orchardson that he painted two pictures before breakfast every day of his life. 'No wonder his pictures are all alike and equally bad,' commented Orchardson sourly. 'He has perfected his imperfections.' In spite of this lack of versatility, the quality of Cooper's paintings remained constant until the 1890s. He showed at the Royal Academy every year in between 1833-1902 (a record for continuous exhibiting) and died at the age of 99.

Claude Cardon (active 1892-1915) British Eye to Eye Signed, oil on canvas 10 x 14in (25.5 x 35.5cm) **£1,700-1,900** *S*

William Albert Clark (20thC)
British
A portrait of the Heifer
'Dene Starette 2nd'
Signed and dated 1930
20 x 24in (50.8 x 60.9cm)
£600-675 *Bon*

Thomas Sidney Cooper (1803-1902) British The End of November 1872
Signed and dated 1872, oil on canvas 48 x 72½in (122 x 183.5)
Exhibited: Royal Academy 1873, No. 235 **£10,000-10,400** *S*

William Sidney Cooper (1854-1927) British
Cattle Watering
Signed and dated 1912, watercolour
8¾ x 11½in (22.2 x 29.2cm)
£530-600 *P(S)*

English Primitive School (19thC)
A Gloucester Old Spot Sow
Oil on board
11⅝ x 13⅜in (29.5 x 34cm)
£900-1,000 *Bon*

Thomas Sidney Cooper (1803-1902) British
Donkey and Sheep in a Meadow
Signed and dated 1880, oil on panel
18 x 13¾in (45.7 x 35cm)
£5,000-5,400 *C*

Peter Graham (1836-1921) British
Misty Moorland
Signed and dated 1874, oil on canvas
15 x 24in (38 x 61cm)
£750-850 *S(SC)*

Andrès Cortés y Aguilar (19thC)
Spanish
Peasants Tending Cattle in a Landscape
Signed, oil on canvas
31 x 49in (79 x 124.5cm)
£2,800-3,200 *S(S)*

H. R. Hall (19thC)
British
Highland Cattle – Loch Achray, Scotland
Signed and inscribed with title
24 x 36in (60 x 90cm)
£550-650 *HSS*

John Frederick Herring, Jnr
(active second half 19thC, d.1907)
British
A Welcome Feed
Signed, oil on board
10 x 13¾in (25 x 35cm)
£5,000-5,300 *S(S)*

English Provincial School (c1850)
Three Prize Pigs – bred by Sir George Wombwell Bt
(The three pigs took first prize at Birmingham in 1860)
oil on canvas
22 x 30in (56 x 76cm)
£3,400-3,700 *S*

Though badly damaged, the present work nearly tripled its original auction estimate. It epitomises the charm of the provincial animal portrait both in its style and its proud inscription, recording the prize-winning triumphs of long dead animals.

Robert Hills (1769-1844) British Ploughing Watercolour
11 x 15in (27.9 x 38cm) **£2,600-2,800** *MS*

George W. Horlor (active 1849-91)
British
The Children of the Mist
Signed and dated 1858, oil on canvas
36 x 55in (51.4 x 139.6cm)
£4,700-5,000 *C*

Gilbert Holiday (1879-1937)
British
The Kelp Cart, Guernsey
Signed, watercolour and bodycolour
12¼ x 9in (31 x 23cm)
£1,900-2,100 *C*

Walter Hunt (1861-1941)
British
Outside the Stable
Signed, oil on canvas
20 x 30in (50.8 x 76.2cm)
£18,750-19,750 *HFA*

Louis Bosworth Hurt (1856-1929)
British
Highland Cattle Grazing
Signed and dated 1882, oil on canvas
24 x 40in (61 x 102cm)
£3,600-3,800 *S*

Franz Van Severdonk (1809-99)
Belgian
Sheep and Lambs
Oil on board, signed and dated 1878, with a similar work (a pair)
7 x 10in (17 x 25cm)
£2,000-2,200 *HSS*

Franz Van Severdonk (1809-99)
Belgian
Cockerels, Pigeons and Ducks in a Landscape
Signed
7 x 10¼in (17.8 x 26cm)
Along with a companion piece (a pair)
£1,900-2,100 *Bon*

Walter Hunt (1861-1941) British
Feeding the Calves
Signed and dated 1931, oil on canvas
24 x 36in (61 x 91.4cm)
£25,000-27,890 *HFA*

Juris Jurans (b.1944) Russian Chickens
Initialled and painted in 1984, oil on canvas
51 x 35in (129.5 x 90cm)
£7,000-8,000 *RMG*

William Joseph Shayer (1811-91) British Wayside Conversation
Signed and dated 1870, oil on canvas
30 x 50in (76.2 x 127cm)
£3,800-4,200 *CSK*

William Grant Stevenson (1849-1919)
British
Feeding a Pet Lamb
Signed, oil on canvas
18 x 24in (46 x 61cm)
£800-850 *S(SC)*

John Macpherson (active 1865-94)
British
Sheep and Lambs Beside a River
Signed
5 x 6½in (12 x 16cm)
£240-280 *LH*

Constant Troyon (1810-65)
French
Milking Time
Signed, oil on canvas
36 x 28¾in (91.5 x 73cm)
£3,400-3,500 *C*

Eugene Verboeckhoven (1799-1881)
Belgian
The Young Shepherd
Oil on board
4¼ x 5¼in (10.5 x 13.5cm)
£1,200-1,500 *S(S)*

Verboeckhoven was phenomenally successful in his own day. His pictures were appreciated with a true 19thC pragmatism and their market value rose and fell along with the number of animals portrayed. A client visiting his studio once asked the price of a painting of a ewe and two lambs. 'A thousand francs for the ewe and two hundred per head of lamb,' replied the artist promptly. On discovering that the client couldn't quite afford this figure, Verboeckhoven's response was typically resourceful and businesslike – 'I'll make it two hundred francs cheaper,' he responded and seizing his brush, painted out one of the lambs.

Dorothea Sharp (1874-1955)
British
The Young Goat Herd
Signed, oil on canvas
32 x 31in (31.2 x 78.74cm)
£22,000-24,000 *Dr*

Charles Frederick Tunnicliffe (1901-79)
British
To the Slaughter
Etching, signed and numbered 6/75 in pencil
11½ x 8½in (29 x 21.5cm)
£300-350 *CSK*

Thomas Woodward (1801-52)
British
A Prize Cow in a Landscape
Bears an inscribed label on stretcher: Gained the Highland First Class Prize for the best cow at Aberdeen in 1840, oil
17¼ x 23½in (44 x 60cm)
£950-1,100 *S(S)*

Along with many other well-connected clients, Queen Victoria and Prince Albert employed Woodward to paint portraits of their favourite animals.

DONKEYS

Apparently a popular subject since all works, except the Thiollet, fetched over their estimate at auction.

Agnes M. Cowieson (20thC)
British
Waiting for Hire, Portobello Sands
11 x 15in (28 x 38cm)
£1,600-1,800 *S(SC)*

Enrico Coleman (1846-1911) Italian
Beasts of Burden
Signed and inscribed Roma, watercolour
13½ x 20½in (34.2 x 52cm)
£4,800-5,300 *Bea*

Louis Marie Dominique Robbe (1806-87) Belgian
A Donkey and Two Chickens in a Barn
Signed
15½ x 23¼ (39.5 x 59cm)
£1,200-1,500 *S(S)*

Alexandre Thiolett (1824-95) French
The Donkey Boy Signed, oil on panel
14 x 11in (35.5 x 28cm) **£2,000-2,300** *C*

HORSES

Sporting painting is one of the most distinctive areas of British Art. The first native-born artists to specialise in the field emerged in the mid-1600s and throughout the 18th and the 19thC, the English patron commissioned paintings of his horses and favourite animals as readily as pictures of his family. In the majority of cases, the standard horse portrait was more of a photographic than an aesthetic production. The thoroughbred horse was the great status symbol of the age and owners wanted their animals accurately and clearly documented. Pictures are often inscribed with details of a horse's show career and parentage, and works constitute a form of pictorial equine Burke's Peerage.

Apart from portraits other types of horse picture that emerge frequently in the salerooms include racing and hunting pictures, coaching scenes, farmyard and country life pictures (patient plough horses at work or in the stable), and related genre scenes: Victorian portrayals of 17th and 18thC cavaliers; sentimental and romantic encounters between rider and his lady, the onlooking horse itself often adopting a suitably sweet and soupy expression.

Follower of Antonio Tempesta (1555-1630) Italian
A Rearing Horse; and a Charger A pair, black and white chalk on light blue paper 11⅞ x 16½in (30.3 x 41.9cm)
£1,520-1,600 *S(NY)*

John Wootton (1686-1765) British
A Match on Newmarket Heath Oil on canvas
24 x 28¾in (61 x 73cm) **£2,000-2,200** *S*

Abraham Van Diepenbeek (1596-1675) Dutch
Trot à Gauche
Red and black chalk, grey wash
8 x 5¾in (20.3 x 14.7cm)
With another drawing attributed to Pieter van Bloemen (a pair)
£380-430 *S(NY)*

Paul Sandby (1725-1809) British Cart Horses Pulling a Timber Wagon
Watercolour over pencil on laid paper 3 x 8¾in (8 x 22cm)
With two other drawings of horses and huntsmen by James Seymour
£2,100-2,300 *S*

19th Century

After Cecil Aldin (1870-1935)
British
The Grand National: First Open Ditch; The Canal Turn; Becher's Brook and Valentines
A set of four reproductions in colours, numbered 220, signed in pencil, published by Richard Wyman and Co Ltd
6¼ x 12in (15.8 x 30.4cm)
£220-280 *Bon*

After Henry Alken (1785-1951) British
A Steeple Chase
A set of four hand-tinted aquatint engravings, engraved by Bentley after H. Alken, published by Fuller 1832, Plates 1-4, original state, maplewood frames (a.f.)
15 x 21in (38 x 53.3cm)
£450-475 *L&E*

After William and Henry Baraud (1810-50) (1811-74)
British
'The Hero' with Alfred Day and John Day Snr
Aquatint by J. Harris after W. and H. Baraud, original rosewood frame
17½ x 27½in (44.5 x 70cm)
£775-825 *CG*

E. Corbet (19thC)
British
'Chief Constable'
Signed and dated 1873, oil on canvas
17½ x 23½in (44.4 x 59.7cm)
£650-750 *Bon*

Painters of horse portraits worked to an established pattern and would often have standard charges: a certain amount for a horse in a stable, more for the horse outdoors with a bit of landscape and still more if you wanted the groom, jockey or a portrait of yourself included, with perhaps a favourite hunting dog by your side.

Willem Jacobus Boogaard (1842-87)
Dutch
A Stable Interior
Signed and indistinctly dated
7¾ x 10¾in (20 x 27cm)
Oil on panel,
with a companion piece (a pair)
£3,900-4,200 *Bon*

Albert Clark (active 1892-1909)
British
Gentleman John
Signed, inscribed with details
of show career on frame,
oil on canvas
17¾ x 23½in (44.5 x 59.5cm)
£1,000-1,200 *S(S)*

English School (19thC)
Study of a Brown Horse and Two Dogs in a Stable
Oil on canvas
18 x 24in (45.7 x 61cm)
£550-600 *Bon*

Follower of Alfred H. Green
(active 1844-62)
British
Before the Departure
Oil on canvas
26 x 32in (66.1 x 81.3cm)
£800-1,000 *CSK*

Heywood Hardy (1843-1933)
British
Saddling Up
Initialled and dated 1883
Oil on panel
8 x 13in (20.3 x 46cm)
£5,100-5,500 *HLG*

Heywood Hardy (1843-1933) British
The New Bridle
Signed, oil on canvas
20 x 30¼in (50.8 x 76.8cm)
£10,200-11,000 *C*

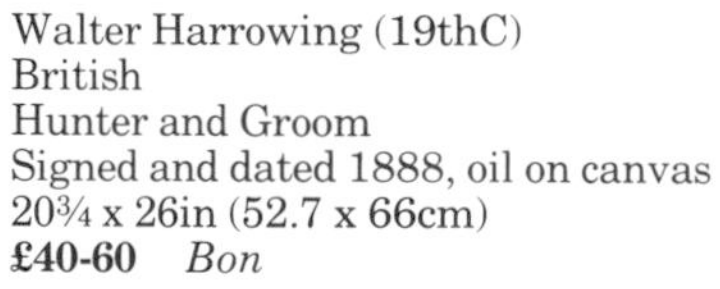

Walter Harrowing (19thC)
British
Hunter and Groom
Signed and dated 1888, oil on canvas
20¾ x 26in (52.7 x 66cm)
£40-60 *Bon*

Captain Adrian Jones (1845-1938)
British
Persimmon
Signed, oil on canvas
11½ x 14½in (29 x 37cm)
£1,600-1,800 *S*

John Frederick Herring Jnr
(1815-1907)
British
A Rest from Labour
Signed and dated 1851,
oil on canvas
15¼ x 20in (38.5 x 51cm)
£4,500-4,700 *S*

After John Frederick Herring Snr (1795-1865) British
'Birmingham' – Winner of the St Leger 1830 Aquatint by R. G. Reeve after Herring, published in 1831 by S. & J. Fuller (Minerva Head Blind Stamp), Ackerman '86
11¼ x 16¼in (28.5 x 41.2cm)
£1,250-1,450 *CG*

Stanley Smith (late 19thC?) British
Loading the Cart
Signed, on canvas board
15½ x 11½in (39.5 x 29cm)
£950-1,050 *CSK*

George Goodwin Kilburne
(1839-1924)
British
Sugar
Signed, watercolour heightened with white
14½ x 20½in (37 x 52cm)
£2,250-2,600 *S*

Follower of William Luker (19thC)
British
A Bay Horse and Two Dogs
Oil on canvas
25 x 30in (63.5 x 76cm)
£1,400-1,600 *S*

Circle of James Pollard (1792-1867)
British
Outside the Village Inn
Oil on paper laid down on canvas
9¾ x 13½in (25 x 34.5cm)
£600-650 *S*

William Tasker (1808-52)
British
The Stable
Signed and dated 1849, watercolour
15¼ x 23½in (38 x 60cm)
£650-735 *BCG*

C. B. Spalding (exhibited 1840-49)
British
'Haidee', a chestnut racehorse, the property of Colonel Crawford, in a stable
Signed and dated 1841, oil on canvas
31½ x 41½in (80 x 105.5cm)
With a companion piece (a pair)
£5,600-6,000 *S*

Haidee, by Langar out of Mermaid, was owned by Colonel Crawford.

Samuel Spode (19thC) British
Voltigeur; The Flying Dutchman (a pair)
Signed and inscribed with title, oil on canvas
17¾ x 23¾in (45 x 60.5cm)
£4,500-4,700 *S(S)*

Jules Jacques Veyrassat (1828-93)
French
Harvest Scene
Signed, oil on canvas
18 x 24in (45.7 x 61cm)
£6,000-6,500 *HLG*

Gilbert S. Wright (active late 19th/early 20thC)
British The Wayward Groom
Signed, oil on canvas 15 x 24in (38 x 61cm)
£15,000-15,500 *HLG*

Gilbert S. Wright
(active late 19th/early 20th)
British
Horse Thieves
Signed, oil on canvas
18 x 26in (46 x 66cm)
£2,800-3,100 *S*

20th Century

John Berry (b.1920)
British
Shire Mare and Foal
Signed and dated 1989
Oil
16 x 24in (40.6 x 61cm)
£2,000-2,200 *Dr*

Miller's is a price GUIDE not a price LIST

John Berry (b.1920) British 'Black Beauty'
Gouache 6 x 11in (15.2 x 28cm) **£425-450** *Dr*

The present work was an original illustration to the version of Black Beauty published by 'Ladybird', for whom Berry worked in the 1960s and 70s. The Driffold Gallery holds the archive collections of 'Ladybird' books illustrations by both Berry and artist Harry Wingfield. 'The pictures have proved extremely successful with everyone from dealers, to serious collectors, to those who simply enjoyed reading the books as children', observes proprietor David Gilbert. 'You could sell Black Beauty a hundred times over.'

Artist John Berry also influenced popular culture in another direction, being the inspiration and illustrator for the original Esso Tiger.

Marino Marini (1901-80)
Italian
Cavaliere
Signed, executed in the early 1950s, gouache, coloured crayon, pen and black ink and wash heightened with white on paper
19⅝ x 13¾in (49.3 x 34.9cm)
£14,500-15,000 *C*

Henry Lamb (1883-1960) British The Stable
Pencil and watercolour 8½ x 9¾in (21.5 x 25cm)
£450-500 *C*

Orovida Pissarro (1893-1968)
British
The Stable Lantern
Signed and dated 1957, oil on canvas
50 x 40in (127 x 102cm)
£2,100-2,200 *C*

Raoul Millais (b.1901)
French
Horses startled by Fire
Signed, oil on canvas
16 x 20in (41 x 51cm)
£3,400-3,600 *C*

Allen Culpeper Sealy (late 19th/early 20thC) British
A Chestnut Racehorse with Jockey Up Signed and dated 1905, oil on canvas 21 x 25¼in (53.3 x 65.5cm) **£1,000-1,250** *CSK*

Harry Wingfield (b.1910) British
The Mare and Foal Signed, gouache
11 x 8in (30 x 20.3cm) **£350-375** *Dr*

The present work was an original illustration for the Ladybird book 'Jane and Peter on the Farm'.

Rowland Wheelwright (1870-1955) British
The Dinner Hour Oil on canvas
40 x 60in (101.6 x 152.6cm)
£13,400-14,600 *C*

COACHING SCENES

Mail and stagecoach scenes are an established theme of 19thC painting. Often produced in pairs, pictures show the loading up of the coach at the wayside inn, the excitement of arrivals and departures, the progress of the stagecoach as it rattled through the English countryside in all seasons and all weathers. In the early 19thC, the stagecoach was the most important form of public transport. London to Edinburgh took only 44 hours at 'the astonishing speed of just under ten miles an hour', and William Hazlitt claimed that the conversation on the stagecoach from London to Oxford was far more interesting and informative than anything one might hear in the colleges themselves. The advent of the railways in the 1830s and 40s brought an end to the world of the stagecoach, and even their vocabulary: carriage and coach, was taken over by the train.

T. Ivester Lloyd (19thC) British The Toll Gate
Signed 9 x 14in (23 x 34cm) **£425-525** *HSS*

W. H. Wheelwright (active second half 19thC)
British
A Coach and Four on the Open Road
Signed and dated 1870, watercolour and bodycolour over pencil
8¼ x 13in (20.5 x 33cm)
And a companion piece (a pair)
£700-800 *S(S)*

HUNTING PRINTS AND PICTURES

'Although the market is generally depressed, good sporting prints have throughout their life been a fairly stable market,' notes specialist dealer Edwin Collins of the Coltsfoot Gallery. 'There is still a strong demand for rare prints: fine early impressions in pristine condition. Quality will always sell because people are afraid that the works won't be around in a few years time. Good watercolours are also still selling, but not at the prices they fetched two or three years ago.'

George Wright (1860-1942) British At the Red Lion
Signed, grisaille, oil on canvas 16 x 24in (40.5 x 61cm)
£1,550-1,700 *S*

19th and 20th Century

Henry Alken Jnr (1810-94) British
'Full Cry' and 'Over the Ditch' (a pair)
Both signed, oil on panel
8¾ x 14½in (22 x 37cm) **£4,600-5,000** *S*

After W. & H. Barraud (19thC) British
'The Meet at Badminton' Engraved by W. Giller, published 1847 by Henry Graves
16¾ x 29in (42.5 x 73.6cm) **£800-875** *CG*

Circle of Henry Alken Jnr (19thC)
British
Hunting Scenes (a set of four)
Signed
12½ x 16½in (31.5 x 42cm)
£1,800-2,000 *S(S)*

Edwin W. Cooper (1785-1833)
British
Mr Maberley, Huntsman to the Surrey Foxhounds
Signed and dated 1819, pen and grey ink and watercolour
11¼ x 18¼in (28.6 x 46.3cm)
£1,700-2,200 *C*

Mr Maberley was huntsman to the Surrey Foxhounds 1812-20. Formerly coachbuilder to George III, Mr Maberley was a keen huntsman, and in 1812 became Master of the Surrey Foxhounds. Maberley had a fiery temper and engaged in a fierce row with Colonel Hylton Joliffe, MP, ex-Colonel of the Coldstream Guards and Master of the Merstham Hounds. The row concerned the digging of a fox, and was finally settled by drawing pistols on Alderstead Heath, both gentlemen firing wide!

Joseph Crawhall (19thC)
British
The Novice
Signed, watercolour and black ink
£2,300-2,500 *S (SC)*

Lionel Dalhousie Robertson Edwards (1878-1966)
British
A Check; Scent Failed
The Dulverton at Bampfylde Clump, South Molton, Devon
Signed, gouache
13½ x 9¾in (34.3 x 24.1cm)
£2,500-2,800 *Bea*

John Emms (1843-1912)
British
Preparing to Go Out
Signed, oil on canvas
28½ x 36¼in (72 x 92cm)
£14,000-14,500 *S*

Charles Edward Johnson (1832-1913) British
Signed and dated 1890, oil on canvas
39½ x 27½in (100.5 x 70cm)
£5,000-5,200 *S (SC)*

English School (19thC)
The Meet
Aquatint with hand-colouring
22 x 29¾in (55.8 x 75.6cm)
Together with three similar
£900-1,200 *Bon*

English School (early 19thC)
Portrait of a Sportsman Oil on canvas
35½ x 27½in (64.8 x 69.8cm)
£1,800-2,200 *Bon*

Prints are a confusing area for the beginner. Two 19thC sporting aquatints might portray the same image, but one could be worth tens of pounds and the other thousands, depending on whether the work is a fine early impression or a later reprint and whether the colouring is original. Other factors also come into play: some hunts are more fashionable than others and specialised sporting subjects will obviously appeal to those involved in that area. To find out more about prints, arm yourself with a good basic reference book which will explain terms and techniques (see Biblio), view auctions and above all visit specialist dealers. As in every other field, it is only through looking at the works themselves, and talking to experts, that one can begin to get some grasp of the subject.

After Francis Calcraft Turner (1795-1865)
British Hawking
Four coloured aquatints by R. G. Reeve, published by I. W. Laird 1839, late impressions, good condition 15¼ x 12¼in (38.5 x 31cm)
£650-750 *S(S)*

James Hardy Jnr (1832-89) British Ready for Action
Signed and dated '78 10 x 15in (26 x 40cm)
£3,200-3,500 *HSS*

George Edward Lodge (1860-1954) British
Woodcock Shooting
Signed and dated 1885, oil on panel
5½ x 9⅜in (14 x 23.8cm)
£2,900-3,100 *C*

Inscribed on the reverse: 'one of George Lodge's quite early sketches from his bedroom wall at Camberley'

John S. Sanderson Wells (active 1890-1940)
British
A Fine Hunting Morn
Signed, oil on canvas
20 x 16in (51 x 40.5cm)
£2,100-2,400 *S*

George Wright (1860-1942)
British
Hunting Scene in Full Cry
Signed, oil on canvas
10 x 17in (25.4 x 43.1cm)
£6,600-7,000 *I*

After Thomas Weaver (1774-1843)
British
John Corbett and his Foxhounds
Engraved by R. Woodman,
published in 1814 by
T. Weaver
Original maple frame
18½ x 24in (47 x 61cm)
£600-695 *CG*

ANIMALS AND WILDLIFE

18th Century

Nicola Viso (first half 18thC) Italian Animals in a River Landscape
Oil on canvas 30 x 50in (76 x 127cm) **£12,200-13,200** *S*

Circle of Samuel Howitt (1765-1822)
British
A Tiger and Tigress; A Lion and Lioness (a pair)
Oil on panel
13 x 18in (33 x 45.8cm)
£1,000-1,200 *CSK*

Follower of Samuel Howitt (1765-1822) British
A Lion and Tiger Fighting in a Cave; A Tiger with its Kill, a Lion Looking On (a pair)
Oil on canvas 20 x 25½in (50.8 x 64.8cm)
£830-900 *CSK*

19th and 20th Century

Follower of Jacques Laurent Agasse (1767-1849) Swiss Two Rabbits Eating Carrots
Oil on panel 5¾ x 8½in (14 x 21.5cm) **£2,300-2,600** *S*

Edward Julius Detmold (1883-1957)
British
The Jungle King
Signed and numbered 2/12, aquatint
12½ x 16¾in (31.7 x 42.5cm)
£1,600-1,800 *Bon*

The story of Edward Detmold and his twin brother Charles is a tragic one. Both were successful artists, working in tandem and specialising in drawings and prints of plants and animals. Their partnership was abruptly terminated in 1908 when Charles committed suicide by inhaling chloroform in a fit of guilt after having chloroformed the family cats on the orders of his uncle. Nearly half a century later, his brother also killed himself.

Joseph Schippers (1868-1950)
Belgian
The Miser
Signed and dated 1915
10 x 13in (25.4 x 33cm)
£1,000-1,300 *Bon*

*'Singeries', monkeys dressed up and 'aping' humans were a popular theme of 19thC painting.
Our own equivalent today is the monkeys in the Typhoo Tea ads*

Eileen Soper (1905-90) British Ring-tailed Lemur and Young
Signed, watercolour 14¼ x 20¾in (36.2 x 52.8cm)
£400-450 *Bon*

Eileen Soper (1905-90)
British
Red Squirrels
Signed, watercolour
15¼ x 11¼in (38.8 x 28.5cm)
£550-630 *Bon*

Arthur Wardle (1864-1949)
British
Tigers at Dusk
Signed, oil on canvas
26 x 32in (66 x 81.3cm)
£13,300-14,000 *C*

T. B. Whaite (19thC)
British
An Artful Dodger
Signed, oil on board, inscribed and dated 1878
16 x 26in (40.7 x 66cm)
£550-650 *Bon*

Pierre Alechinsky
(b.1927)
Belgian
En Connaissance
de Cause
Signed, titled and
dated 1974,
acrylic on paper
laid down on canvas
45 x 60½in (114 x 154cm)
£35,000-45,000 *S*

Frank Auerbach (b.1931)
British
Seated Model in Studio IV
Oil on wood
12 x 6in (30.5 x 15.2cm)
£22,000-30,000 *S(NY)*

John Baldessari (20thC)
American (?)
Stain
Vinyl paint and oil tint on
photograph mounted on
paperboard in two parts
Overall: 89½ x 57¼in
(227.3 x 145.4cm)
£10,000-12,000 *S(NY)*

Karel Appel (b.1921)
Dutch Animal
Signed and dated
1955, oil on canvas
21⅝ x 18⅛in
(54.9 x 46cm)
£25,000-30,000
S(NY)

Horst Antes (b.1936) German
Figur, die Kleinen Kopf Tragt
Signed, titled, dated 1972 and
inscribed *Agnatu* on the
reverse, oil on canvas
59 x 47¼in (150.3 x 120cm)
£28,000-35,000 *S*

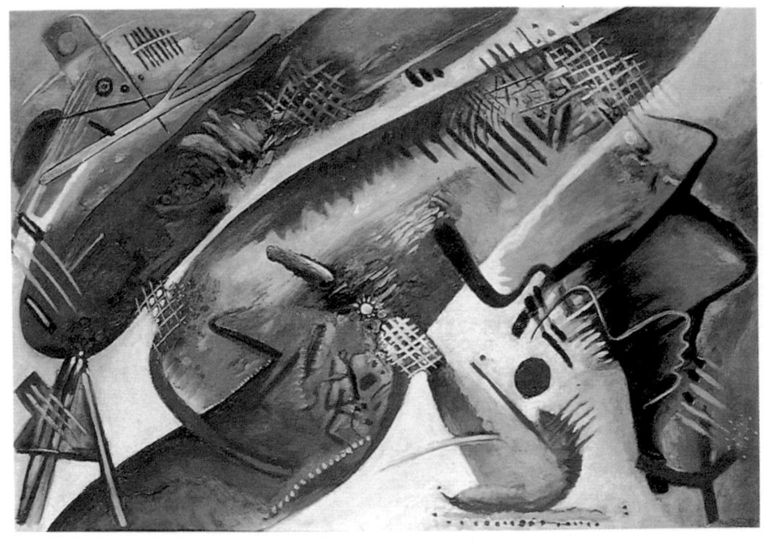

Rudolf Bauer (20thC)
German
Presto 7
Signed, oil on panel
29¼ x 40¾in (74.3 x 103.5cm)
£22,000-24,000 *S(NY)*
Painted in 1919

Afro (Basaldella) (b.1912)
Italian
Untitled
Signed and dated 52,
oil on canvas
21¼ x 29¼in (54 x 74.3cm)
£22,000-28,000 *S(NY)*

Victor Brauner (1903-1966)
Rumanian
Etre Retracte en Chien
1950, oil on canvas
21¼ x 25½in (54 x 65cm)
£115,000-125,000 *MAY*

Corneille (b.1922)
Dutch
Lumiere du Sud I
Signed and dated '59,
oil on canvas
31 x31in (79 x 79cm)
£29,000-34,000 *S*

Brian Clarke (20thC)
British
Words, Words, Words
(for ECF)
1989, oil on canvas
75 x 59in (190 x 150cm)
£16,500-17,500 *MAY*

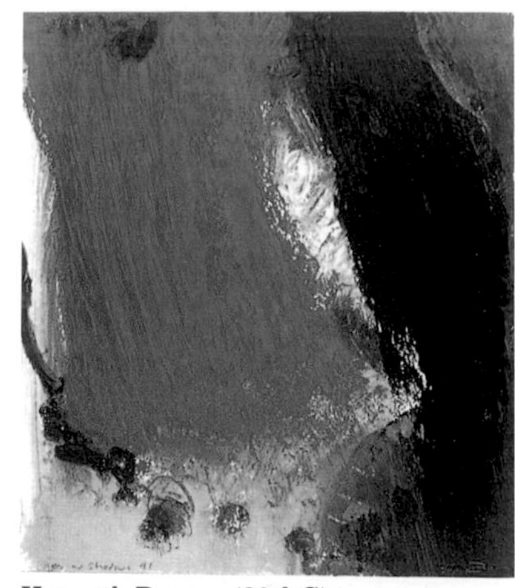

Kenneth Draper (20thC)
British
Edges and Shadows
Pastel
16 x 14in (41 x 36cm)
£900-1,100 *OLG*

Richard Diebenkorn (b.1922)
American
Ocean Park No.42
Signed with initials and dated 71,
oil on canvas
93 x 81in (236.2 x 205.7cm)
£250,000-275,000 *S(NY)*

Friedel Dzubas (b.1915)
American
Cold Hedge
Signed, titled and dated 73, oil on canvas
39 x 39in (99.1 x 99.1cm)
£9,000-9,500 *S(NY)*

Jim Dine (b.1935)
American
Hearts
Signed and dated 1968, enamel and
turpentine on paper
29½ x 31¼in (74.9 x 79.4cm)
£13,000-16,000 *S(NY)*

Jean Dubuffet (1901-1985)
French
Site avec 3 Personnages
Signed with initials and dated 81,
acrylic on paper mounted on canvas
26⅜ x 19⅝in (67 x 49.8cm)
£32,000-37,000 *S(NY)*

Helen Frankenthaler (b.1928)
American
Yellow Crater
Signed, titled and dated 63-64, oil on canvas
$80\frac{3}{4}$ x $68\frac{3}{4}$in (205.1 x 174.6cm)
£83,000-93,000 *S(NY)*

Sam Francis (b.1923)
American
Untitled
Acrylic on canvas
36 x $71\frac{3}{4}$in (91.4 x 182.2cm)
£65,000-75,000 *S(NY)*
Painted in 1982

Emil Filla (1882-1953)
Czech
L'Escargot
Signed and dated 42, oil on canvas
14 x 18in (35 x 45.7cm)
£5,000-5,300 *C*

Philip Guston (b.1912)
American
Painter and Model
Signed, titled and dated 1969, oil on masonite
30 x 40in (76.2 x 101.6cm)
£110,000-125,000 *S(NY)*

William Gear (b.1915)
British
In the Garden
Signed and dated '48
22 x 15in (56 x 38cm)
£1,100-1,500 *CSK*

Albert Gleizes (1881-1953)
French
L'homme dans les Buildings
Signed, titled and dated *NY 1920*,
gouache on board, mounted on board
$14\frac{7}{8}$ x $9\frac{1}{8}$in (37.8 x 23.2cm)
£13,000-15,000 *S(NY)*

Hans Hartung (1904-1989)
French
T1971-H14
Signed and dated '71 and titled on the stretcher, oil on canvas
60½ x 98¼in (154 x 250cm)
£50,000-60,000 *S*

Jean Hélion (b.1904)
French
Equilibre
Signed and dated *Paris '34,* oil on canvas
8½ x 10½in (21.5 x 26.5cm)
£28,000-35,000 *S*

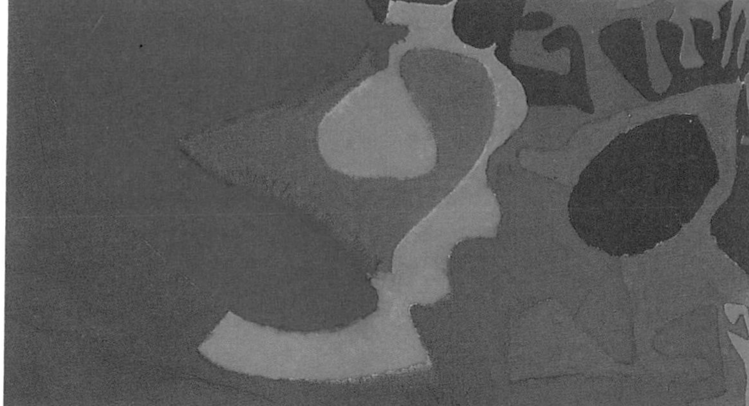

Patrick Heron (b.1920)
British
Design for Carpet
Signed and dated 1978 on reverse, gouache
9 x 15in (23 x 39.4cm)
£3,300-3,500 *Wa*

Ivon Hitchens (1893-1979)
British
Surroundings of Water
Signed and dated '72, inscribed on a label on the stretcher *"Surroundings of Water" 1973 oil painting, presented to Mr Owen Roberts M.P.S. in May 1974,* oil on canvas
16 x 29¼in (40.5 x 74cm)
£8,600-9,000 *C*

Fernand Léger (1881-1955)
French
Composition
Signed and dated 46,
oil on canvas
$21^{1}/_{4}$ x $24^{3}/_{4}$in (54 x 65cm)
£120,000-140,000 *S*

André Lanskoy (1902-1976)
Russian
Abstrait
Signed, gouache and pastel
on paper
Sheet: $25^{1}/_{2}$ x $19^{5}/_{8}$in
(64.8 x 49.8cm)
£4,600-5,000 *S(NY)*

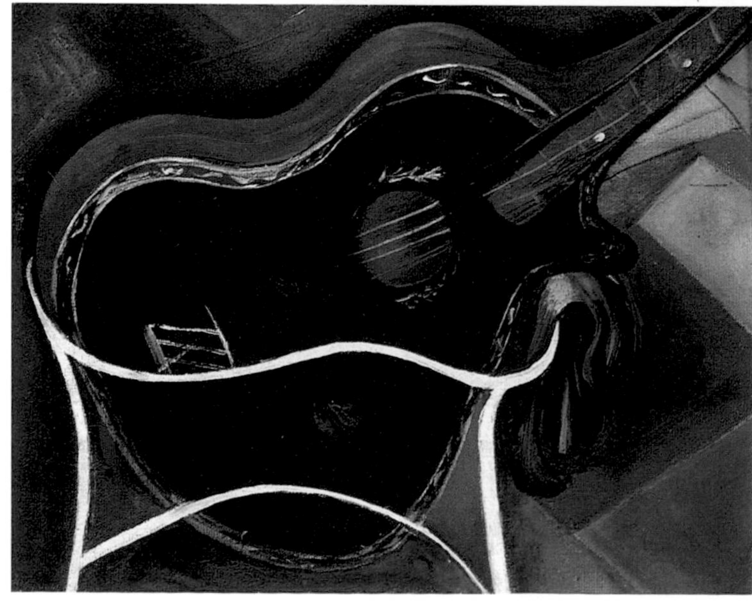

Peter Lanyon (1918-1964)
British
Foggia Guitar
Signed and dated 44, also
signed, inscribed with title
and *RAF Escape Map / Italy*
and dated 1944 on the
reverse, oil on linen map
laid on board
$11^{1}/_{2}$ x 14in (29 x 35.5cm)
£4,000-4,500 *S*

Jean Lurçat (1892-1966)
French
Acapulco
Signed in the weave, woven tapestry
$100^{3}/_{4}$ x $171^{1}/_{4}$in (256 x 437cm)
£8,000-8,500 *S*
Executed in 1961 and woven in the studio of Suzanne Goubely-Gatien at Aubusson

John Mackay (20thC)
British (?)
Urban Landscape
Signed
40 x 46in (101.6 x 116.9cm)
£3,000-3,400 *CSK*

Jean Lucebert (b.1924)
Dutch
Thessaurier Baby
Signed and dated *XII'60*, oil on canvas
$39^{1}/_{2}$ x $31^{1}/_{2}$in (100 x 80cm)
£14,500-16,000 *S(NY)*

Alberto Magnelli (1888-1971)
Italian
Entente secrète, 1948
Signed and dated 48, oil on canvas
18 x $21^{1}/_{2}$in (46 x 55cm)
£22,500-27,500 *C(R)*

René Magritte (1898-1967)
Belgian
Le Savoir
Signed, titled on reverse, pencil, black crayon, watercolour and collage with musical score
$13^{5}/_{8}$ x $10^{1}/_{2}$in (34.6 x 26.8cm)
£40,000-45,000 *S*

Richard Mortensen (b.1910)
Danish
Restonica
Signed, titled and dated, oil on canvas
38 x 51in (97 x 130cm)
£9,000-9,500 *S*

Jean Metzinger (1883-1956)
French
Composition aux Verre, Poires et deux de Carreau
Signed, oil on canvas
8⅝ x 13¾in (22 x 35cm)
£14,500-17,000 *C*

André Masson (1896-1988)
French
Le Migrateur
Signed and dated 1957, oil on canvas
47⅝ x 39⅜in (121 x 100cm)
£45,000-55,000 *S*

Joan Miró (1893-1983)
Spanish
Oiseaux
19 x 14¼in (48.3 x 36.2cm)
£30,000-35,000 *S(NY)*
Executed in 1971

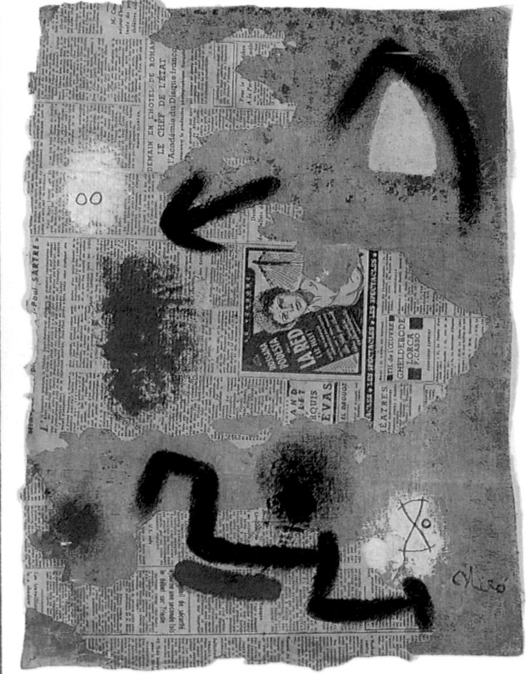

James Rosenquist (b.1933)
American
The Bird of Paradise approaches the Hot Water Plant
Painted in 1988, oil and acrylic on canvas
96 x 84in (243.8 x 213.4cm)
£83,000-90,000 *S(NY)*

Mimmo Paladino (b.1948)
Italian
Silenzioso,1979
Titled, signed and dated 1979, oil on canvas
59 x 86½ x 7⅝in (150 x 220 x 20cm)
£22,500-27,500 *C(R)*

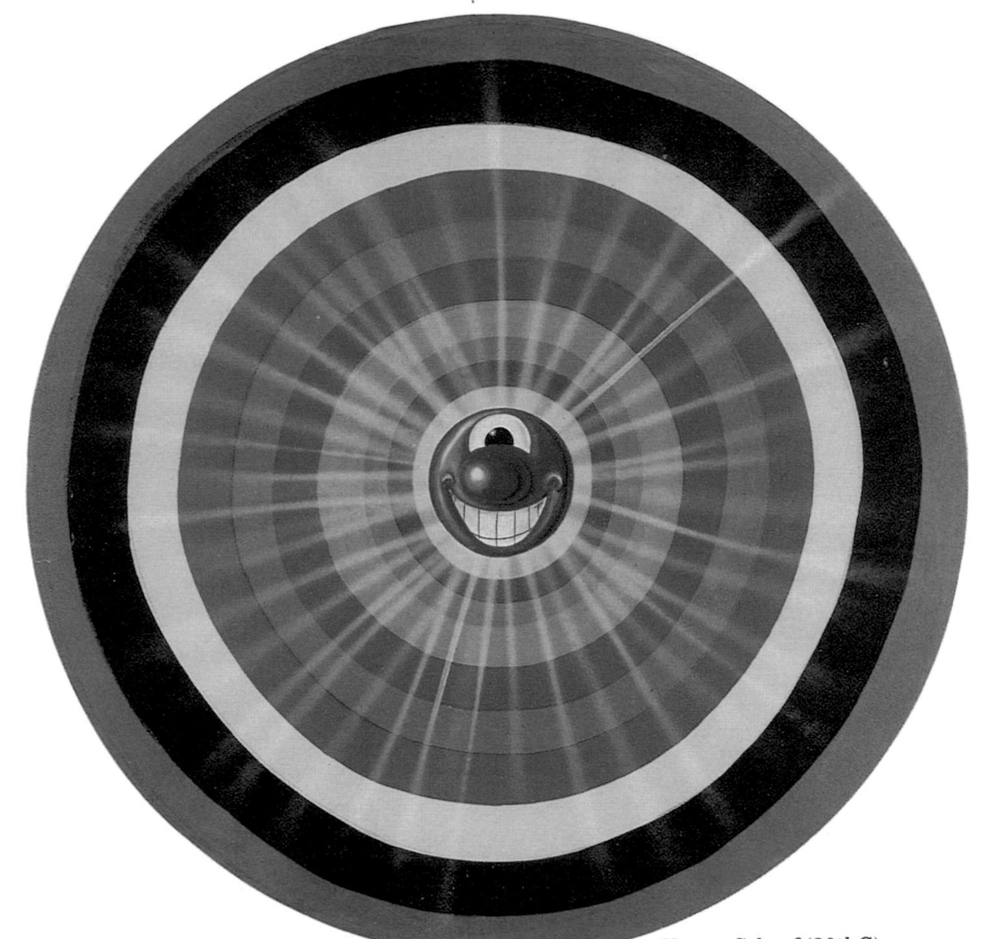

Kenny Scharf (20thC)
Starring the Star
Signed, titled and dated Dec 85, acrylic and spray enamel on canvas
Diameter 48in (121.9cm)
£5,800-6,500 *S(NY)*

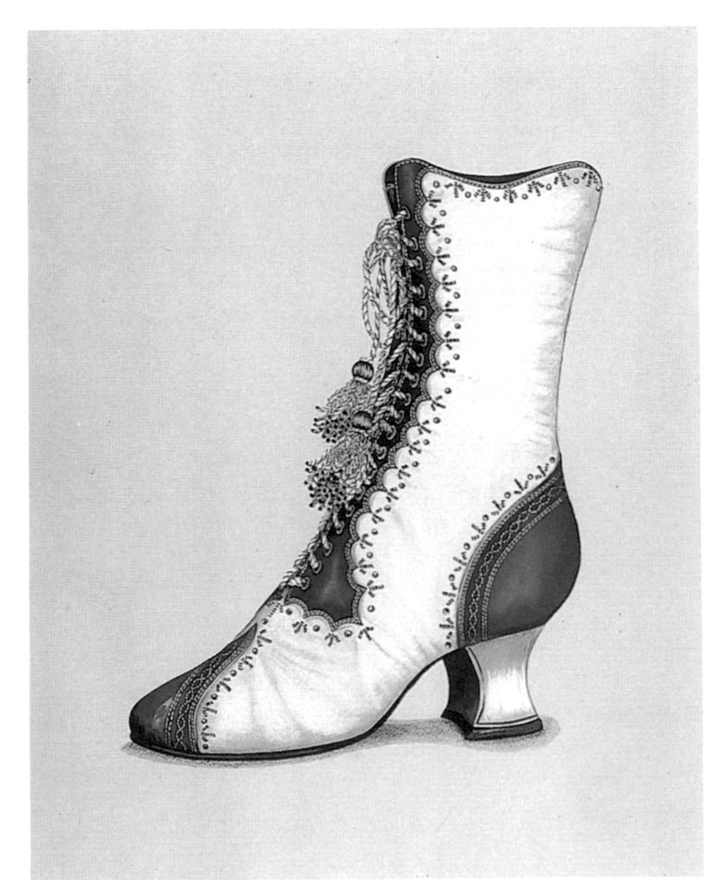

Fiona Saunders (19thC)
Blue laced boot with scalloped edges and fringe, c1870
Watercolour heightened with gouache
18 x 16in (46 x 41cm)
£1,400-1,500 *HOP*

José María Sicilia (b.1954)
Spanish
Untitled
Signed and dated 4.85,
acrylic on canvas
39½ x 39½in (100.3 x 100.3cm)
£21,000-25,000 *S(NY)*

Frank Stella (b.1935)
American
Imola Three II (A. 164; T. 602:FS61)
Woodcut printed in colours, with relief, 1984,
signed in pencil, dated, and numbered 12/30
(total edition includes 10 artist's proofs), on TGL
handmade paper, with the blindstamp of the
publisher, Tyler Graphics Ltd, the full sheet,
printed to the edges, framed.
Sheet size 66 x 51¼in (167.7 x 130.3cm)
£17,000-20,000 *S(NY)*

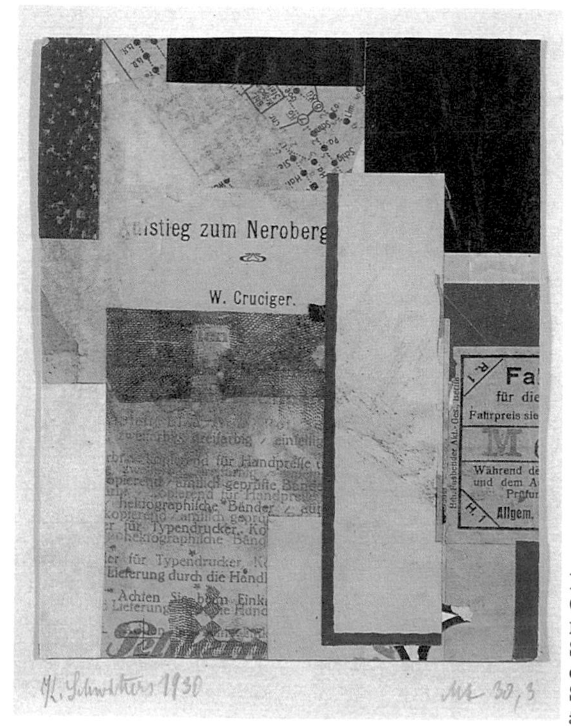

Kurt Schwitters (1887-1948)
German
M.Z.30,3
Signed, dated with the title *1930, M.Z.30,3*
on the artist's mount, collage
Sheet Size 12¾ x 8¾in (32.2 x 22.2cm)
£39,000-45,000 *S*

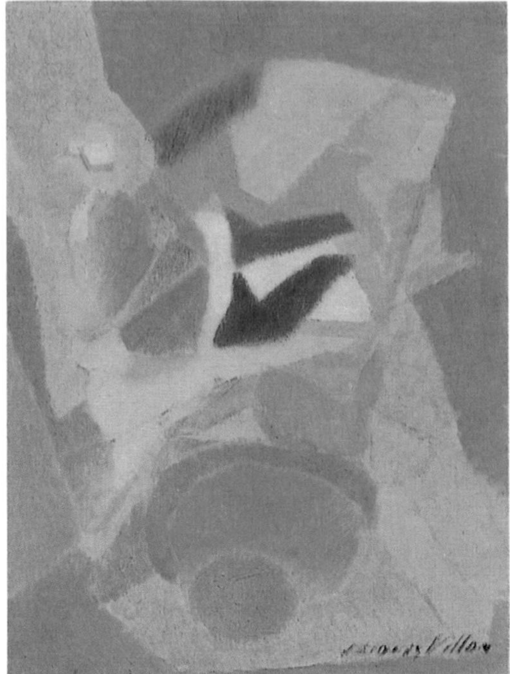

Jacques Villon (1875-1963)
French
Le Pigeon à la Tasse
Signed, dated and inscribed, painted in 1948, oil on canvas
13 x $9\frac{1}{2}$in (33 x 24.2cm)
£9,500-10,000 *C*

Antoni Tàpies (b.1923)
Spanish
Claredad
Signed and titled, executed in 1953, oil and sand on canvas
$36\frac{1}{4}$ x $25\frac{1}{2}$in (92 x 65cm)
£31,000-36,000 *S*

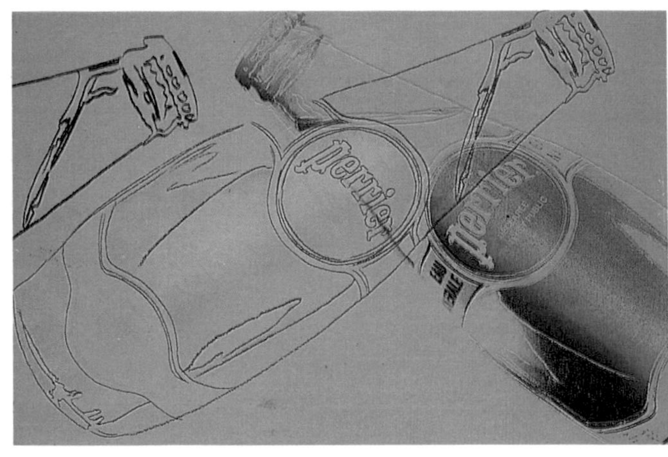

Andy Warhol (1930-1986)
American
Untitled
Signed on the overlap, acrylic and silkscreen on canvas
$20\frac{1}{4}$ x 30in (51.3 x 76.3cm)
£17,000-18,000 *S*

Edward Wadsworth (1889-1949)
British
Study for the Bexhill Mural
Signed and dated 1935, watercolour and gouache, squared for transfer
$21\frac{1}{2}$ x 29in (54.5 x 73.5cm)
£10,500-11,500 *S*

Malcolm Morley (b.1931)
Age of Catastrophe
Painted in 1976, oil on canvas
60 x 96in (152.4 x 243.8cm)
£160,000-200,000 *S(NY)*

Anna Airy (1882-1964)
British
The Boat Train
Signed, watercolour
14 x 13¾in (35.6 x 34.8cm)
£7,500-9,500 *DM*

Robert Timmis (1919-1960)
British
Fares, R.A.
Signed, oil on canvas
35 x 46in (89 x 116.8cm)
£18,500-19,000 *HFA*

Michael Coulter (b.1937)
British
Train and Kestrel
Watercolour
13½ x 18in (34 x 46cm)
£800-850 *PHG*

Jack Butler Yeats
(1871-1957)
British
Dawn, Holyhead
Signed, oil on canvas
14 x 18in (33.5 x 45.5cm)
£34,000-40,000 *S*
Painted in 1920, this work is set on the boat train between Dublin and London, and the figure looking out of the window is probably the artist

Christophe Huet (d.1759) French
La boisson chaude, la boisson froide, le repas froid pendant la chasse and le repas froid dans le parc:
A set of four paintings (two shown) All oil on canvas, unframed
Two shown:119½ x 53¼in (303.5 x 135.3cm)
£95,000-115,000 *S(NY)*

Leon Bakst (1866-1924)
Russian
Helene de Sparte: Costume design for Pollux
25 x 18in (63.5 x 45.7cm)
£8,800-9,500 *S(NY)*

Giuseppe Galli Bibiena (1696-1756)
Italian
A circular Courtyard and Colonnade: Design for the Stage
Pen and brown ink, watercolour
17⅛ x 26in (43.5 x 66cm)
£16,500-18,500 *S(NY)*

Above left:
Isabelle Brent (b.1961)
British
Birds
Watercolour and gold leaf
4¾ x 4½in (12 x 11cm)
£240-255 *PHG*

Circle of Jean Baptiste Pillement (1727-1808)
French
Chinese Musicians in Stylised Gardens with Birds and Flowers: A set of three Chinoiserie paintings mounted as a screen
All oil on canvas
Each section: 63¾ x 20in (161.9 x 50.8cm)
£9,000-9,500 *S(NY)*

SPORT AND GAMES

Please also refer to the Animal Section.

Dighton (Publisher) (19thC)
British
A Striking View of Richmond, and Molineux
Etchings, with hand colouring
13 x 9in (33 x 22.8cm)
£90-110 *Bon*

Bill Richmond, "The Black Terror", and Tom Molineux enjoyed great success in the British ring as the first two negro boxers, but neither could whip Tom Cribb, the British Champion. Richmond was knocked out by Cribb in 1805, and Molineux "The Moor" succumbed twice in 1810 and 1811.

After J. Jackson (19thC) British Tom Cribb, Champion of England Aquatint by George Hunt, with hand colouring, published by J. Moore, 1842 19 x 15½in (48.3 x 39.4cm) Together with a hand coloured aquatint after Henry Meyer depicting Deaf Burke, framed. **£210-250** *Bon*

H. Thornton (19thC)
British
The Clerk of the Course
Signed and dated Decr. 1835, pen and ink (heightened)
13¾ x 10¾in (35 x 27cm)
£1,200-1,400 *S(S)*

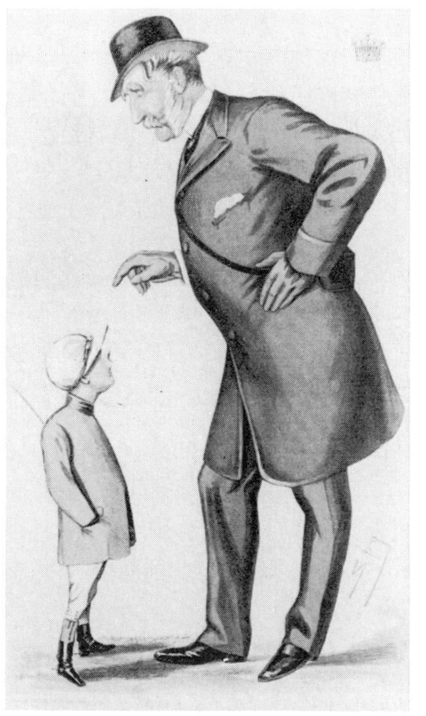

Vanity Fair (Publishers) (19thC)
British
The Turf (Lord Dorchester)
Lithograph, printed in colours by Vincent Brooks Day and Son, 24 March 1877, and 17 others
12¼ x 7¼in (31.2 x 18.4cm)
£180-250 *Bon*

Vanity Fair (Publishers) (19thC)
British
A Jockey
Lithograph printed in colours by Vincent Brooks Day and Son, 3 September 1887, and 4 others
11⅞ x 7¼in (30.2 x 18.4cm)
£100-125 *Bon*

Francis Cecil Boult (active late 19thC)
British
Polo
Signed and dated 1890, oil on canvas
24 x 36in (61 x 91.5cm)
£6,400-6,800 *S*

After Lowes Cato Dickinson (1819-1908)
British
The Marylebone Cricket Club at Lords Cricket Ground
2 photogravures, published by Dickinson and Foster 1895, each signed in pencil, and another
19¼ x 39¾in (49 x 101cm)
£410-450 *S(S)*

After William Drummond and Charles J. Basébe (19thC)
British
The Cricket Match between Sussex and Kent at Brighton
Engraving by G. H. Phillips, with hand colouring, published by E. Gambart & Co., 1849, framed
23¼ x 35½in (59.1 x 90.2cm)
£450-550 *Bon*

John Strickland Goodall (b1908)
British
Cowes Week
Signed, watercolour and gouache
7 x 10in (17.5 x 25cm)
£1,100-1,200 *SRB*

'Despite the recession, we have found that pictures by Goodall still sell well and his prices have remained unchanged,' note Sussex dealers Susan and Robert Botting. 'He is a good draughtsman, an extremely popular painter and many of his works have been made into greetings cards. Generally speaking, there is still a demand for good quality works by collectable artists, lower quality works are more difficult to place and have dropped in price.'

Stanley Roy Badmin (1906-89)
British
A Game of Water-Polo
Signed, inscribed and dated 1932, Wareham V. Pool, watercolour
6¾ x 10in (17 x 25.5cm)
£1,450-1,650 *C*

Robert Medley (b1905) British Summer Eclogue No. 1 – Cyclists
Signed and dated 1950, oil on canvas 51¼ x 63in (130 x 160cm) **£6,100-6,500** *S*

Tony Smith (b1932)
British
Sierra and BMW Saloon
Car Championship,
Donnington Park 1986
Signed and dated 1987, oil
20 x 30in (50.8 x 76.2cm)
£750-850 *Dr*

Sam Rabin (1902-91)
American
The Straight Left
Mixed media
19 x 26in (48.2 x 66cm)
£1,700-1,800 *JD*

George Bellows (1882-1925)
American
Dempsey and Firpo (M.181; B.89)
Lithograph, 1923-24, signed and
titled in pencil,
from edition of 103
18¼ x 22⅜in (46.5 x 56.8cm)
£7,600-8,000 *S(NY)*

Bellows was an outstanding sportsman himself at University and boxing matches were one of his favourite subjects. A member of the Ash Can School of artists, who flourished in America in the early 20thC, Bellows concentrated on urban scenes, presented in a muscular and vigorous style. Dempsey and Firpo is the best known of the lithographs produced in the last 10 years of his life, and reflects the artist's growing interest in formal balance and pictorial symmetry.

BULLFIGHTING AND SPANISH GENRE PICTURES

The romance of Spain has captured the imagination of many artists. Pictures can range vastly in quality from powerful evocations of the bullfight and scenes of Spanish life to endless clichéd visions of raven-haired, dark-eyed beauties with their fans and mantillas.

Antonio Cabral y Bejarano (1822-91)
Spanish
A Spanish Lady with a Fan
Signed and dated Sevilla 1855 on reverse, oil on canvas
23¾ x 15½in (60 x 39cm)
£1,900-2,200 *S*

J*** Péris Brell (19thC) Spanish
A Matador; A Picador; A Toreador
Three, all signed, one dated Valencia '86, another '86 and another Valencia 1887, oil on canvas
Two 21½ x 13¾in (55 x 35cm)
One 26¾ x 19in (68 x 48cm)
£5,600-6,000 *S*

Richard Geiger (b1870) Austrian
A Gypsy Girl Signed, oil on canvas
31 x 23in (78.8 x 58.4cm) **£950-1,000** *CSK*

Dudley Hardy (1867-1922)
British
To the Bull Ring
Signed and inscribed, oil on canvas
28¼ x 24in (71.5 x 61cm)
£2,000-2,200 *C*

Francisco José de Goya y Lucientes (1746-1828)
Spanish
Dibersion de Espana (D.288; H.285)
Crayon lithograph, 1825, from the Bulls of Bordeaux
11¾ x 16⅛in (30 x 41cm)
£178,000-200,000 *S(NY)*

Goya made his first lithographs in 1819 when he was 73 years old. These were very experimental and technically not entirely successful. However, by the time he moved to Bordeaux, only 5 years later, he was in command of the medium. The Bulls of Bordeaux are crayon lithographs that Goya drew directly on the stone, creating highlights with a scraper and revising as he went along. His freedom of working is astonishing even today.

Robert Kemm (active 1874-85)
British
The Matador's Sweetheart
Signed R. Kemm, oil on canvas
35½ x 27½in (90.2 x 69.8cm)
£2,800-3,000 *C*

Indulis Zarins (20thC)
Russian
The Matador, The Suit of Lights
Oil on canvas
39in (99cm) sq.
£11,800-12,000 *CE*

John Frederick Lewis (1805-76)
British Spanish Peasants
Watercolour over pencil heightened
with bodycolour 12 x 16½in (30.5 x 42cm)
£9,000-9,400 *S*

TRANSPORT

English School (c1860)
Design for the Interior of the Metropolitan Line Station at King's Cross
Pencil and watercolour with white heightening
24⅞ x 32in (63.2 x 81.2cm)
£800-850 *C*

The Metropolitan Line was built in 1864 and was the first underground line in the world. The station was destroyed by bomb damage on 16 October 1940.

Sir Robert Ponsonby Staples, Bt. (1853-1943)
British
The Tram Ride
Signed, dated Feb 19 and inscribed 'Attempt Effect of Rain on Windows with shoplights shining through', pencil and coloured crayons
10¼ x 14½in (26 x 36.8cm)
£2,400-2,600 *DM*

Staples could not afford to take cabs and usually went about London on a bicycle which he learned to ride in Battersea Park, the fashionable rendezvous for cyclists, in 1895. Sometimes, however, when he took the tram or omnibus he would draw his fellow passengers who must have been amused and curious about him.

John Sloan (1871-1951)
American
Subway Stairs (M.221)
Etching, 1926, signed, titled and inscribed 'N.Y. April 1926'
6⅞ x 5in (17.5 x 12.8cm)
£1,200-1,400 *S(NY)*

DECORATIVE DESIGNS, MISCELLANEOUS

Circle of Hans Holbein II (1497/8-1543)
German
Design for a Scabbard of a Dagger: The Dance of Death
Black chalk, pen and black ink, black and grey wash
1¾ x 10¾in (4.3 x 27.5cm)
£2,300-2,500 *C*

The present drawing is a project for the decoration of the scabbard of a Swiss 'Holbein' dagger. It depicts the Dance of Death, a popular motif for the decoration of such scabbards.

Attributed to Domenico Rignano (active 16thC) Italian
Design for a Wall Tomb
Inscribed, black chalk, pen and brown ink, brown wash
17 x 11½in (43.4 x 29.7cm)
£720-770 *C*

Johann Esaias Nilson (1721-88)
German
Design for a Frontispiece: Faith seated under an Awning, a terraced Garden beyond
Signed and dated 1757, black chalk, pen and black ink, grey wash heightened with white
7¼ x 10¼in (18.3 x 26cm)
£2,900-3,200 *S(NY)*

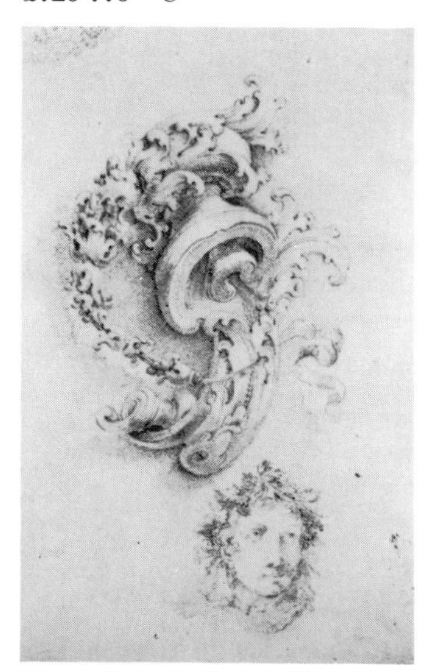

Mauro Antonio Tesi (1730-66)
Italian
Design for an ornamental acanthus spray, a Portrait of a Man wearing a wreath of vineleaves, and a subsidiary study of leaves (recto); an architectural study (verso)
Black chalk, pen and brown ink, brown wash (recto), black lead (verso)
10⅝ x 6¾in (27 x 17.2cm)
£900-950 *S(NY)*

Circle of Daniel Lindtmayer (1552-1607)
Swiss
Designs for a Frieze with Armorial Shields and Putti
Inscribed DLN 16010, black chalk, pen and black ink, grey wash
7¾ x 12½in (19.3 x 31.7cm)
and 3 other drawings.
£1,100-1,300 *S(NY)*

Rex Whistler (1905-44)
British
Chimneypiece Design for 5 Belgrave Square
Pencil, pen and black ink and watercolour heightened with white and gold
14½ x 9¼in (37 x 23.5cm)
£2,700-3,000 *S*

Painted in 1935, this work is a preliminary design for the decorated chimneypiece at 5 Belgrave Square, the home of Sir Henry (Chips) Channon. In his diary under 9th September 1935 Channon wrote: 'Today we spent with Rex Whistler whom I have persuaded to paint a fresco for our drawing room. He is chetif, mild and has faultless taste, even genius.'

School of Como (late 17thC)
Design for a Fountain with Neptune riding a Chariot, and alternative side elevations with herons and eagles
Inscribed, black chalk, pen and brown ink, watercolour
16½ x 15¾in (41.9 x 40.3cm)
£2,700-3,000 *C*

French School (c1820)
Design for a Chandelier
Inscribed in brown ink above: Restauration
Pen and black ink and watercolour
9¼ x 7in (23.8 x 17.8cm)
£560-600 *S*

Robert Adam (1728-92)
British
Design of a chimney piece for the dining room at Moccas Court, Herefordshire Inscribed, dated, coloured washes over pen and black ink 13 x 18½in (33 x 47cm)
£4,500-5,000 *S*

Moccas Court was built for Sir George Cornewall who commissioned designs from Robert Adam, which were extensively revised and simplified by a local architect Anthony Keck. Building began in 1775 and fitting out the interior continued until about 1783. The house still stands but, as often happened in the 1950s and 60s, the fireplace was torn out.

THEATRICAL DESIGNS

Léon Bakst (1866-1924)
Russian
Phaedre: Costume Design for a Slave (or Minoan woman)
Stamped with signature, gouache, silver paint and pencil on paper
12 x 9in (30.5 x 22.9cm)
£7,000-7,500 *S(NY)*

The tragedy Phaedre, written by Gabriele d'Annunzio, music by Ildebrando Pizzetti, costumes and decors by Bakst, was revived by Ida Rubinstein at the Théâtre National de l'Opéra, Paris on June 7, 1923.

Giuseppe Galli Bibiena (1696-1756)
Italian
A Palatial Loggia, a Courtyard Beyond: Design for the Stage
Pen and brown ink, brown, grey and blue wash
17⅛ x 26in (43.5 x 66cm)
£8,200-8,600 *S(NY)*

Sir Cecil Beaton (1904-80)
British
Two Knights, from Picnic at Tintagel; ballet by Frederick Ashton, music Arnold Bax New York City Ballet, City Centre, New York
Watercolour
14 x 9½in (35.5 x 24cm)
£900-1,050 *MP*

Leslie Hurry (1909-78)
British
Timon of Athens (Shakespeare), 1956, Old Vic (Michael Benthall): Preliminary Costume Design for a Young Athenian
Signed and inscribed, pen, black ink and watercolour with a fabric swatch, unframed
17¼ x 11¼in (44 x 28.5cm)
Together with 2 unframed costume designs from the same production.
£850-950 *C*

Leslie Hurry (1909-78)
British
The Queen of Spades (Tchaikovsky), 1966, Sadler's Wells Opera (Anthony Besch): Costume Design for the Masque and Domino Cloaks for the Masque
Signed and inscribed, pen, coloured inks and watercolour with fabric swatches, unframed
15¼ x 11¼in (38.5 x 28.5cm)
Together with an unframed costume design for Sourin and a prop design for a Mask from the same production.
£600-700 *C*

Sir Osbert Lancaster (b1908) British
Set Design for L'Italian Algeri
Watercolour, collage
11 x 15in (28 x 38cm)
£950-1,050 *C*

Locate the source

The source of each illustration in Miller's can be found by checking the code letters below each caption with the list

Carel Weight (b1908)
British
For Children, The Witches are Here
Signed, oil on canvas, 1984
83½ x 44½in (212 x 113cm)
£12,200-13,000 *S*

FAIRIES AND FANTASY PICTURES

Etheline E. Dell (active 1885-91)
British
Fairies and a Field Mouse
Signed, pencil, watercolour and bodycolour
8½ x 7½in (21.6 x 19cm)
£5,600-6,000 *C*

The artist specialised in domestic and fairy subjects, exhibiting at the Royal Academy, Suffolk Street, and the New Watercolour Society.

Richard Dadd (1817-86)
British
Contradiction: Oberon and Titania
Signed and dated, and inscribed, oil on canvas
24 x 29¾in (61 x 75.5cm)
£1,700,000-2,000,000 *C*

Dadd is famous as the 'mad painter'. He was one of 7 children, 4 of whom died insane. He enjoyed a brilliant early artistic career, concentrating on imaginative works and gaining a great reputation for his fairy pictures. In 1834, after a gruelling artistic tour of the Middle East, he succumbed to the family sickness and believing that he was the agent of the Egyptian God Osiris, who had commanded him to exterminate the devil, murdered his father. He was committed to Bethlem Hospital where the present work was painted during the years 1854-58. Its inspiration was 'A Midsummer Night's Dream' and the quarrel between Oberon and Titania over the Indian changeling boy. Like 'The Fairy Feller's Master-Stroke' in the Tate Gallery, 'Contradiction' is remarkable for its teeming wealth of magical detail controlled with a gemlike precision of form and creating a vision of halucinatory brilliance. When auctioned at Christie's in June 1992 it set a new record for a Victorian painting.

Henry Barnabus Bright (1824-76)
British
The Frog Bandits
Signed, pencil, watercolour and bodycolour
14¼ x 27in (36.2 x 68.6cm)
£3,600-4,000 *C*

ABSTRACT AND MODERN

'Confidence is returning to the contemporary market,' claims Susan Sterling of Christie's, speaking at the end of the 1991/92 season and immediately after Christie's successful July sale of Contemporary Art which included properties from the estate of collector Frederik Roos. 'Prices might not have increased dramatically since 1991, but levels of interest have. You now stand a chance of more people vying for a specific lot and a competitive bidding pattern has been reintroduced.'

In the contemporary field, as in other areas, many of those competing figures have been private buyers rather than dealers. 'The trade is simply not spending the money that private people are prepared to pay,' notes Sterling. 'Many dealers are still severely affected by the slump in the market, and during the past year two of London's foremost contemporary dealers, John Kasmin and Wolfgang Fischler, have closed down their galleries.'

The most successful works in the auction rooms have tended to be good quality items, fresh to the market, with sales of specific private collections (such as the Roos estate) inspiring particular interest. 'The more contemporary works are enjoying a stronger market than they were four years ago,' notes Sterling. Yet whilst 1992 saw new price records set for living artists, including Malcolm Morley and Anselm Kiefer, other areas of the modern market performed less well. 'Prices are still a lot lower than they were in 1989 for abstract art from the 50s. Demand is still there but not the former high prices. Take Jean Dubuffet, for example. In 1989 and 1990 his works made record figures, today his prices have fallen, in some instances by as much as 50%, but at these new levels there is still tremendous activity.'

Sterling is cautiously enthusiastic about the future. 'Though there are bound to be difficult times ahead, I wouldn't expect to see any further reductions in prices. Things look a lot more hopeful than they did at the beginning of the season.'

Eileen Agar (1904-91) British
Abstract Composition
Signed, oil on canvas
23½ x 19¼in (59.5 x 49cm)
£2,000-2,200 *C*

Pierre Alechinsky (b1927)
Belgian
On Le Dit Mais On Dit Tant
Signed, titled and dated 1963 on the stretcher, oil on canvas
24 x 19¾in (61 x 50cm)
£17,800-18,800 *S*

Stuart Armfield (b1916)
British
Prayer
Signed and dated 56, oil on panel
22 x 30in (55.9 x 76.2cm)
£1,300-1,600 *S(NY)*

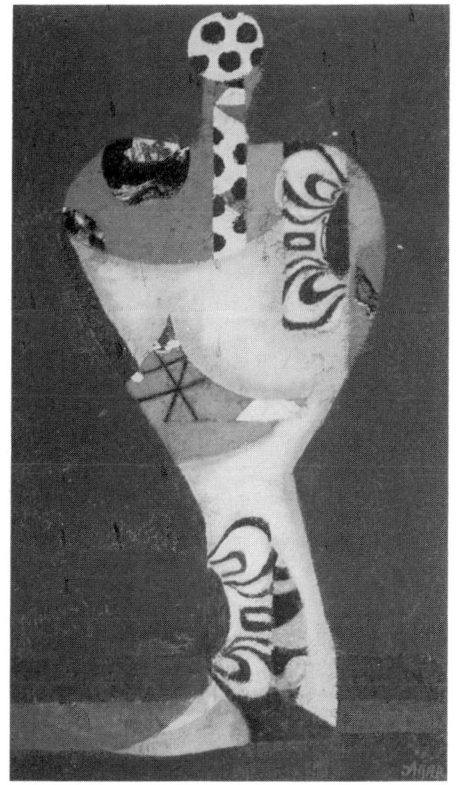

Eileen Agar (1904-91)
British
Vase Transformed
Signed, inscribed and dated 1944, oil on canvas
24 x 14in (61 x 35.5cm)
£5,300-5,600 *C*

Arman (b1930) Spanish
XXIVeme Caprice de Paganini
Signed and dated 1962, cut violin on painted board
32⅛ x 25⅛in (81.6 x 64cm)
£35,000-40,000 *C*

Karel Appel (b1921)
Untitled
Signed and dated 69, acrylic on paper laid down on canvas
30 x 22in (76.2 x 55.9cm)
£7,000-7,400 *S(NY)*

Richard Artschwager (b1923)
American
Expression Impression
Signed and dated 66, acrylic on celotex
27 x 33⅛in (68.5 x 84.2cm)
£11,000-12,000 *S(NY)*

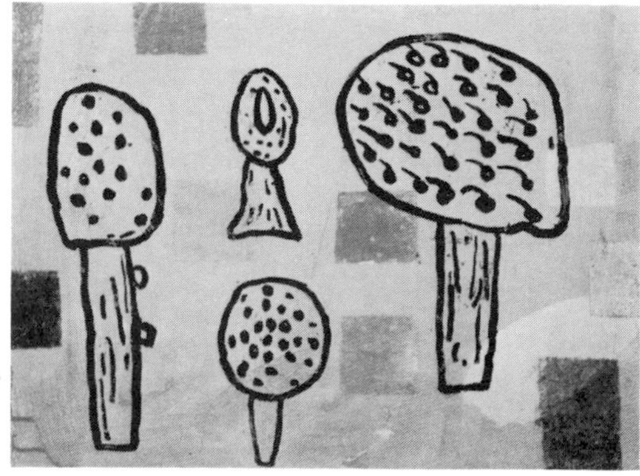

Donald Baechler (b1956)
American
Abstract Painting with Four Trees
Signed with initials, titled and dated 85, polyurethane and acrylic on canvas
18 x 24in (45.7 x 61cm)
£3,500-3,800 *S(NY)*

Jean-Michel Atlan (1913-60)
French
L'Oiseau Bleu
Signed, dedicated A Alice and indistinctly inscribed, oil on canvas, c1945-56
£7,800-8,200 *S*

'For me a picture cannot be the result of a preconceived idea,' claimed Atlan in 1953. 'The part played by chance is too important and... is decisive in creation. At the outset there is a rhythm which tends to develop itself; it is the perception of this rhythm which is fundamental and it is on its development that the vital quality of the work depends.'

Jean Michel Basquiat (1960-88)
American
Orange Sports Figure
Acrylic, oil stick and spray paint on canvas, 1982
60 x 48in (152.4 x 121.9cm)
£38,000-45,000 *S(NY)*

Raz Barfield (b1968)
British
The Blue Mask
Mixed media collage on board, signed with initials and dated 91
7 x 10in (18 x 25cm)
£200-250 *Bon*

Shona Barr (b1965)
British
Mimulus
Oil on canvas
28in (71cm) sq.
£1,200-1,400 *FCG*

Georg Baselitz (b1938)
German
Graue Hunde, Drei Streifen
Signed and dated 68, oil on canvas
63¾ x 51⅛in (161.9 x 129.9cm)
£212,000-240,000 *S(NY)*

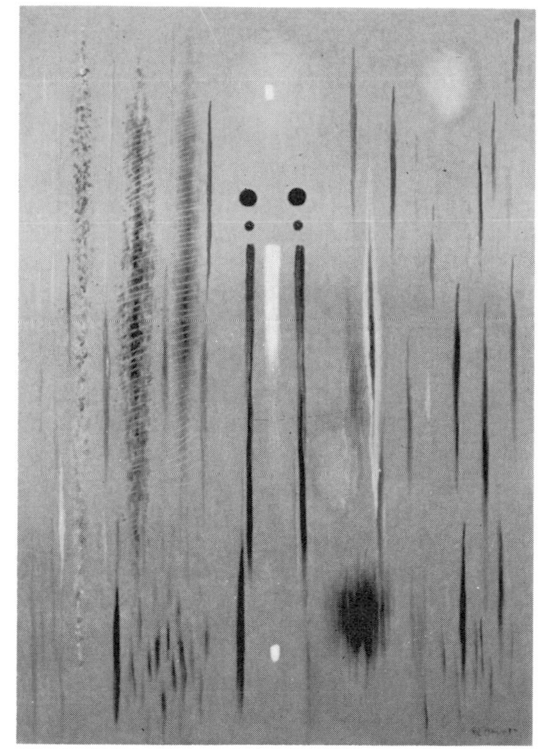

Rudolf Bauer (1889-1954)
Polish American
Spirituality
Signed, oil on canvas, 1938
45¾ x 31½in (116.2 x 80cm)
£8,600-9,000 *S(NY)*

Ross Bleckner (b1949)
American
Untitled
Signed and dated 1981, oil and wax on canvas
108 x 77¾in (274.3 x 197.5cm)
£8,600-9,000 *S(NY)*

Bernd and Hilla Becher (20thC)
American
Fachwerkhäuser des Siegener Industriegebiets
Titled and dated 1976, 16 black and white photographs
£16,000-17,000 *S*

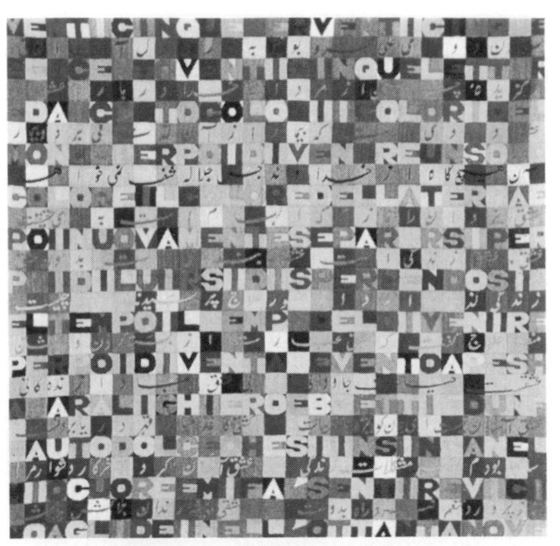

Aligherio Boetti (b1940) Italian
Alfabeto
Signed on overlap, embroidered fabric, 1988, unframed
41½ x 42½in (105.5 x 108cm)
£6,700-7,200 *C*

Aligherio Boetti (b1940)
Italian
Larga approssimazione grande tolleranza (1989)
Signed, embroidered fabric
10in (25cm) sq.
£900-1,200 *S(R)*

John Boyd (20thC)
British
Cuboid II
Oil on board
23 x 16in (59 x 41cm)
£1,300-1,400 *VCG*

Georges Braque (1882-1963)
French
L'Atelier (V.165)
Lithograph printed in colours, 1961, signed in pencil, printed by Mourlot, published by Musées Nationaux, Paris, framed
17 x 20⅝in (43 x 52.2cm)
£4,200-4,600 *S(NY)*

Victor Brauner (1903-66)
Romanian/French
Sans Titre
Signed and dated 1939, oil on canvas
44⅞ x 57½in (114 x 146cm)
£180,000-200,000 *S*

In the mid-1930s Brauner produced a series of paintings about mutilations to the eye, which proved strangely prophetic when in 1938 he was involved in a fight with two other artists and indeed lost an eye. This event stimulated a group of paintings called Lycanthropes, executed between 1938 and 39. In true surrealist manner these depict hybrids: woman/animal, animal/ object, elements combined from the vegetable and human worlds and painted in a restricted range of glowing muted colours. These pictures were dominated by disturbing female spectres symbolising, as one critic has noted: 'the supernatural conflict between the artist and his demons'.

Allin Braund (b1915) British
House in the Valley
Lithograph in colours
16 x 23½in (40.6 x 59cm)
£230-250 *SCG*

Alexander Calder (1898-1976) American Composition
Signed with initials, oil on canvas 19¼ x 45¼in (49 x 115cm)
£23,000-28,000 *S*

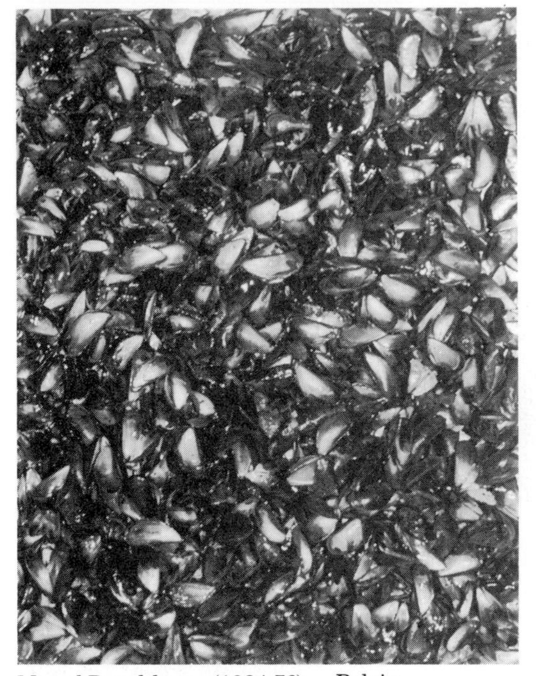

Marcel Broodthaers (1924-76) Belgian
Panneau de Moules
Panel encrusted with mussel shells, some painted blue on the inside, 1965
31½ x 23⅝in (80 x 60cm)
£90,000-100,000 *C*

Marcel Broodthaers (1924-76)
Belgian
La Malediction de Magritte
Signed, inscribed with title and dated 1966, wood, paper, glass and cotton wool
30¾ x 24½ x 12½in (78 x 62 x 32cm)
£190,000-210,000 *C*

Broodthaers was a poet and writer, who did not decide to become an artist until the age of 40. 'I too asked myself if I couldn't sell something and become successful in life...' he announced at the opening of his first exhibition in 1964. He made objects using everything from eggshells to suitcases, his imaginative assemblages providing a bizarre and surreal commentary on everyday life. Broodthaers sold most of his work directly to private collectors and it appears only rarely on the market today. Huge interest was therefore inspired when nine works from a Belgian private collection came up for sale at Christie's in July '92 – 'I've never seen such excitement at a modern sale,' commented one Christie's press officer. All the works sold way above estimate, one piece making 10 times its expected figure.

John Bratby (1928-92)
British
The Sunflower
Signed and dated 1973, oil on canvas
30 x 20in (76.2 x 50.8cm)
£2,800-3,000 *GG*

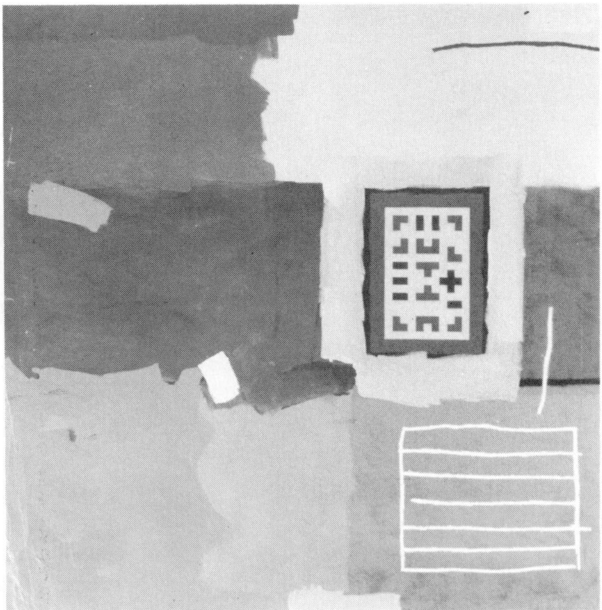

Brian Clarke (b1953)
British
11.02.89 (For DJFC)
Oil on canvas
79in (200cm) sq.
£19,500-20,000 *MAY*

Alexander Calder (1898-1976)
American
Untitled
Signed with initial and dated '44, gouache on paper
30½ x 23in (77.5 x 58.4cm)
£8,600-9,000 *S(NY)*

Christo (b1935)
Bulgarian/American
The Umbrellas (joint project for Japan and USA)
Signed, inscribed with title and dated 1989, collage with fabric, coloured crayon, gouache, pencil and diagram on card
Top panel: 12 x 30½in (30.5 x 77.5cm)
Bottom panel: 26¼ x 30½in (66.7 x 77.5cm)
£24,000-30,000 *C*

Peter Brüning (b1929)
German
Ohne Titel
Signed and dated 1961, oil on canvas
27½ x 38⅛in (70 x 90cm)
£29,000-35,000 *C*

Christo (b1935)
Bulgarian/American
Wrapped Monument to General G. H. Dufor
Signed, titled and dated 1975, fabric, string, coloured crayon and pencil on card
27½ x 19¾in (70 x 50cm)
£10,500-11,500 *S*

Modesto Cuixart (b1925)
Spanish
Composition
Signed and dated 1960, oil on canvas
39½ x 32in (100 x 81cm)
£6,900-7,400 *S*

Enzo Cucchi (b1950)
Italian
Palla Santa
Signed, titled and dated 1979-80, oil on canvas
24½ x 37¾in (62.2 x 95.9cm)
£11,500-12,000 *S(NY)*

Salvador Dali (1904-89)
Spanish
Moïse et le Monothéisme
Signed, gouache, watercolour, coloured chalks, pen and ink and etching on paper, 1974
25½ x 19⅝in (64.7 x 49.8cm)
£28,000-35,000 *C*

A reproduction of this work was used to illustrate Sigmund Freud's Moïse et le Monothéisme published in 1974.

Oscar Dominguez (1906-58)
Spanish
Mujeres con Pajaro y Pez
Signed, gouache on paper, 1947
18¼ x 20¾in (46.3 x 52.6cm)
£9,400-9,800 *C*

Joseph Davie (b1965) British
Animula
Etching and collage, 1991
9 x 8⅜in (23 x 21cm)
£325-350 *HOU*

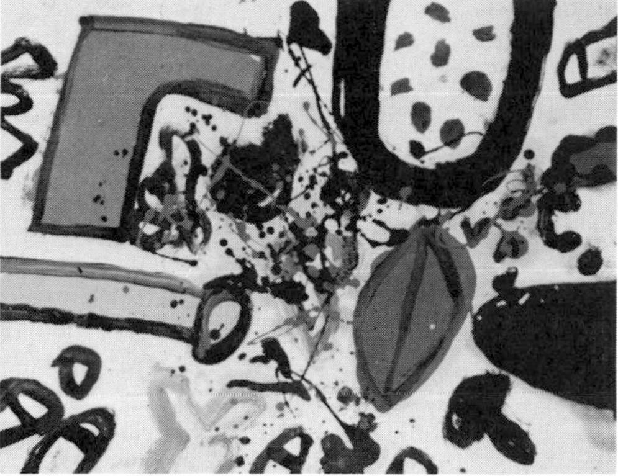

Alan Davie (b1920) British
Marvellous Feeling
Signed, titled and dated '61, oil on paper laid down on canvas
16¼ x 21in (41.5 x 53.5cm)
£4,200-4,600 *S*

Terry Frost (b1915) British
Mars Yellow
Oil on canvas
25 x 30in (63.5 x 76cm)
£13,500-14,000 *MAY*

Maurits Cornelis Escher (1898-1972) Dutch
Sun and Moon (Bol/Kist/Locker/Wierda 357)
Woodcut printed in colours, 1948, signed in pencil, numbered No. 11/20 and inscribed hontmode, eigendruck, on Japan paper, in good condition
10 x 10¾in (25.3 x 27.3cm)
£3,500-3,800 *S(NY)*

Jean Dubuffet (1901-85)
French
Paysage Tricolore IV (Aux Ruines d'un Chateau)
Signed with initials and dated 74, vinyl on canvas
76¾ x 51¼in (195 x 130.2cm)
£115,000-130,000 *S(NY)*

Jean Dubuffet was the champion of l'Art Brut, a term he himself coined to describe the work of madmen, prisoners, children, all those whose creations took place outside the confines and 'parrot-like processes' of the art world. He incorporated its elements into his own work, using chance and automatism, playing with a range of different materials from silver foil to butterfly wings, continually experimenting with new ideas. 'There is only one healthy diet for artistic creation: permanent revolution,' he claimed defiantly. 'After each meal brush away the crumbs and set the table afresh. Are you really going to hand out 300 year old steaks and mutton in your dining-room? Bon appétit!' Though opinion is divided about the quality of his work, no-one ever questioned its variety or exhuberance: 'Art should always make people laugh a little and frighten them a little,' advised Dubuffet. 'Anything but bore them.'

Sam Francis (b1923) American
Deux Magots
Signed, oil on canvas
36¼ x 24⅛in (92.1 x 61.3cm)
£78,000-90,000 *S(NY)*

Painted c1959, Deux Magots is a summation of Francis's important style of the 1950s as well as a transitional work which contains elements of the Blue Ball series of the early 1960s.
Francis began painting at the age of 21 during a long recuperation in hospital from spinal tuberculosis. Confined to his bed, he was fascinated by the play of light upon the ceiling, both by its patterns and its substance, which acted as an inspiration to his work. In 1950 he moved to Paris and in 1957 embarked on a world tour spending much time in Japan. On his return, his works evinced a profound Japanese influence, the drips of paint on white canvasses with their asymmetrical play between colour and empty space have been compared to Japanese haboku (flung ink) landscapes, relating to 'the Oriental use of the silence and voids of the white spaces as artistic means of expression.'

Jean Dubuffet (1901-85)
French
Personnage
Signed with initials and dated mars '64, ink on paper
8¾in x 7in (22 x 17.5cm)
£5,000-5,500 *S*

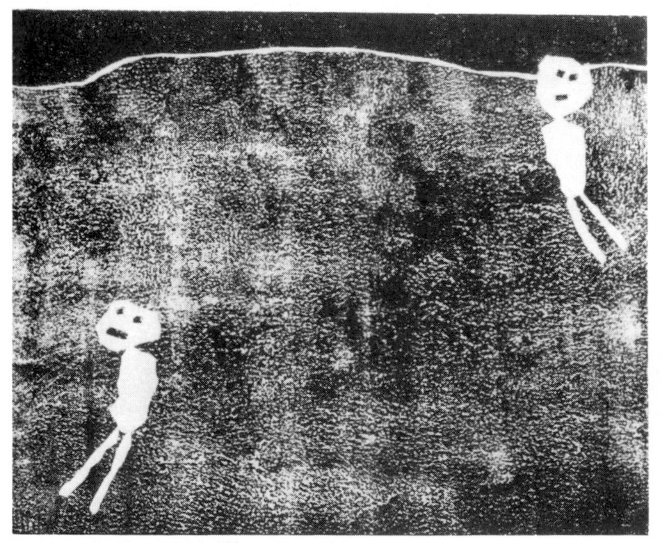

Jean Dubuffet (1901-85) French
La Pierre (L.XVI, p.223)
Lithograph printed in colours, 1962, and 5 colour proofs, each initialled in pencil and inscribed
11⅞ x 15⅞in (30.2 x 40.4cm)
£4,600-5,000 *S(NY)*

Hamish Fulton (b1946)
British
Road Dust (Iceland)
Black and white photograph mounted on card
54 x 43½in (137.2 x 110.5cm)
£3,600-4,000 *C*

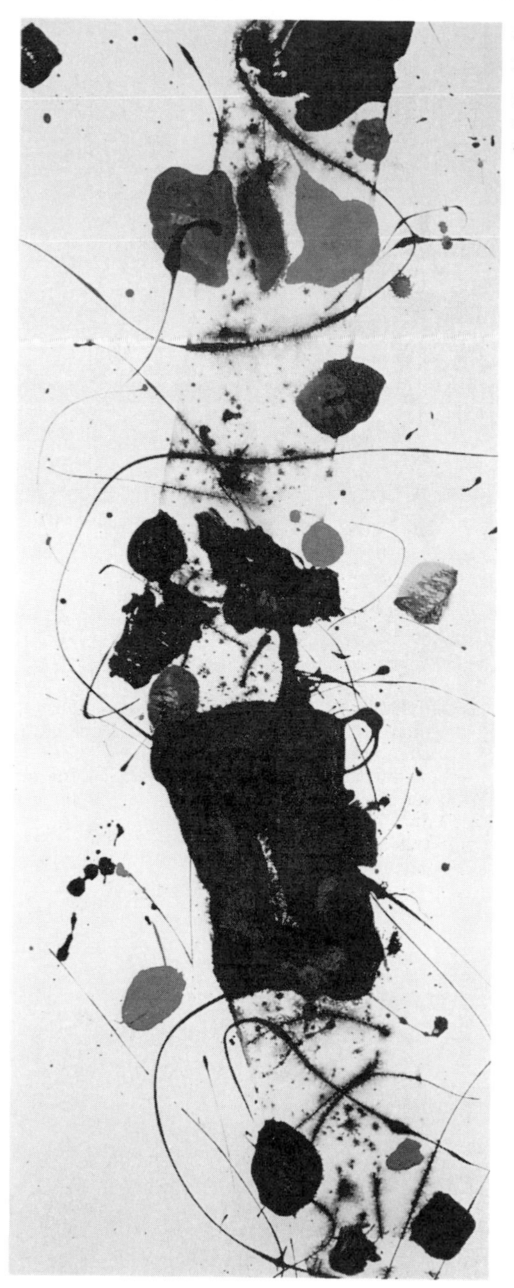

Sam Francis (b1923)
American
Untitled
Signed and dated 1984, oil on canvas
55 x 21¼in (139.7 x 54cm)
£38,000-45,000 *S(NY)*

Sam Francis (b1923)
American
No Class Virus
Acrylic on paper, 1984
15⅛ x 10¼in (38.4 x 26cm)
£3,800-4,300 *S(NY)*

William Gear (b1915)
British
Black 100L, 1958
Oil on canvas
24 x 20in (61 x 51cm)
£4,300-4,500 *JB*

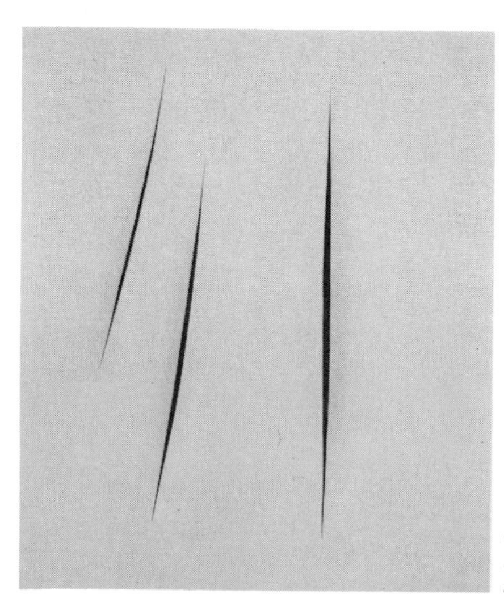

Lucio Fontana (1899-1968)
Italian
Concetto Spaziale-Attese
Signed and titled, oil on canvas
25½ x 21¼in (64.7 x 54cm)
£38,000-45,000 *S(NY)*

Gilbert and George (b1934 & 1942)
British
Tower Bridge Flag
Signed, inscribed and dated 1981, on paper label, 49 postcards mounted on card
37½ x 49⅛in (95.3 x 124.8cm)
£6,800-7,500 *C*

Juan Gris (1887-1927)
Spanish
L'Apero
Pencil
12¾ x 9⅜in (32.5 x 23.3cm)
£29,000-35,000 *S*

Executed c1920, this work is a study for one of four lithographs which Gris made as illustrations for Max Jacob's Ne coupez pas, mademoiselle, ou les erreurs des P.T.T., published in Paris in 1921.

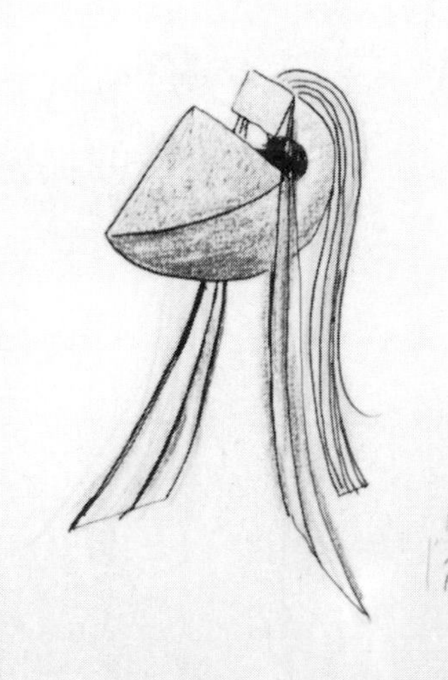

Julio González (1876-1942)
Spanish
Étude Pour Le Cagoulard
Signed with initials, dated 1935, pen and Indian ink, pencil and wax crayons
9½ x 6⅜in (24 x 16.2cm)
£8,300-8,600 *S*

Philip Guston (1913-80)
American
Rug III
Signed, titled and dated 1976, oil on canvas
69 x 110⅜in (175.3 x 280.4cm)
£300,000-325,000 *S(NY)*

By the late 1960s, Guston had moved away from abstraction, turning his attention to the everyday things that surrounded him. 'I knew I wanted to go on and to deal with concrete objects,' he explained. 'I got stuck on shoes, shoes on the floor. I must have done hundreds of paintings of shoes, books, hands, buildings and cars, just everyday objects. And the more I did the more mysterious these objects became. The visible world is abstract and mysterious enough, I don't think one needs to depart from it in order to make art.'

Teresa Grealish (b1969)
British
Filter
Mixed media collage, on board
60in (152.5cm) sq.
£400-450 *Bon*

Barbara Hepworth (1903-75)
British
Design for a Sculpture
Pencil, pen and ink and coloured crayon
15¾ x 12in (40 x 30.3cm)
£6,700-7,200 *S*

Executed c1936, this is a design for the carving Darkwood Spheres of 1936.
Barbara Hepworth is a model for any working mother. As well as having one son by her first marriage to sculptor John Skeaping, she had triplets by her second to Ben Nicholson. 'A woman artist is not deprived by cooking or having children, nor by nursing children with measles (even in triplicate),' she wrote, 'one is in fact nourished by this rich life, provided one always does some work each day; even a single half hour, so that the images grow in one's mind. I detest a day of no work, no music, no poetry.'

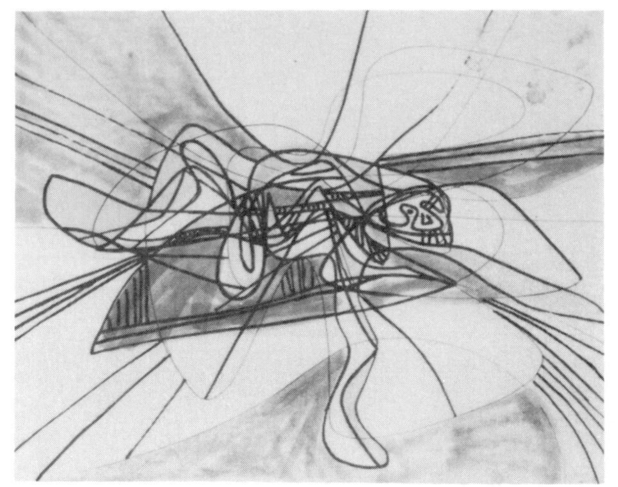

Stanley Hayter (1901-89)
British
The Fly
Signed and dated 20.5.45, watercolour and ink on paper
25¼ x 29½in (64.1 x 74.9cm)
£900-1,000 *S(NY)*

Georg Herold (20thC)
German
Russian Cocaine
Beluga caviar, shellac, asphaltum and acrylic on canvas
60 x 48in (152.4 x 121.89cm)
£6,300-6,800 *S(NY)*

Beluga caviar is without doubt the most esoteric and expensive painting material included in this year's Price Guide.

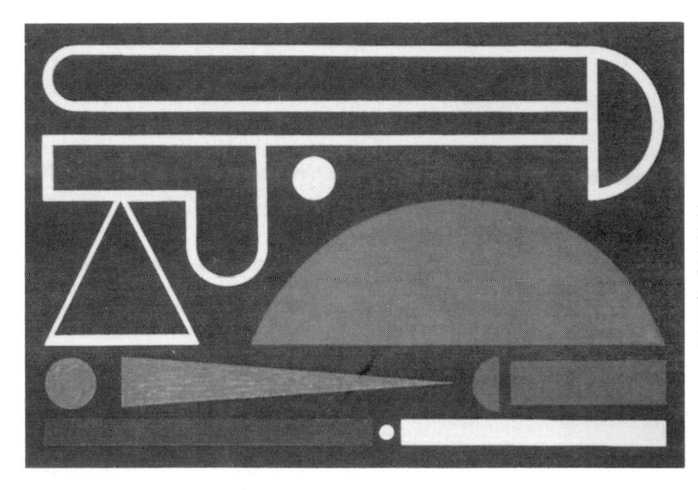

Auguste Herbin (1882-1960)
French
Nuit
Signed, titled and dated 1953, gouache and pencil on paper
8¾ x 12½in (22 x 31.5cm)
£6,700-7,200 *S*

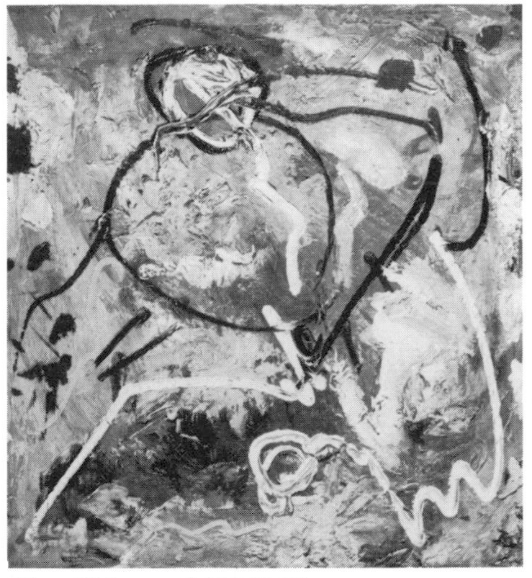

Hans Hofmann (1880-1966)
German
Le Dragon
Oil on board, 1947
22⅝ x 21⅜in (57.5 x 54.3cm)
£26,000-30,000 *S(NY)*

David Hockney (b1937)
British
Afternoon Swimming (T.266:DH53)
Lithograph printed in colours, 1980, signed in white crayon, dated '79, numbered 24/55, on Arches Cover mouldmade paper, with the blindstamp of the publisher Tyler Graphics Ltd., the full sheet, in good condition
31¾ x 39½in (80.5 x 100.3cm)
£21,000-25,000 *S(NY)*

Ivon Hitchens (1893-1979) British
Early Daffodils in Spring Woodland
Signed and dated 75, oil on canvas
16½ x 35in (42 x 91.5cm)
£8,900-9,400 *S*

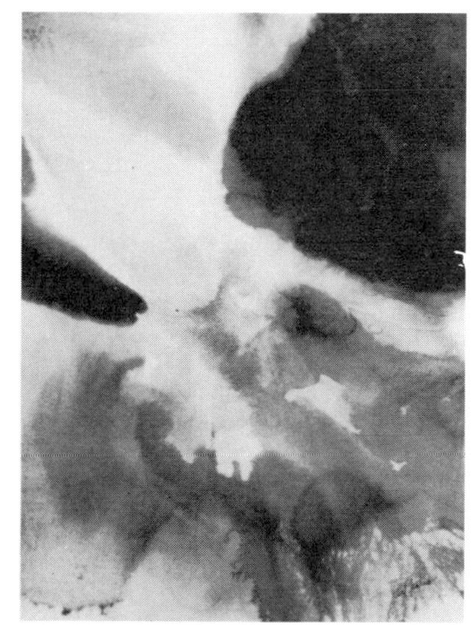

Paul Jenkins (b1923)
American
Sonnor-Spark-Blue
Signed, titled and dated Paris 1959, watercolour on paper
29½ x 22in (75 x 56cm)
£1,400-1,600 *S*

Anselm Kiefer (b1945)
German
Dein Goldenes Haar, Margarethe (Your Golden Hair, Margaret)
Oil and straw on photograph, 1981
23 x 32½in (58.4 x 82.6cm)
£16,000-17,000 *S(NY)*

Lezar M. Hidekel (b1904) Russian
Suprematist Composition
Signed with initials, oil on canvas
26 x 32¼in (66 x 82cm)
£3,100-3,500 *S*

Heidi Jukes (b1963)
British
Alice Fisk, 1991
Mixed media
21 x 22in (53.5 x 56cm)
£500-575 *LG*

Friedensreich Hundertwasser (b1928)
Austrian
Versaumter Frühling – Das Schwarze Loch
Signed, titled, numbered 633 and dated 17-OKT.1966, watercolour, egg, oil, polyvinyl and gold leaf on paper, mounted on jute and canvas
20½ x 28¼in (52.1 x 71.8cm)
£39,000-45,000 *S(NY)*

As the Oxford Companion to 20th Century Art reports disapprovingly, much of this artist's creativity appears to have centred around his own name. Born Friedrich Stowasser, he changed the 'Sto' (Czech for hundred) into the German 'hundert' and extended his first name to 'Friedensreich' (trans. Kingdom of Peace), which he claimed symbolised the new life of peace and joy to which his work would introduce a fallen and corrupted civilisation. For good measure he often added Regenstad (rainy day) on to his last name, on the grounds that he felt happy on rainy days because colours were more luminous. 'This exaggerated concern with the name,' sniffs the Oxford Companion, 'was a sympton of the braggadocio and conceit which were apparent in his work as well as his life.'

Wassily Kandinsky (1866-1944)
Russian
Schwarze Linien (R. 184)
Lithograph, 1924, signed in pencil and numbered 8/50, printed by Graphischen Druckerei des Staatalichen Bauhauses, Weimar, on wove paper
9⅞ x 8⅝in (25 x 22cm)
£2,100-2,500 *S(NY)*

Jasper Johns (b1930)
American
Corpse and Mirror (Screenprint) (F.211) Silkscreen printed in colours, 1976, signed in pencil, dated and numbered 55/65, on ivory Nishinouchi Kizuki Kozo paper, published by the artist and Simca Print Artists, Tokyo
36¼ x 46⅞in (92 x 119cm)
£29,000-35,000 *S(NY)*

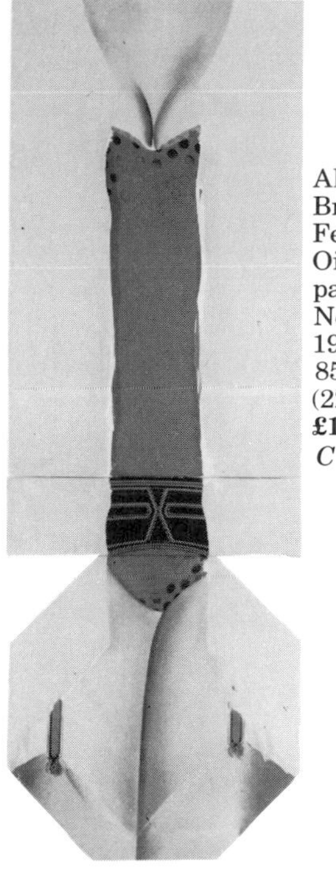

Allen Jones (b1937)
British
Female Medal
Oil on 3 canvas panels, painted in New York in 1964
85½ x 30¼in (222.5 x 76.6cm)
£13,300-14,000 *C*

Wassily Kandinsky (1866-1944) Russian Composition
Signed with initials, dated 30, Indian ink on paper
6¼ x 8¾in (15.9 x 22.2cm)
£17,000-18,000 *S(NY)*

Edmund Kapp (1890-1978)
British
Trio on Red Brick, 1978
Mixed media
30 x 22in (76 x 56cm)
£4,250-4,500 *JB*

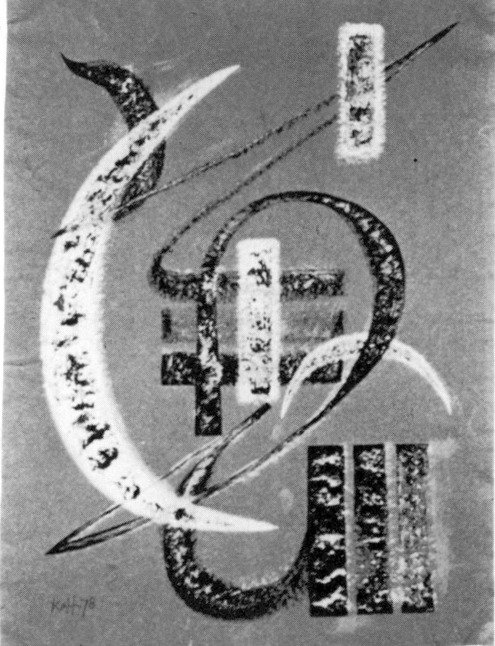

Stephen Kellett (20thC)
British
The New Forest, 1990
Watercolour and wax on paper
27 x 40in (69 x 101.5cm)
£600-700 *LG*

On Kawara (b1933)
Japanese
I Got Up At...
Stamped with the artist's name and dated July 12, 1973 through July 31, 1973, 20 colour postcards of Nova Scotia with black ink stamped on reverse
3½ x 5½in (8.9 x 14cm) each
£9,500-10,000 *S(NY)*

Peter Kinley (1926-88) British
Yellow Flower 1966-67 Oil on canvas
60 x 50in (152.4 x 127cm) **£8,100-8,500** *Bon*

R. B. Kitaj (b1932)
American
Rock Garden (The Nation)
Oil on canvas, 1981
48in (121.9cm) sq.
£80,000-90,000 *S(NY)*

In Rock Garden (The Nation), Kitaj portrays the homeless Jewish nation not in patriotic or geographic terms, but as a community of shared history, values and culture. 'The Jews have been called a Spiritual nation... a people who lived without a territory for two millennia, always ready to move, as the Spirit moves... the Spiritual in art appeals to me and a Spiritual nation can belong to a Spiritual art; and even form one as rarely before.' (R. B. Kitaj, First Kiasporist Manifesto, London, 1989).

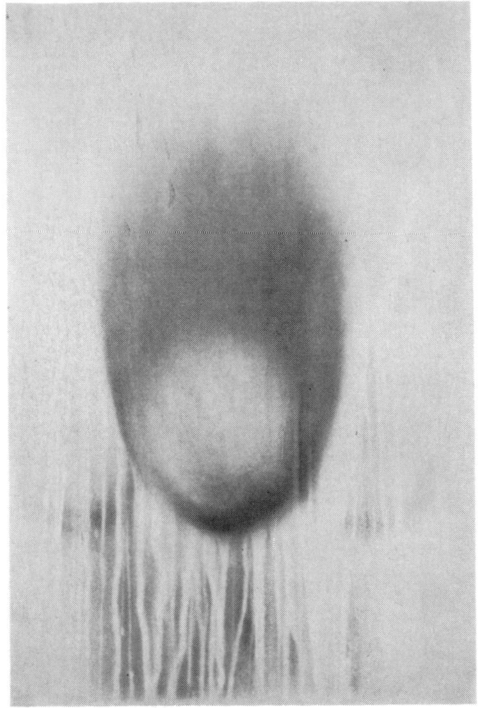

Yves Klein (1928-62) French
Feu nr F2
Burnt cardboard mounted on board
57½ x 38½in (146 x 97cm)
£83,000-90,000 *C*

Executed in 1961 at the Centre d'Essai du Gaz de France, Plaine Saint-Denis. Klein experimented with unorthodox methods, including in the present instance making pictures with the use of a flame-thrower. As with many 20thC artists, Klein's importance lies as much in the symbolic value of his actions, as in the works of art these actually produced. Self-consciously theatrical, Klein's work was designed to provoke a strong response, for some critics he is one of the more significant artists of his generation, whilst others would have been happier had he turned the flame-thrower up to its fullest destructive capacity.

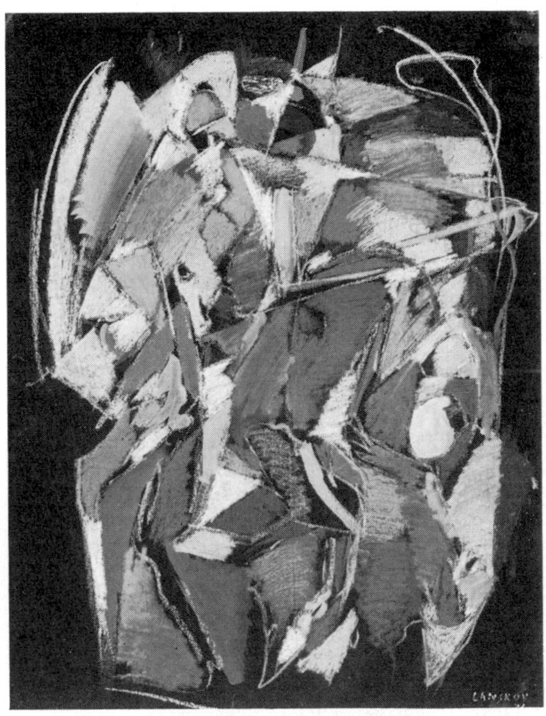

André Lanskoy (1902-76)
Russian/French
Abstract composition on black ground
Signed, gouache and pastel on paper
25½ x 19⅝in (65 x 49cm)
£5,800-6,300 *S(NY)*

André Lanskoy (1902-76)
Russian/French
Signed, dated 11 Aoút 71 on the reverse, oil on canvas
39 x 25½in (99.1 x 64.8cm)
£13,800-14,300 *S(NY)*

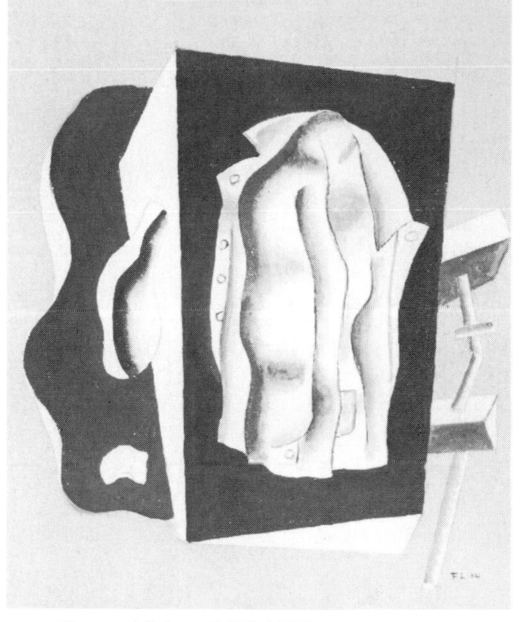

Fernand Léger (1881-1955)
French
Le Veston
Signed with initials and dated lower right F.L.34, gouache and pencil on paper
19 x 16¼in (48.5 x 41.5cm)
£16,600-17,600 *C*

For a short while between 1928 and 1934 Léger turned his back on his mechanical universe and concentrated on the human body and any article of clothing that displayed its imprint, trousers, belts, gloves and jackets.

Peter Lanyon (1918-64)
British
Antigone
Signed and dated 62, also on reverse, inscribed with title on the stretcher, oil on canvas
72 x 48in (183 x 122cm)
£35,500-40,500 *S*

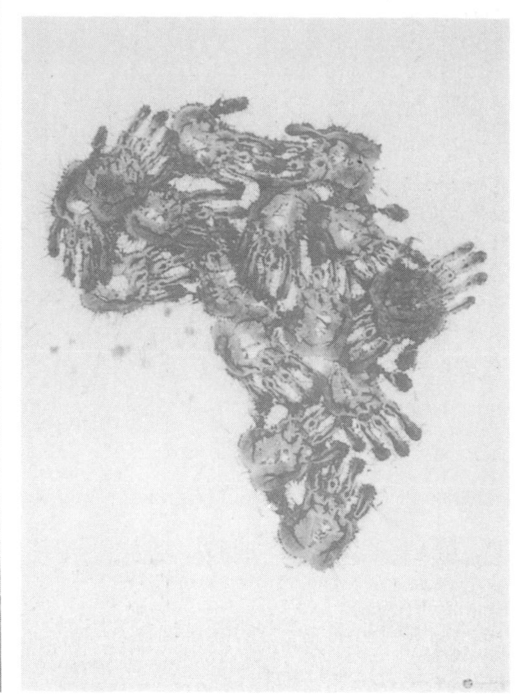

Richard Long (b1945)
British
Mud Hand Africa Map
Signed, titled, stamped with the monogram and dated 1985, River Avon mud on paper
44 x 32¼in (112 x 82cm)
£15,500-16,500 *S*

Peter Lanyon (1918-64)
British
Strange Coast
Signed, also signed, inscribed with title and Aug: 1960 on the reverse, oil on board
45½ x 17½in (114.5 x 44.5cm)
£15,500-16,000 *S*

El Lissitzky (1890-1947)
Russian
Proun VIII
Lithograph printed in black and grey, 1923, from the portfolio, Proun, 1.Kestner-Mappe, signed in pencil, on simili-Japan, the full sheet, printed to the edges
23¼ x 17in (59 x 43.3cm)
£11,000-12,000 *S(NY)*

Jacques Lipchitz (1891-1973) French
Guitariste
Signed, gouache, oil and sand on panel, 1918
10¾ x 8½in (27.3 x 21.6cm)
£76,000-86,000 *S(NY)*

Simon Linke (b1958) American
Lee Krasner October 1986
Oil on canvas
72 x 72in (183 x 183cm)
£6,300-6,800 *S(NY)*

Bruce McLean (b1944) British
'Bien oh yeah'
Original screenprint 1991
Signed in pencil and numbered, from the edition of 200. It was published specially for, and is accompanied by the book 'Bruce McLean Prints 1978-1991' edited by Jeremy Hunt, image and paper
11½ x 30½in (29 x 77.5cm)
£380-400 *WO*

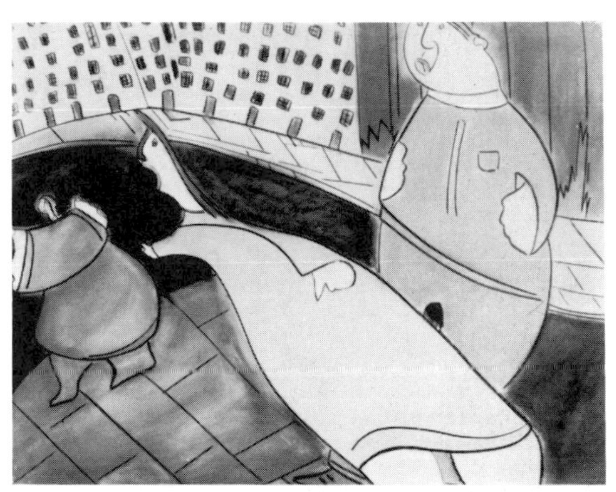

Albert Loudon (b1942) British
Song of the Metropolis Pastel
18 x 22in (46 x 56cm)
£900-1,000 *BG*

Tom MacDonald (20thC) British
Nursery Tale
Oil on board, together with two other oils by the same hand
12 x 18½in (30.5 x 47cm)
£150-180 *Bon*

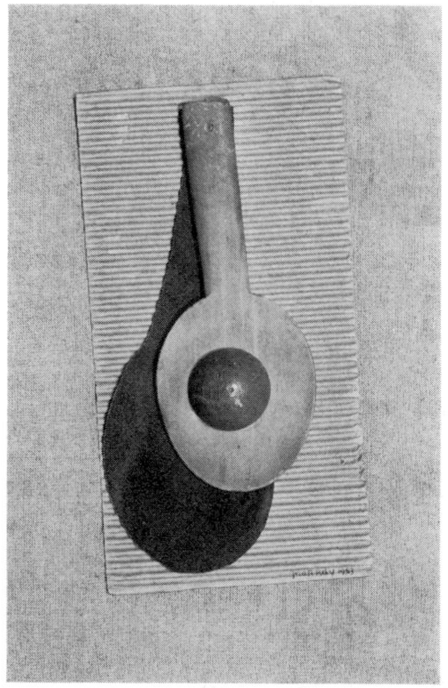

Man Ray (1890-1977) American
Ombre de Cuir Signed and dated 1953, signed and inscribed Optical Hopes and Illusions on the stretcher, leather, wood, corrugated cardboard and hessian
13½ x 9¼in (34 x 23.5cm)
£12,700-13,500 *S*

Conroy Maddox (b1912) British
The Late Sleeper
Oil on canvas, 1973
32 x 24in (81.5 x 61.5cm)
£4,300-4,500 *JB*

Conroy Maddox (b1912) British
The Statue
Oil on canvas, 1983
30 x 24in (76.5 x 61.5cm)
£2,300-2,500 *JB*

Georges Mathieu (b1921)
French
Composition
Signed and dated '65, watercolour and collage on paper
27½ x 20⅛in (70 x 51cm)
£2,400-2,600 *S*

René Magritte (1898-1967) French
Tête d'Homme
Signed, gouache on paper, c1930
9 x 7in (22.8 x 17.8cm)
£10,000-10,400 *C*

Agnes Martin (b1912) American
Happy Valley
Signed, titled and dated 1967 on the reverse, acrylic, pencil and ink on canvas
72 x 72in (182.9 x 182.9cm)
£105,000-115,000 *S(NY)*

Happy Valley is a classic example of Martin's early paintings of 1960-67. Her canvasses measuring 72in square were prepared with an acrylic base of white, off white or buff. Verticals and horizontals were ruled on the canvas in pencil with the use of a T-Square and stretched strings. Many of her works, like Happy Valley, took their titles from nature, the artist's response to the natural world being filtered through her reading in Chinese philosophy. In Eastern thought, art which represents only an external likeness is dead and empty, and the artist must seek to capture the spirit or essence of an object. Martin wanted to evoke through her paintings the same feelings inspired by the beauties of nature: 'When people go to the ocean, they like to see it all day... I want to draw a response like this... an experience of simple joy.'

Man Ray (1890-1977)
American
King Lear (Shakespearean Equation)
Signed with initials, dated 48, watercolour on paper
12 x 16in (30.5 x 40.6cm)
£8,500-9,500 *S(NY)*

This work is part of a series of paintings entitled 'Shakespearean Equations'. Man Ray originally photographed these objects, which were much admired by the Surrealists, and showed them in London in 1936. In Hollywood, however, he used them as subject matter for a series of paintings to which he gave titles taken from Shakespeare's play. Man Ray stated 'In returning to the mathematical objects as a source of material for my 'Shakespearean Equation', I proposed to myself to take liberties not only with the legends but with the forms themselves, their composition, and by addition of colour to make them as arbitrary as the most creative work could be.'

Alastair Michie (b1921)
British
Lochside 2, 1991
Acrylic on board
18⅞ x 14in (48 x 36cm)
£700-800 *HOU*

Joan Miró (1893-1983)
Spanish
Dog Barking at the Moon (M.189)
Lithograph printed in colours, 1952, signed, dated and numbered 19/80 in white crayon
14⅜ x 21½in (36.5 x 54.6cm)
£6,300-6,800 *S(NY)*

Louis Marcoussis (1883-1941)
Polish/French
La Table (Lafranchis 62; Milet 52)
Etching and engraving printed in colours, 1930, signed in pencil and numbered 22/120
9⅝ x 7in (25.5 x 17.8cm)
£4,600-5,000 *S(NY)*

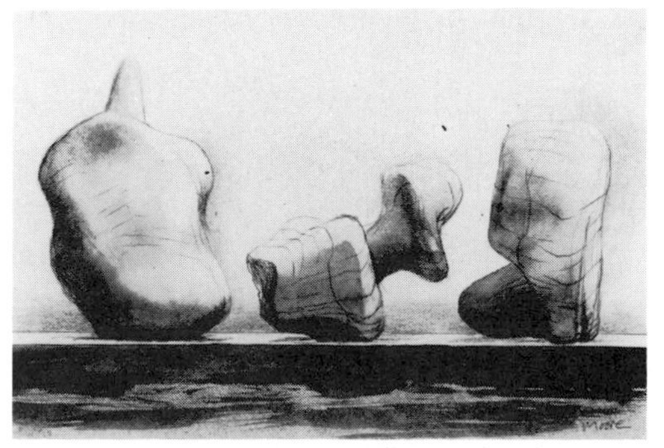

Henry Moore (1898-1986)
British
Idea for Sculpture – Reclining Figure (Notebook No. 2, Drawing No. 12)
Signed, charcoal and wash over pencil, c1975
7 x 10in (17.5 x 25.4cm)
£7,200-7,700 *S*

Oscar Mellor (20thC)
British?
The Vicissitudes of Affection
1989, oil
24 x 16in (61.5 x 41cm)
£750-800 *JB*

Desmond Morris (b1928)
British
The Bull, 1957
Oil on canvas
7 x 15in (18 x 38cm)
£2,300-2,500 *JB*

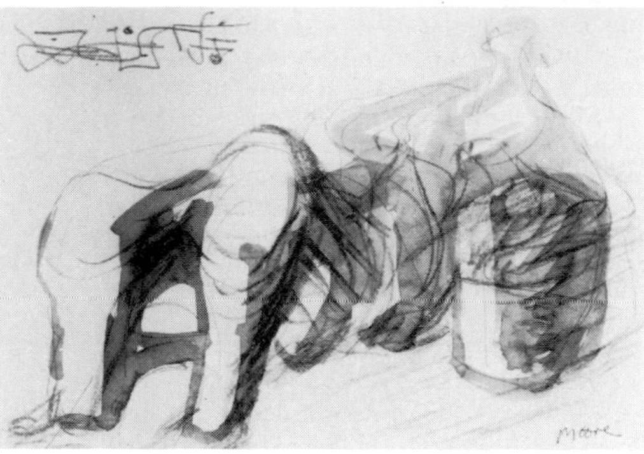

Henry Moore (1898-1986) British
Reclining Figure
Page 27 from Life Drawings and Single Seated Figures Notebook (1972-74), signed, watercolour and crayon on paper
6⅞ x 10in (17.5 x 25.4cm)
£2,700-3,000 *Bon*

Henry Moore Foundation Archive Number HMF 73/4 (67)

Kenneth Noland (b1924) American Beauty Spot
Signed, titled and dated 1969, acrylic on canvas
5½ x 102in (14 x 259.1cm)
£11,500-12,500 *S(NY)*

Ben Nicholson (1894-1982) British
1933, Collage with Spanish Postcard
Signed and dated on the overlap, dedicated and dated on the stretcher for Herbert and Ludo Sept. 1933, oil and pencil with collage of paper and printed fabric on canvas, in the artist's painted frame 19⅝ x 29½in (50 x 75cm)
£190,000-210,000 *S*

This important painting was originally the property of Sir Herbert Read, the most influential art critic of his generation and champion both of abstraction and Surrealism between which this picture hovers. It was painted at a period when the notion of abstraction was shifting from the distorted perception of objects to what Read himself defined as 'a geometrical art which is entirely contained within the relationship of forms, colours, lines and surfaces, without any suggestions of natural objects'. The work shows Nicholson on the edge of an artistic breakthrough that was soon to be achieved in his abstract reliefs.

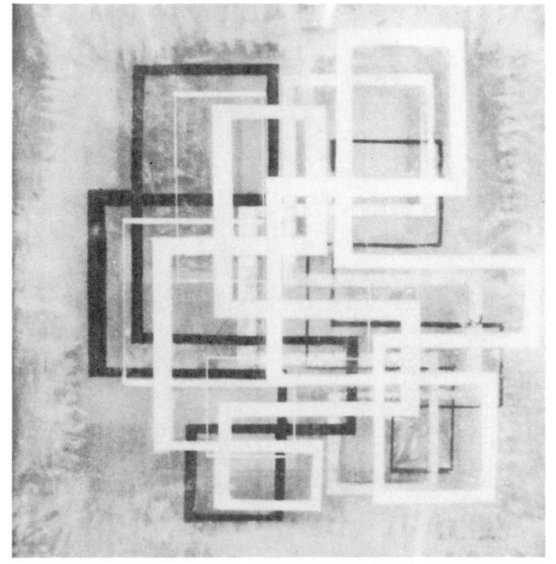

Irene Rice Pereira (b1907) Copper Light
Signed and titled on reverse, mixed media collage on parchment and panel, c1950
18 x 17in (45.7 x 43.2cm) **£3,400-3,700** *S(NY)*

Rebecca Pitt (b1970)
British
Having arrived at a Beginning
On board with ceramic centrepiece
41 x 41in (104 x 104cm)
£600-700 *Bon*

Antoine Pevsner (1886-1962)
Russian
Fond Vert
Signed, and incised 1923, absorbed chemical painting
14⅛ x 11⅛in (35.5 x 28.2cm)
£35,500-38,000 *S(NY)*

Antoine Pevsner worked closely with his younger brother, the sculptor Naum Gabo, in Moscow during the post-Revolutionary years, both playing significant roles as teachers and artists in the development of the Russian Avant-Garde.

He was constantly experimenting with various media for use in his paintings including oil, encaustic and metal. In 1923 he produced a work entitled Peinture Chimique Absorbée in which the medium is described as a mixture of ether, vinegar, powdered pigment and anyline. This work is an absorbed chemical painting, its colours produced by oxidisation, possibly induced by the application of heat.

Alan Reynolds (b1926) British
Legend in Early Autumn 55
Signed, dated and inscribed lower left Reynolds 68 for Robert and Lillian with love, inscribed again on a label on the reverse Legend in Early Autumn 55, watercolour and bodycolour
13¼ x 16½in (33.5 x 42cm)
£2,800-3,200 *C*

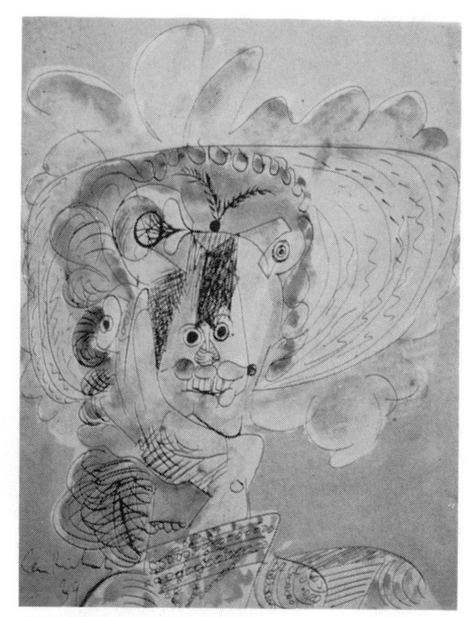

Ceri Richards (1903-71)
British
Costerwoman
Signed and dated 39, watercolour, pen and black ink
15 x 10¾in (38 x 27.5cm)
£1,600-1,800 *C*

Gerhard Richter (b1932)
German
Untitled
Signed, numbered 36/50 and dated 1989, oil on photograph mounted to plexiglass
35 x 55in (88.9 x 139.7cm)
£2,900-3,200 *S(NY)*

Gerhard Richter (b1932)
German
Korsika (Sonne)
Signed and dated on the reverse okt, 68, oil on canvas
33⅝ x 35⅝in (85.5 x 90.5cm)
£83,000-90,000 *C*

Philip Ridley (20thC)
British
The Knife I, The Holding 1991
Charcoal on paper
27½ x 19½in (70 x 49cm)
£600-650 *LG*

Diego Rivera (1886-1957)
Mexican
Mujer Con Alcatraces
Signed and dated 1945, oil on canvas
47⅝ x 47½in (121 x 120.7cm)
£1,610,000-2,000,000 *S(NY)*

The calla lily was a favourite motif of Rivera's. First appearing as a subsidiary detail in paintings of the 1920s, it became increasingly dominant in his later works and a central element of the composition. Rivera sought to create what one critic has described as a heroic and straightforward style 'that would both exploit the formal discoveries of modern art and be immediately comprehensible to the people'. The symbolic significance of the lily would have been familiar to his catholic audience, the flower being the symbol of purity, associated particularly with the Virgin Mary, as well as many other saints.

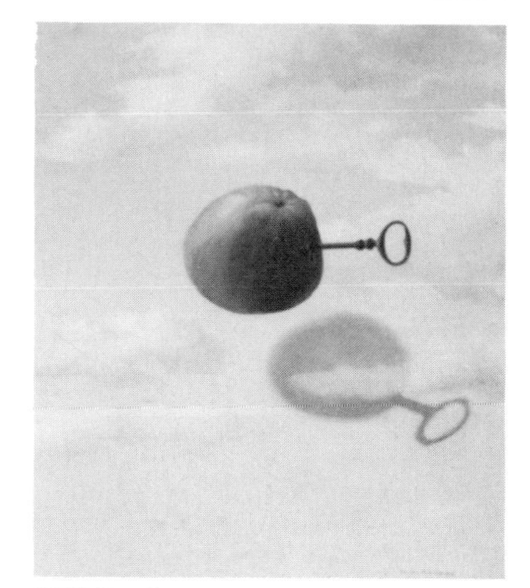

Willi Rondas (20thC)
Belgian
The Key of Gravity, or The Gravity of The Key, 1967
Oil on board
20 x 16in (51 x 41cm)
£500-550 *JB*

David Royle (20thC)
British
Le Déjeuner Sur L'Herbe III
Oil on cotton
54 x 72in (137 x 182.5cm)
£5,800-6,000 *BG*

Pierre Roy (b1880-?)
French
Composition Aux Poids Et Mesures
Signed, oil on canvas
36¼ x 23⅝in (92 x 60cm)
£31,000-35,000 *S*

Roy had a curious method of working which consisted of first making a fully accurate and detailed maquette of an object of his choice and then reproducing it on canvas. When asked by someone why he did not simply photograph the maquette he replied: 'La photographie n'est pas ressemblante.'

Kurt Schwitters (1887-1948)
German
Das Herz Geht Zur Mühle
Signed with the initials and dated 1919, watercolour and red crayon
10¼ x 8in (26 x 20.5cm)
£10,000-10,500 *S*

This work belongs to a series of some 40 watercolours in which Schwitters first developed Dadaism, combining seemingly unconnected objects and motifs in order to create a narrative which defies logical interpretation. 'I play off sense against nonsense,' he explained in 1920. 'I prefer nonsense, but that is a purely personal matter. I feel sorry for nonsense because up to now it has so rarely been artistically moulded; that is why I love nonsense. Here I must mention Dadaism, which like myself, cultivates nonsense.'

Michael Sandle (b1936) British
Artist's visual of Million Pound Monument opened by H.M. Queen in Malta, May 1992
Watercolour
30 x 24in (76 x 61cm)
£2,800-3,200 *GO*

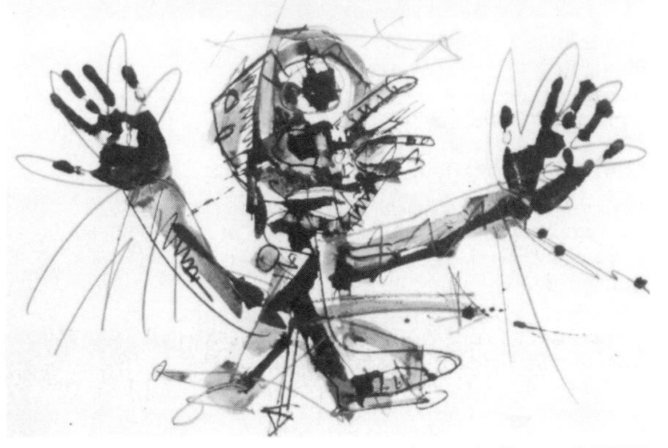

Antonio Saura (b1930)
Spanish
Untitled
Signed and dated 66, gouache and ink on paper
29⅞ x 40⅛in
(76 x 102cm)
£8,600-9,000 *S(NY)*

Mario Schifano (b1934)
Italian
Coca Cola (1970)
Signed
27½ x 39in (70 x 100cm)
£2,500-3,000 *S(R)*

Kenny Scharf (20thC) American
Solsu N Luis Violetch
Signed, titled and dated 84 on the reverse, acrylic and spray enamel on canvas
25½ x 36in (64.8 x 91.4cm)
£5,200-5,500 *S(NY)*

Kenny Scharf (20thC)
American
In Ecstasy
Signed and dated '82 on the stretcher, acrylic and spray paint on canvas
89½ x 107½in (227.3 x 273.1cm)
£12,900-13,500 *S(NY)*

Charles Smith (20thC)
British
Red Wave
Linoleum cut printed in colours, 1938, on laid Japan paper
9¾ x 11¾in (24.8 x 30cm)
£1,100-1,300 *S(NY)*

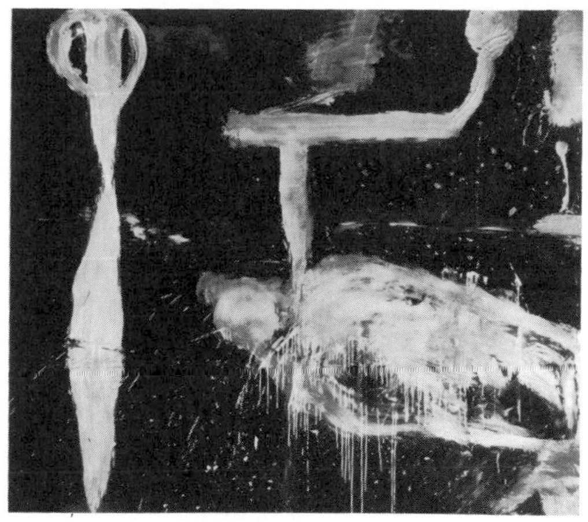

Julian Schnabel (b1951) American
Maria Callas No. 4 Oil on velvet 108 x 122in (274.3 x 309.9cm) **£166,000-186,000** *S(NY)*

Painted in 1982, Maria Callas No. 4 is from a series of 4 works painted on velvet devoted to the American/Greek soprano (1923-77).

Frank Stella (b1936) American
Steller's Albatross, 5X
Mixed media on aluminium
120 x 165in (304.8 x 419.1cm)
£190,000-210,000 *S(NY)*

Executed in 1976, this work belongs to the Exotic Bird series.

Frank Stella (b1936)
American
Double Concentric Squares
Acrylic on canvas, c1973
81 x 161in (205.7 x 408.9cm)
£125,000-140,000 *S(NY)*

Emil Schumacher (b1912) German Tecins Signed and dated '62, titled on the reverse, oil on board 30¼ x 71¼in (77 x 181cm) **£91,000-100,000** *S*

Tancredi (1927-64)
Italian
Composizione astratta, 1958
Signed and dated '58, oil on canvas
35½ x 45in (90 x 115cm)
£24,000-26,000 *C(R)*

John Tunnard (1900-71)
British
Focal Point
Signed and dated '43, oil on board
48 x 60in (122 x 153cm)
£19,500-23,500 *S*

In 1943, Messrs. John Lewis sponsored an exhibition entitled 'The Four Freedoms', for which leading artists were invited to collaborate with a poet to produce a picture to accompany a poem. Tunnard chose Cecil Day Lewis and his poem is reproduced on the reverse of this work.

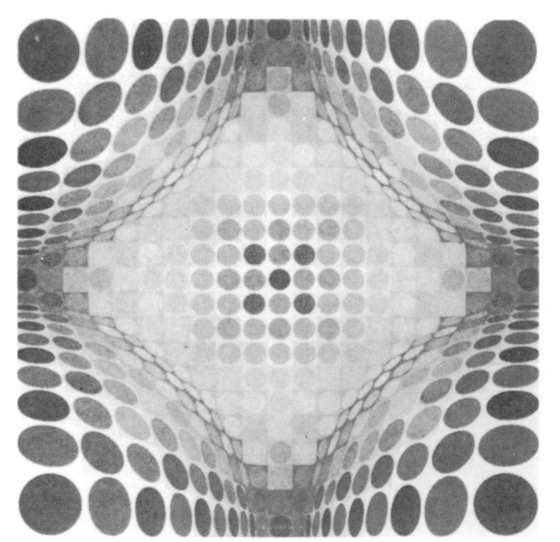

Victor Vasarely (b1908)
Hungarian
Ond-Bv
Signed, titled and dated 1968
Acrylic on board
18⅞ x 18⅞in (47.9 x 47.9cm)
£6,900-7,500 *S(NY)*

Graham Sutherland (1903-80)
British
The Shipwreck
Signed and dated 1978, gouache, watercolour, pastel and pencil on paper laid down on board
14¼ x 13⅜in (36 x 34cm)
£10,200-11,000 *S*

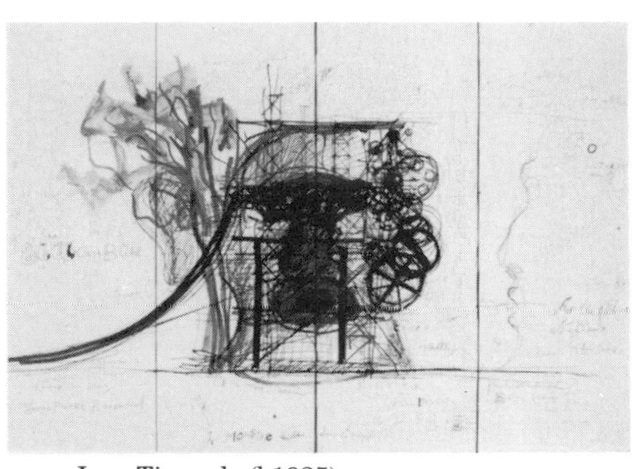

Jean Tinguely (b1925)
French
Le Monstre Dans La Forêt
Watercolour, felt tip pen, ball point and pencil on paper, 1970
23 x 31¾in (58.5 x 80.5cm)
£6,700-7,200 *S*

Tim Walton (20thC)
British?
The Ghost has no Home
Oil on linen
50 x 40in (127 x 101.6cm)
£3,300-3,500 *JB*

John Welson (20thC) British
Interior, 1978 Oil on board
30 x 24in (76 x 61.5cm)
£1,300-1,500 *JB*

Bob White (20thC)
British
Learning to Fly 4
Oil on board
48 x 30in (122 x 76cm)
£1,100-1,200 *BG*

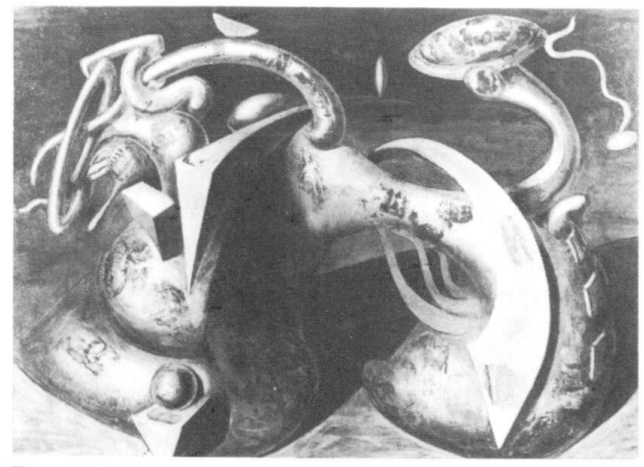

Fiona Weedon (b1954)
British
Hypothetical Noumenon
Signed and dated 1990 on reverse, unframed
56 x 77in (142 x 195.5cm)
£700-800 *Bon*

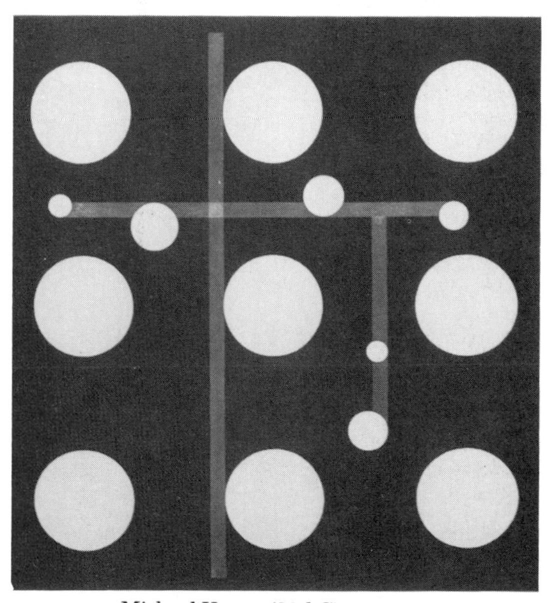

Michael Young (20thC)
American
Rhizome
Signed, titled and dated 1986 on the reverse, sand, earth and acrylic on canvas
82 x 78in (208.3 x 198.1cm)
£4,000-4,500 *S(NY)*

Christopher Wool (b1955)
American
Untitled (W6)
Signed, inscribed with title and dated on the reverse W 6 1990, enamel on aluminium
108 x 72in (274.3 x 183cm)
£28,000-35,000 *C*

DIRECTORY OF GALLERIES

This directory is in no way complete. If you wish to be included in next year's directory or if you have a change of address or telephone number, please could you inform us by July 1st 1993. Entries will be repeated in subsequent editions unless we are requested otherwise. Finally we would advise readers to make contact by telephone before a visit, therefore avoiding a wasted journey, which nowadays is both time consuming and expensive.

London

Abbey Mills Gallery,
Merton Abbey Mills,
Riverside Craft Village,
Meranton Way, SW19
Tel: 081-542 5035

L'Acquaforte,
49a Ledbury Road, W11
Tel: 071-221 3388

Thomas Agnew & Sons,
43 Old Bond Street, W1
Tel: 071-629 6176

Alberti Gallery,
114 Albert Street,
Camden Town, NW1
Tel: 071-485 8976

Alpine Gallery,
74 South Audley Street, W1Y 5FF
Tel: 071-491 2948

Alton Gallery,
72 Church Road,
Barnes, SW13
Tel: 081-748 0606

Michael Appleby,
7 St James's Chambers,
2-10 Ryder Street, SW1Y 6QA
Tel: 071-839 7635

Argile Gallery,
7 Blenheim Crescent, W11
Tel: 071-792 0888

Art Collection,
3-5 Elyston Street, SW3 3NT
Tel: 071-584 4664

Art of Africa,
158 Walton Street, SW3 2JZ
Tel: 071-584 2326

Art Space Gallery,
84 St Peter's Street, N1 8JS
Tel: 071-359 7002

Bankside Gallery,
48 Hopton Street, SE1 9JH
Tel: 071-928 7521

Stephen Bartley Gallery,
62 Old Church Street, SW3
Tel: 071-352 8686

Baumkotter Gallery,
63a Kensington Church Street,
W8 4BA
Tel: 071-937 5171

Beardsmore Gallery,
22-24 Prince of Wales Road,
Kentish Town, NW5
Tel: 071-485 0923

Beaton-Brown Gallery,
20 Motcomb Street,
Belgravia, SW1X 8LB
Tel: 071-823 2240

Chris Beetles Ltd
10 Ryder Street,
St James's, SW1
Tel: 071-839 7551

Belgrave Gallery,
22 Mason's Yard,
Duke Street, SW1
Tel: 071-930 0294

Blason Gallery,
351 Kennington Lane, SE11 5QY
Tel: 071-735 5280

Blond Fine Art
Unit 10
Canalside Studios,
2-4 Orsman Road, N1 5QJ
Tel: 071-739 4383

John Bonham & Murray Feely,
46 Porchester Road, W2
Tel: 071-221 7208

Anna Bornholt Gallery,
3-5 Weighhouse Street, W1
Tel: 071-499 6114

Boundary Gallery,
98 Boundary Road, NW8
Tel: 071-624 1126

Brod Gallery,
24 St James's, SW1A 1HA
Tel: 071-839 3871

Browse & Darby Gallery,
19 Cork Street, W1
Tel: 071-734 7984

Bruton Street Gallery,
28 Bruton Street, W1
Tel: 071-499 9747

Burlington Paintings,
12 Burlington Gardens, W1X 1LG
Tel: 071-734 9984

Cadogan Contemporary,
108 Draycott Avenue, SW3
Tel: 071-581 5451

Caelt Gallery,
182 Westbourne Grove, W11 2RH
Tel: 071-229 9309

Camden Art Gallery,
22 Church Street, NW8
Tel: 071-262 3613

Duncan Campbell Fine Art,
15 Thackeray Street, W8 5ET
Tel: 071-937 8665

Lucy B. Campbell Gallery,
123 Kensington Church Street,
W8 7LP
Tel: 071-727 2205

Catto Gallery,
49 Ladbroke Grove, W11 3AR
Tel: 071-221 7765

Rupert Cavendish Antiques,
98 Waterford Road, SW6
Tel: 071-384 2642

Lumley Cazalet Ltd,
24 Davies Street, W1
Tel: 071-491 4767

Century Gallery,
Westley Richards & Sons,
100/102 Fulham Road,
Chelsea, SW3 6HS
Tel: 071-581 1589

Anna-Mei Chadwick,
64 New King's Road,
Parsons Green, SW6
Tel: 071-736 1928

Churzee Studio Gallery,
17 Bellevue Road,
Wandsworth Common, SW17 7EG
Tel: 081-767 8113

Connaught Brown Gallery,
2 Albemarle Street, W1
Tel: 071-408 0362

Cooling Gallery,
2-4 Cork Street, W1
Tel: 071-409 3500

Cooper Fine Arts Ltd,
768 Fulham Road, SW6 5SJ
Tel: 071-731 3421

Cox & Co
37 Duke Street,
St James's, SW1
Tel: 071-930 1987

Curwen Gallery,
4 Windmill Street, W1
Tel: 071-636 1459

John Denham Gallery,
50 Mill Lane,
West Hampstead, NW6 1NJ
Tel: 071-794 2635

Colin Denny Ltd,
18 Cale Street, SW3
Tel: 071-584 0240

Vanessa Devereux Gallery,
11 Blenheim Crescent, W11
Tel: 071-221 6836

Sebastian D'Orsai Ltd,
39 Theobalds Road, WC1
Tel: 071-609 1275

Dover Street Gallery,
13 Dover Street, W1X 3PH
Tel: 071-409 1540

Drey Gallery,
R16/17 Chenil Galleries,
181-3 King's Road, SW3 5EB
Tel: 071-351 2921

Drian Galleries,
7 Porchester Place,
Marble Arch, W2
Tel: 071-723 9473

Durini Gallery,
150 Walton Street, SW3 2JJ
Tel: 071-581 1237

Eagle Gallery,
159 Farringdon Road, EC1
Tel: 071-833 2674

Ealing Gallery,
78 St Mary's Road,
Ealing, W5
Tel: 081-840 7883

East West,
8 Blenheim Crescent, W11
Tel: 071-229 7981

Eaton Gallery,
34 Duke Street,
St James's, SW1Y 6DF
Tel: 071-930 5950

Editions Graphiques Gallery,
3 Clifford Street, W1
Tel: 071-734 3944

England & Co,
14 Needham Road, W11 2RP
Tel: 071-221 0417

Entwistle Gallery,
37 Old Bond Street, W1
Tel: 071-409 3484

Example Art,
903 Fulham Road, SW6
Tel: 071-384 1130

Finchley Fine Art Galleries,
983 High Road,
North Finchley, N12
Tel: 081-446 4848

Fleur de Lys Gallery,
227a Westbourne Grove, W11
Tel: 071-727 8595

Flowers East,
199 Richmond Road, E8
Tel: 081-985 3333

Frith Street Gallery,
60 Frith Street, W1
Tel: 071-494 1550

Gallery K,
101-103 Heath Street,
Hampstead, NW3 6SS
Tel: 071-794 4949

The Gallery on Church Street,
12 Church Street, NW8
Tel: 071-723 3389

Jill George Gallery,
38 Lexington Street, W1
Tel: 071-439 7343

Martyn Gregory Gallery,
34 Bury Street,
St James's, SW1
Tel: 071-839 3731

Gruzelier Modern &
Contemporary Art,
16 Maclise Road,
West Kensington, W14 0PR
Tel: 071-603 4540

Laurence Hallett
Tel: 071-828 8606

Hamilton Fine Arts,
186 Willifield Way,
Hampstead, NW11 6YA
Tel: 081-455 7410

Hardware Gallery,
277 Hornsey Road,
Islington, N7 6RZ
Tel: 071-272 9651

Marina Henderson Gallery,
11 Langton Street, SW10
Tel: 071-352 1667

Hicks Gallery,
2 & 4 Leopold Road,
Wimbledon SW19
Tel: 081-944 7171

Hildegard Fritz-Denneville Fine
Arts Ltd,
31 New Bond Street, W1Y 9HD
Tel: 071-629 2466

Holland Gallery,
129 Portland Road, W11 4LW
Tel: 071 727 7198

Holland & Holland Gallery,
31 Bruton Street, W1
Tel: 071-499 9383

Stephanie Hoppen Ltd,
17 Walton Street, SW3
Tel: 071-589 3678

Dennis Hotz Fine Art Ltd,
9 Cork Street, W1
Tel: 071-287 8324

Houldsworth Fine Art,
4-6 Bassett Road, W10
Tel: 081-969 8197

Christopher Hull Gallery,
17 Motcomb Street, SW1X 8LB
Tel: 071-235 0500

Sally Hunter Gallery,
11 Halkin Arcade,
Motcomb Street, SW1X 8JT
Tel: 071-235 0934

Hyde Park Gallery,
16 Craven Terrace, W2
Tel: 071-402 2904

Indar Pasricha Fine Arts,
22 Connaught Street, W2 2AF
Tel: 071-724 9541

Malcolm Innes Gallery,
172 Walton Street, SW3 2JL
Tel: 071-584 0575/5559

JPL Fine Arts,
26 Davies Street, W1
Tel: 071-493 2630

David James Gallery,
3 Halkin Arcade,
Motcomb Street, SW1
Tel: 071-235 5552

Gillian Jason Gallery,
42 Inverness Street, NW1
Tel: 071-267 4835

Oscar and Peter Johnson Ltd,
Lowndes Lodge Gallery,
27 Lowndes Street, SW1
Tel: 071-235 6464

E. Joseph,
1 Vere Street, W1
Tel: 071-493 8353

Annely Juda Fine Art,
23 Dering Street, W1
Tel: 071-629 7578

Beryl Kendall,
The English Watercolour Gallery,
2 Warwick Place,
Little Venice, W9
Tel: 071-286 9902

David Ker Fine Art,
85 Bourne Street, SW1
Tel: 071-730 8365

King Street Galleries,
17 King Street,
St James's, SW1
Tel: 071-930 3993

Knapp Gallery,
Regent's College,
Inner Circle,
Regent's Park, NW1 4NS
Tel: 071-487 7540

Stephen Lacey Gallery,
Redcliffe Square, SW10 9JX
Tel: 071-370 7785

Lamont Gallery,
65 Roman Road, E2
Tel: 081-981 6332

Leleco Art Gallery,
5 Britannia Road, SW6
Tel: 071-371 5804

Lisson Gallery,
67 Lisson Street, NW1
Tel: 071-724 2739

Llewellyn Alexander (Fine
Paintings) Ltd,
124-126 The Cut,
Waterloo, SE1
Tel: 071-620 1322

Maas Gallery,
15a Clifford Street,
New Bond Street, W1
Tel: 071-734 2302

Mall Galleries,
The Mall,
Nr Trafalgar Square, SW1
Tel: 071-930 6844

Mark Gallery,
9 Porchester Place,
Marble Arch, W2
Tel: 071-262 4906

Mathaf Gallery,
24 Motcomb Street, SW1
Tel: 071-235 0010

Mathon Gallery,
Pied Bull Yard
68-69 Great Russell Street, WC1
Tel: 071-242 4443

Mayor Gallery,
22a Cork Street, W1
Tel: 071-734 3558

Mercury Gallery,
26 Cork Street, W1
Tel: 071-734 7800

Merrifield Studios,
110 Heath Street, NW3
Tel: 071-794 0343

Roy Miles Gallery,
29 Bruton Street, W1
Tel: 071-495 4747

Mistral Galleries,
10 Dover Street, W1
Tel: 071-499 4701

Montpelier Studio,
4 Montpelier Street, SW7
Tel: 071-584 0667

Moreton Street Gallery,
40 Moreton Street, SW1
Tel: 071-834 7773

Guy Morrison,
91 Jermyn Street, SW1
Tel: 071-839 1454

Narwhal Invit Art Gallery,
55 Linden Gardens, W4 2EH
Tel: 081-747 1575

Guy Nevill Fine Paintings,
251a Fulham Road, SW3
Tel: 071-351 4292

New Grafton Gallery,
49 Church Road,
Barnes, SW13 9HH
Tel: 081-748 8850

Opus 1 Gallery,
25a Maddox Street, W1
Tel: 071-495 2570

O'Shea Gallery,
89 Lower Sloane Street, SW1
Tel: 071-730 0081

Park Walk Gallery,
20 Park Walk,
Chelsea, SW10
Tel: 071-351 0410

Michael Parkin Fine Art Ltd,
11 Motcomb Street, SW1
Tel: 071-235 8144

Paton Gallery,
2 Langley Court, WC2
Tel: 071-379 7854

W. H. Patterson,
19 Albemarle Street, W1X 3HA
Tel: 071-629 4119

Piccadilly Gallery,
16 Cork Street, W1
Tel: 071-499 4632

Pike Gallery,
145 St John's Hill, SW11 1TQ
Tel: 071-223 6741

Polak Gallery,
21 King Street,
St James's, SW1
Tel: 071-839 2871

Primrose Hill Gallery,
81 Regent's Park Road, NW1 8UY
Tel: 071-586 3533

Pyms Gallery,
13 Motcomb Street,
Belgravia, SW1X 8LB
Tel: 071-235 3050

Raab Gallery,
9 Cork Street, W1X 1PD
Tel: 071-734 6444

Railings Gallery,
5 New Cavendish Street, W1
Tel: 071-935 1114

Sue Rankin Gallery,
40 Ledbury Road, W11 2AB
Tel: 071-229 4923

Anthony Reynolds Gallery,
5 Dering Street, W1R 9AB
Tel: 071-491 0621

Benjamin Rhodes Gallery,
4 New Burlington Place, W1
Tel: 071-434 1768

Richmond Gallery,
8 Cork Street, W1
Tel: 071-437 9422

Royal Exchange Art Gallery,
14 Royal Exchange, EC3
Tel: 071-283 4400

Salama-Caro Gallery,
5/6 Cork Street, W1
Tel: 071-734 9179

Karsten Schubert Ltd,
85 Charlotte Street, W1P 1LB
Tel: 071-631 0031

Mark Senior,
240 Brompton Road, SW3
Tel: 071-589 5811

Sheen Gallery,
370 Upper Richmond Road West,
East Sheen, SW14
Tel: 081-878 1100

John Spink,
14 Darlan Road, SW6 5BT
Tel: 071-731 8292

Spink & Son Ltd
5, 6 & 7 King Street,
St James's, SW1Y 6QS
Tel: 071-930 7888

Splinter Gallery,
The Old Conveniences,
227 Goldhawk Road,
Ravenscourt Park,
Hammersmith, W12 8EU
Tel: 081-741 3399

Stern Art Dealers,
46 Ledbury Road, W11
Tel: 071-221 3489

Oliver Swann Galleries,
170 Walton Street, SW3
Tel: 071 581 4229

Talent Store Gallery,
11 Eccleston Street, SW1W 9LX
Tel: 071-730 8117

Tesser Galleries,
106 Heath Street, NW3 1DR
Tel: 071-794 7971

Thompson Gallery,
38 Albemarle Street, W1X 3FB
Tel: 071-499 1314

Todd Gallery,
1-5 Needham Road, W11
Tel: 071-792 1404

The Totteridge Gallery,
61 Totteridge Lane, N20
Tel: 081-446 7896

Tryon & Moorland Gallery,
23/24 Cork Street, W1X 1HB
Tel: 071-734 6961

20th Century Gallery,
821 Fulham Road, SW6
Tel: 071-731 5888

Ben Uri Art Gallery,
21 Dean Street, W1
Tel: 071-437 2852

Rafael Valls Gallery,
11 Duke Street,
St James's, SW1Y 6BN
Tel: 071-930 1144

Gisela van Beers,
34 Davies Street, W1Y 1LG
Tel: 071-408 0434

Waddington Gallery,
10 Cork Street, W1
Tel: 071-437 8611

Walker-Bagshawe,
73 Walton Street, SW3
Tel: 071-589 4582

Waterman Fine Art Ltd,
74a Jermyn Street,
St James's, SW1Y 6NP
Tel: 071-839 5203

Westbourne Gallery,
331 Portobello Road, W10 5SA
Tel: 081-960 1867

Wilkins & Wilkins,
1 Barrett Street, W1A 6DN
Tel: 071-935 9613

Wiseman Originals,
34 West Square,
Lambeth, SE1
Tel: 071-587 0747

Wolsely Fine Arts plc,
4 Grove Park, SE5 8LT
Tel: 071-274 8788

Christopher Wood Gallery,
141 New Bond Street,
Belgravia, W1
Tel: 071-235 9141

Wykeham Galleries,
51 Church Road,
Barnes, SW13 9HH
Tel: 081-741 1277

Wyllie Gallery,
12 Needham Road, W11
Tel: 071-727 0606

Avon

Adam Gallery,
13 John Street,
Bath, BA1 2JL
Tel: (0225) 480406

Alexander Gallery,
122 Whiteladies Road,
Bristol
Tel: (0272) 734692

Alma Gallery,
29 Alma Vale Road,
Clifton,
Bristol, BS8 2HL
Tel: (0272) 237157

Arnolfini Gallery,
16 Narrow Quay,
Bristol, BS1 4QA
Tel: (0272) 299191

Beaux Arts,
York Street,
Bath, BA1 1NG
Tel: (0225) 464850

Cleveland Bridge Gallery,
8 Cleveland Place East,
Bath, BA1 5DG
Tel: (0225) 447885

David Cross Gallery,
30 Boyces Avenue,
Clifton,
Bristol, BS8 4AA
Tel: (0272) 732614

Ginger Gallery,
84/86 Hotwell Road,
Bristol, BS8 4UB
Tel: (0272) 292527

Kingsley Gallery,
Upper Langridge Farm,
Lansdown,
Bath, BA1 9BW
Tel: (0225) 421714

Pelter/Sands Art Gallery,
43-45 Park Street,
Bristol
Tel: (0272) 293988

St James Gallery,
9b Margarets Buildings,
Bath, BA1 2LP
Tel: (0225) 319197

Saville Row Gallery,
1 Saville Row,
Alfred Street,
Bath
Tel: (0225) 334595

Toll House Gallery,
Clevedon Pier Trust Ltd,
The Beach,
Clevedon
Tel: (0275) 878846

The Patricia Wells Gallery,
Morton House,
Lower Morton,
Thornbury,
Bristol, BS12 1RA
Tel: (0454) 412288

Bedfordshire

Charterhouse Gallery Ltd,
14 Birds Hill,
Heathand Reach,
Leighton Buzzard, LU7 0AQ
Tel: (052523) 379

Woburn Fine Arts,
12 Market Place,
Woburn
Tel: (0525) 290624

Berkshire

Marian & John Alway Fine Art,
Riverside Corner,
Windsor Road,
Datchet, SL3 9BT
Tel: (0753) 541163

The Collectors Gallery,
8 Bridge Street,
Caversham Bridge,
Caversham,
Nr Reading
Tel: (0734) 483663

Emgee Gallery,
60 High Street,
Eton, SL4 6AA
Tel: (0753) 856329

Graham Gallery,
Highwoods,
Burghfield Common,
Nr Reading, RG7 3BG
Tel: (0734) 832320

Jaspers Fine Arts Ltd,
36 Queen Street,
Maidenhead
Tel: (0628) 36459

Omell Galleries in Windsor,
Goswell Hill,
134 Peascod Street,
Windsor, SL4 1DR
Tel: (0753) 852271

Paravicini,
7 Bridge Street,
Hungerford
Tel: (0488) 685173

Buckinghamshire

Christopher Cole (Fine Paintings) Ltd,
1 London End,
Beaconsfield
Tel: (0494) 671274

Angela Hone Watercolours,
The Garth,
31 Mill Road,
Marlow, SL7 1QB
Tel: (0628) 484170

Images in Watercolour,
8 The Lagger,
Chalfont St Giles
Tel: (02407) 5592

David Messum,
The Studio,
Lordswood,
Marlow, SL7 2QS
Tel: (0628) 486565

Mon Galerie,
The Old Forge,
The Broadway,
Old Amersham
Tel: (0494) 721705

Penn Barn Gallery,
By the Pond,
Elm Road,
Penn, HP10 8LU
Tel: (0494 81) 5691

Van Riemsdijk Fine Art,
Seven Gables,
Stockwell Lane,
Wavendon
Tel: (0908) 582621

Cheshire

Baron Fine Art
68 Watergate Street,
Chester, CH1 2LA
Tel: (0244) 342520

Betley Court Gallery,
Betley,
Nr Crewe, CW3 9BH
Tel: (0270) 820652

Harper Fine Paintings,
'Overdale',
Woodford Road,
Poynton,
Nr Stockport
Tel: (0625) 879105

Cleveland

E. & N. R. Charlton Fine Art,
69 Cambridge Avenue,
Marton,
Nr Middlesbrough
Tel: (0642) 319642

Cornwall

Art & Antiques,
9 St Nicholas Street,
Bodmin
Tel: (0208) 74408

The Broad Street Gallery,
9 Broad Street,
Penryn, TR10 8JL
Tel: (0326) 377216

Copperhouse Gallery,
14 Fore Street,
Hayle
Tel: (0736) 752787

David Lay,
The Penzance Auction House,
Alverton,
Penzance, TR18 4RE
Tel: (0736) 61414

Penandrea Gallery,
12 Higher Fore Street,
Redruth
Tel: (0209) 213134

St Breock Gallery,
St Breock Churchtown,
Wadebridge
Tel: (0208) 812543

Tony Sanders Penzance Gallery,
14 Chapel Street,
Penzance
Tel: (0736) 66620

Tamar Gallery,
5 Church Street,
Launceston
Tel: (0566) 774233

Cumbria

The Gallery,
54 Castlegate,
Penrith
Tel: (0768) 65538

Derbyshire

Ashbourne Fine Art,
Agnes Meadow Farm,
Offcote,
Ashbourne
Tel: (0335) 44072

Devon

A-B Gallery,
67 Fore Street,
Salcombe
Tel: (0548) 842764

Birbeck Gallery,
45 Abbey Road,
Torquay
Tel: (0803) 297144

Honiton Galleries,
205 High Street,
Honiton
Tel: (0404) 42404

New Gallery,
Abele Tree House,
9 Fore Street,
Budleigh Salterton
Tel: (039 544) 3768

Beverley J. Pyke,
The Gothic House,
Bank Lane,
Totnes
Tel: (0803) 864219

Dorset

Alpha Gallery,
21a Commercial Road,
Swanage
Tel: (0929) 423692

Dorchester Gallery,
10a High East Street,
Dorchester, DT1 1HS
Tel: (0305) 251144

Hampshire Gallery,
18 Lansdowne Road,
Bournemouth
Tel: (0202) 551211

Peter Hedley Gallery,
10 South Street,
Wareham
Tel: (0929) 551777

York House Gallery,
32 Somerset Road,
Boscombe,
Bournemouth
Tel: (0202) 391034

East Sussex

Barclay Antiques,
7 Village Mews,
Little Common,
Bexhill-on-Sea
Tel: (0797) 222734

Barnes Gallery,
8 Church Street,
Uckfield
Tel: (0825) 762066

John Day of Eastbourne Fine Art,
9 Meads Street,
Eastbourne
Tel: (0323) 25634

Old Post House Antiques,
Old Post House,
Playden,
Nr Rye
Tel: (079 7280) 303

Rye Art Gallery,
Easton Rooms,
107 High Street,
Rye, TN31 7JE
Tel: (0797) 223218

E. Stacy-Marks Ltd,
24 Cornfield Road,
Eastbourne
Tel: (0323) 20429

Towner Art Gallery,
High Street,
Old Town,
Eastbourne
Tel: (0323) 411688

Essex

Barn Gallery,
Parvilles Farm,
Hatfield Heath,
Nr Bishop's Stortford
Tel: (0279) 731228

Brandler Gallery,
1 Coptfold Road,
Brentwood, CM14 4BM
Tel: (0277) 222269

Chappel Galleries,
Colchester Road,
Chappel, Nr Colchester, CO6 2DE
Tel: (0206) 240326

Simon Hilton,
Flemings Hill Farm,
Great Easton,
Dunmow
Tel: (0279) 850107

Richard Iles Gallery,
10a, 10 & 12 Northgate Street,
Colchester
Tel: (0206) 577877

Gloucestershire

Astley House Fine Art,
Astley House,
London Road,
Moreton-in-Marsh
Tel: (0608) 50601

Gerard Campbell,
Maple House,
Market Place,
Lechlade
Tel: (0367) 52267

The Cotswold Galleries,
The Square,
Stow-on-the-Wold
Tel: (0451) 30586

John Davies Fine Paintings,
Church Street,
Stow-on-the-Wold, GL54 1BB
Tel: (0451) 31698/31790

Fosse Gallery,
The Square,
Stow-on-the-Wold
Tel: (0451) 31319

David Howard,
42 Moorend Crescent,
Cheltenham
Tel: (0242) 243379

Kenulf Fine Art Ltd
5 North Street,
Winchcombe,
Cheltenham, GL54 5LH
Tel: (0242) 603204

Manor House Gallery,
Manor House,
Badgeworth Road,
Cheltenham
Tel: (0452) 713953

Heather Newman Gallery,
Milidduwa,
Mill Lane,
Cranham
Tel: (0452) 812230

Ogle Fine Art,
1 Wellington Square,
Cheltenham
Tel: (0242) 231011

Priory Gallery,
The Priory,
Station Road,
Bishops Cleeve,
Cheltenham, GL52 4HH
Tel: (0242) 673226

Turtle Fine Art,
29 & 30 Suffolk Parade.
Cheltenham
Tel: (0242) 241646

Upton Lodge Galleries,
No 6 Long Street,
Tetbury, GL6 8AQ
Tel: (0666) 503416

Greater Manchester

Corner House,
70 Oxford Street, M1 5NH
Tel: 061-228 7621

The Fulda Gallery,
19 Vine Street,
Salford
Tel: 061-792 1962

Hampshire

Alresford Gallery,
36 West Street,
Alresford,
Winchester
Tel: (0962) 735286

Bell Fine Art,
67b Parchment Street,
Winchester
Tel: (0962) 860439

Fleet Fine Art Gallery,
1/2 King's Parade,
King's Road,
Fleet
Tel: (0252) 617500

On Line Gallery,
76 Bedford Place,
Southampton, SO1 2DF
Tel: (0703) 330660

J. Morton Lee,
Cedar House,
Bacon Lane,
Hayling Island, PO11 0DN
Tel: (0705) 464444

Petersfield Bookshop,
16a Chapel Street,
Petersfield
Tel: (0730) 263438

Hereford & Worcester

Coltsfoot Gallery,
Hatfield,
Leominster, HR6 0SF
Tel: (056 882) 277

Hay Loft Gallery,
Berry Wormington,
Broadway, WR12 7NH
Tel: (0242) 621202

Haynes Fine Art,
69 High Street,
Broadway,
Worcester, WR12 7DP
Tel: (0386) 852649

The Kilvert Gallery,
Ashbrook House,
Clyro,
Hay-on-Wye, HR3 5RZ
Tel: (0497) 820831

Lismore Gallery,
3 Edith Walk,
Great Malvern
Tel: (0684) 568610

Mathon Gallery,
Mathon Court,
Mathon
Nr Malvern
Tel: (0684) 892242

Hertfordshire

Countrylife Gallery,
41 Portmill Lane,
Hitchin, SG5 1DJ
Tel: (0462) 433267

Gallery One Eleven,
111 High Street,
Berkhampstead, HP4 2JF
Tel: (0442) 876333

McCrudden Gallery,
23 Station Road,
Rickmansworth
Tel: (0923) 772613

Carole Thomas Fine Arts,
Grange Farm Cottages,
Hexton,
Nr Hitchin, SG5 3AH
Tel: (0582) 883337

Humberside

Steven Dews Fine Art,
66-70 Princes Avenue,
Hull
Tel: (0482) 42424

Isle of Wight

The Gallery,
High Street,
Yarmouth
Tel: (0983) 760784

The Marine Gallery,
1 Bath Road,
Cowes
Tel: (0983) 200124

Vectis Fine Arts,
2 Ivy Cottages,
Newchurch
Tel: (0983) 865463

Kent

Bank Street Gallery,
3-5 Bank Street,
Sevenoaks, TN13 1UW
Tel: (0732) 458063

Clare Gallery,
21 High Street,
Royal Tunbridge Wells, TN1 1UT
Tel: (0892) 538717

Mistral Galleries,
12 Market Square,
Westerham

Platform Gallery,
136 Sandgate Road,
Folkestone, CT20 2BY
Tel: (0732) 458063

Pratt Contemporary Art,
The Gallery,
Ightham,
Sevenoaks, TN15 9HH
Tel: (0732) 882326

Sundridge Gallery,
9 Church Road,
Sundridge,
Nr Sevenoaks
Tel: (0959) 564104

The Weald Gallery,
High Street,
Brasted,
Nr Westerham
Tel: (09595) 62672

Lancashire

Peter Haworth,
Howe Hill,
Cow Brow,
Carnforth
Tel: (05395 67) 656

Neill Gallery,
4 Portland Street,
Southport, PR8 1JU
Tel: (0704) 549858

Studio Arts Gallery,
6 Lower Church Street,
Lancaster
Tel: (0524) 68014

Leicestershire

Fine Art of Oakham Ltd,
4 High Street,
Oakham,
Rutland, LE15 6AL
Tel: (0572) 755221

Foulds-Field Fine Art,
2 Bidford Court,
Bidford Close,
Leicester
Tel: (0533) 824364

Goldmark Gallery,
Orange Street,
Uppingham,
Rutland, LE15 9SQ
Tel: (0572) 821424

The Old House Gallery,
13-15 Market Place,
Oakham
Tel: (0572) 755538

Merseyside

Lyver & Boydell Galleries,
15 Castle Street,
Liverpool
Tel: 051-236 3256

Middlesex

Hampton Hill Gallery,
203 & 205 High Street,
Hampton Hill, TW12 1NP
Tel: 081-977 1379

Midlands

Driffold Gallery,
The Smithy,
78 Birmingham Road,
Sutton Coldfield, B72 1QR
Tel: 021-355 5433

Graves Gallery,
No 3 The Spencers,
Augusta Street,
Hockley,
Birmingham, B18 6JA
Tel: 021-212 1635

Halcyon Gallery,
30 Marshall Street,
Birmingham, B1 1LE
Tel: 021-616 1313

Midlands Contemporary Art,
Newhall Court,
59 George Street,
Birmingham
Tel: 021-233 9818

Sport & Country Gallery,
Northwood House,
121 Weston Lane,
Bulkington,
Nuneaton, CV12 9RX
Tel: (0203) 314335

Norfolk

Bank House Gallery,
71 Newmarket Road,
Norwich, NR2 2HW
Tel: (0603) 633380

The Coach House,
Townhouse Road,
Old Costessey,
Nr Norwich
Tel: (0603) 742977

Crome Gallery,
34 Elm Hill,
Norwich, NR3 1HG
Tel: (0603) 622827

The Fairhurst Gallery,
13 Bedford Street,
Norwich
Tel: (0603) 614214

Humbleyard Fine Art,
3 Fish Hill,
Holt
Tel: (0263) 713362

Staithe Lodge Gallery,
Staithe Lodge,
Swafield,
Nr North Walsham
Tel: (0692) 402669

Northamptonshire

Savage Fine Art,
Alfred Street,
Northampton, NN1 5EY
Tel: (0604) 20327

North Yorkshire

Sutcliffe Galleries,
5 Royal Parade,
Harrogate, HG1 2SZ
Tel: (0423) 562976

Nottinghamshire

Anthony Mitchell Fine Paintings,
Sunnymede House,
11 Albemarle Road,
Woodthorpe,
Nottingham, NG5 4FE
Tel: (0602) 623865

Oxfordshire

Bohun Gallery,
15 Reading Road,
Henley-on-Thames, RG8 1AB
Tel: (0491) 576228

The Burford Gallery,
Classica House,
High Street,
Bloxham,
Nr Banbury
Tel: (099 382) 2305

H. C. Dickens,
High Street,
Bloxham,
Nr Banbury, OX15 4LT
Tel: (0295) 721949

Horseshoe Antiques & Gallery,
97 High Street,
Burford
Tel: (099 382) 3244

The Barry M. Keene Gallery,
12 Thameside,
Henley-on-Thames
Tel: (0491) 577119

The Oxford Gallery,
23 High Street,
Oxford, OX1 4AH
Tel: (0865) 242731

Brian Sinfield Gallery,
Grafton House,
128 High Street,
Burford
Tel: (0993) 822603

Wren Gallery,
4 Bear Court,
High Street,
Burford, OX18 4RR
Tel: (0993) 823495

Shropshire

Gallery 6,
6 Church Street,
Broseley
Tel: (0952) 882860

Haygate Gallery,
40 Haygate Road,
Wellington,
Telford
Tel: (0952) 248553

The Jane Marler Gallery,
Dawes Mansion,
Church Street,
Ludlow
Tel: (0584) 874160

Teme Valley Antiques,
1 The Bull Ring,
Ludlow
Tel: (0584) 874686

Somerset

Julian Armytage,
The Old Rectory,
Wayford,
Nr Crewkerne, TA18 8QG
Tel: (0460) 73449

Martin Dodge Interiors Ltd,
Southgate,
Wincanton, BA9 9EB
Tel: (0225) 462202

Heale Gallery,
Curry Rivel, T10 0PQ
Tel: (0458) 251234

Plympton Gallery,
31 West Street,
Ilminster
Tel: (0460) 54437

Staffordshire

Victoria Des Beaux Arts Ltd,
11 Newcastle Street,
Burslem,
Stoke-on-Trent, ST6 3QB
Tel: (0782) 836490

Wavertree Gallery,
Berkeley Court,
Borough Road,
Newcastle-under-Lyme
Tel: (0782) 712686

Suffolk

Equus Art Gallery,
Sun Lane,
Newmarket, CB8
Tel: (0638) 560445

Simon Carter Gallery,
23 Market Hill,
Woodbridge, IP12 4LX
Tel: (0394) 382242

Mangate Gallery,
The Old Vicarage,
Laxfield,
Nr Woodbridge, IP13 8DT
Tel: (0986) 798524

John Russell Gallery,
Orwell Court,
13 Orwell Place,
Ipswich, IP4 1BD
Tel: (0473) 212051

West Sussex

Susan & Robert Botting,
Felpham,
Nr Bognor Regis
Tel: (0243) 584515

Sheila Hinde Fine Art,
Idolsfold House,
Nr Billingshurst
Tel: (0403) 77576

Vosper Gallery,
Old Station House,
London Road,
East Grinstead, RH19 1YZ
Tel: (0342) 315057

Surrey

Alba Gallery,
3 Station Approach,
Kew Gardens,
Richmond
Tel: 081-948 2672

Boathouse Gallery,
The Towpath,
Manor Road,
Walton-on-Thames, KT12 2PG
Tel: (0932) 242718

Bourne Gallery,
31-33 Lesbourne Road,
Reigate, RH2 7JS
Tel: (0737) 241614

P. & J. Goldthorpe,
Bicton Croft,
Deanery Road,
Godalming
Tel: (0483) 414356

Tyne & Wear

The Dean Gallery,
42 Dean Street,
Newcastle-upon-Tyne
Tel: 091-232 1208

MacDonald Fine Art,
2 Ashburton Road,
Gosforth
Tel: 091-284 4214

Vicarage Cottage Gallery,
Preston Road,
North Shields, NE29 9PJ
Tel: 091-257 0935

Warner Fine Art,
208 Wingrove Road,
Fenham,
Newcastle-upon-Tyne
Tel: 091-273 8030

Warwickshire

Colmore Galleries Ltd,
52 High Street,
Henley-in-Arden, B95 5AN
Tel: (0564) 792938

Coughton Galleries Ltd,
Coughton Court,
Coughton,
Nr Alcester
Tel: (0789) 762642

The Chadwick Gallery,
2 Doctors Lane,
Henley-in-Arden, B95 5AN
Tel: (0564) 794820

Fine Lines Fine Art,
The Old Rectory,
31 Sheep Street,
Shipston on Stour, CV36 4AE
Tel: (0608) 662323

Wiltshire

Courcoux & Courcoux,
90-92 Crane Street,
Salisbury, SP1 2QD
Tel: (0722) 333471

Lacewing Fine Art Gallery,
124 High Street,
Marlborough, SN8 1LZ
Tel: (0672) 514580

Lantern Gallery,
Hazeland House,
Kington St Michael, SN14 6JJ
Tel: (024 975) 0306

Summerleaze Gallery,
East Knoyle,
Salisbury
Tel: (0747) 830790

Worcestershire

John Noott Galleries,
14 Cotswold Court,
Broadway
Tel: (0386) 852787

Yorkshire

Kentmere House Gallery,
53 Scarcroft Hill,
York, YO2 1DF
Tel: (0904) 656507

James Starkey Fine Art,
Highgate,
Beverley
Tel: (0482) 881179

The Titus Gallery,
1 Daisy Place,
Saltaire,
Shipley, BD18 4NA
Tel: (0274) 581894

Walker Galleries Ltd,
6 Montpelier Gardens,
Harrogate, HG1 2TF
Tel: (0423) 567933

Scotland

Ancrum Gallery,
3 Capelaw Road,
Colinton,
Edinburgh, EH3 0HG
Tel: (083) 53340

Laurance Black Ltd,
45 Cumberland Street,
Edinburgh, EH3 6RA
Tel: 031-557 4545

Bourne Fine Art,
4 Dundas Street,
Edinburgh, EH3 6HZ
Tel: 031-557 4050

Calton Gallery,
10 Royal Terrace,
Edinburgh, EH7 5AB
Tel: 031-556 1010

Flying Colours Gallery,
35 William Street,
West End,
Edinburgh, EH3 7LW
Tel: 031-225 6776

Gatehouse Gallery,
Rouken Glen Road,
Giffnock,
Glasgow, G46 7UG
Tel: 041-620 0235

Hanover Fine Arts,
22a Dundas Street,
Edinburgh, EH3 6JN
Tel: 031-556 2181

William Hardie Gallery,
141 West Regent Street,
Glasgow, G2
Tel: 041-221 6780

Paul Hayes Gallery,
71 High Street,
Auchterarder,
Perthshire PH3 1BN
Tel: (0764) 62320

Malcolm Innes Gallery,
67 George Street,
Edinburgh, EH2 2JG
Tel: 031-226 4151

Barclay Lennie Fine Art,
203 Bath Street,
Glasgow, G2 4HZ
Tel: 041-226 5413

The McEwan Gallery,
Glengarden,
Ballater,
Aberdeenshire AB35 5UB
Tel: (03397) 55429

Open Eye Gallery,
75/79 Cumberland Street,
Edinburgh, EH3
Tel: 031-557 1020

Portfolio Gallery,
43 Candlemaker Row,
Edinburgh, EH1 2QB
Tel: 031-220 1911

Wales

Rowles Fine Art,
Station House Gallery,
Llansantffraid,
Powys SY22 6AD
Tel: (0691) 828478

Martin Tinney Gallery,
6 Windsor Place,
Cardiff, CF1 3BX
Tel: (0222) 641411

Michael Webb Fine Art,
Cefn-Llwyn,
Bodorgan,
Anglesey,
Gwynedd LL62 5DN
Tel: (0407) 840336

Channel Islands

Coach House Gallery,
Les Islets,
St Peters,
Guernsey
Tel: (0481) 65339

DIRECTORY OF SPECIALISTS

GALLERY HIRE

London

Academia Italiana,
24 Rutland Gate, SW7 1BB
Tel: 071-225 3474

Kensington Gallery,
202 Kensington Park Road,
W11 1NR
Tel: 071-792 9875

Marsden Fine Art,
21 Dulwich Village, SE21 7BT
Tel: 071-836 6252

RESTORERS

London

Bates and Baskcomb,
191 St John's Hill, SW11 1TH
Tel: 071-223 1629

John Campbell Master Frames,
164 Walton Street, SW3
Tel: 071-584 9268

Chapman Restorations,
10 Theberton Street, N1 0QX
Tel: 071-226 5565

The Conservation Studio,
The Studio,
107 Shepherds Bush Road, W6 7LP
Tel: 071-602 0757

Cooper Fine Arts Ltd,
768 Fulham Road, SW6 5SJ
Tel: 071-731 3421

Deansbrook Gallery,
134 Myddleton Road, N22 4NQ
Tel: 081-889 8389

P. Dowling,
Chenil Galleries,
181-183 Kings Road, SW3 5EB
Tel: 071-376 5056

Harries Fine Art,
712 High Road,
North Finchley, N12 9QD
Tel: 081-445 2804

Lamont Gallery,
65 Roman Road, E2
Tel: 081-981 6332

Plowden & Smith Ltd,
190 St Ann's Hill, SW18 2RT
Tel: 081-874 4005

Relcy Antiques,
9 Nelson Road, SE10 9JB
Tel: 081-858 2812

Woolcock Framing,
8 Huguenot Place,
Wandsworth, SW18
Tel: 081-874 2008

Jane Zagel,
31 Pandora Road, NW6 1PS
Tel: 071-794 1663

Avon

International Fine Art
Conservation Studios,
43-45 Park Street,
Bristol, BS1 5NL
Tel: (0272) 293480

Pelter/Sands Art Gallery,
43-45 Park Street,
Bristol
Tel: (0272) 293988

Cambridgeshire

Alan Candy,
Old Manor House,
4 Cambridge Street,
Godmanchester,
Huntingdon
Tel: (0480) 453198

Essex

Terry Hilliard,
The Barn,
Master Johns,
Thoby Lane,
Mountnessing,
Brentwood
Tel: (0277) 354717

Pearlita Frames Ltd
30 North Street,
Romford, RM11 2LB
Tel: (0708) 760342

Gloucestershire

David Bannister,
26 Kings Road,
Cheltenham,
Gloucester, GL52 6BG
Tel: (0242) 514287

Keith Bawden,
Mews Workshop,
Montpelier Retreat,
Cheltenham, GL50 2XG
Tel: (0242) 230320

Cleeve Picture Framing,
Coach House Workshops,
Stoke Road,
Bishops Cleeve,
Cheltenham
Tel: (0242) 672785

Hampshire

Printed Page,
2-3 Bridge Street,
Winchester, SO23 9BH
Tel: (0962) 854072

Middlesex

Hampton Hill Gallery,
203 & 205 High Street,
Hampton Hill, TW12 1NP
Tel: 081-977 1379

Northamptonshire

Broadway Fine Art,
61 Park Avenue South,
Abington,
Northampton, NN3 3AB
Tel: (0604) 32011

Nottinghamshire

Mark Roberts,
1 West Workshops,
Tan Gallop,
Welbeck,
Nr Worksop, S80 3LW
Tel: (0909) 484270

Surrey

Boathouse Gallery,
The Towpath,
Manor Road,
Walton-on-Thames, KT12 2PG
Tel: (0932) 242718

Limpsfield Watercolours,
High Street,
Limpsfield
Tel: (0883) 717010

S. & S. Picture Restoration Studios,
The Rookery,
Frensham,
Farnham, GU10 3DU
Tel: (025 125) 3673

Wiltshire

D. M. Beach,
52 High Street,
Salisbury, SP1 2PG
Tel: (0722) 333801

Scotland

Alder Arts,
57 Church Street,
Highland,
Inverness, IV1 1DR
Tel: (0463) 243575

Fiona Butterfield,
Overhall,
Kirkfieldbank,
Lanark,
Strathclyde, ML11 9TZ
Tel: (0555) 66291

FRAMERS

London

John Campbell Master Frames,
164 Walton Street, SW3
Tel: 071-584 9268

Chelsea Frameworks,
106 Finborough Road, SW10
Tel: 071-373 0180

Cooper Fine Arts Ltd,
768 Fulham Road, SW6 5SJ
Tel: 071-731 3421

Court Picture Framers,
8 Bourdon Street, W1X 9HX
Tel: 071-493 3265

Trevor Cumine,
133 Putney Bridge Road,
SW15 2PA
Tel: 081-870 1525

Deansbrook Gallery,
134 Myddleton Road, N22 4NQ
Tel: 081-889 8389

John Jones Frames Ltd,
Unit 4,
Finsbury Park Trading Estate,
Morris Place, N4 3JG
Tel: 071-281 5439

Lamont Gallery,
65 Roman Road, E2
Tel: 081-981 6332

Porcelain & Pictures Ltd,
The Studio,
Gastein Road, W6 8LT
Tel: 071-385 7512

Railings Gallery,
5 New Cavendish Street, W1
Tel: 071-935 1114

Woolcock Framing,
8 Huguenot Place,
Wandsworth, SW18
Tel: 081-874 2008

Essex

Pearlita Frames Ltd,
30 North Street,
Romford, RM11 2LB
Tel: (0708) 760342

Gloucestershire

Cleeve Picture Framing,
Coach House Workshops,
Stoke Road,
Bishops Cleeve,
Cheltenham
Tel: (0242) 672785

Surrey

Boathouse Gallery,
The Towpath,
Manor Road,
Walton-on-Thames, KT12 2PG
Tel: (0932) 242718

Limpsfield Watercolours,
High Street,
Limpsfield
Tel: (0883) 717010

LIGHTING

London

Chatsworth Commercial Lighting,
6 Highbury Corner, N5 1RD
Tel: 071-609 9829

Kent

St John A. Burch,
Myrtle House,
Headcorn Road,
Grafty Green, ME17 2AR
Tel: (0622) 850381

INSURANCE

London

Crowley Colosso Ltd,
Ibex House,
Minories, EC3N 1JJ
Tel: 071-782 9782

Miller Art Insurance,
Dawson House,
5 Jewry Street, EC3N 2EX

J. H. Minet,
Minet House,
100 Leman Street, E1 8HG
Tel: 071-481 0707

Dorset

Gibbs Hartley Cooper,
Beech House,
28-30 Wimborne Road,
Poole, BH15 2BJ
Tel: (0202) 660866

Oxfordshire

Penrose Forbes,
29-30 Horsefair,
Banbury, OX16 0NE
Tel: (0295) 259892

West Sussex

Bain Clarkson Ltd,
Harlands Road,
Haywards Heath, RH16 1GA
Tel: (0444) 414141

ART CONSULTANTS

London

Art Image,
1/5 The Garden Market,
Chelsea Harbour, SW10 0XE
Tel: 071-352 8181

Arts Direction,
60 Albert Court,
Prince Consort Road,
Knightsbridge, SW7 2BH
Tel: 071-823 8800

PHOTOGRAPHERS

London

Prudence Cuming Associates Ltd,
28/29 Dover Street, W1
Tel: 071-629 6430

Darkroom Associates Ltd,
Unit 15,
7 Chalcot Road, NW1 8LH
Tel: 071-586 4024

PICTURE PLAQUES

London

Picture Plaques,
142 Lambton Road, SW20 0TJ
Tel: 081-879 7841

Somerset

Berkeley Studio,
The Old Vicarage,
Castle Cary, BA7 7EJ
Tel: (0963) 50748

SHIPPERS

London

Featherston Shipping,
24 Hampton House,
15-17 Ingate Place, SW8 3NS
Tel: 071-720 0422

GLASS

London

Rankins (Glass) Company,
The London Glass Centre,
24-34 Pearson Street, E2 8JD
Tel: 071-729 4200

SECURITY

London

Ambassador Security Group plc,
4 Blake House,
Admirals Way,
Docklands, E14 9UF
Tel: 071-538 1327

Simba Security Systems Ltd,
Security House,
Occupation Road,
Walworth, SE17 3BE
Tel: 071-703 0485

SERVICES

London

Art Loss Register,
The Hogg Group,
1 Portsoken Street, E1
Tel: 071-480 4000

Bibliography

Antique Collectors' Club (pub.) – *The British Portrait 1660-1960* – 1990
E. H. H. Archibald – Dictionary of Sea Painters – Antique Collectors' Club, 1980.

Arts Council of Great Britain – *British Sporting Painting 1650-1850* – 1974 Arts Council of Great Britain – The Modern Spirit: American Painting 1908-1935 – 1977

Wendy Baron – *The Camden Town Group* – Scholar Press 1979.

Charles Baudelaire – *Art in Paris 1845-1862* – Phaidon, Oxford 1981.

E. Benezit – *Dictionnaire des Peintres, Sculpteurs, Dessinateurs et Graveurs* – 10 vol – Paris 1976.

Michael Bryan – *Dictionary of Painters and Engravers* – 2 vols – George Bell and Sons 1889.

Ian Crofton – *A Dictionary of Art Quotations* – Routledge 1988.

Bernard Denvir (ed.) – *The Impressionists at First Hand* – Thames and Hudson – 1987.

Dictionary of National Biography.

David Hugh Farmer – *The Oxford Dictionary of Saints* – Oxford University Press 1987.

Edmond and Jules de Goncourt – *French Eighteenth Century Painters* – Phaidon, Oxford 1981.

Donald Hall and Pat Corrington Wykes – *Anecdotes of Modern Art* – Oxford University Press 1990.

James Hall – *Dictionary of Subjects and Symbols in Art* – John Murray 1979.

Martin Hardie – *Watercolour Painting in Britain* – 3 vols – B. T. Batsford Ltd 1966/67/68.

Nancy G. Heller – *Women Artists, An Illustrated History* – Virago 1987.

Philip Hook and Mark Poltimore – *Popular 19th Century Painting* – Antique Collectors' Club 1986.

Edward Lucie-Smith – *The Thames and Hudson Dictionary of Art Terms* – 1988.

Jeremy Maas – *Victorian Painters* – Barrie & Jenkins 1988.

Huon Mallalieu (ed.) – *The Popular Antiques Yearbook* – 1985/1987/1988 (3 vols), Phaidon-Christie's.

Huon Mallalieu – *How to Buy Pictures* – Phaidon-Christie's 1984.

Madeleine Marsh – *Art Detective* – Pelham Books 1993 – An invaluable guide to identifying your picture.

Harold Osborne (ed.) – *The Oxford Companion to Twentieth Century Art* – Oxford University Press 1988.

H. Ottley – *Dictionary of Recent and Living Painters and Engravers* – Henry G. Bohn – 1866.

Betty Radice – *Who's Who in the Ancient World* – Penguin Books 1984.

Richard and Samuel Redgrave – *A Century of British Painters* – Phaidon, Oxford 1981.

Jakob Rosenberg, Seymour Slive and E. H. ter Kuile – *Dutch Art and Architecture 1600-1800* – Penguin Books 1982.

John Rothenstein – *Modern English Painters* – Macdonald 1984.

Frances Spalding – *20th Century Painters and Sculptors* – Antique Collectors' Club, 1990.

Ellis Waterhouse – *The Dictionary of 16th and 17th Century British Painters* – Antique Collectors' Club 1988.

Ellis Waterhouse – *The Dictionary of British 18th Century Painters* – Antique Collectors' Club 1981.

Ellis Waterhouse – *Painting in Britain 1530 to 1790* – Penguin Books 1978.

Christopher Wood – *The Dictionary of Victorian Painters* – Antique Collectors' Club, 1978.

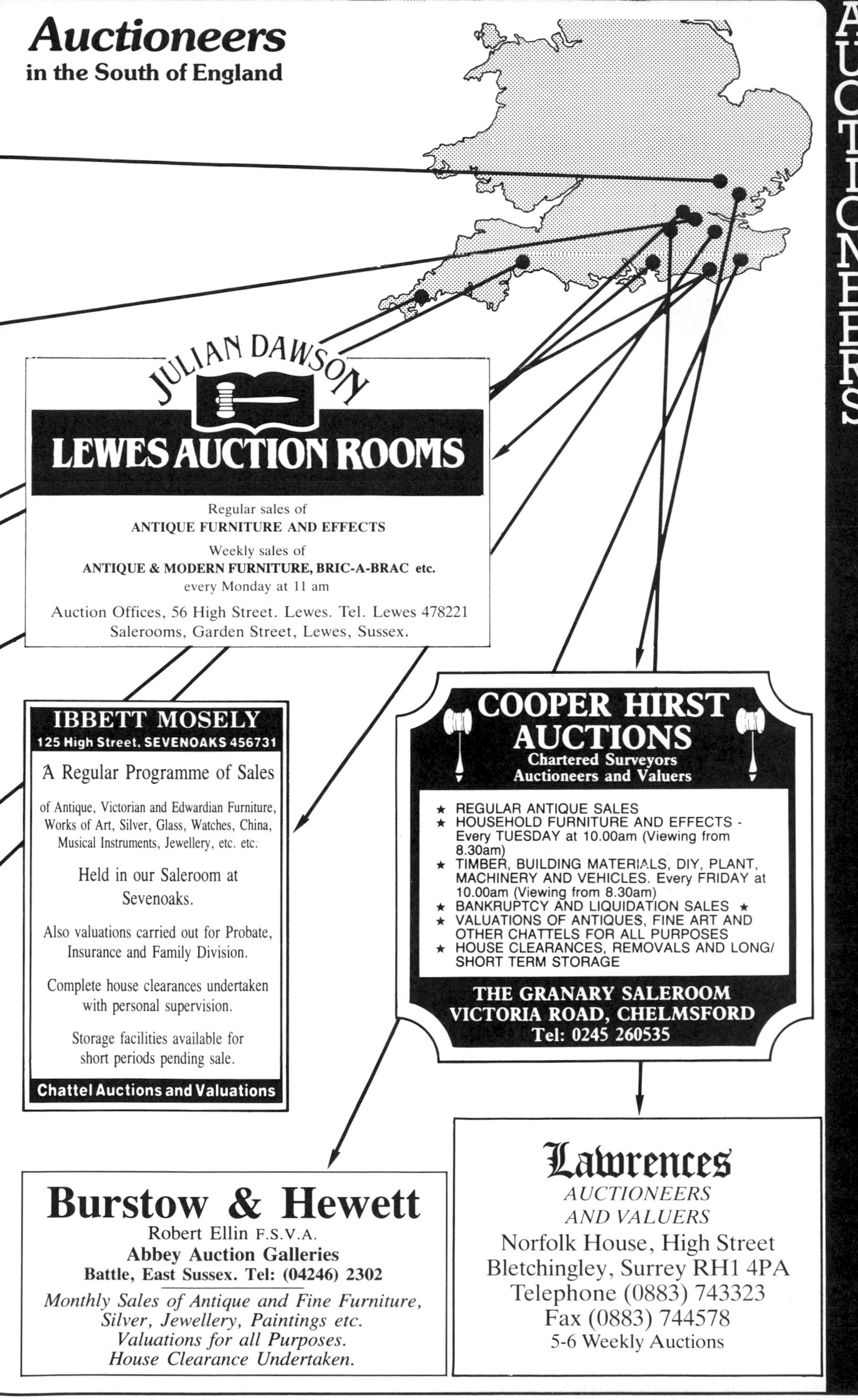
Auctioneers
in the South of England
JULIAN DAWSON
LEWES AUCTION ROOMS
Regular sales of
ANTIQUE FURNITURE AND EFFECTS
Weekly sales of
ANTIQUE & MODERN FURNITURE, BRIC-A-BRAC etc.
every Monday at 11 am
Auction Offices, 56 High Street. Lewes. Tel. Lewes 478221
Salerooms, Garden Street, Lewes, Sussex.
IBBETT MOSELY
125 High Street, SEVENOAKS 456731
A Regular Programme of Sales
of Antique, Victorian and Edwardian Furniture, Works of Art, Silver, Glass, Watches, China, Musical Instruments, Jewellery, etc. etc.
Held in our Saleroom at Sevenoaks.
Also valuations carried out for Probate, Insurance and Family Division.
Complete house clearances undertaken with personal supervision.
Storage facilities available for short periods pending sale.
Chattel Auctions and Valuations
COOPER HIRST
AUCTIONS
Chartered Surveyors
Auctioneers and Valuers
★ REGULAR ANTIQUE SALES
★ HOUSEHOLD FURNITURE AND EFFECTS - Every TUESDAY at 10.00am (Viewing from 8.30am)
★ TIMBER, BUILDING MATERIALS, DIY, PLANT, MACHINERY AND VEHICLES. Every FRIDAY at 10.00am (Viewing from 8.30am)
★ BANKRUPTCY AND LIQUIDATION SALES ★
★ VALUATIONS OF ANTIQUES, FINE ART AND OTHER CHATTELS FOR ALL PURPOSES
★ HOUSE CLEARANCES, REMOVALS AND LONG/SHORT TERM STORAGE
THE GRANARY SALEROOM
VICTORIA ROAD, CHELMSFORD
Tel: 0245 260535
Burstow & Hewett
Robert Ellin F.S.V.A.
Abbey Auction Galleries
Battle, East Sussex. Tel: (04246) 2302
Monthly Sales of Antique and Fine Furniture, Silver, Jewellery, Paintings etc.
Valuations for all Purposes.
House Clearance Undertaken.
Lawrences
AUCTIONEERS
AND VALUERS
Norfolk House, High Street
Bletchingley, Surrey RH1 4PA
Telephone (0883) 743323
Fax (0883) 744578
5-6 Weekly Auctions

A Thoroughbred Amongst Auctioneers

FINE ART VALUERS AND AUCTIONEERS SINCE 1834

Monthly Fine Art Sales including sizeable picture sections

Weekly Victoriana Sales

All Enquiries:
Locke & England, 18 Guy Street, Royal Leamington Spa, Warwickshire CV32 4RT
TEL: (0926) 889100 FAX: (0926) 470608

CUMBRIA AUCTION ROOMS

Fine Art, Antiques and Furniture Auctioneers and Valuers

Regular Catalogue Sales of Antiques and Works of Art

Weekly Sales of General Furniture and Effects

12 LOWTHER STREET, CARLISLE, CUMBRIA CA3 8DA

Telephone: Carlisle (0228) 25259

Victoria Hall Salerooms
Little Lane, Ilkley, West Yorkshire LS29 8EA
(Tel 0943 816363)

Independent
Furniture and Fine Arts Auctioneers for three generations. Now fully extended and computerised premises with two salerooms and carefully graded general and specialist sales every week.

Lithgow Sons & Partners
(Established 1868)
North East Auctioneers

Antique House
Station Road, Stokesley
Middlesbrough
Cleveland TS9 7AB
Tel: 0642 710158
Fax: 0642 712641

William H. Brown

FINE ART

— Fine Art Auctioneers and Valuers —

SALES

- *Regular auction sales of antique and fine art at our main salerooms*
- *Regular auction sales of general furniture and effects at all salerooms*
- *Contents sales on vendors' premises*
- *Total House clearance for executors*

VALUATIONS
Valuations and Inventories for Insurance, Probate, Capital Transfer, Capital Gains Tax and Family Division

ADVICE
Free Advisory Service at the Salerooms

SALEROOMS

William H. Brown
(Ken Green)
10 Regent Street
Barnsley
South Yorkshire
S70 2EJ
(0226) 299221

William H. Brown
(Francis Beal)
Paskells Rooms
14 East Hill
Colchester
Essex CO1 2QX
(0206) 868070

*William H. Brown
(Suki Burnett)
Stanilands Auction Rooms
28 Netherhall Road
Doncaster
South Yorkshire
DN1 2PW
(0302) 367766

*William H. Brown
(Robert R. Woods)
Morphets
4-6 Albert Street
Harrogate
North Yorkshire
HG1 1JL
(0423) 530030

William H. Brown
(Ray Young)
The Warner Auction Rooms
16-18 Halford Street
Leicester LE1 1JB
(0533) 519777

*William H. Brown
(James Fletcher)
Olivers Rooms
Burkitts Lane
Sudbury
Suffolk CO10 6HB
(0787) 880305

Brown & Merry
(Stephen J. Hearn)
Brook Street
Tring, Hertfordshire
HP23 5EF
(044282) 6446

REGIONAL OFFICES

1 Market Place
Beverley
North Humberside
HU17 8BB
(0482) 870832

19 Market Square
Northampton
NN1 2DX
(0604) 231866

37-39 Church Street
Sheffield S1 2GL
(0742) 769062

48 Goodramgate
York YO1 2LF
(0904) 621138

*Denotes Members of The Society of Fine Art Auctioneers

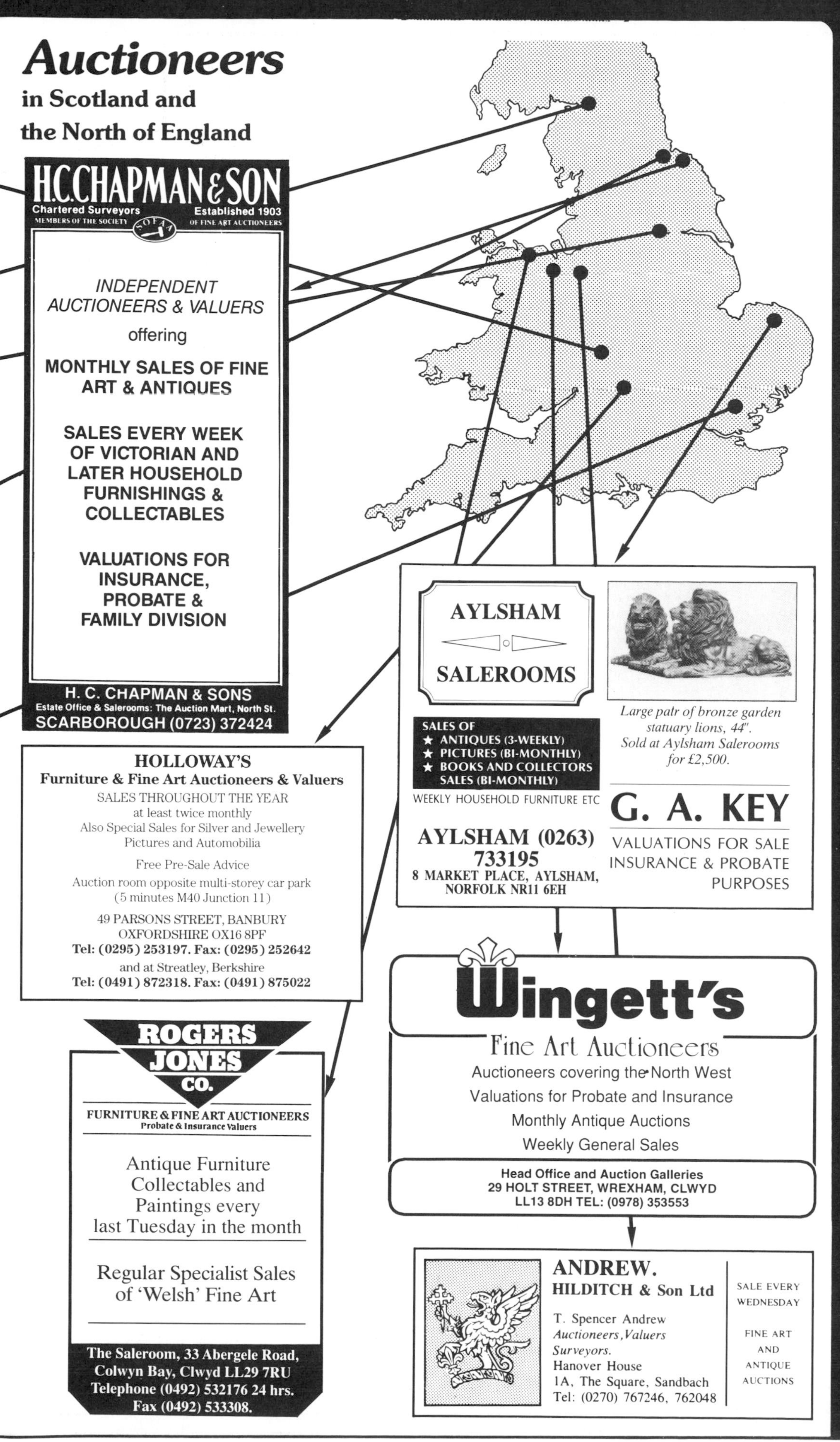
Auctioneers
in Scotland and
the North of England
H.C.CHAPMAN & SON
Chartered Surveyors
Established 1903
MEMBERS OF THE SOCIETY OF FINE ART AUCTIONEERS
SOFAA
INDEPENDENT
AUCTIONEERS & VALUERS
offering
MONTHLY SALES OF FINE
ART & ANTIQUES
SALES EVERY WEEK
OF VICTORIAN AND
LATER HOUSEHOLD
FURNISHINGS &
COLLECTABLES
VALUATIONS FOR
INSURANCE,
PROBATE &
FAMILY DIVISION
H. C. CHAPMAN & SONS
Estate Office & Salerooms: The Auction Mart, North St.
SCARBOROUGH (0723) 372424
AYLSHAM
SALEROOMS
Large pair of bronze garden
statuary lions, 44".
Sold at Aylsham Salerooms
for £2,500.
SALES OF
★ ANTIQUES (3-WEEKLY)
★ PICTURES (BI-MONTHLY)
★ BOOKS AND COLLECTORS
SALES (BI-MONTHLY)
WEEKLY HOUSEHOLD FURNITURE ETC
G. A. KEY
AYLSHAM (0263)
733195
8 MARKET PLACE, AYLSHAM,
NORFOLK NR11 6EH
VALUATIONS FOR SALE
INSURANCE & PROBATE
PURPOSES
HOLLOWAY'S
Furniture & Fine Art Auctioneers & Valuers
SALES THROUGHOUT THE YEAR
at least twice monthly
Also Special Sales for Silver and Jewellery
Pictures and Automobilia
Free Pre-Sale Advice
Auction room opposite multi-storey car park
(5 minutes M40 Junction 11)
49 PARSONS STREET, BANBURY
OXFORDSHIRE OX16 8PF
Tel: (0295) 253197. Fax: (0295) 252642
and at Streatley, Berkshire
Tel: (0491) 872318. Fax: (0491) 875022
Wingett's
Fine Art Auctioneers
Auctioneers covering the North West
Valuations for Probate and Insurance
Monthly Antique Auctions
Weekly General Sales
Head Office and Auction Galleries
29 HOLT STREET, WREXHAM, CLWYD
LL13 8DH TEL: (0978) 353553
ROGERS
JONES
CO.
FURNITURE & FINE ART AUCTIONEERS
Probate & Insurance Valuers
Antique Furniture
Collectables and
Paintings every
last Tuesday in the month
Regular Specialist Sales
of 'Welsh' Fine Art
The Saleroom, 33 Abergele Road,
Colwyn Bay, Clwyd LL29 7RU
Telephone (0492) 532176 24 hrs.
Fax (0492) 533308.
ANDREW.
HILDITCH & Son Ltd
T. Spencer Andrew
Auctioneers, Valuers
Surveyors.
Hanover House
1A, The Square, Sandbach
Tel: (0270) 767246, 762048
SALE EVERY
WEDNESDAY
FINE ART
AND
ANTIQUE
AUCTIONS

INDEX

H

I

J

K

L

M